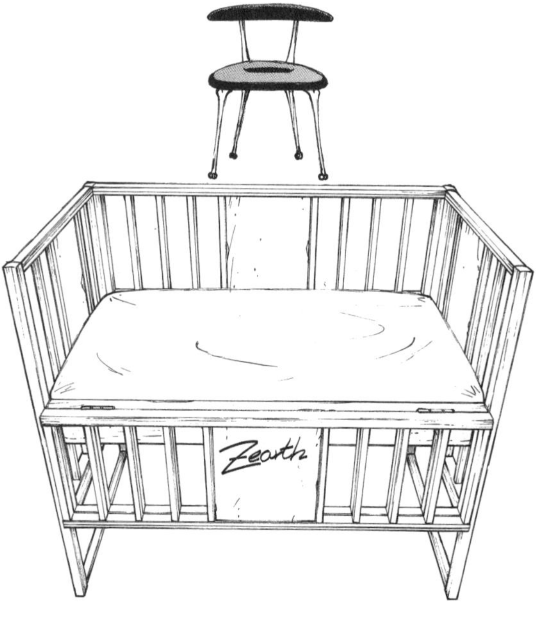
Zearth

BOKURANO
OURS

5

MOHIRO
KITOH

CHARACTER INFORMATION
—BOYS—

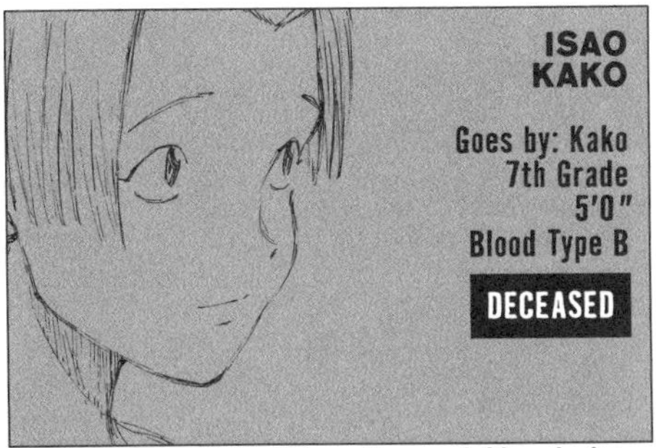
ISAO
KAKO
Goes by: Kako
7th Grade
5'0"
Blood Type B
DECEASED

Stabbed to death by Chizu after panicking during his battle.

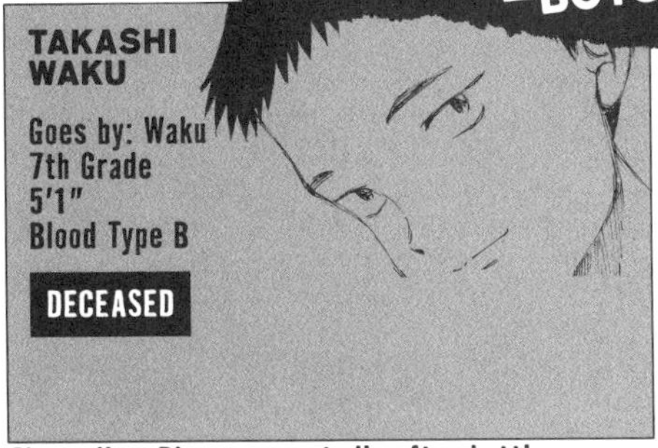
TAKASHI
WAKU
Goes by: Waku
7th Grade
5'1"
Blood Type B
DECEASED

First pilot. Dies unexpectedly after battle.

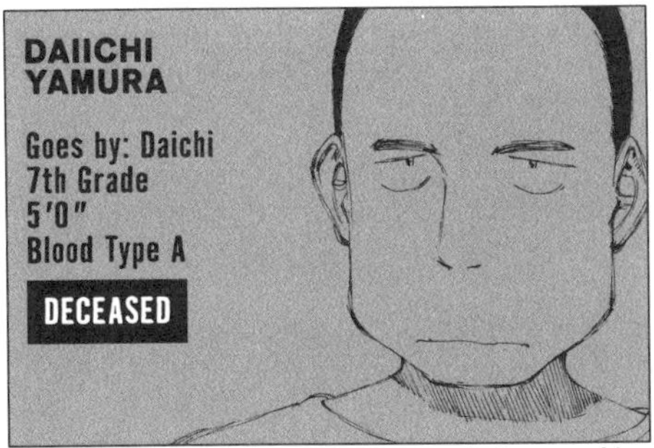
DAIICHI
YAMURA
Goes by: Daichi
7th Grade
5'0"
Blood Type A
DECEASED

A heroic type who faces death bravely to save his three younger siblings.

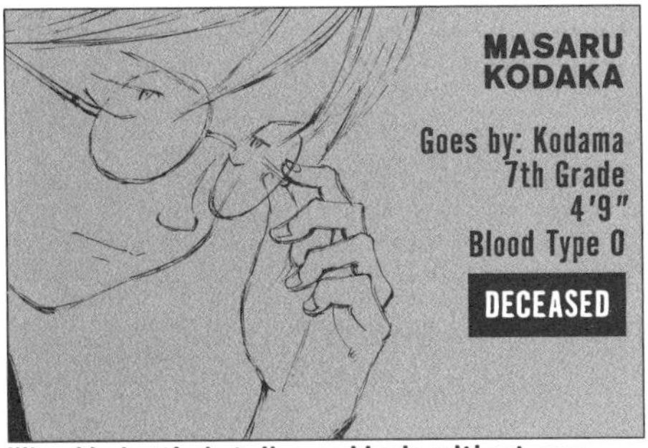
MASARU
KODAKA
Goes by: Kodama
7th Grade
4'9"
Blood Type O
DECEASED

Wins his battle but dies suddenly without ever knowing why.

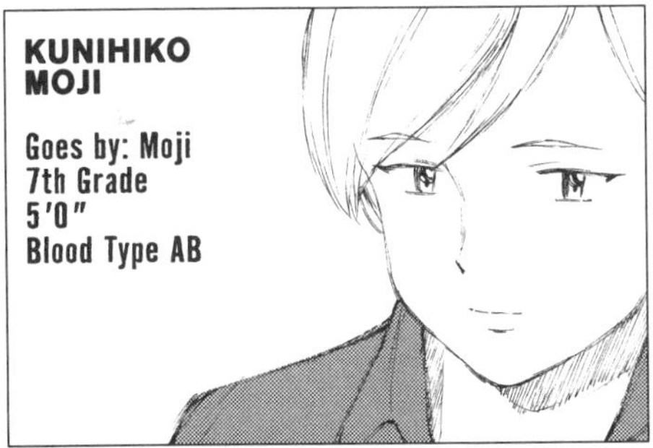
KUNIHIKO
MOJI
Goes by: Moji
7th Grade
5'0"
Blood Type AB

Arranges to donate his heart to an ailing friend after his death.

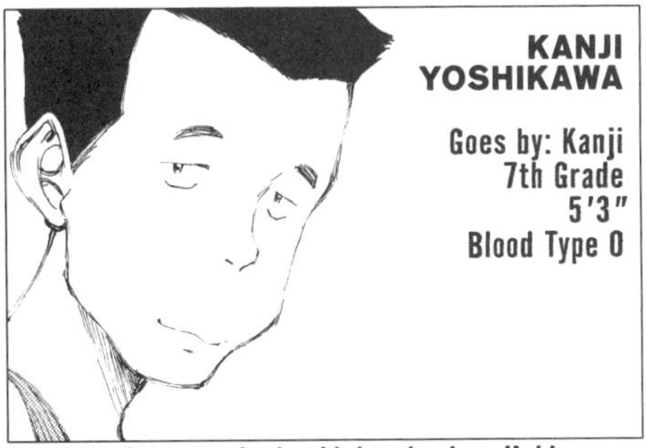
KANJI
YOSHIKAWA
Goes by: Kanji
7th Grade
5'3"
Blood Type O

Attends the same junior high school as Ushiro.

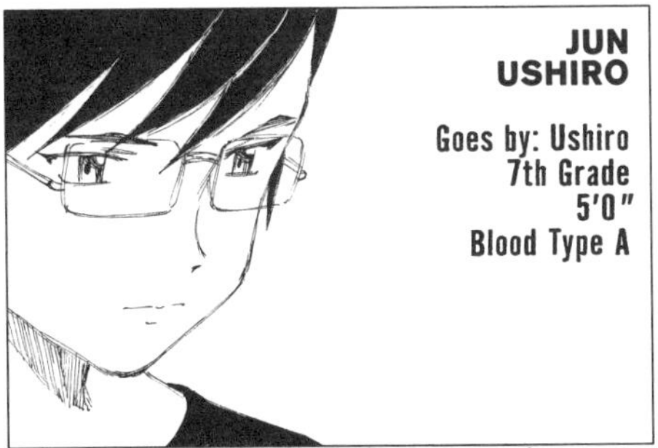
JUN
USHIRO
Goes by: Ushiro
7th Grade
5'0"
Blood Type A

Kana's older brother. Somewhat egocentric.

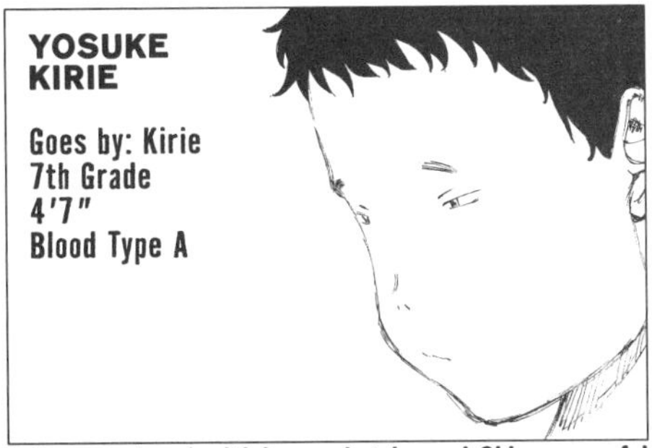
YOSUKE
KIRIE
Goes by: Kirie
7th Grade
4'7"
Blood Type A

Introverted and withdrawn, but he and Chizu were friends.

CHARACTER INFORMATION
—GIRLS—

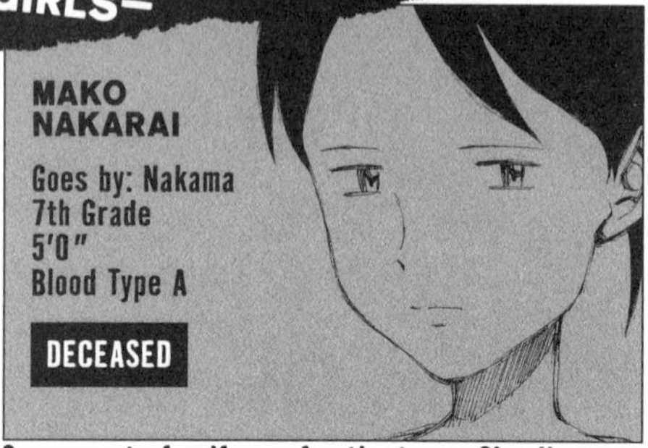
MAKO NAKARAI
Goes by: Nakama
7th Grade
5′0″
Blood Type A
DECEASED

Sews a set of uniforms for the team. She dies thinking of her mother.

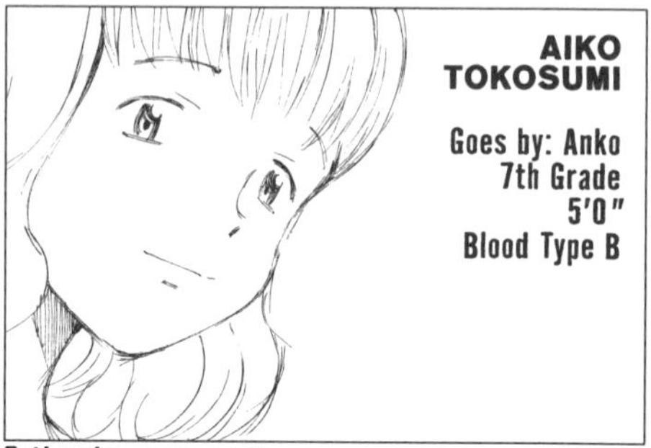
AIKO TOKOSUMI
Goes by: Anko
7th Grade
5′0″
Blood Type B

Father is a newscaster.

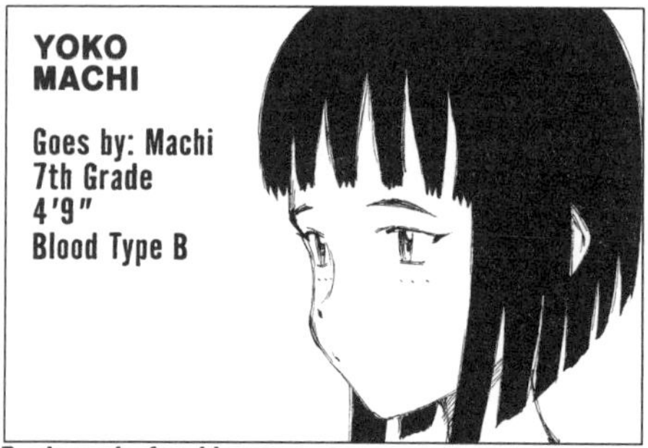
YOKO MACHI
Goes by: Machi
7th Grade
4′9″
Blood Type B

Trademark: freckles.

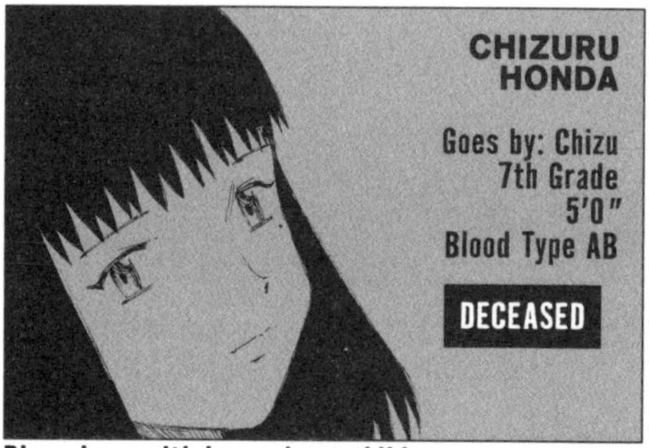
CHIZURU HONDA
Goes by: Chizu
7th Grade
5′0″
Blood Type AB
DECEASED

Dies along with her unborn child.

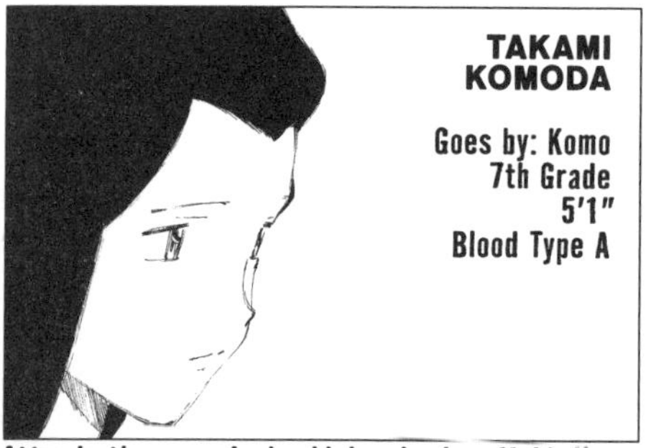
TAKAMI KOMODA
Goes by: Komo
7th Grade
5′1″
Blood Type A

Attends the same junior high school as Maki. Her father is a high-ranking military officer.

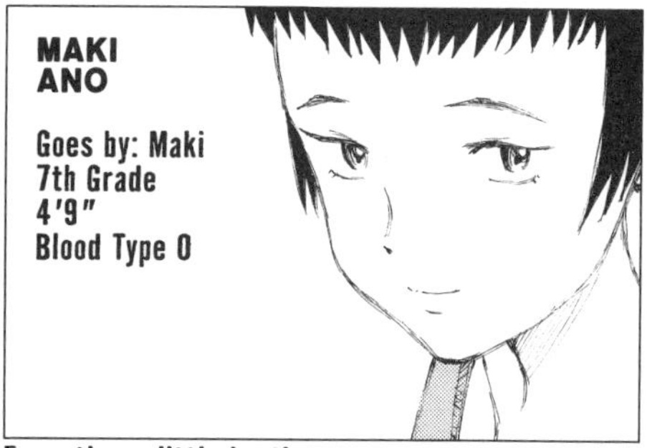
MAKI ANO
Goes by: Maki
7th Grade
4′9″
Blood Type O

Expecting a little brother.

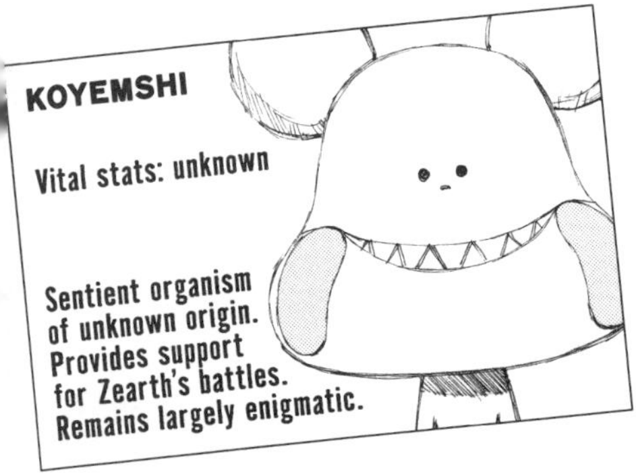
KOYEMSHI
Vital stats: unknown
Sentient organism of unknown origin. Provides support for Zearth's battles. Remains largely enigmatic.

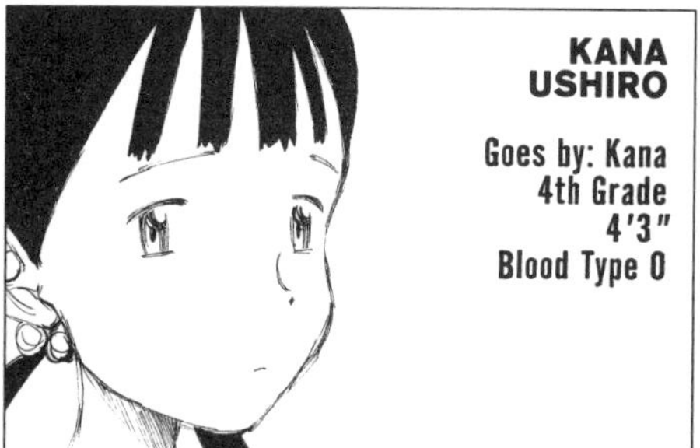
KANA USHIRO
Goes by: Kana
4th Grade
4′3″
Blood Type O

Jun Ushiro's younger sister. Her older brother bullies her.

CONTENTS

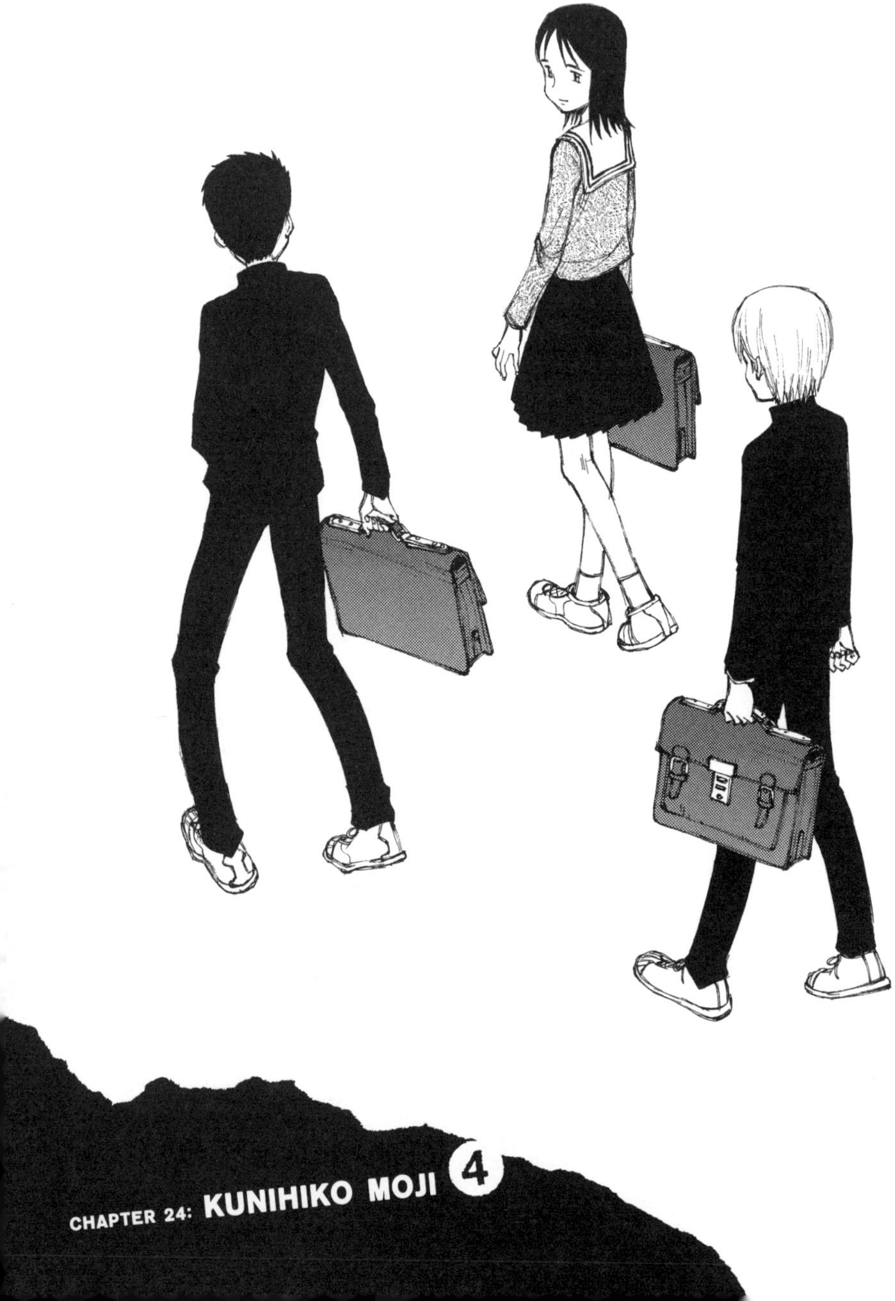

CHAPTER 24: KUNIHIKO MOJI 4

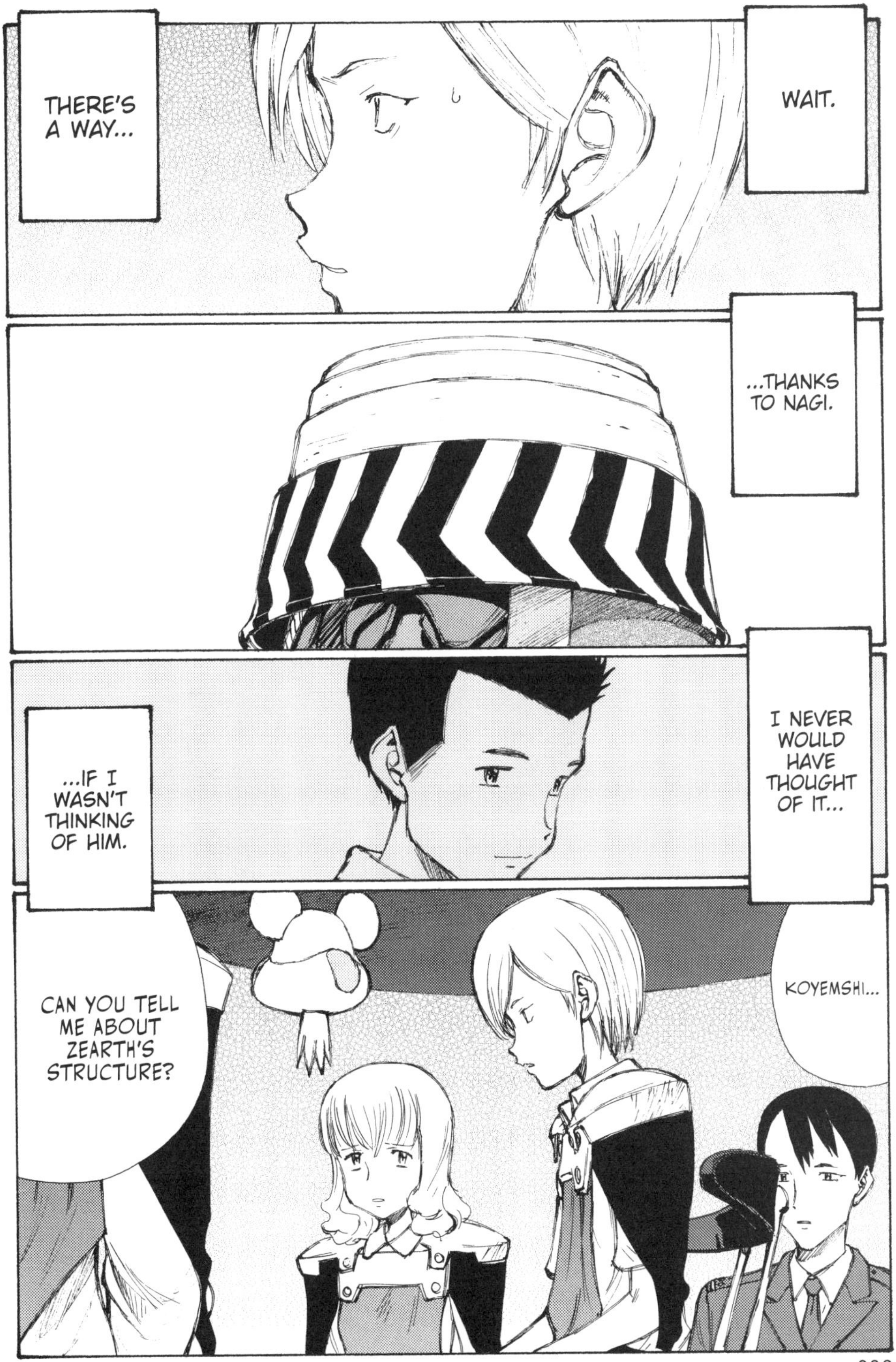
WAIT.
THERE'S A WAY...
...THANKS TO NAGI.
I NEVER WOULD HAVE THOUGHT OF IT...
...IF I WASN'T THINKING OF HIM.
KOYEMSHI...
CAN YOU TELL ME ABOUT ZEARTH'S STRUCTURE?

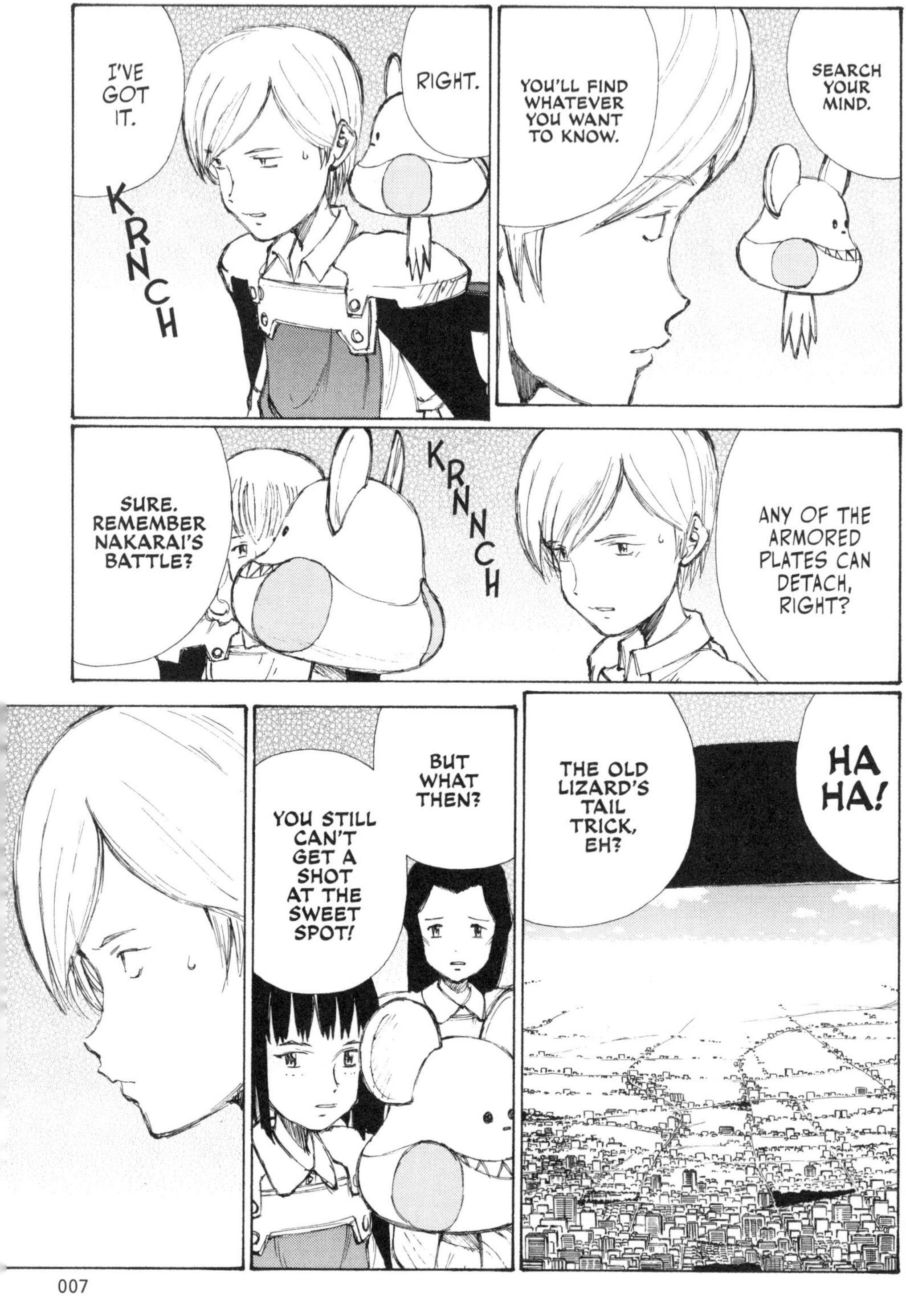
SEARCH YOUR MIND.
YOU'LL FIND WHATEVER YOU WANT TO KNOW.
RIGHT.
I'VE GOT IT.
KRNCH
ANY OF THE ARMORED PLATES CAN DETACH, RIGHT?
KRNNCH
SURE. REMEMBER NAKARAI'S BATTLE?
HA HA!
THE OLD LIZARD'S TAIL TRICK, EH?
BUT WHAT THEN?
YOU STILL CAN'T GET A SHOT AT THE SWEET SPOT!

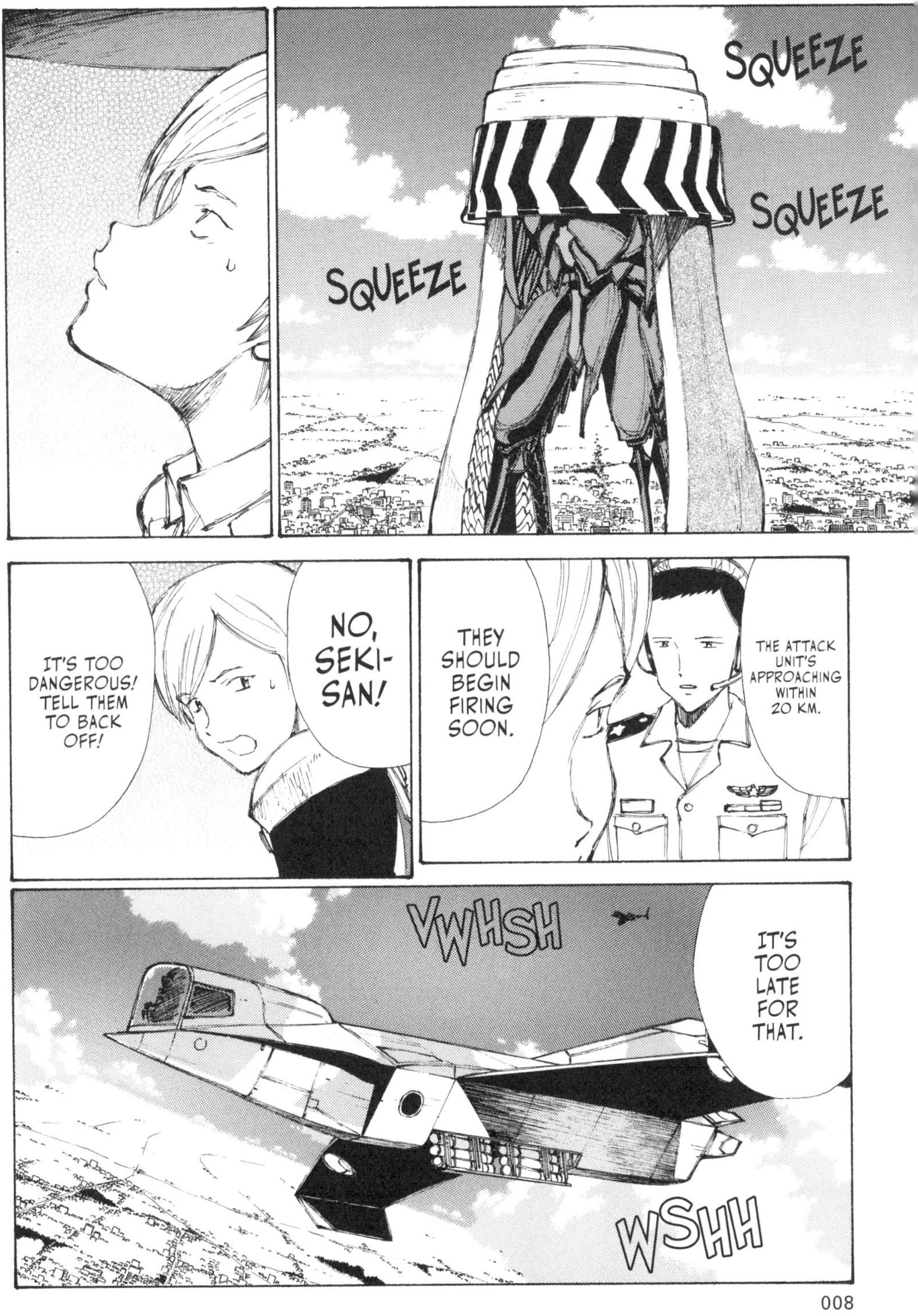
SQUEEZE
SQUEEZE
SQUEEZE
THE ATTACK UNIT'S APPROACHING WITHIN 20 KM.
THEY SHOULD BEGIN FIRING SOON.
NO, SEKI-SAN!
IT'S TOO DANGEROUS! TELL THEM TO BACK OFF!
IT'S TOO LATE FOR THAT.
VWHSH
WSHH

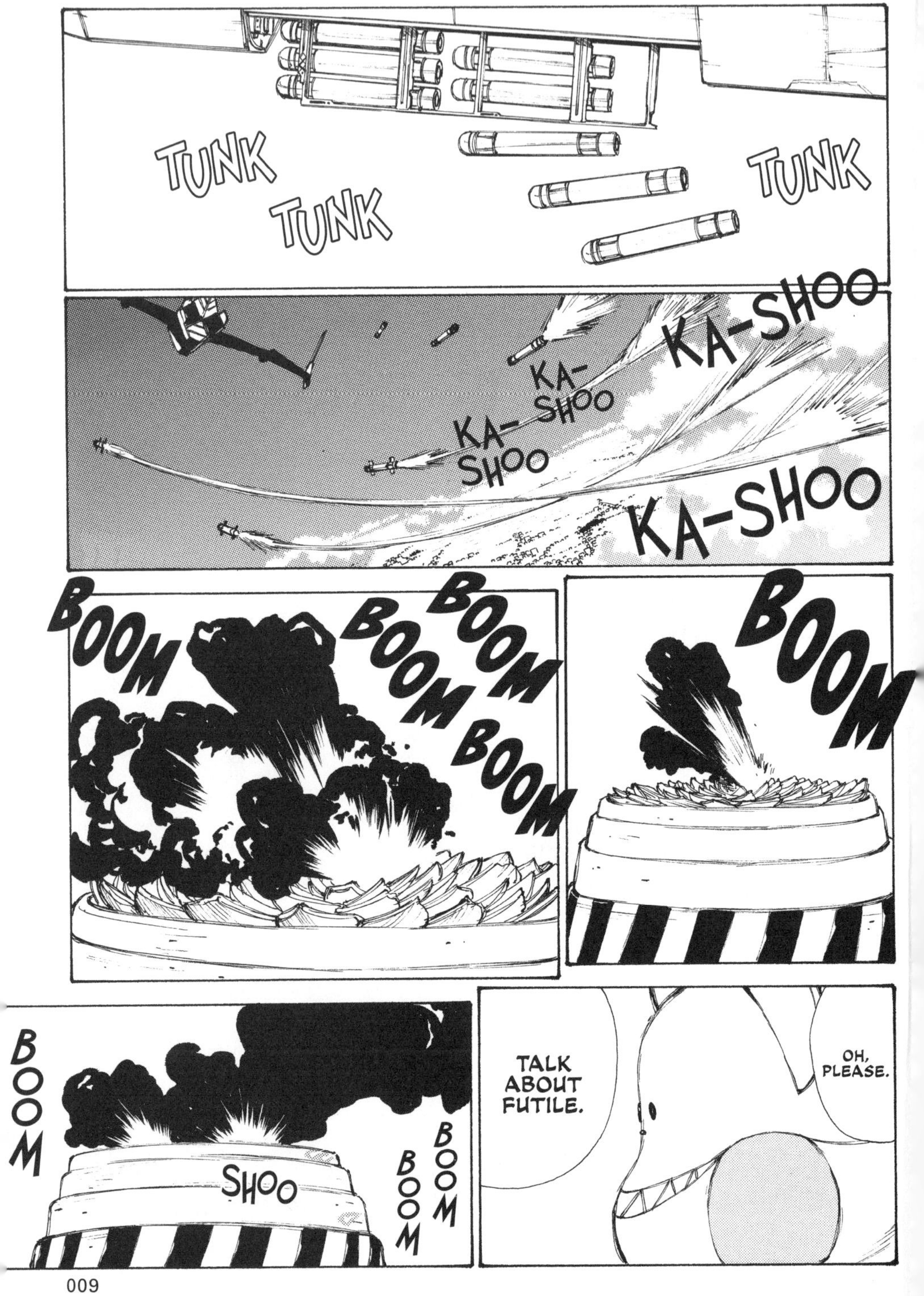
TUNK
TUNK
TUNK
KA-SHOO
KA-SHOO
KA-SHOO
KA-SHOO
BOOM
BOOM
BOOM
BOOM
BOOM
OH, PLEASE.
TALK ABOUT FUTILE.
BOOM
BOOM
BOOM
SHOO
BOOM

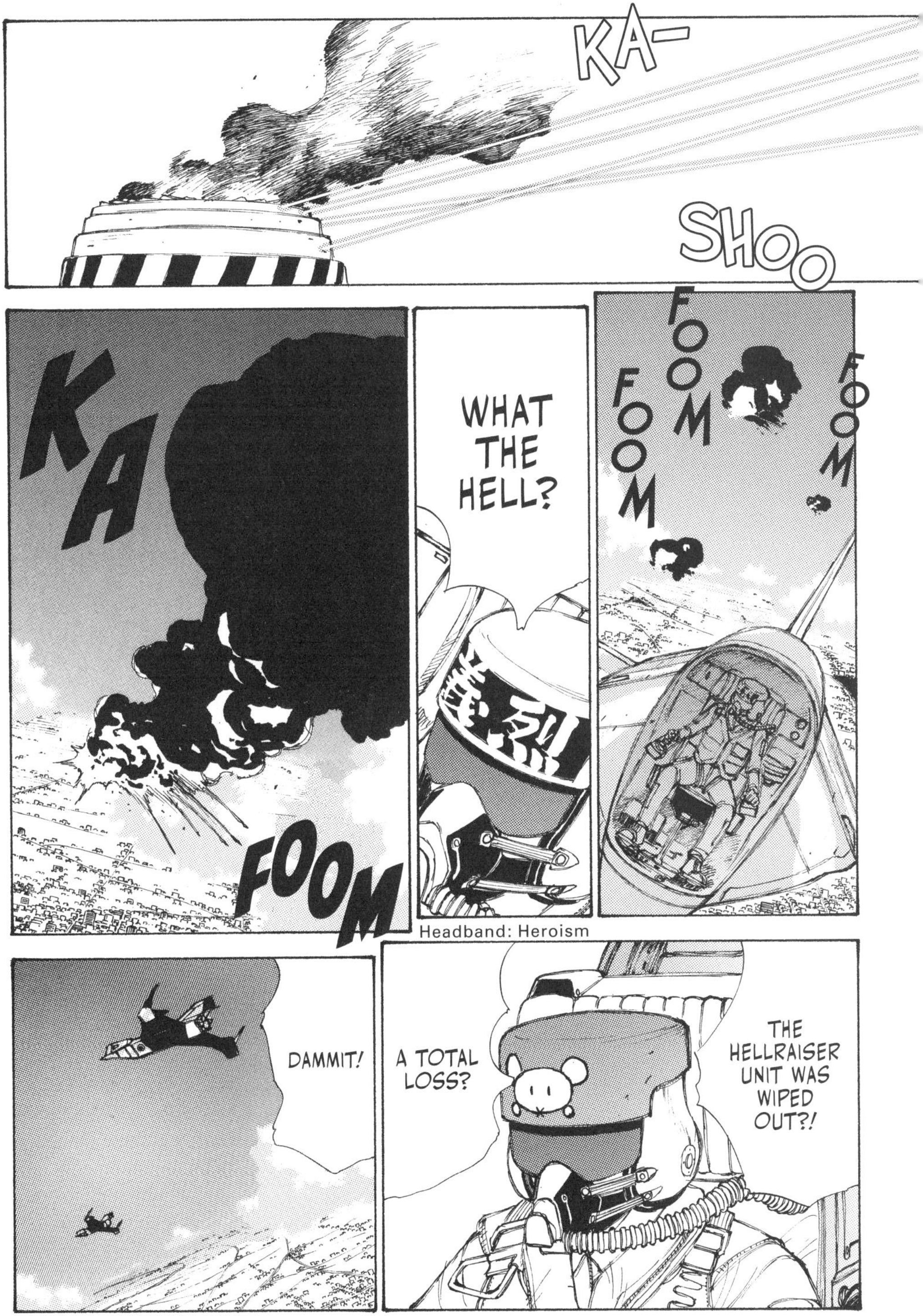
KA-
SHOO
FOOM
FOOM
FOOM
WHAT THE HELL?
KA
FOOM
Headband: Heroism
THE HELLRAISER UNIT WAS WIPED OUT?!
A TOTAL LOSS?
DAMMIT!

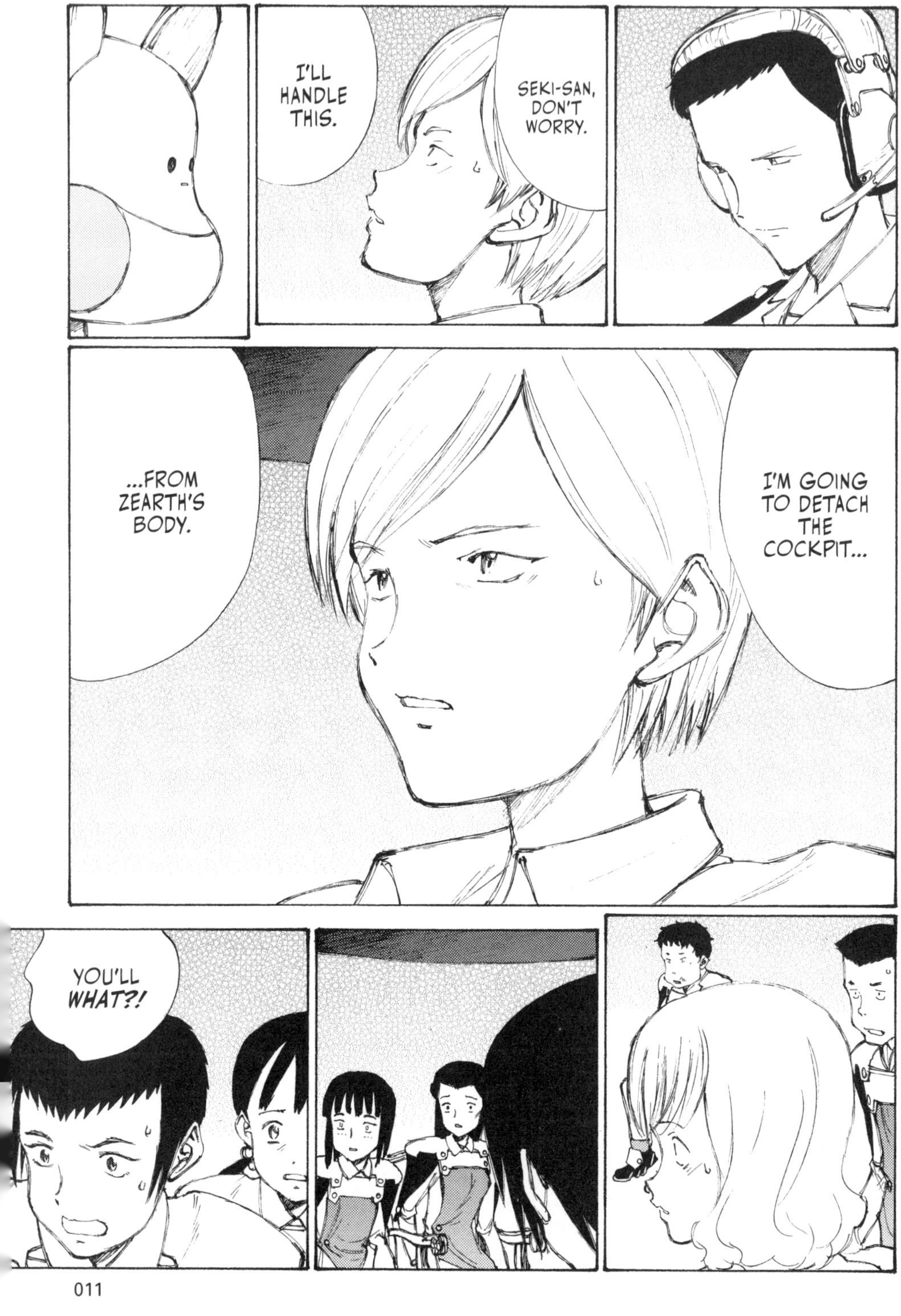
SEKI-SAN, DON'T WORRY.
I'LL HANDLE THIS.
I'M GOING TO DETACH THE COCKPIT...
...FROM ZEARTH'S BODY.
YOU'LL *WHAT?!*

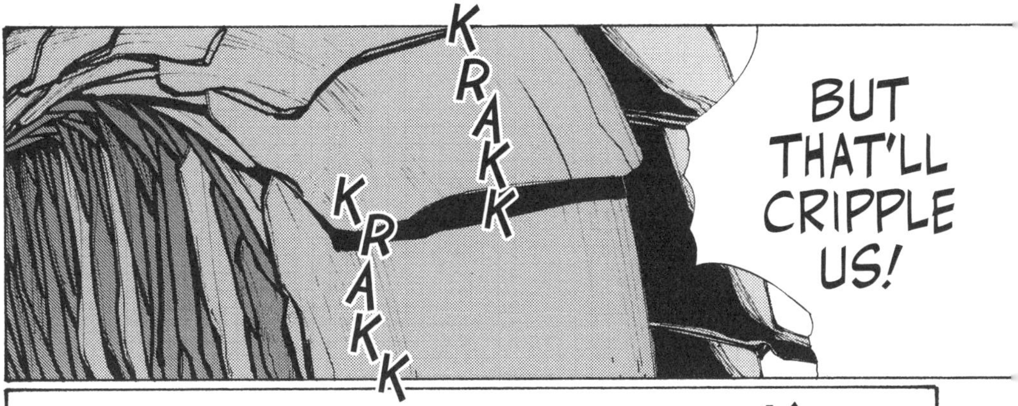
BUT THAT'LL CRIPPLE US!
KRAKK
KRAKK

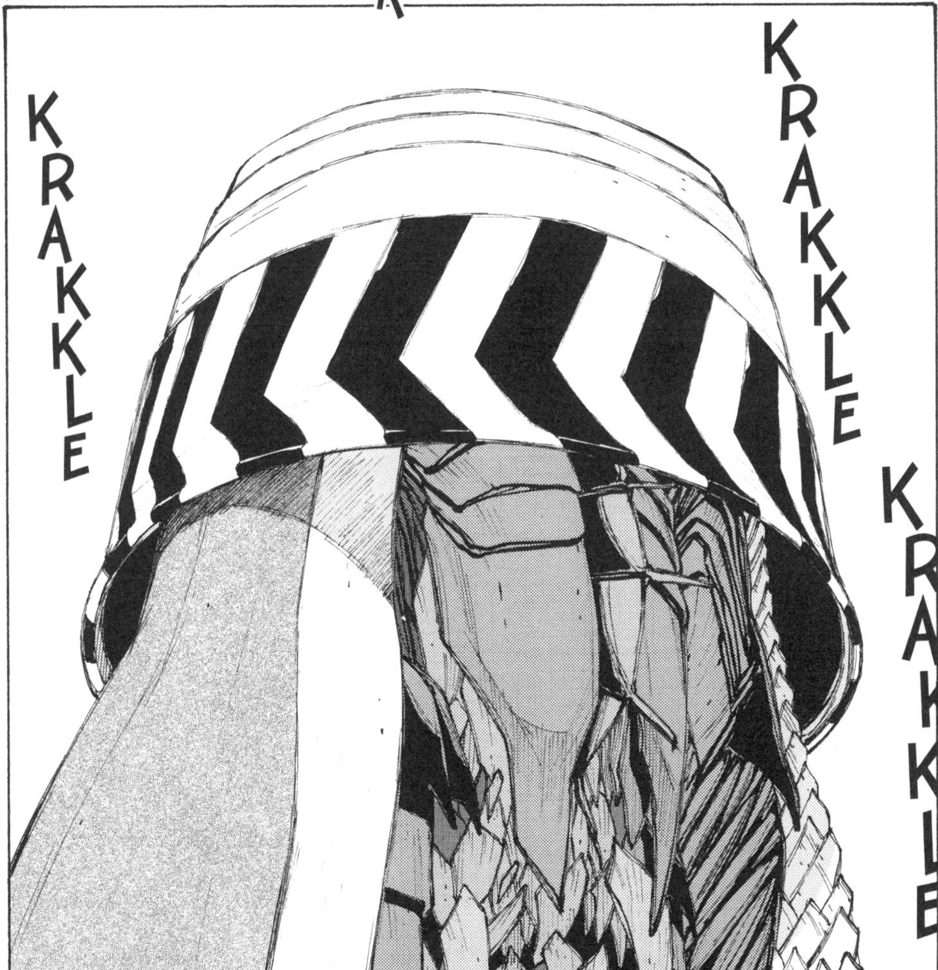
KRAKKLE
KRAKKLE
KRAKKLE

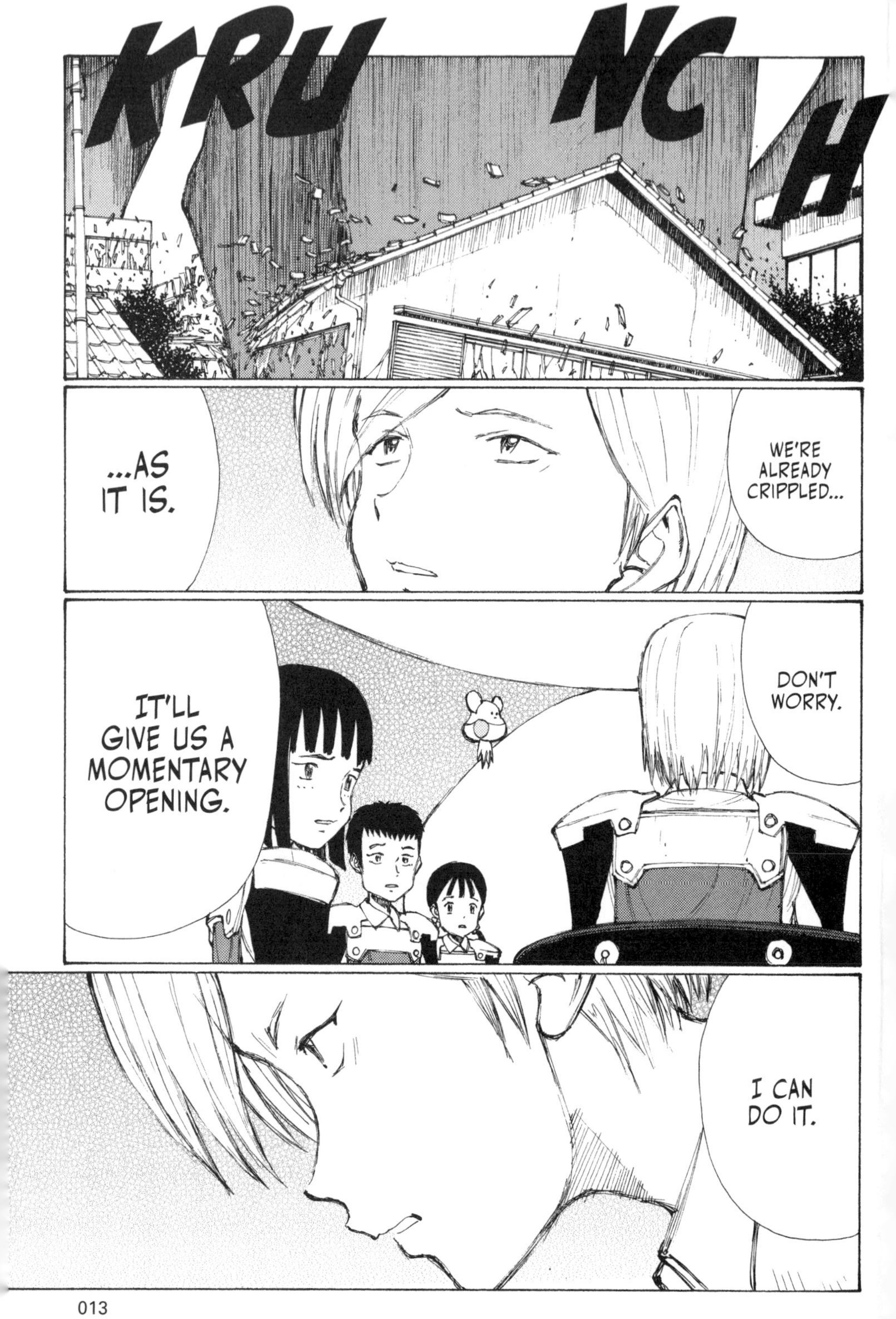
KRUNCH
WE'RE ALREADY CRIPPLED...
...AS IT IS.
DON'T WORRY.
IT'LL GIVE US A MOMENTARY OPENING.
I CAN DO IT.

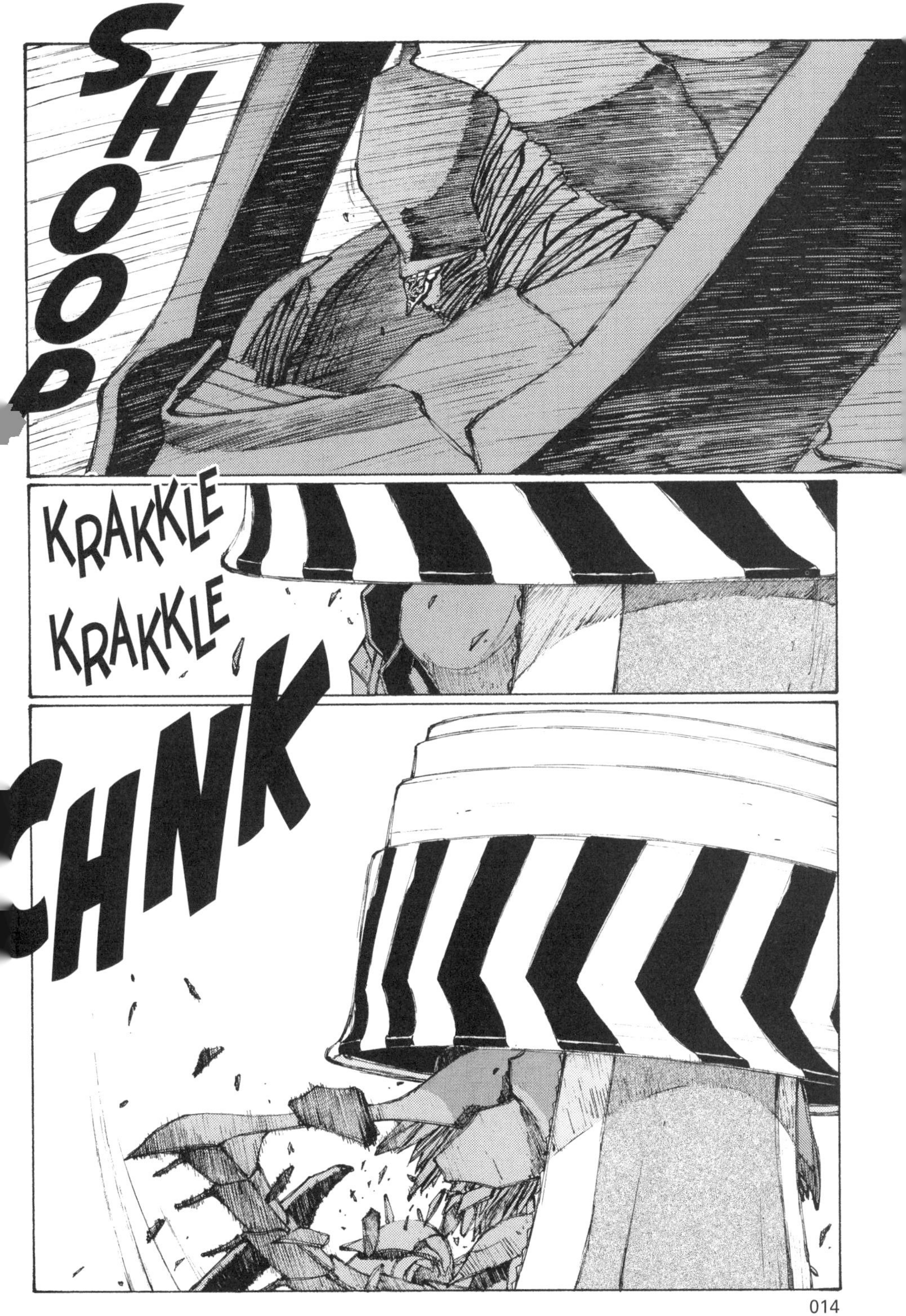
SHOOD
KRAKKLE
KRAKKLE
CHNK

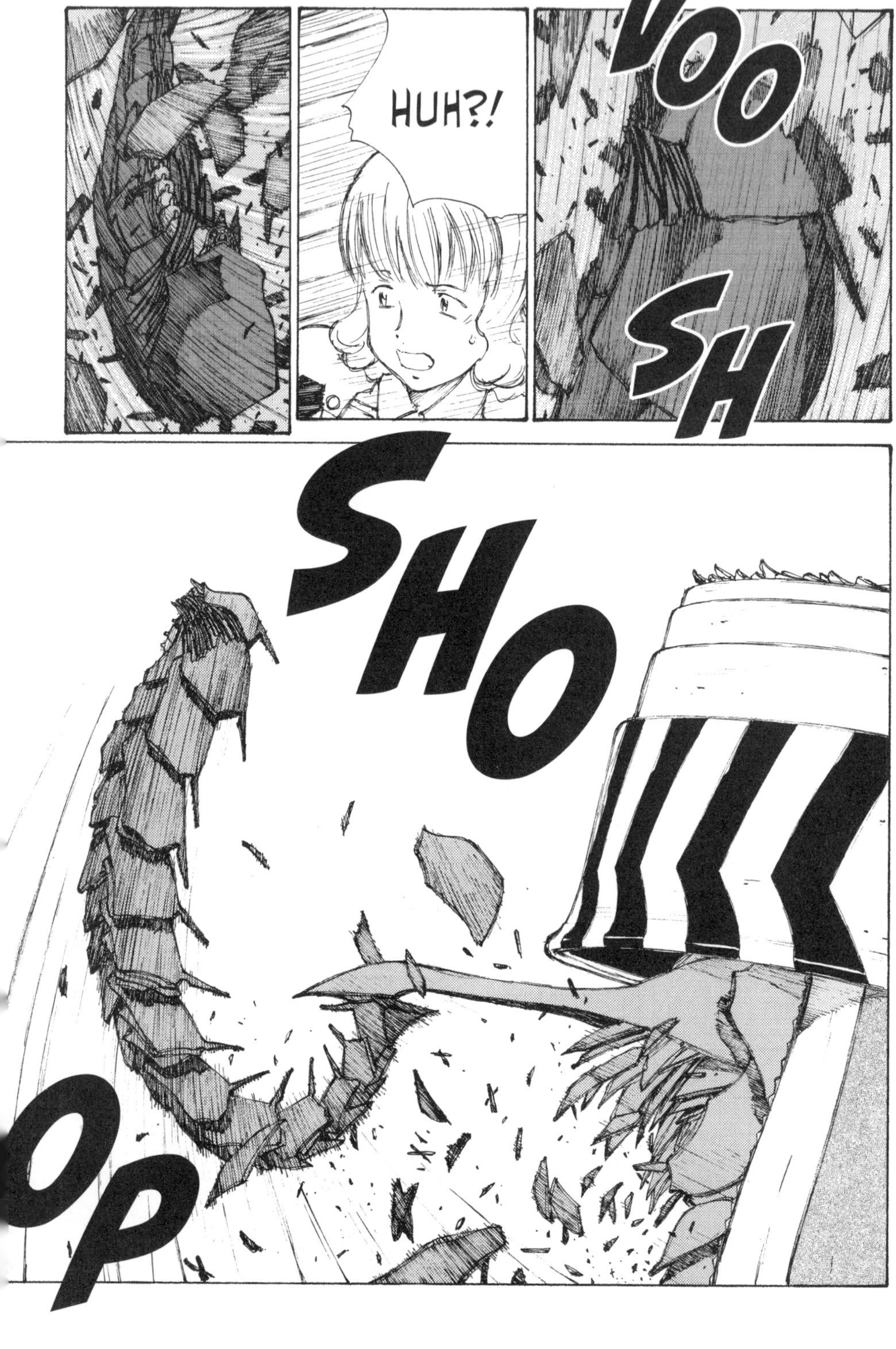
VOO
SH
HUH?!
SHO
OP

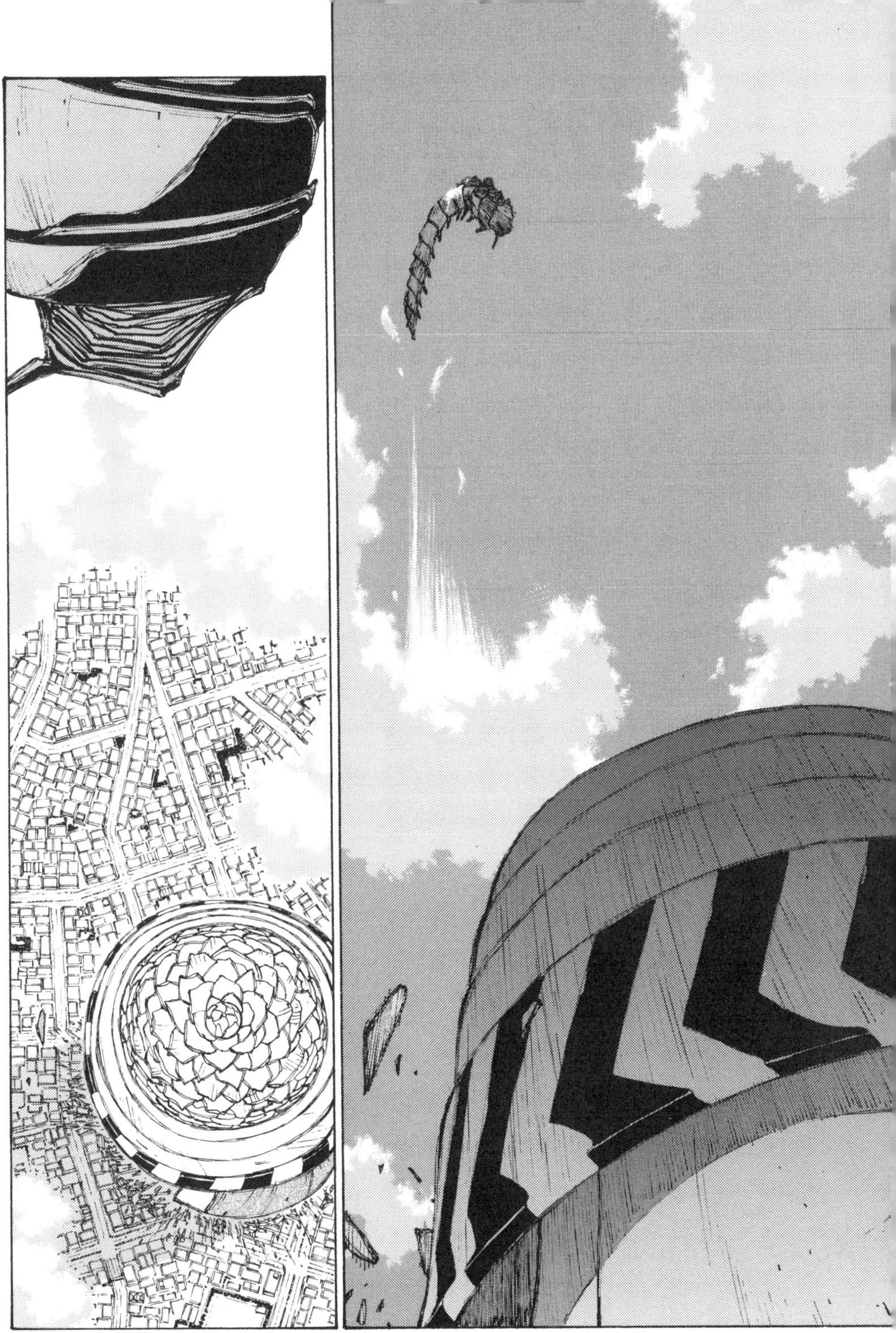

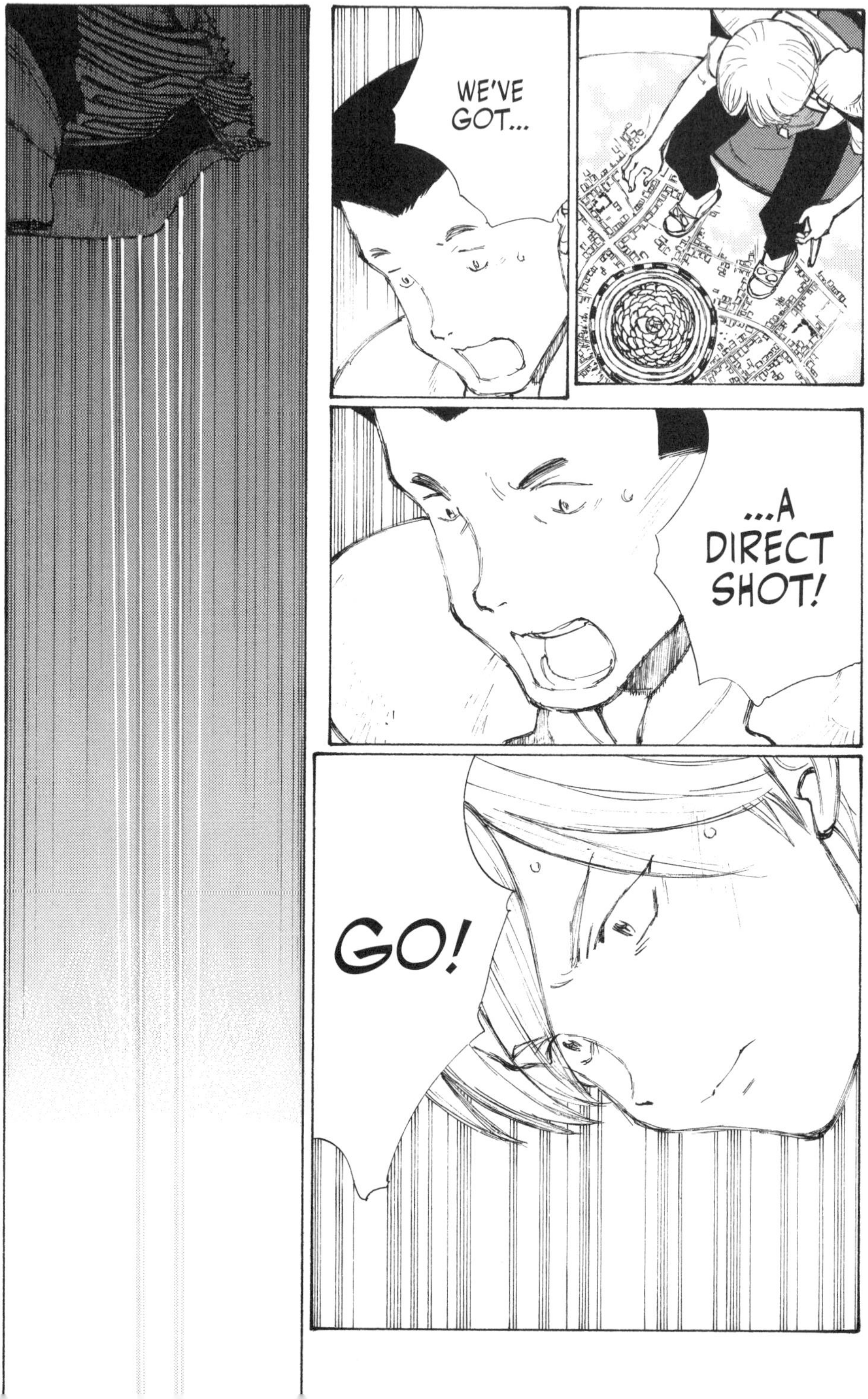
WE'VE GOT...
...A DIRECT SHOT!
GO!

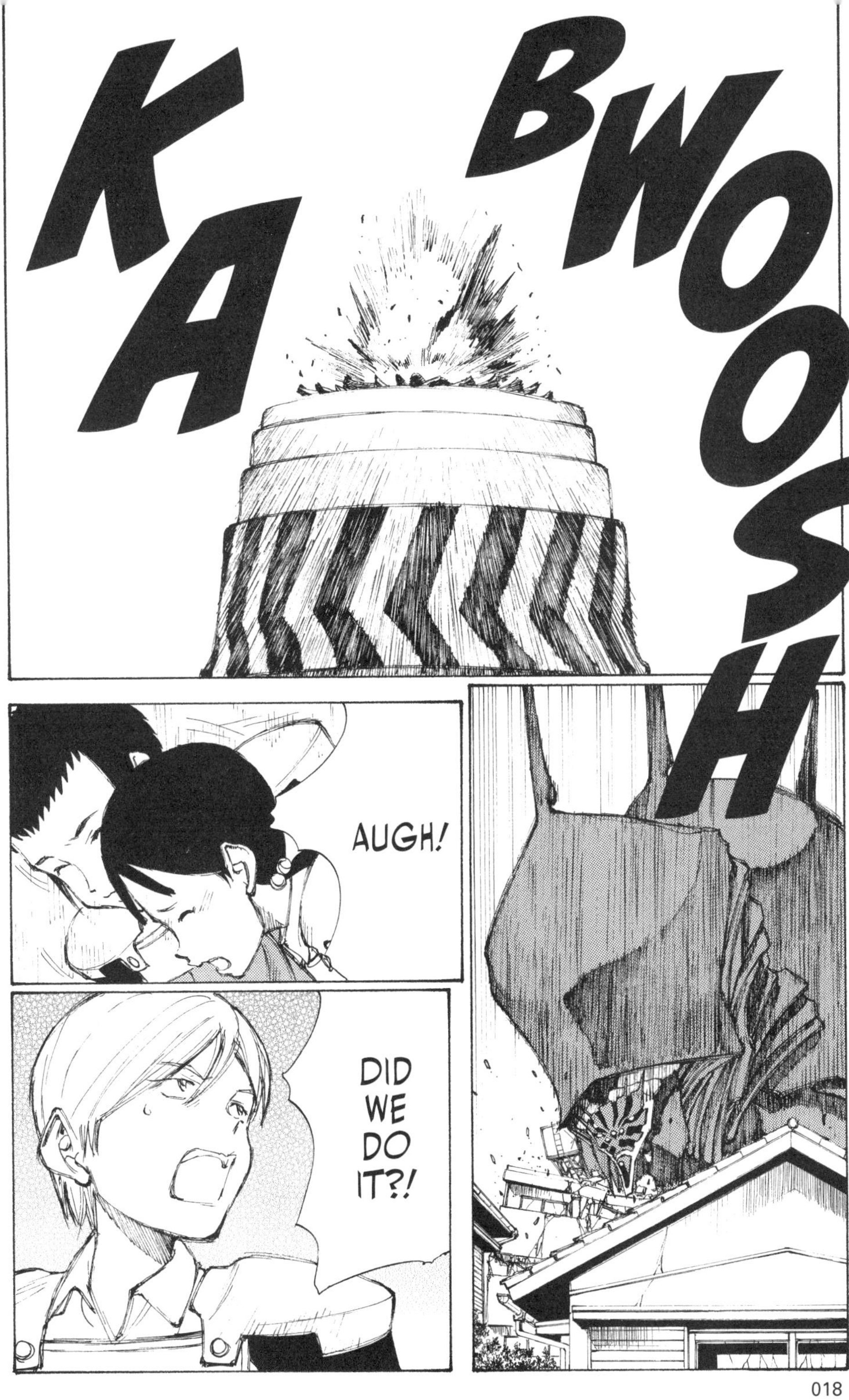
KA
BWOOSH
AUGH!
DID WE DO IT?!

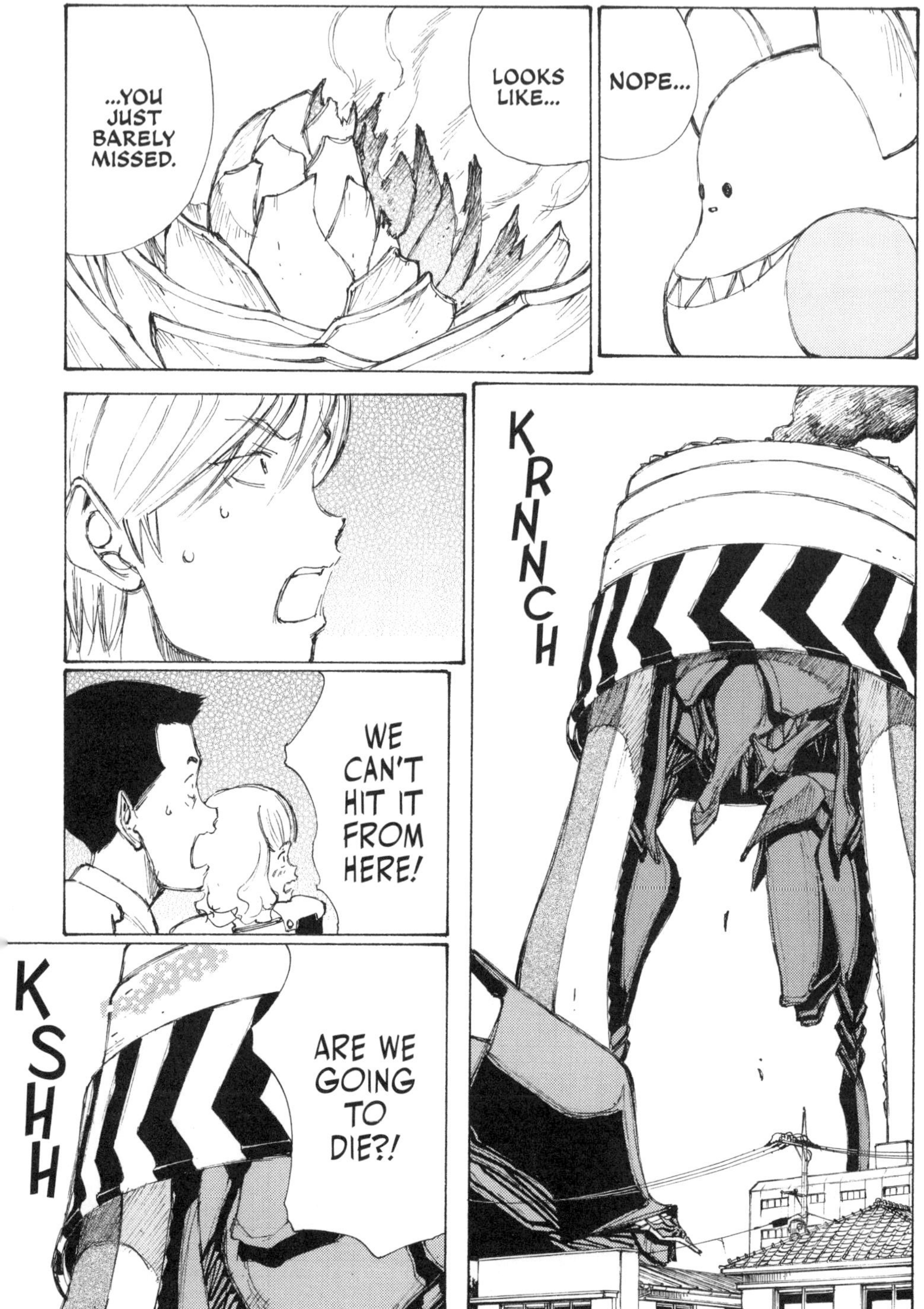
NOPE...
LOOKS LIKE...
...YOU JUST BARELY MISSED.
KRNNNCH
WE CAN'T HIT IT FROM HERE!
ARE WE GOING TO DIE?!
KSHH

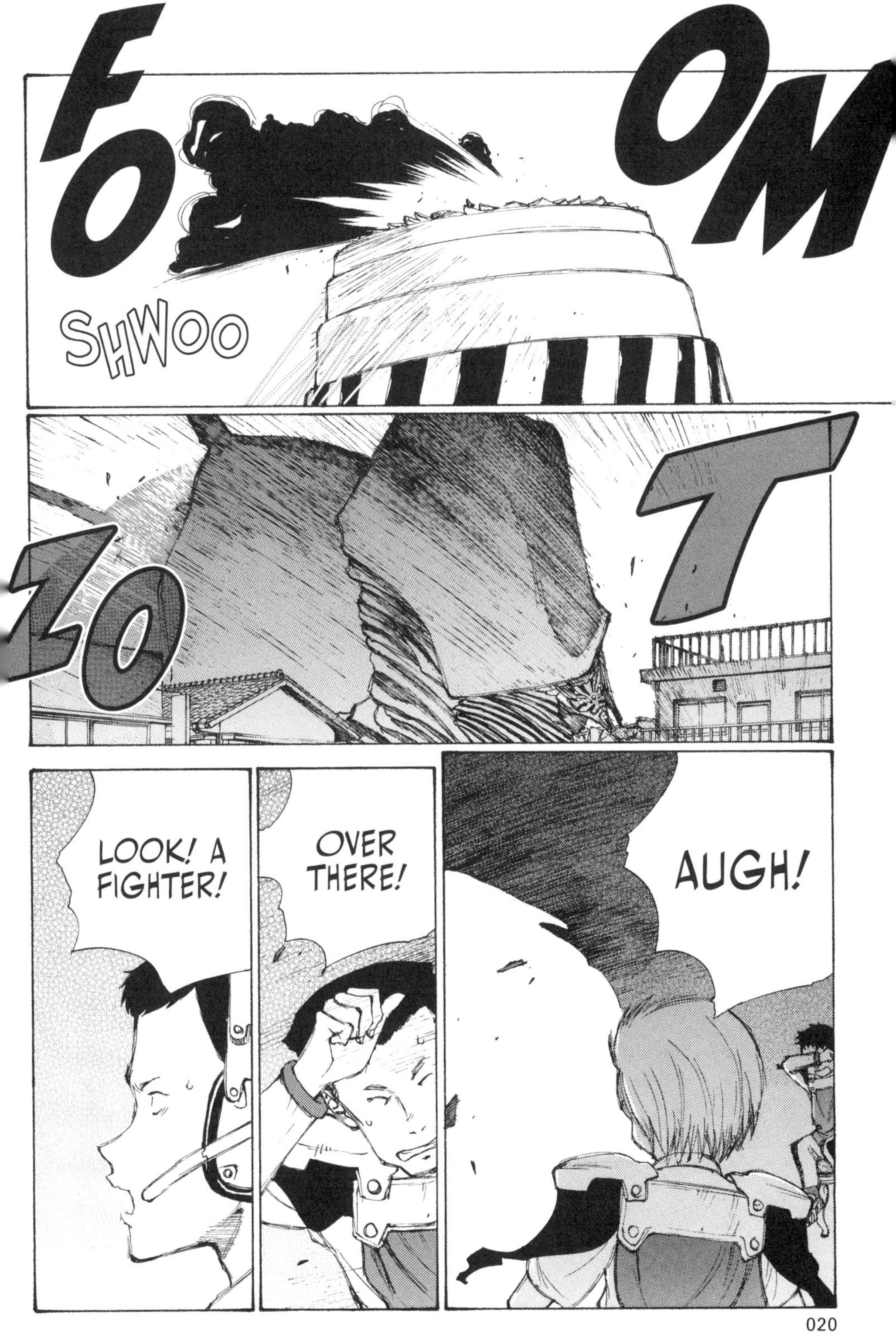
FOOM
SHWOO
ZOT
AUGH!
OVER THERE!
LOOK! A FIGHTER!

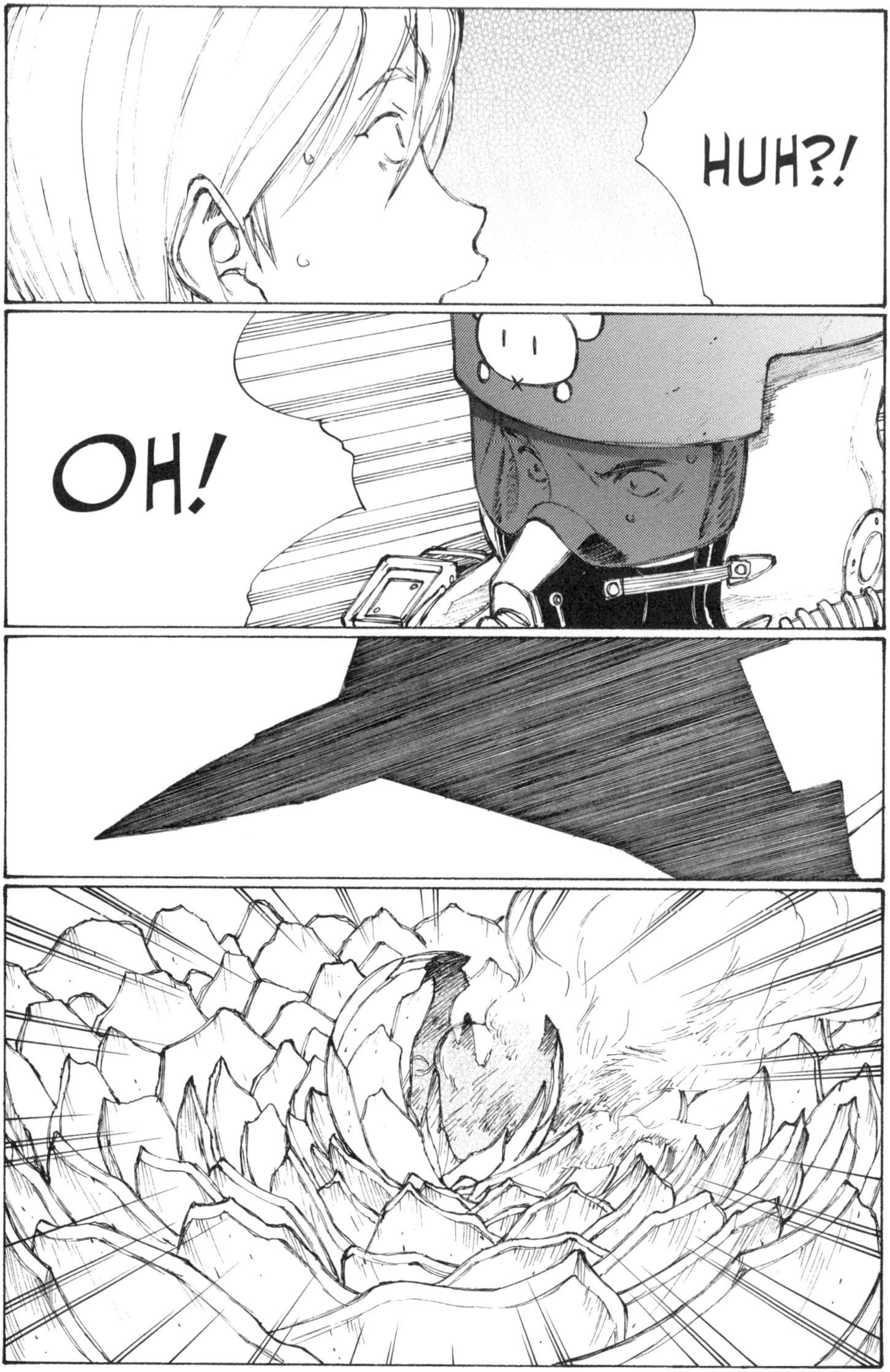
HUH?!
OH!

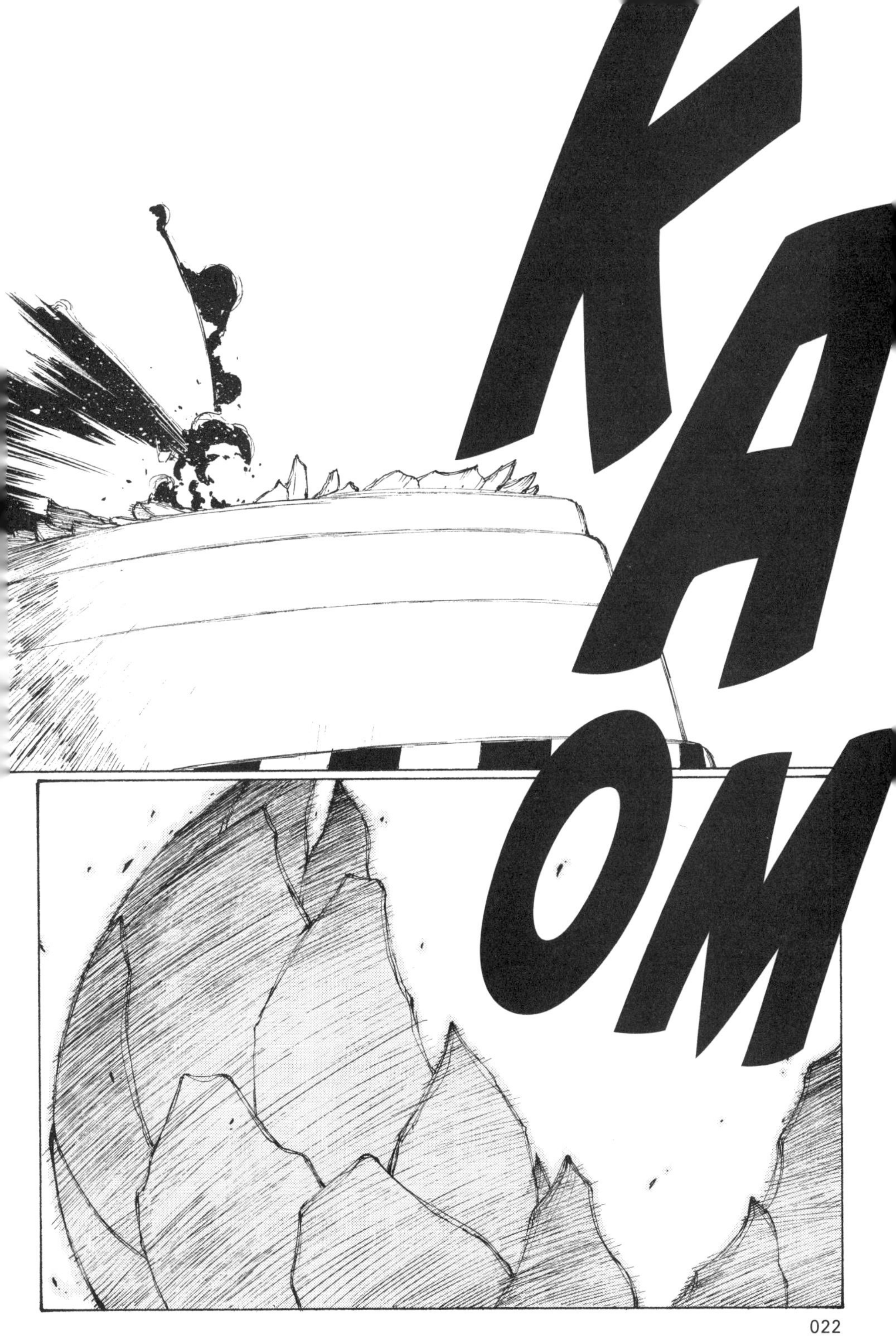
KAAOM

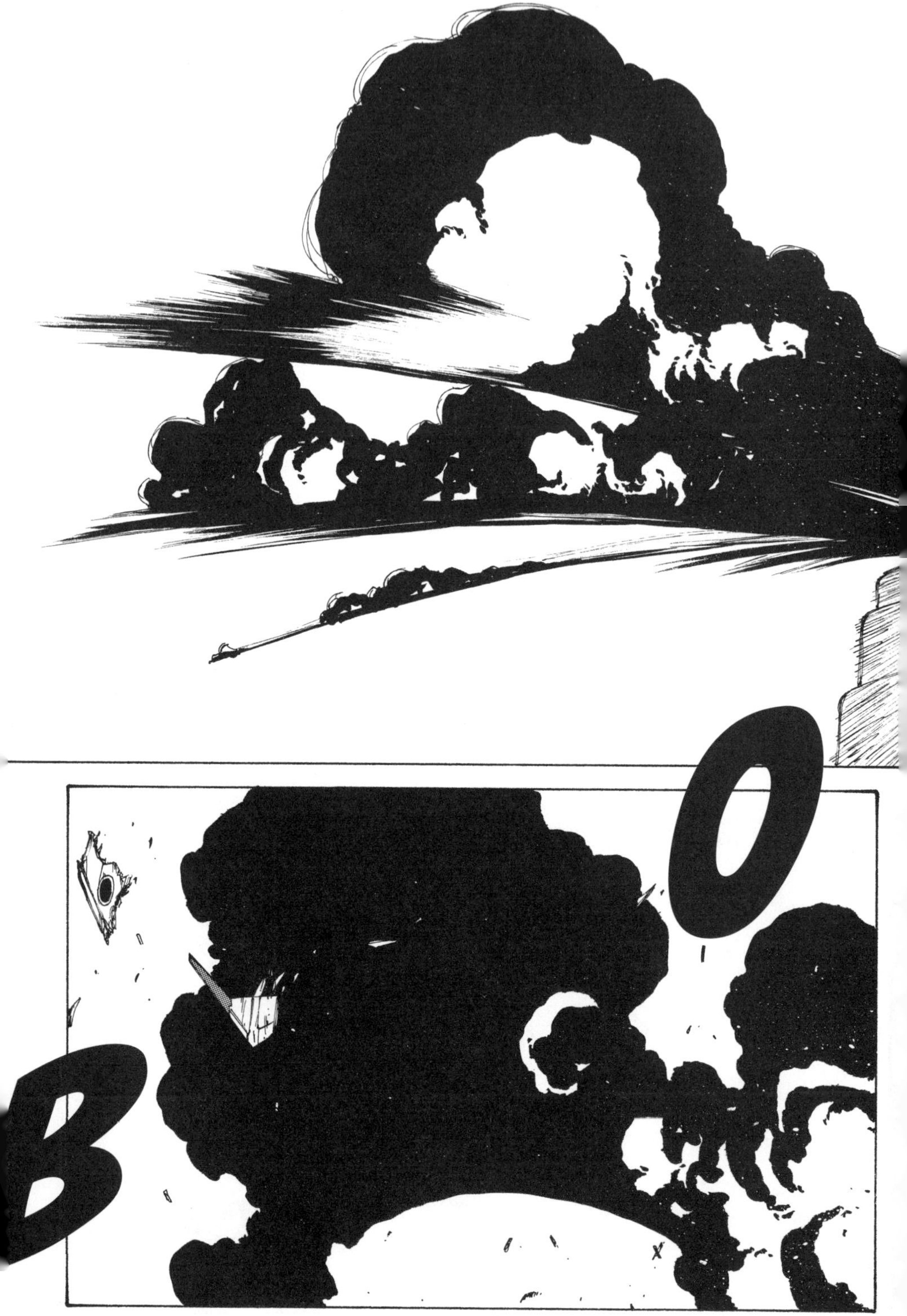
B
O

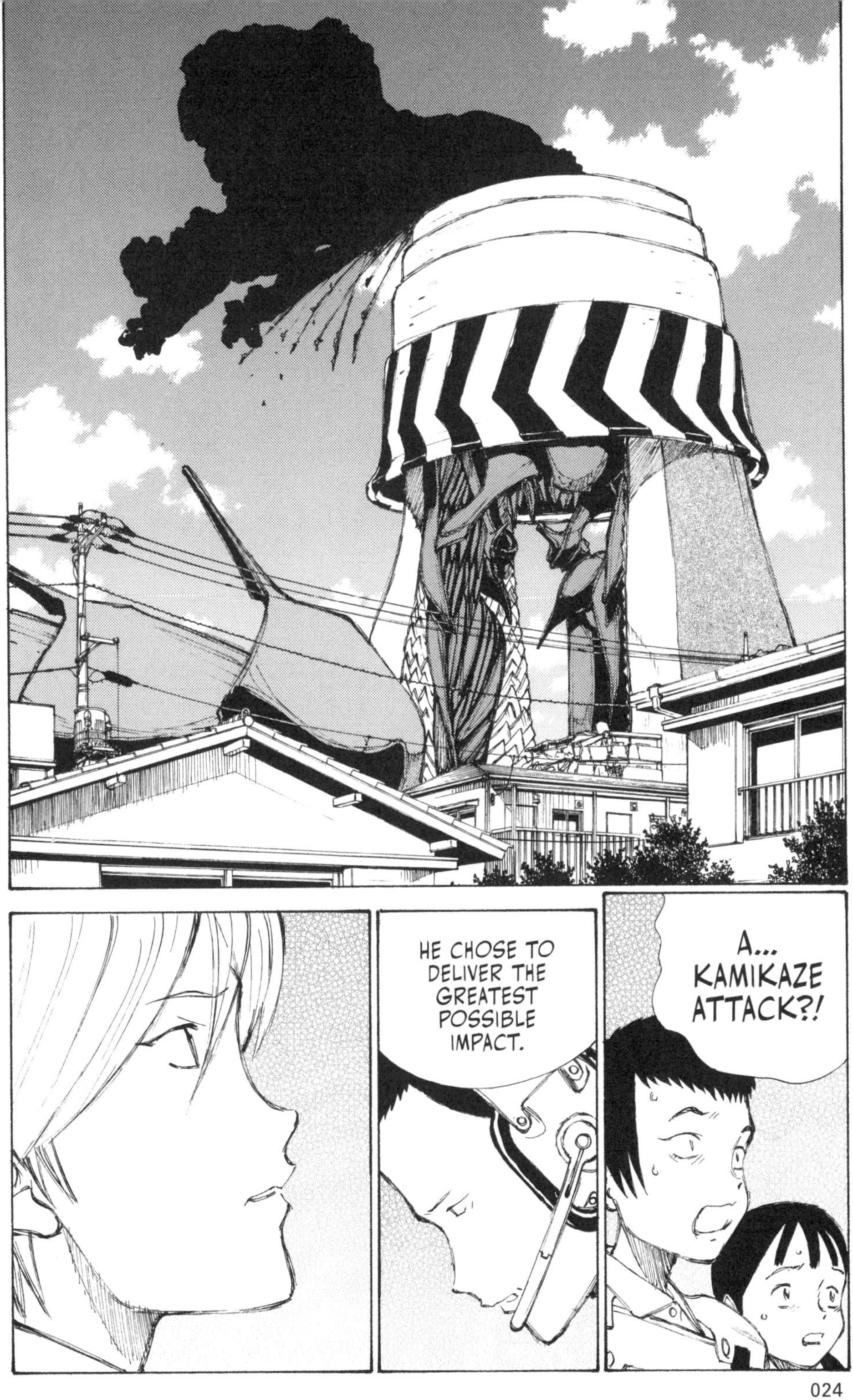
A... KAMIKAZE ATTACK?!
HE CHOSE TO DELIVER THE GREATEST POSSIBLE IMPACT.

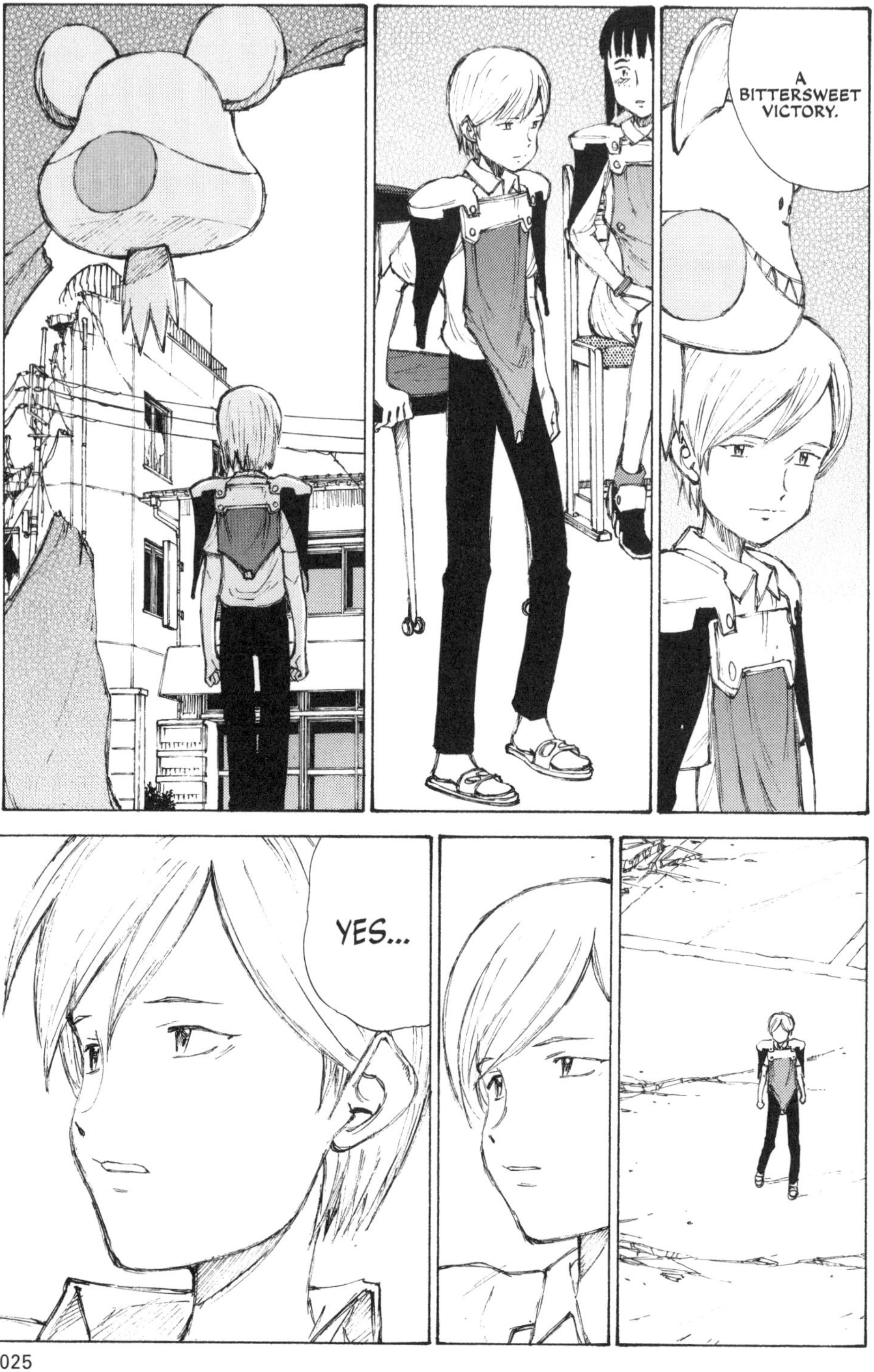
A BITTERSWEET VICTORY.
YES...

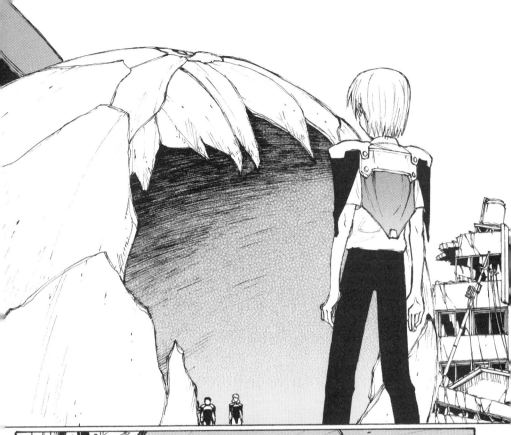

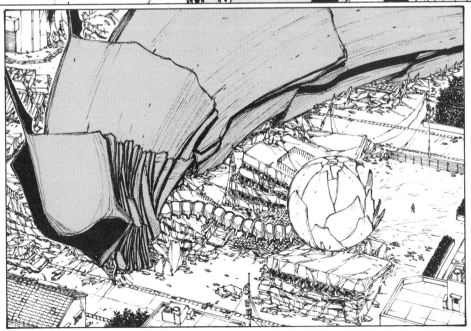

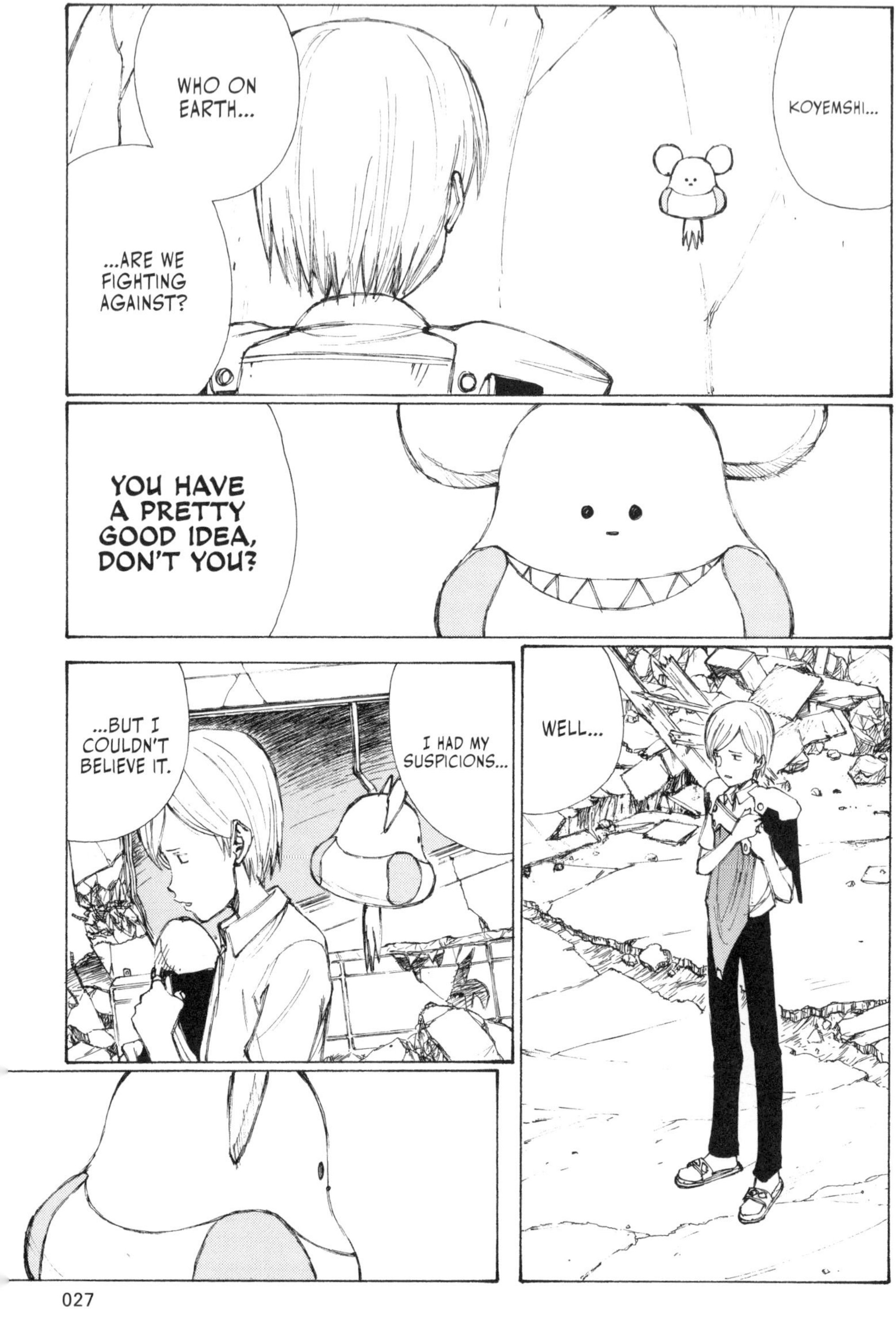
KOYEMSHI...
WHO ON EARTH...
...ARE WE FIGHTING AGAINST?
YOU HAVE A PRETTY GOOD IDEA, DON'T YOU?
WELL...
I HAD MY SUSPICIONS...
...BUT I COULDN'T BELIEVE IT.

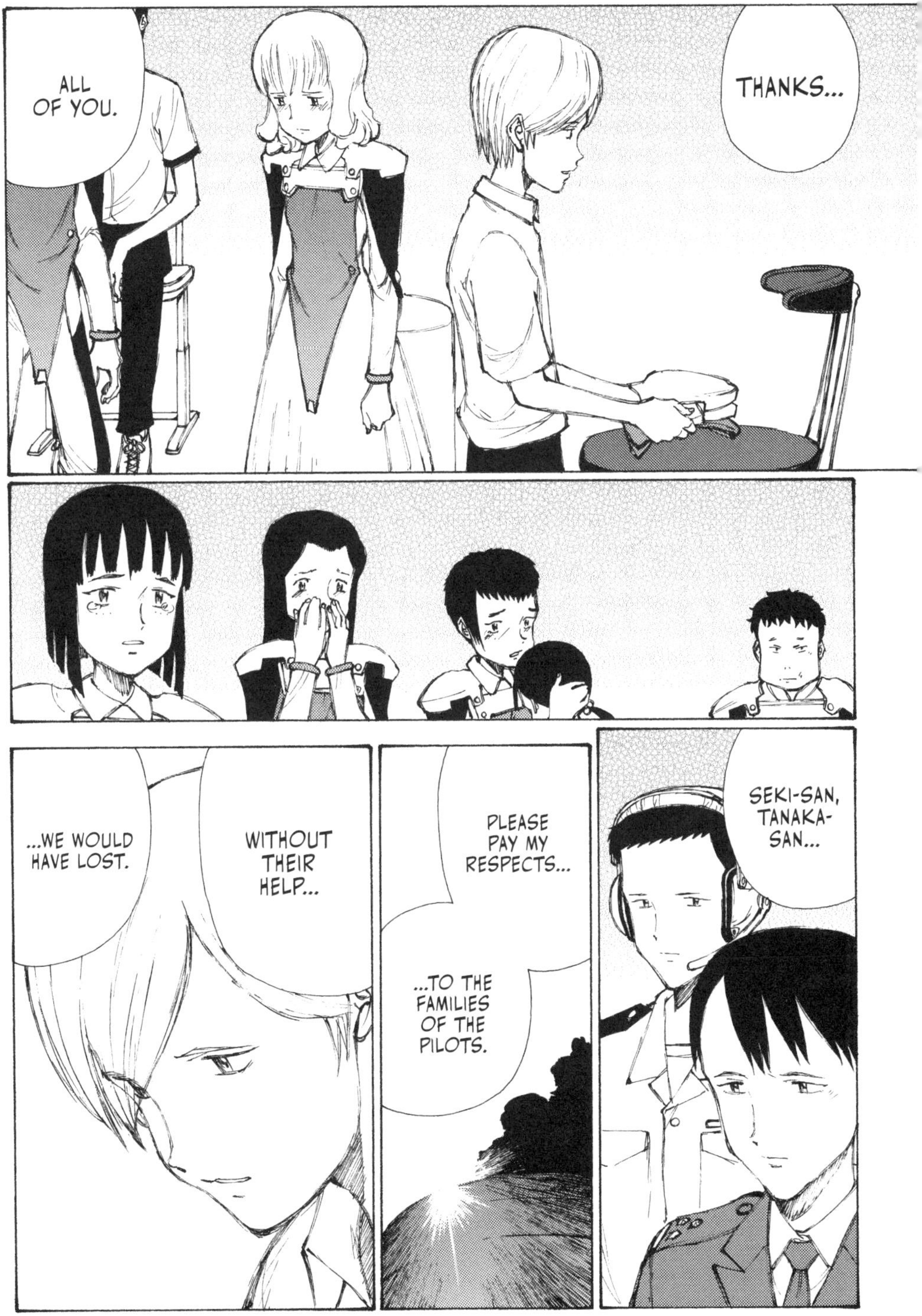
THANKS...
ALL OF YOU.
SEKI-SAN, TANAKA-SAN...
PLEASE PAY MY RESPECTS...
...TO THE FAMILIES OF THE PILOTS.
WITHOUT THEIR HELP...
...WE WOULD HAVE LOST.

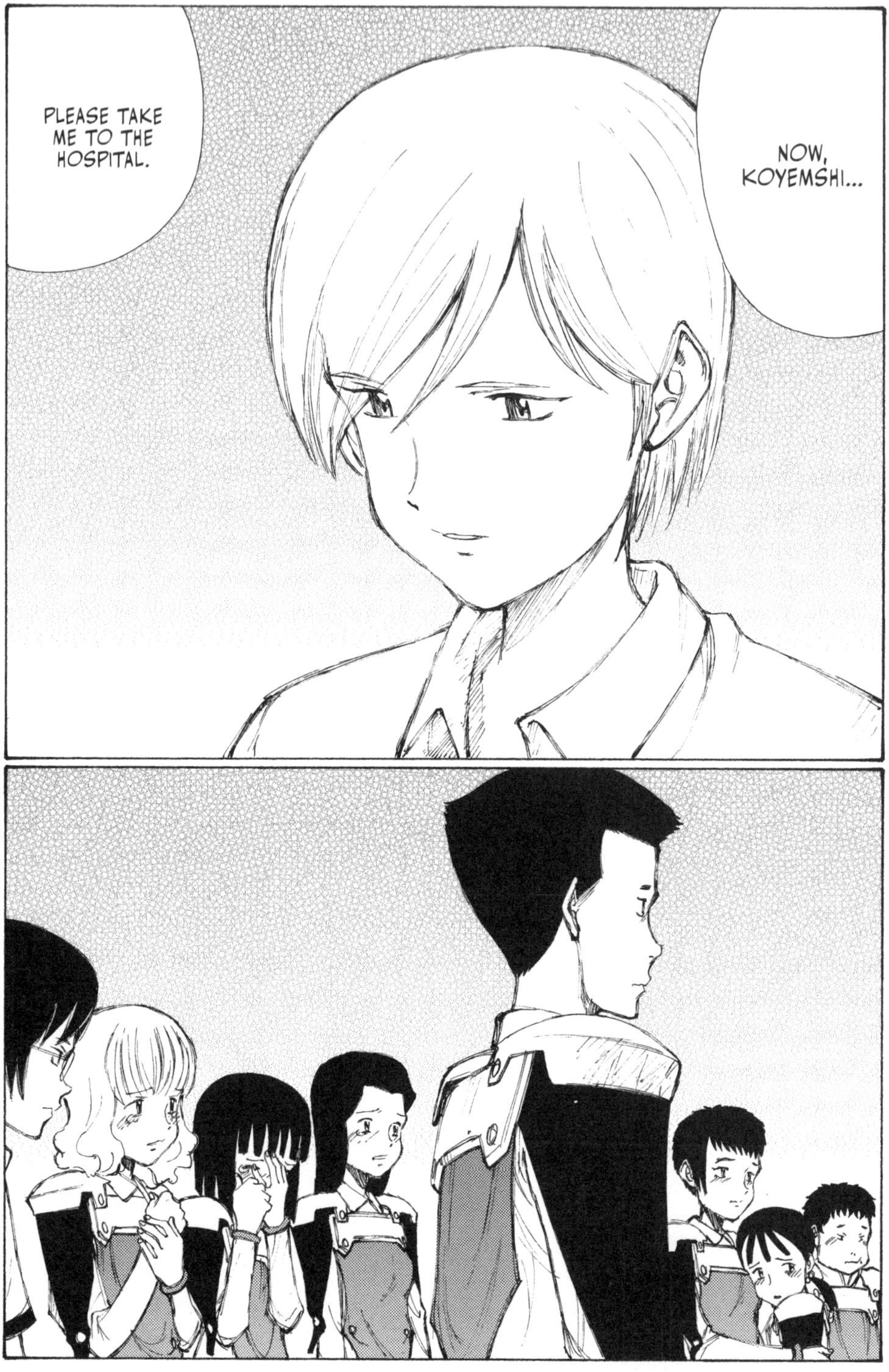
NOW, KOYEMSHI...
PLEASE TAKE ME TO THE HOSPITAL.

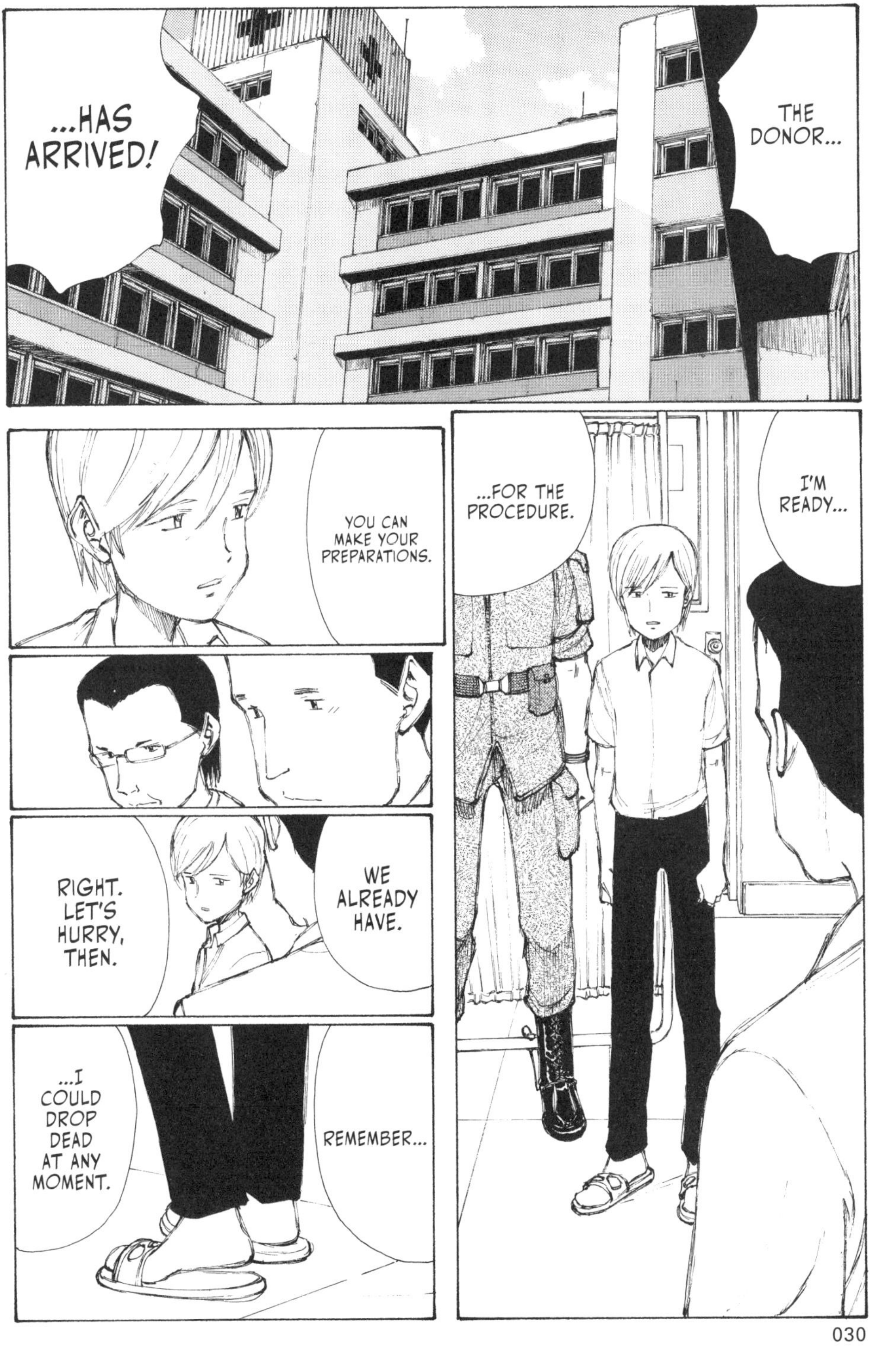
THE DONOR...
...HAS ARRIVED!
I'M READY...
...FOR THE PROCEDURE.
YOU CAN MAKE YOUR PREPARATIONS.
WE ALREADY HAVE.
RIGHT. LET'S HURRY, THEN.
REMEMBER...
...I COULD DROP DEAD AT ANY MOMENT.

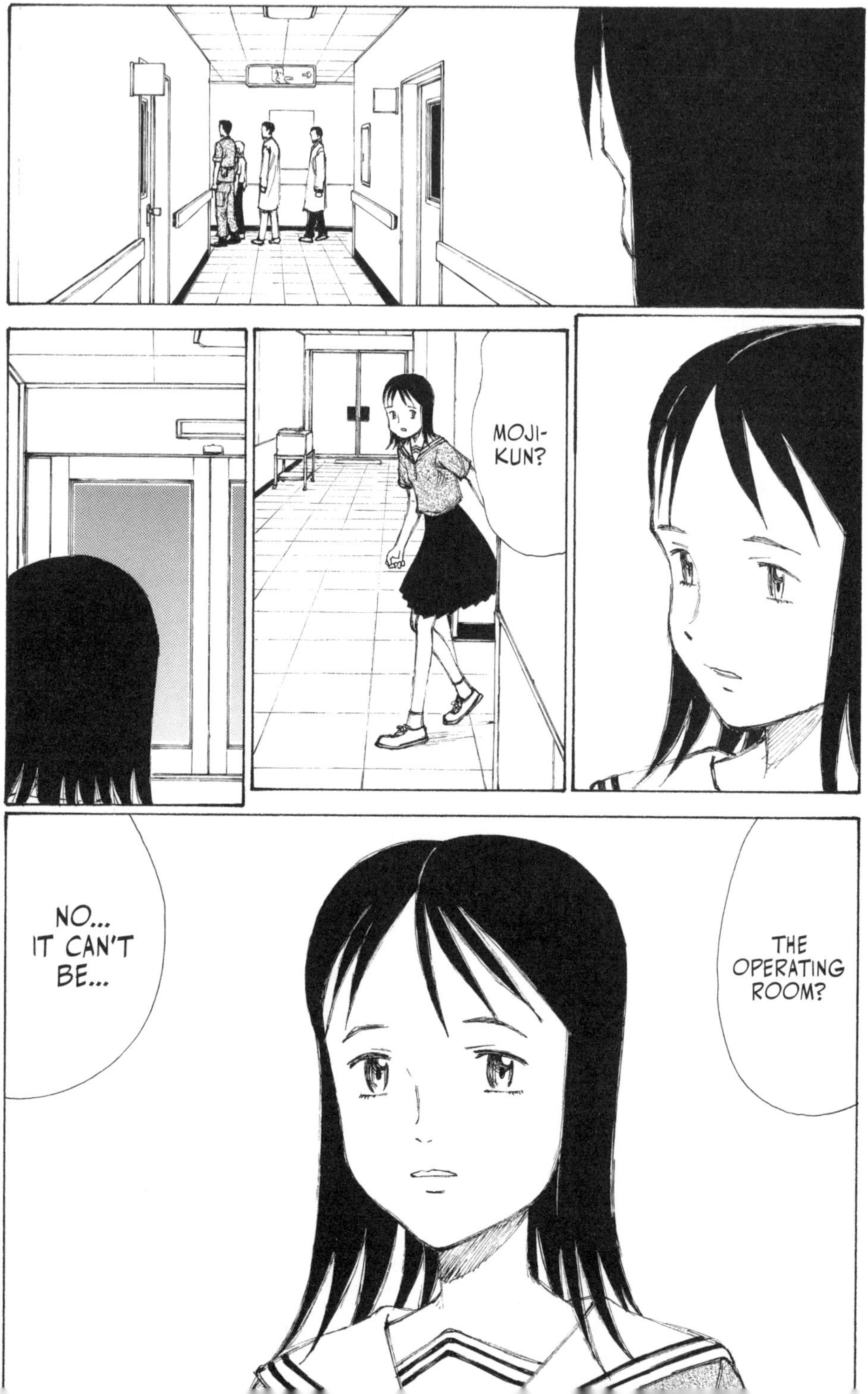
MOJI-KUN?
THE OPERATING ROOM?
NO... IT CAN'T BE...

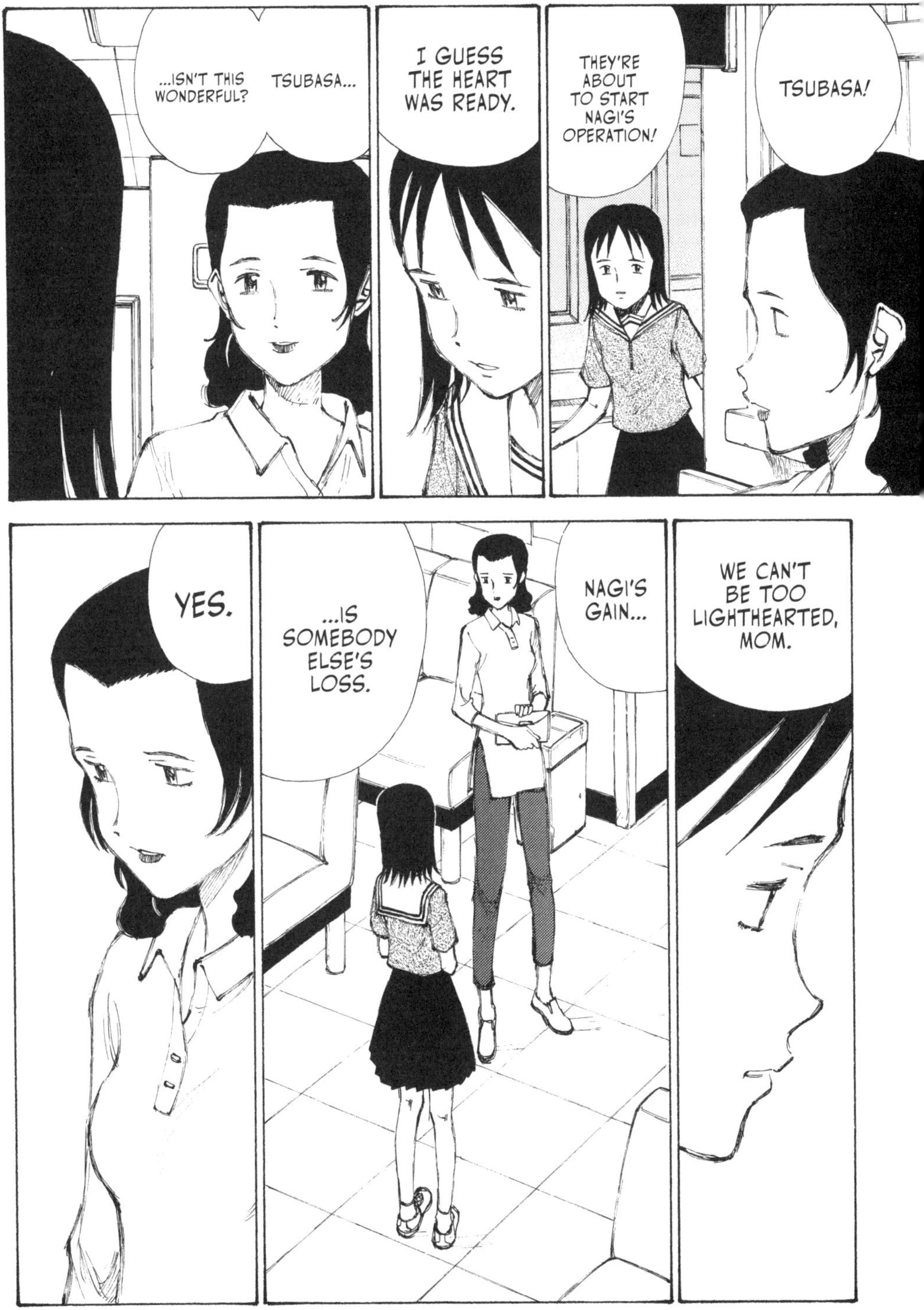
TSUBASA!
THEY'RE ABOUT TO START NAGI'S OPERATION!
I GUESS THE HEART WAS READY.
TSUBASA...
...ISN'T THIS WONDERFUL?
WE CAN'T BE TOO LIGHTHEARTED, MOM.
NAGI'S GAIN...
...IS SOMEBODY ELSE'S LOSS.
YES.

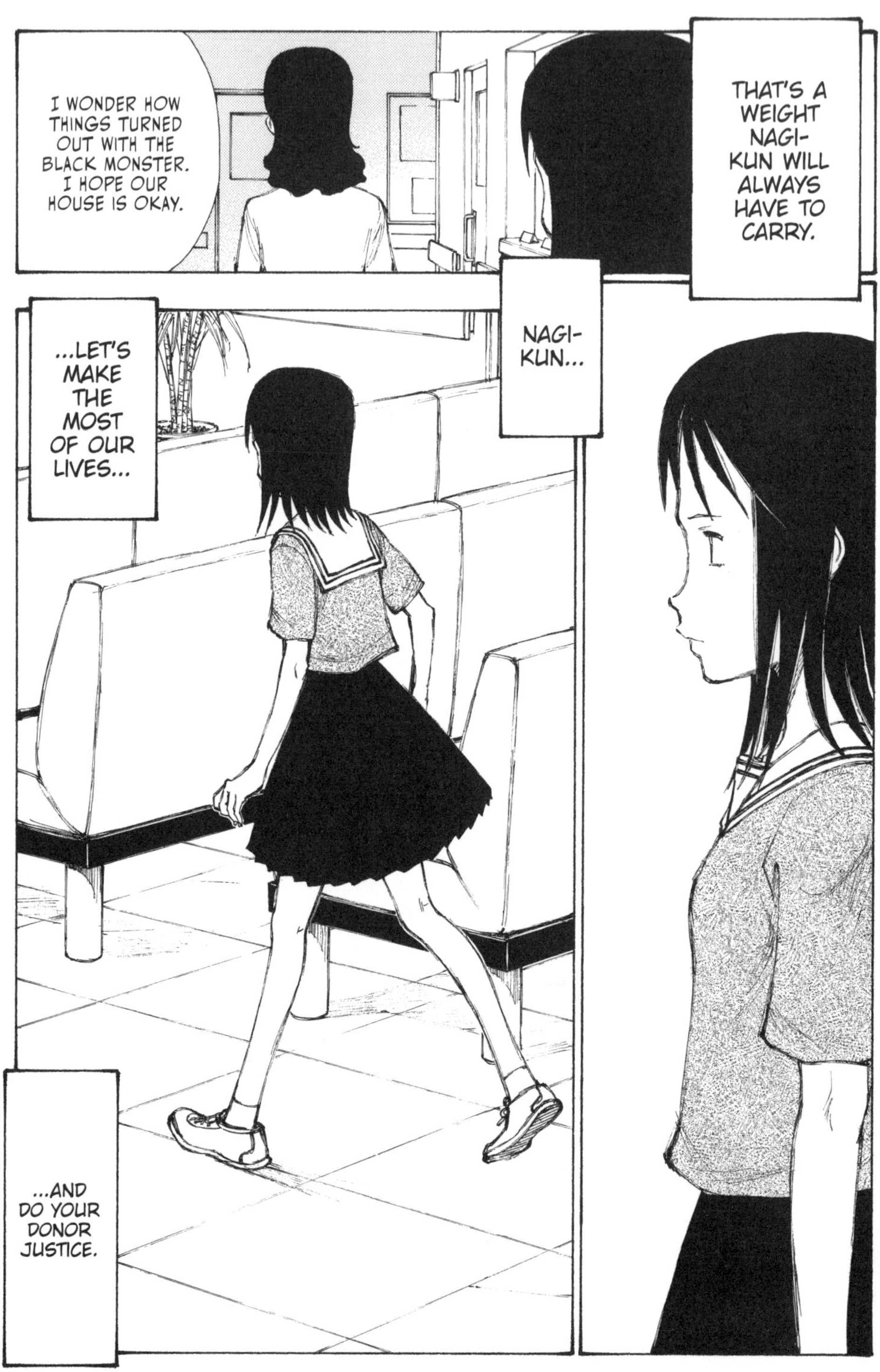
THAT'S A WEIGHT NAGI-KUN WILL ALWAYS HAVE TO CARRY.
I WONDER HOW THINGS TURNED OUT WITH THE BLACK MONSTER. I HOPE OUR HOUSE IS OKAY.
NAGI-KUN...
...LET'S MAKE THE MOST OF OUR LIVES...
...AND DO YOUR DONOR JUSTICE.

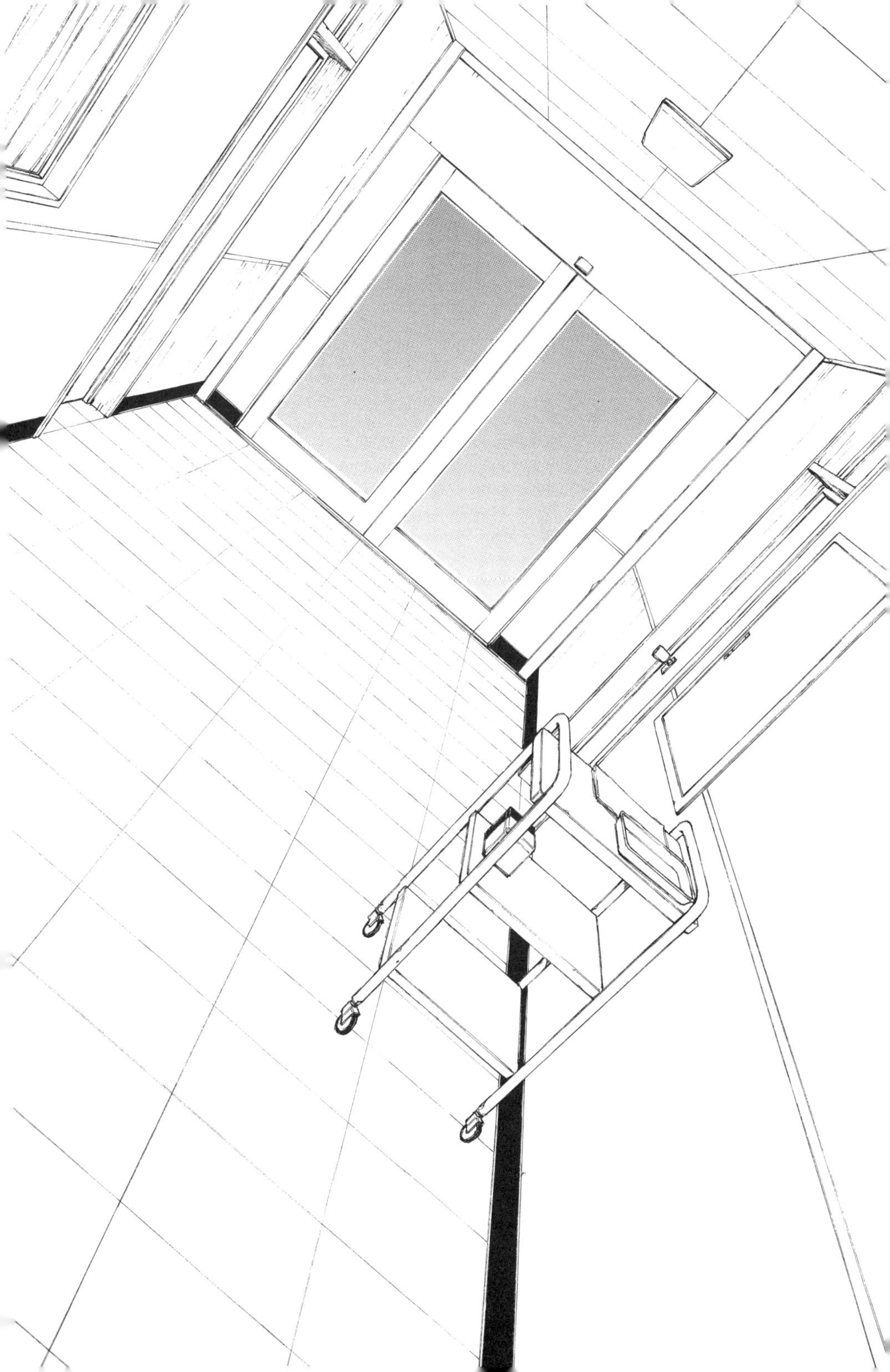

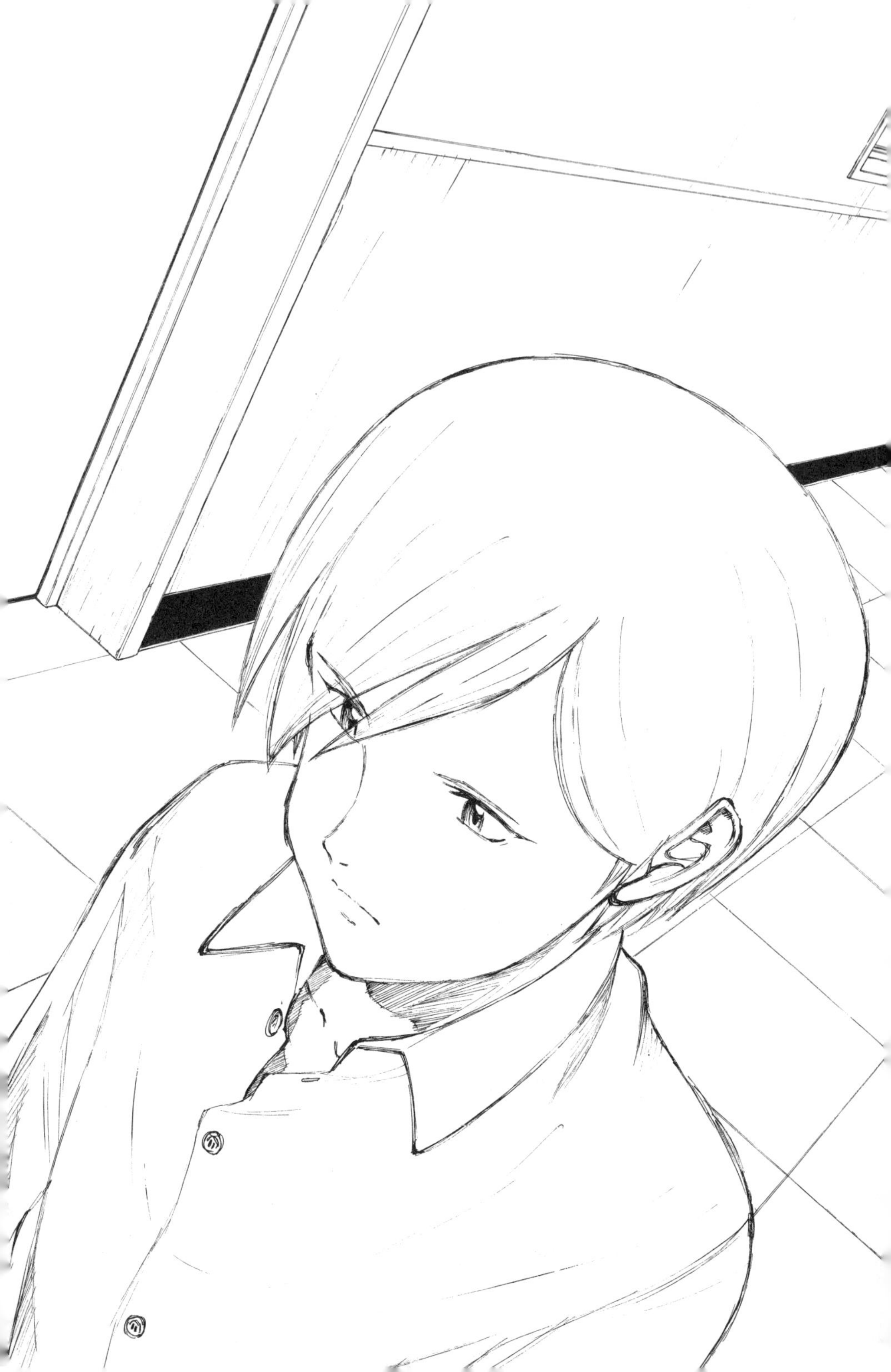

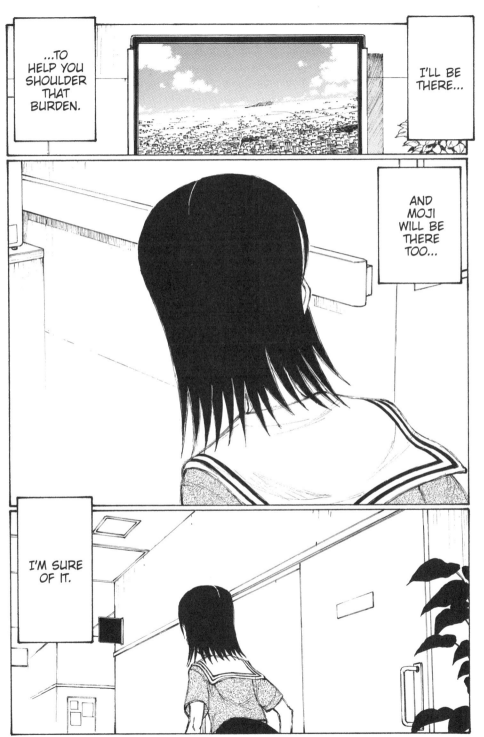

...TO HELP YOU SHOULDER THAT BURDEN.

I'LL BE THERE...

AND MOJI WILL BE THERE TOO...

I'M SURE OF IT.

036

CHAPTER 25: MAKI ANO 1

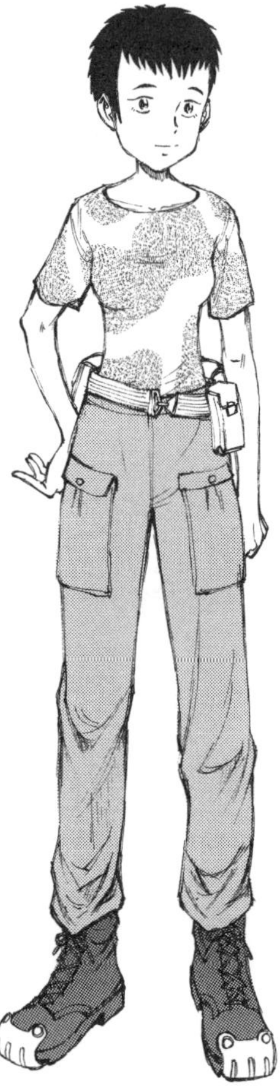

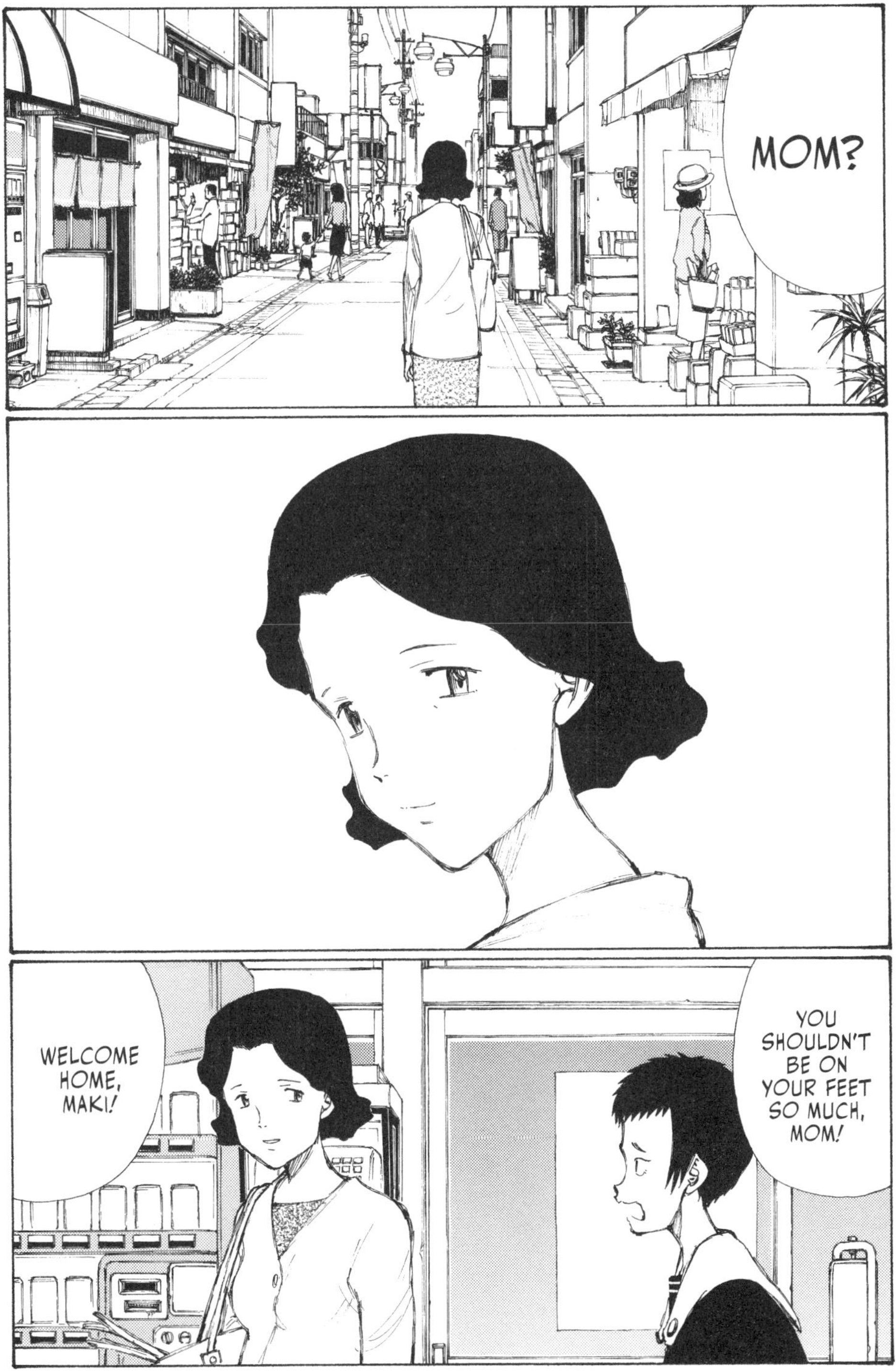
MOM?
YOU SHOULDN'T BE ON YOUR FEET SO MUCH, MOM!
WELCOME HOME, MAKI!

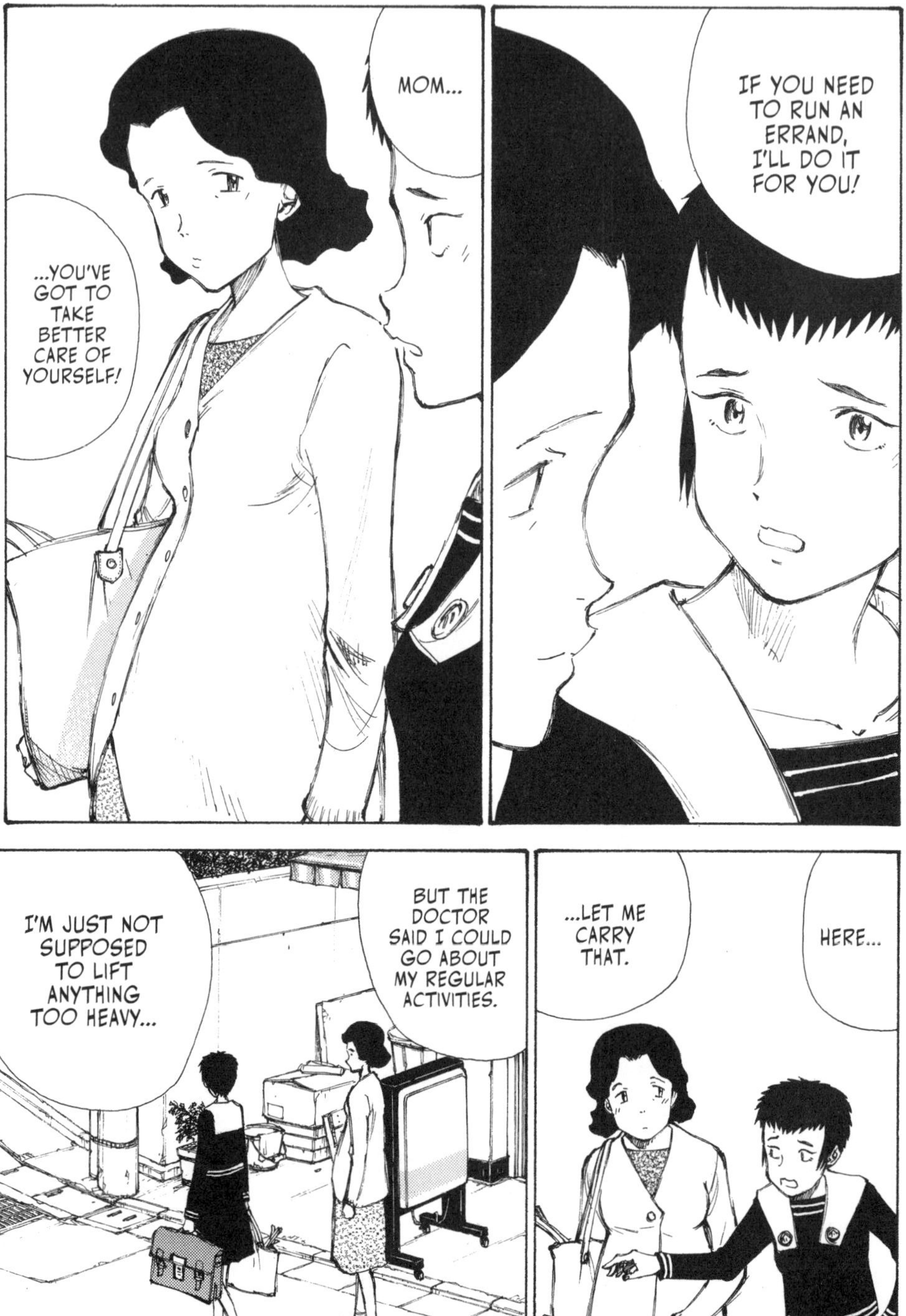
IF YOU NEED TO RUN AN ERRAND, I'LL DO IT FOR YOU!
MOM...
...YOU'VE GOT TO TAKE BETTER CARE OF YOURSELF!
HERE...
...LET ME CARRY THAT.
BUT THE DOCTOR SAID I COULD GO ABOUT MY REGULAR ACTIVITIES.
I'M JUST NOT SUPPOSED TO LIFT ANYTHING TOO HEAVY...

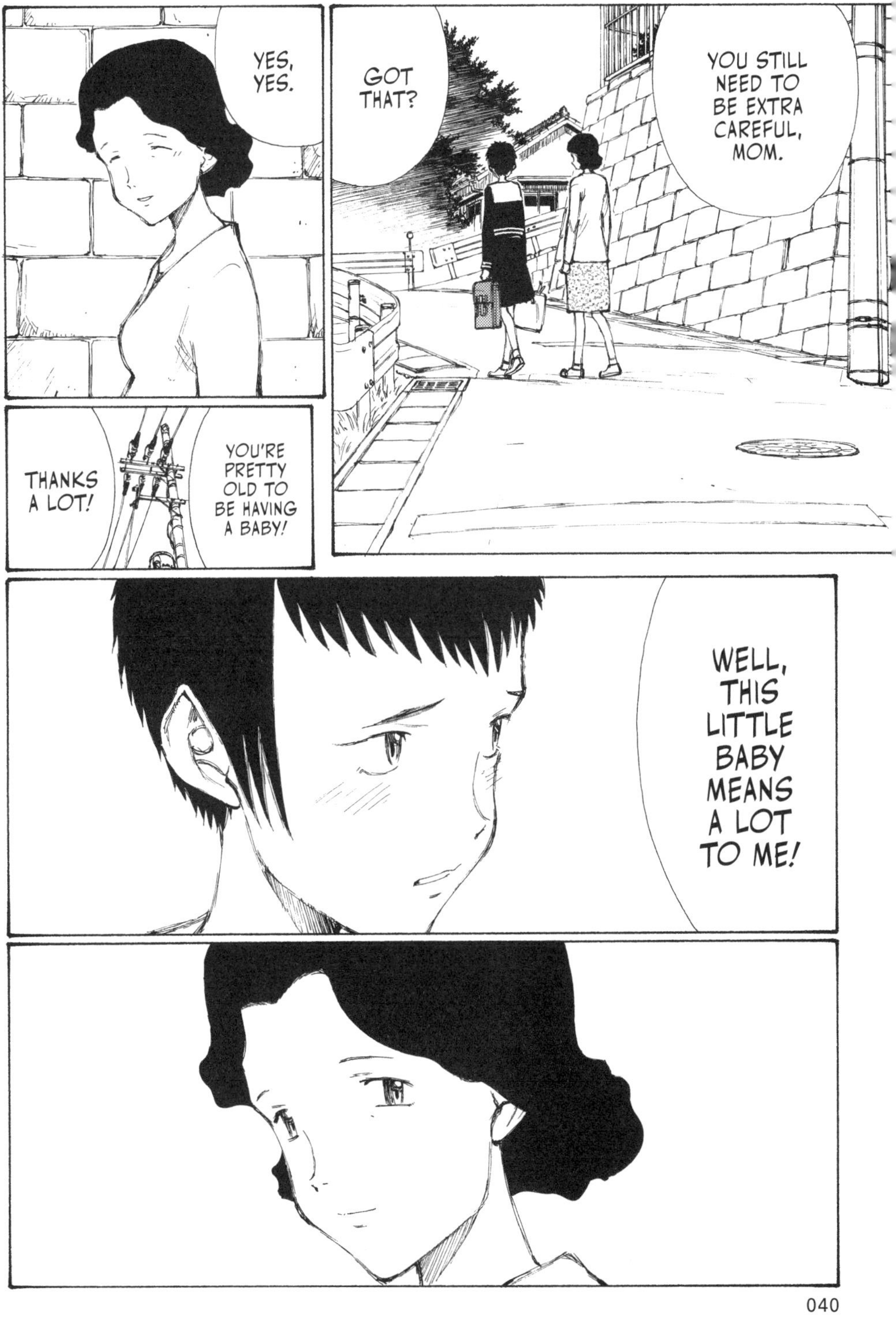
YOU STILL NEED TO BE EXTRA CAREFUL, MOM.
GOT THAT?
YES, YES.
YOU'RE PRETTY OLD TO BE HAVING A BABY!
THANKS A LOT!
WELL, THIS LITTLE BABY MEANS A LOT TO ME!

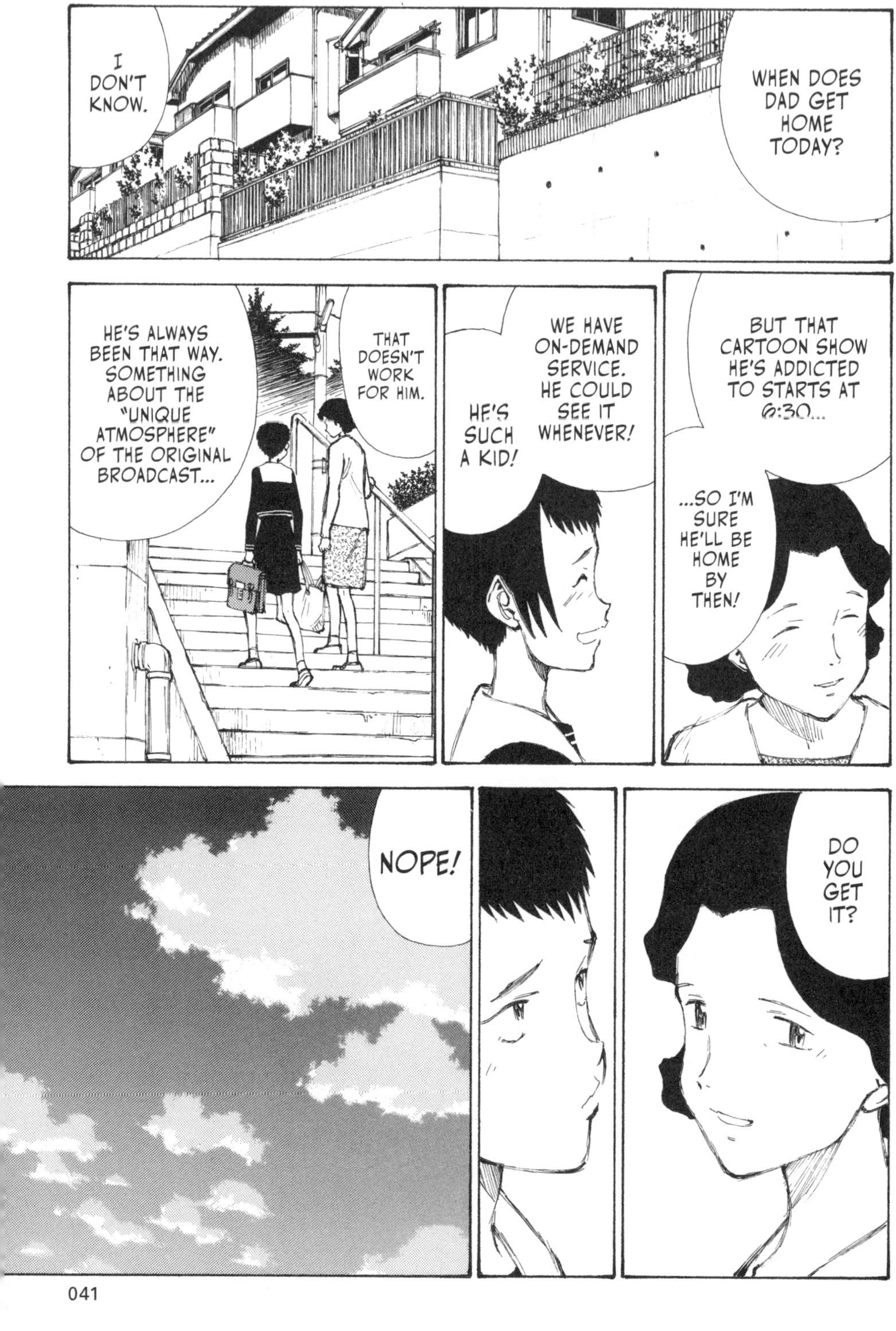
WHEN DOES DAD GET HOME TODAY?
I DON'T KNOW.
BUT THAT CARTOON SHOW HE'S ADDICTED TO STARTS AT 6:30...
...SO I'M SURE HE'LL BE HOME BY THEN!
WE HAVE ON-DEMAND SERVICE. HE COULD SEE IT WHENEVER!
HE'S SUCH A KID!
THAT DOESN'T WORK FOR HIM.
HE'S ALWAYS BEEN THAT WAY. SOMETHING ABOUT THE "UNIQUE ATMOSPHERE" OF THE ORIGINAL BROADCAST...
DO YOU GET IT?
NOPE!

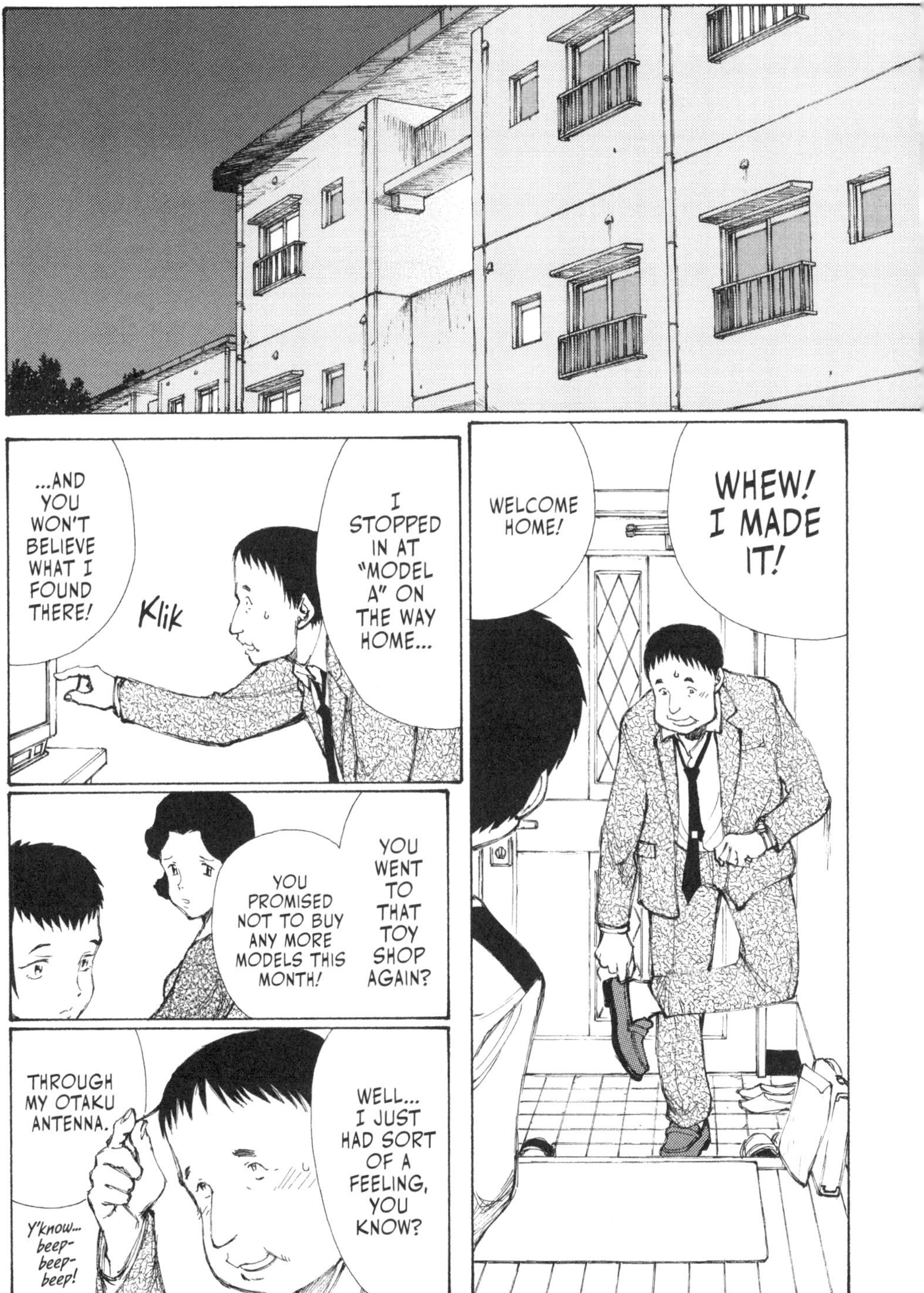
WHEW! I MADE IT!
WELCOME HOME!
I STOPPED IN AT "MODEL A" ON THE WAY HOME...
Klik
...AND YOU WON'T BELIEVE WHAT I FOUND THERE!
YOU WENT TO THAT TOY SHOP AGAIN?
YOU PROMISED NOT TO BUY ANY MORE MODELS THIS MONTH!
WELL... I JUST HAD SORT OF A FEELING, YOU KNOW?
THROUGH MY OTAKU ANTENNA.
Y'know... beep-beep-beep!

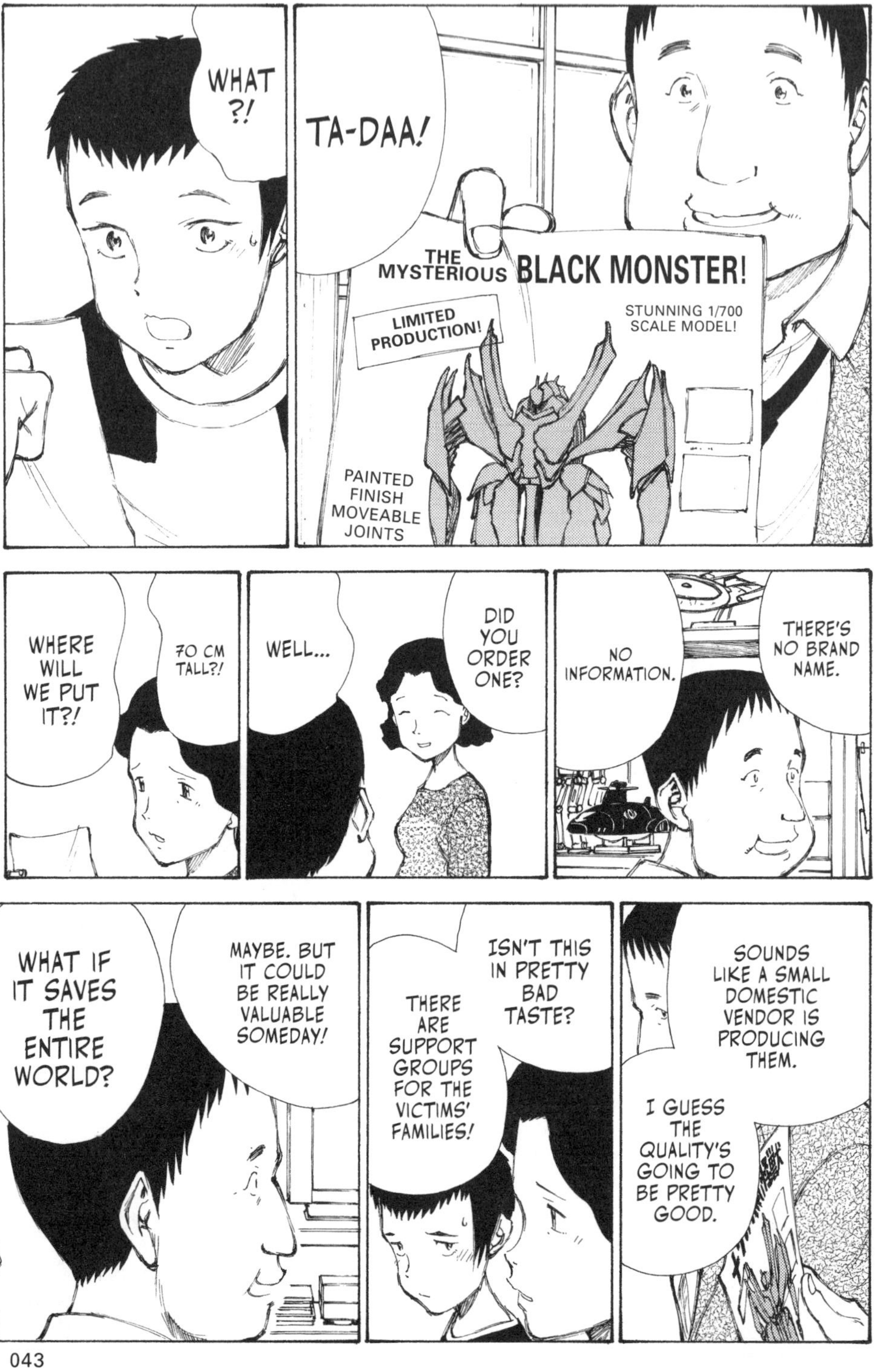
TA-DAA!
THE MYSTERIOUS BLACK MONSTER!
STUNNING 1/700 SCALE MODEL!
LIMITED PRODUCTION!
PAINTED FINISH MOVEABLE JOINTS
WHAT?!
THERE'S NO BRAND NAME.
NO INFORMATION.
DID YOU ORDER ONE?
WELL...
70 CM TALL?!
WHERE WILL WE PUT IT?!
SOUNDS LIKE A SMALL DOMESTIC VENDOR IS PRODUCING THEM.
I GUESS THE QUALITY'S GOING TO BE PRETTY GOOD.
ISN'T THIS IN PRETTY BAD TASTE?
THERE ARE SUPPORT GROUPS FOR THE VICTIMS' FAMILIES!
MAYBE. BUT IT COULD BE REALLY VALUABLE SOMEDAY!
WHAT IF IT SAVES THE ENTIRE WORLD?

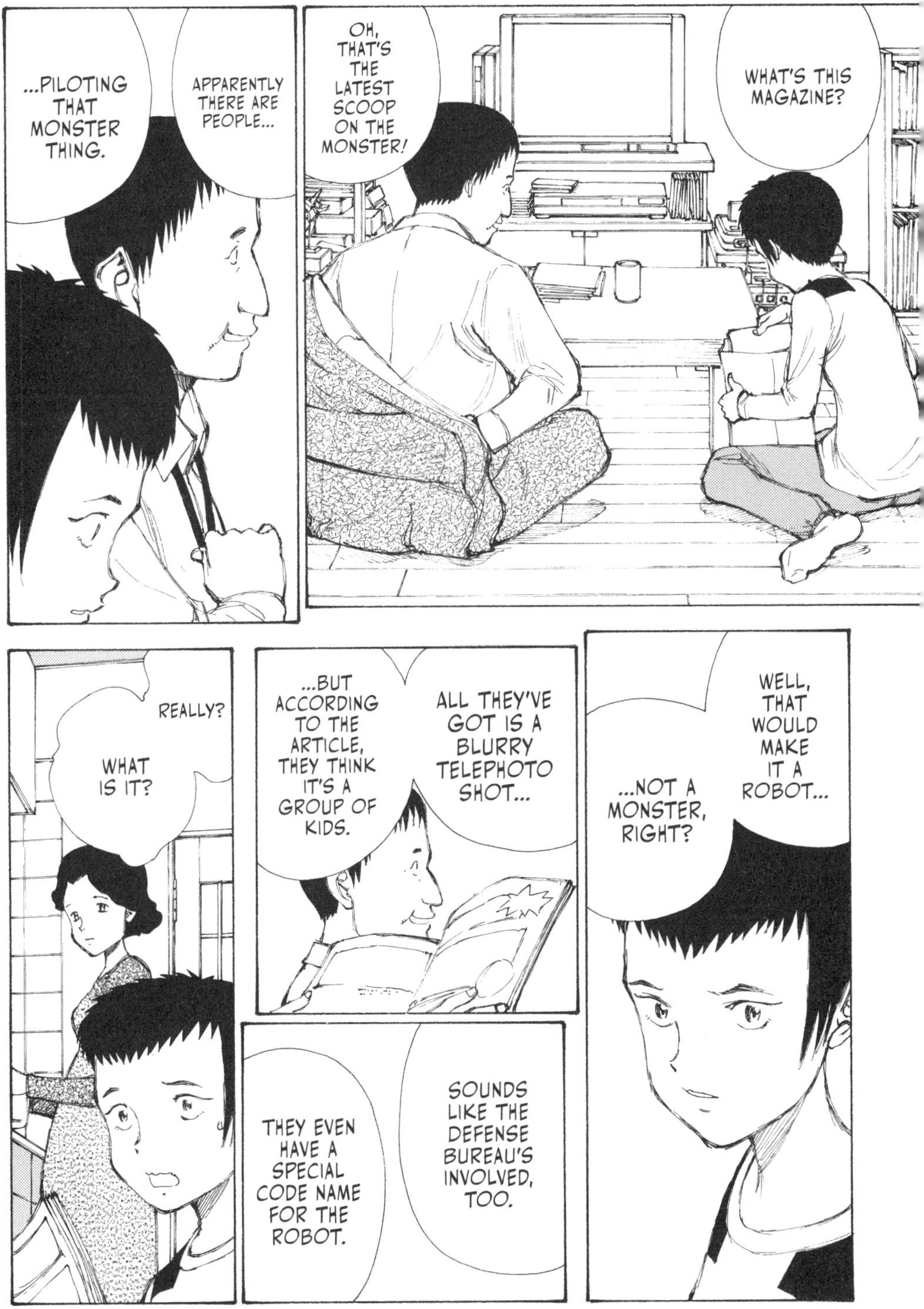
WHAT'S THIS MAGAZINE?
OH, THAT'S THE LATEST SCOOP ON THE MONSTER!
APPARENTLY THERE ARE PEOPLE...
...PILOTING THAT MONSTER THING.
WELL, THAT WOULD MAKE IT A ROBOT...
...NOT A MONSTER, RIGHT?
ALL THEY'VE GOT IS A BLURRY TELEPHOTO SHOT...
...BUT ACCORDING TO THE ARTICLE, THEY THINK IT'S A GROUP OF KIDS.
SOUNDS LIKE THE DEFENSE BUREAU'S INVOLVED, TOO.
THEY EVEN HAVE A SPECIAL CODE NAME FOR THE ROBOT.
REALLY?
WHAT IS IT?

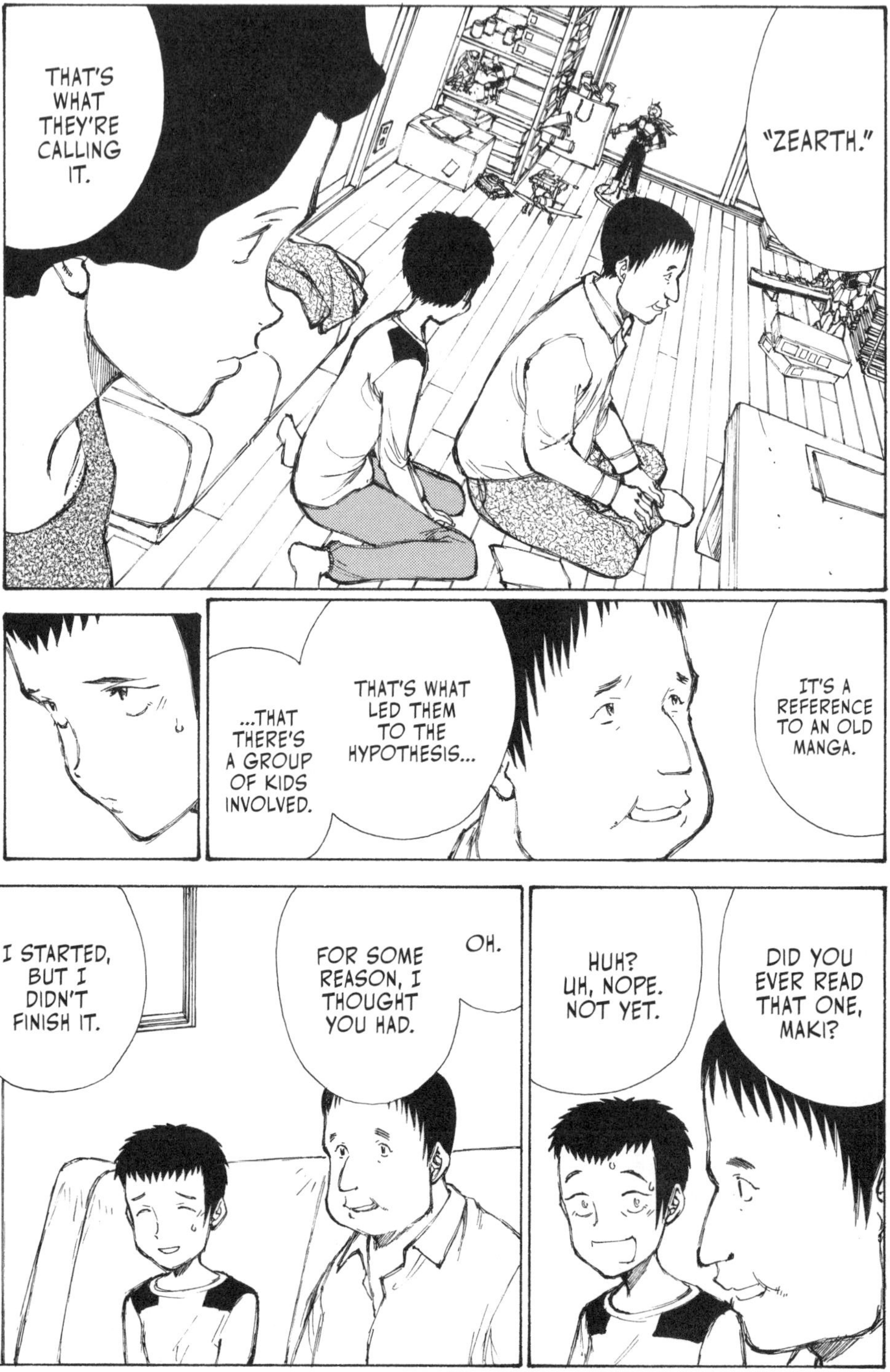
"ZEARTH."
THAT'S WHAT THEY'RE CALLING IT.
IT'S A REFERENCE TO AN OLD MANGA.
THAT'S WHAT LED THEM TO THE HYPOTHESIS...
...THAT THERE'S A GROUP OF KIDS INVOLVED.
DID YOU EVER READ THAT ONE, MAKI?
HUH? UH, NOPE. NOT YET.
OH.
FOR SOME REASON, I THOUGHT YOU HAD.
I STARTED, BUT I DIDN'T FINISH IT.

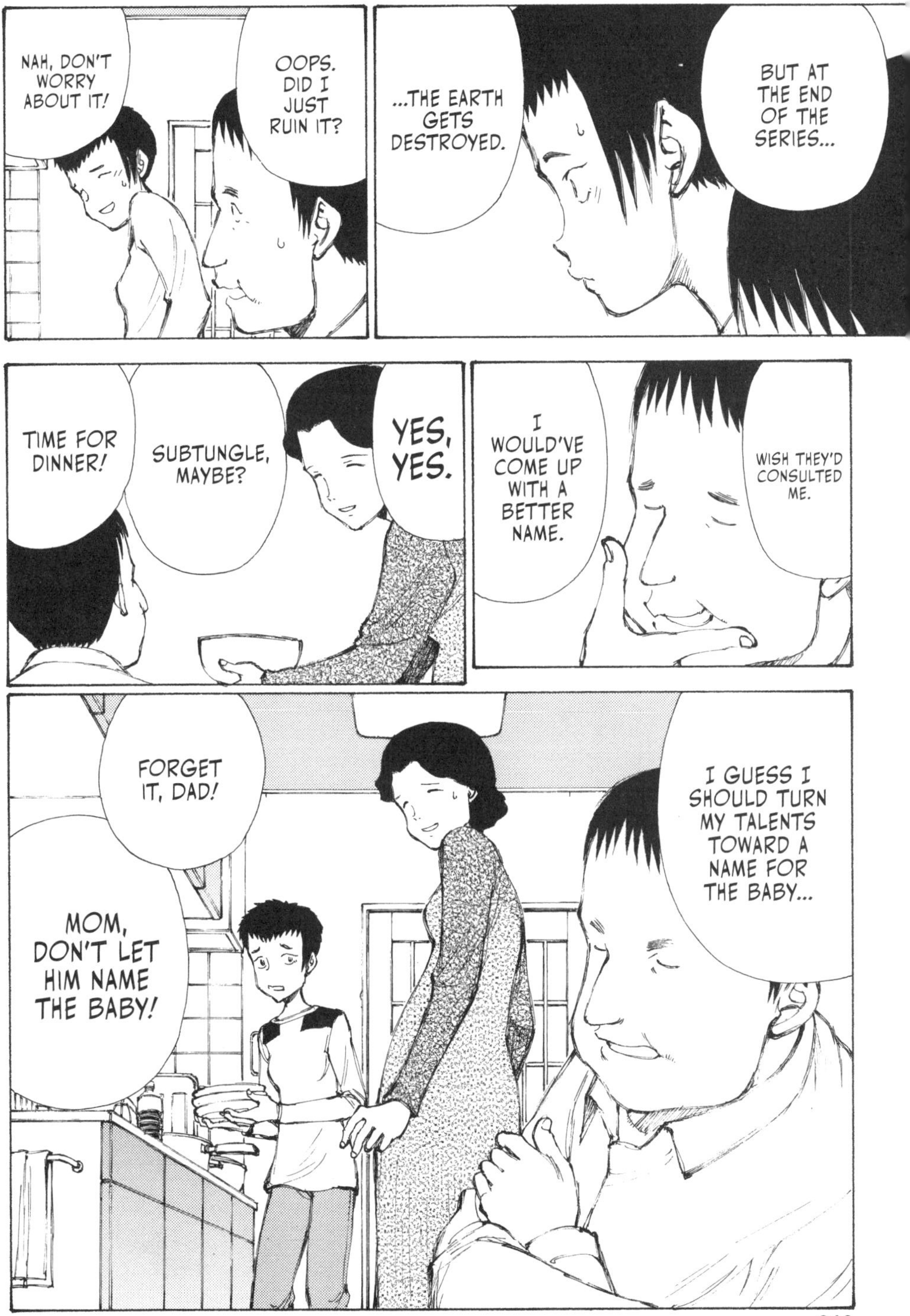
BUT AT THE END OF THE SERIES...
...THE EARTH GETS DESTROYED.
OOPS. DID I JUST RUIN IT?
NAH, DON'T WORRY ABOUT IT!
WISH THEY'D CONSULTED ME.
I WOULD'VE COME UP WITH A BETTER NAME.
YES, YES.
SUBTUNGLE, MAYBE?
TIME FOR DINNER!
I GUESS I SHOULD TURN MY TALENTS TOWARD A NAME FOR THE BABY...
FORGET IT, DAD!
MOM, DON'T LET HIM NAME THE BABY!

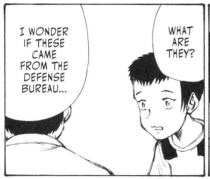

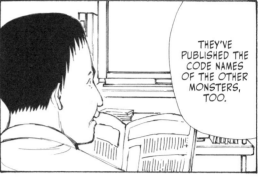

THEY'VE PUBLISHED THE CODE NAMES OF THE OTHER MONSTERS, TOO.
WHAT ARE THEY?
I WONDER IF THESE CAME FROM THE DEFENSE BUREAU...
NOT COUNTING ZEARTH...
...THE FIRST MONSTER WAS ARACHNE.
NEXT WAS BAYONET.
THEN CANCER...
DRUM...
THEY'RE FOLLOWING THE ALPHABET, I SEE...
ENIGMA...
FIG...
AND THE LAST ONE...
...WAS GONTA!

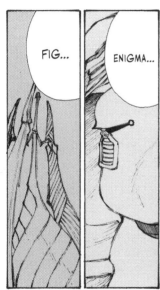

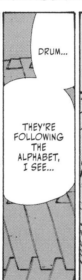

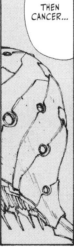

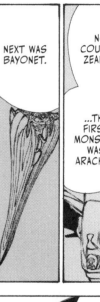

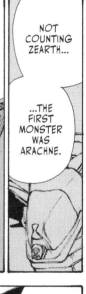

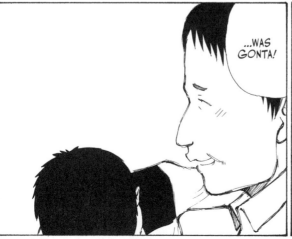

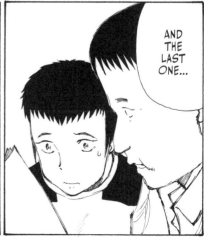

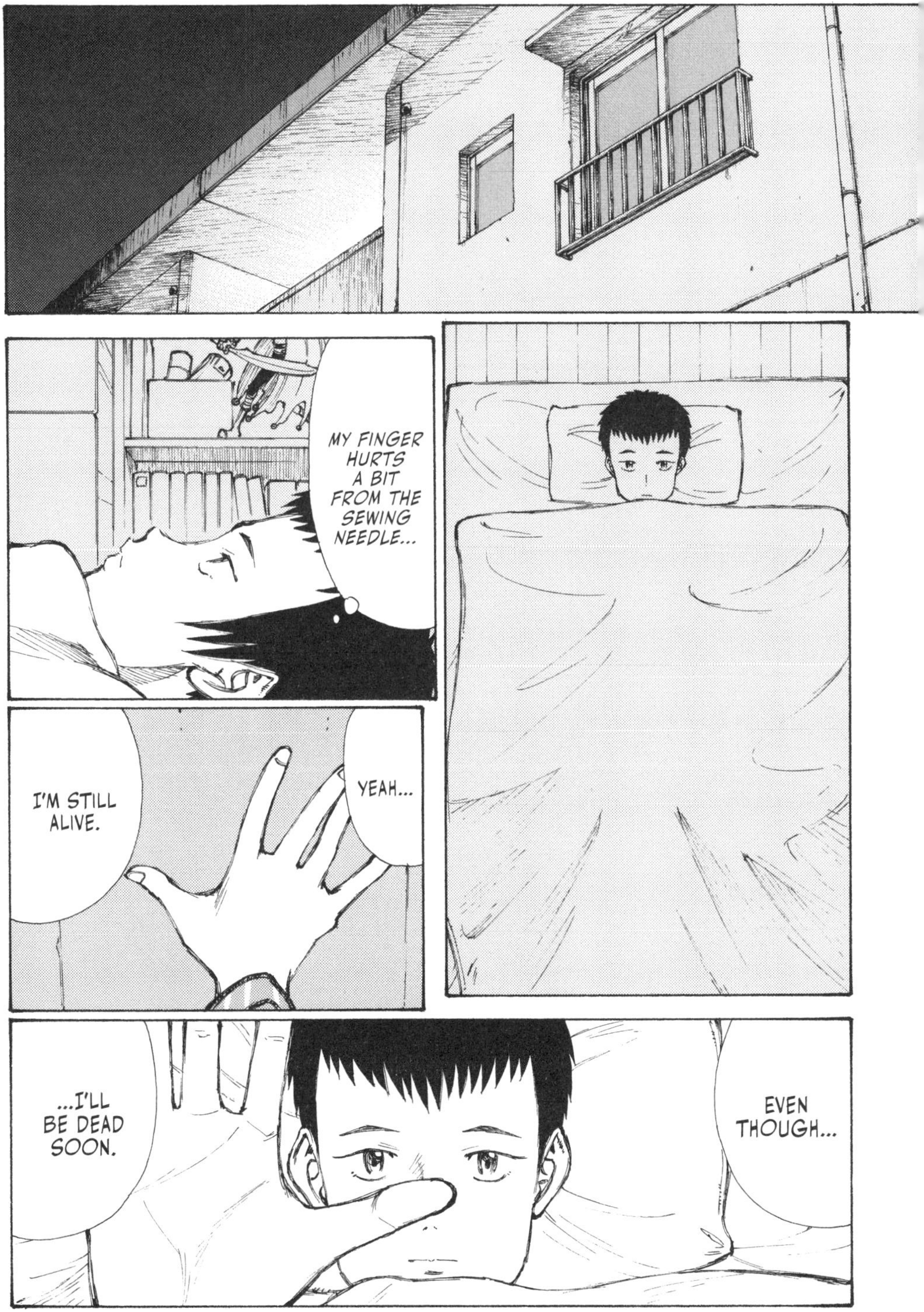
MY FINGER HURTS A BIT FROM THE SEWING NEEDLE...
YEAH...
I'M STILL ALIVE.
EVEN THOUGH...
...I'LL BE DEAD SOON.

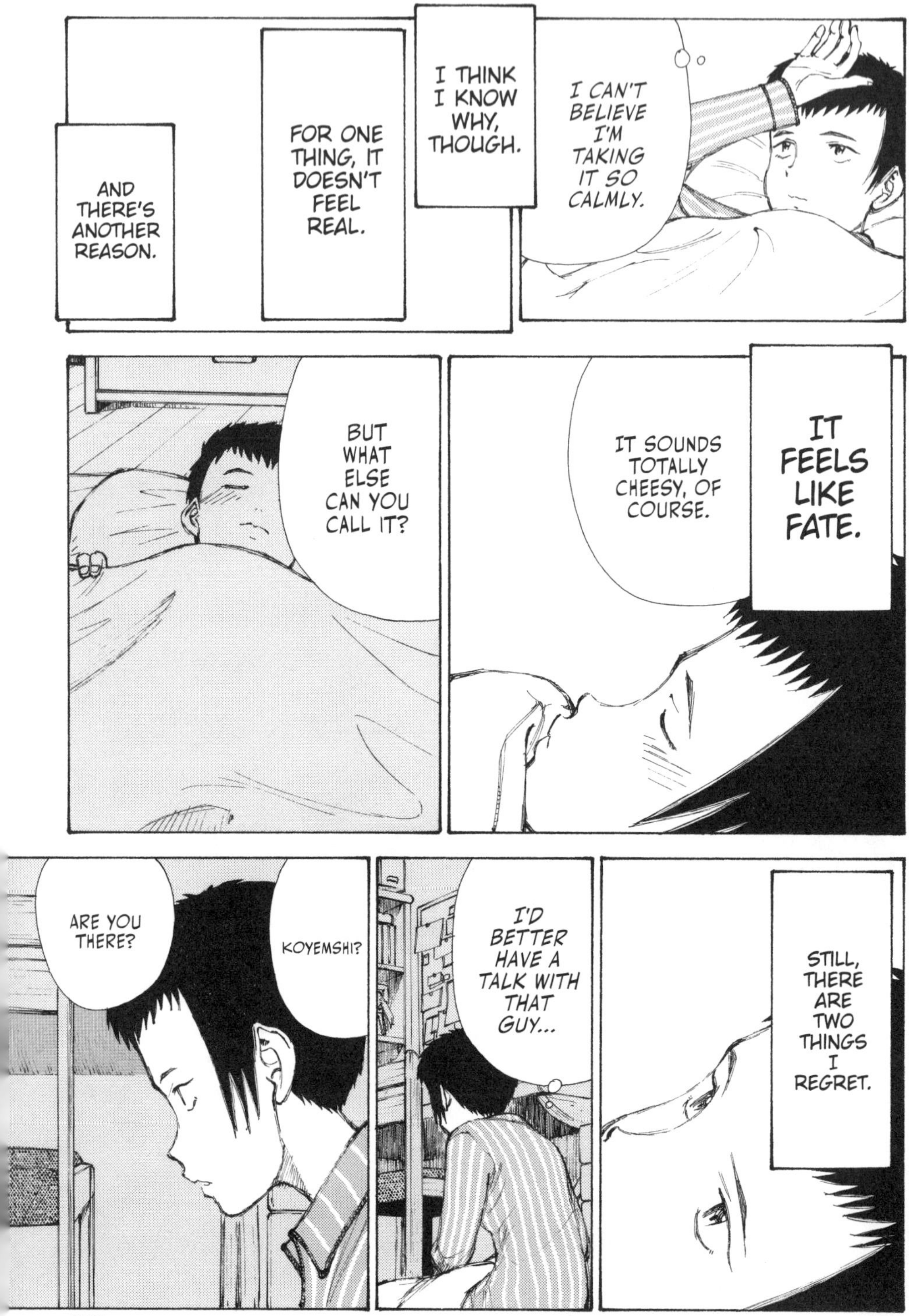
I CAN'T BELIEVE I'M TAKING IT SO CALMLY.
I THINK I KNOW WHY, THOUGH.
FOR ONE THING, IT DOESN'T FEEL REAL.
AND THERE'S ANOTHER REASON.
IT FEELS LIKE FATE.
IT SOUNDS TOTALLY CHEESY, OF COURSE.
BUT WHAT ELSE CAN YOU CALL IT?
STILL, THERE ARE TWO THINGS I REGRET.
I'D BETTER HAVE A TALK WITH THAT GUY...
KOYEMSHI?
ARE YOU THERE?

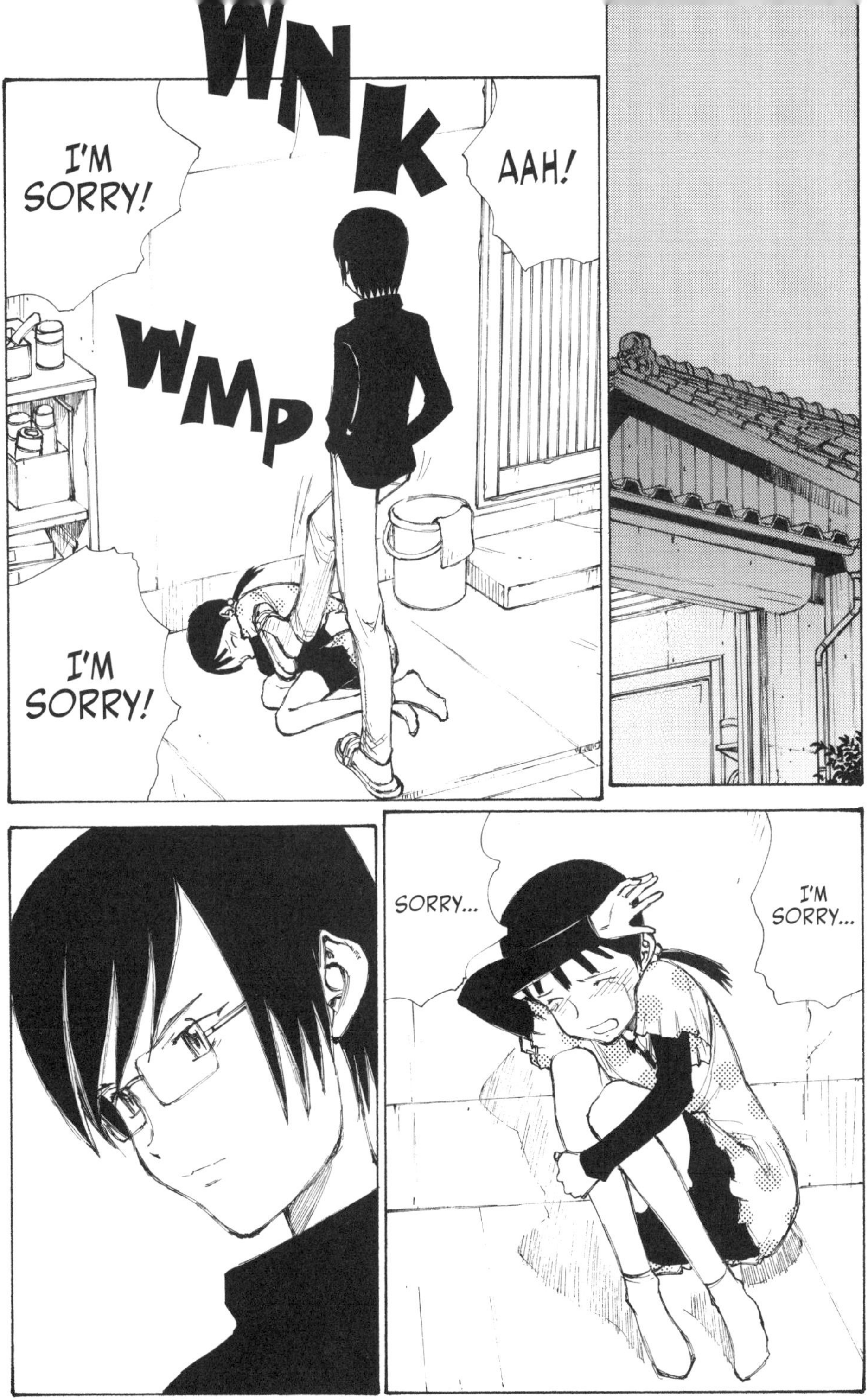
AAH!
WNK
I'M SORRY!
WMP
I'M SORRY!
I'M SORRY...
SORRY...

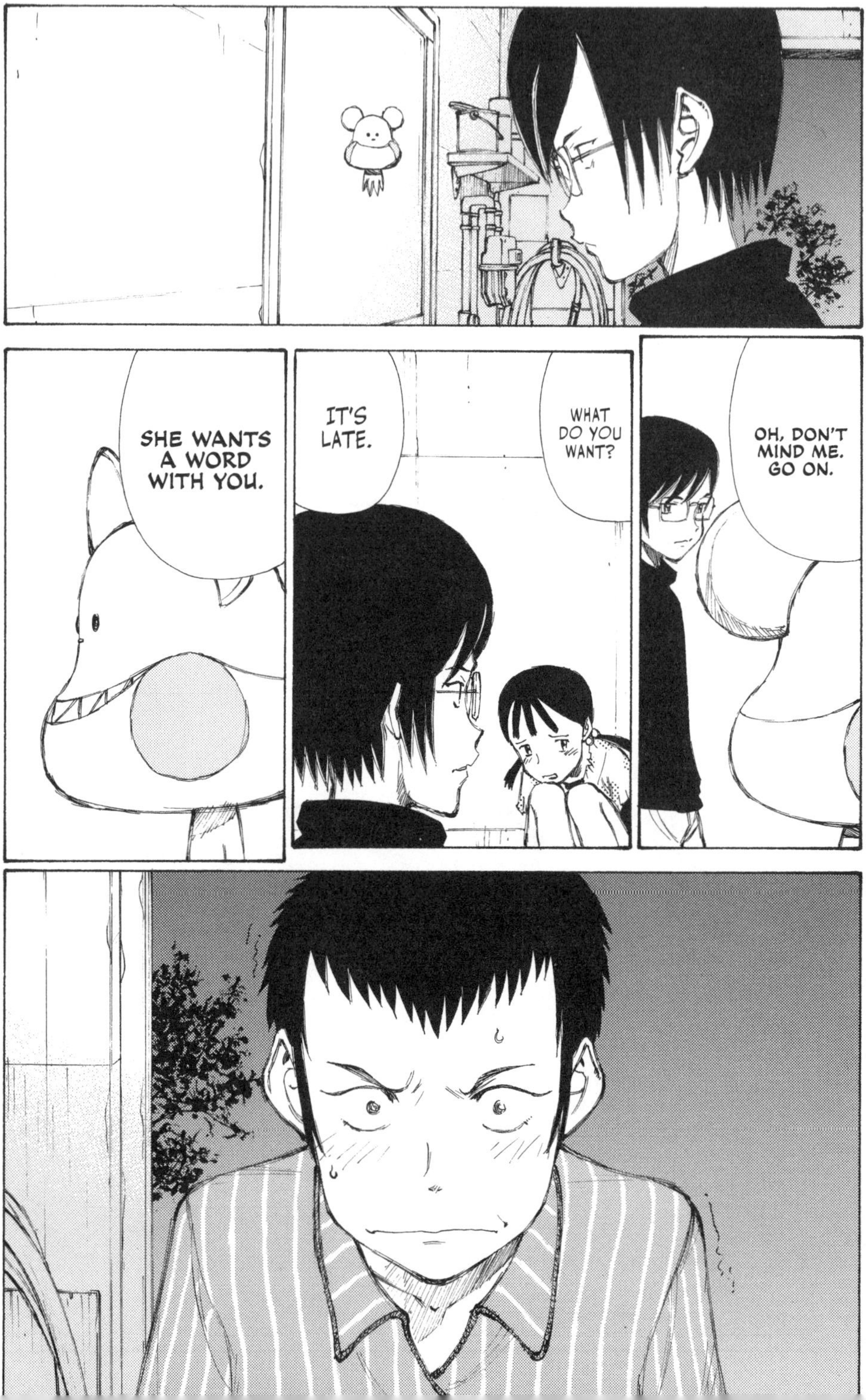
OH, DON'T MIND ME. GO ON.
WHAT DO YOU WANT?
IT'S LATE.
SHE WANTS A WORD WITH YOU.

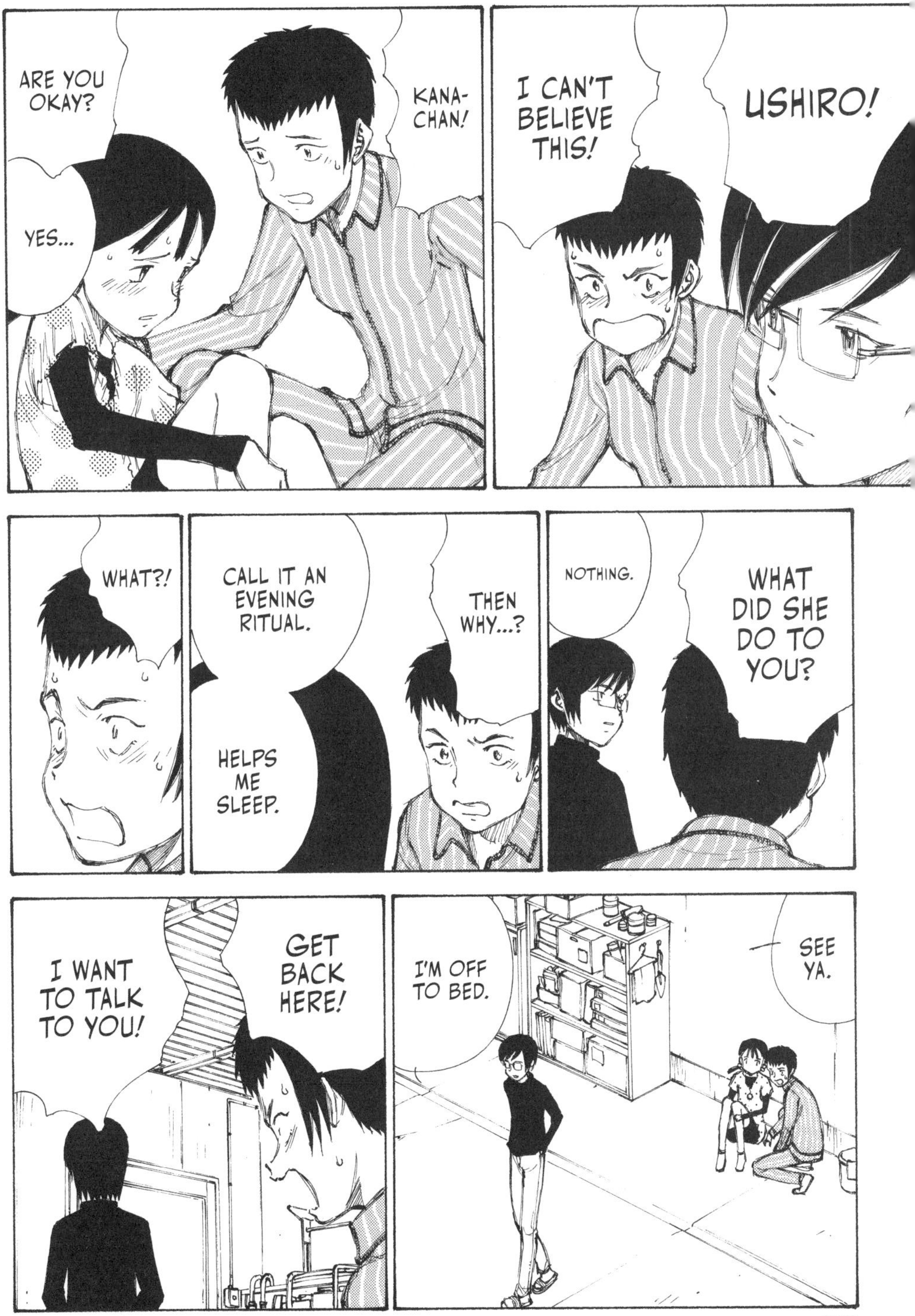
USHIRO!
I CAN'T BELIEVE THIS!
KANA-CHAN!
ARE YOU OKAY?
YES...
WHAT DID SHE DO TO YOU?
NOTHING.
THEN WHY...?
CALL IT AN EVENING RITUAL.
HELPS ME SLEEP.
WHAT?!
SEE YA.
I'M OFF TO BED.
GET BACK HERE!
I WANT TO TALK TO YOU!

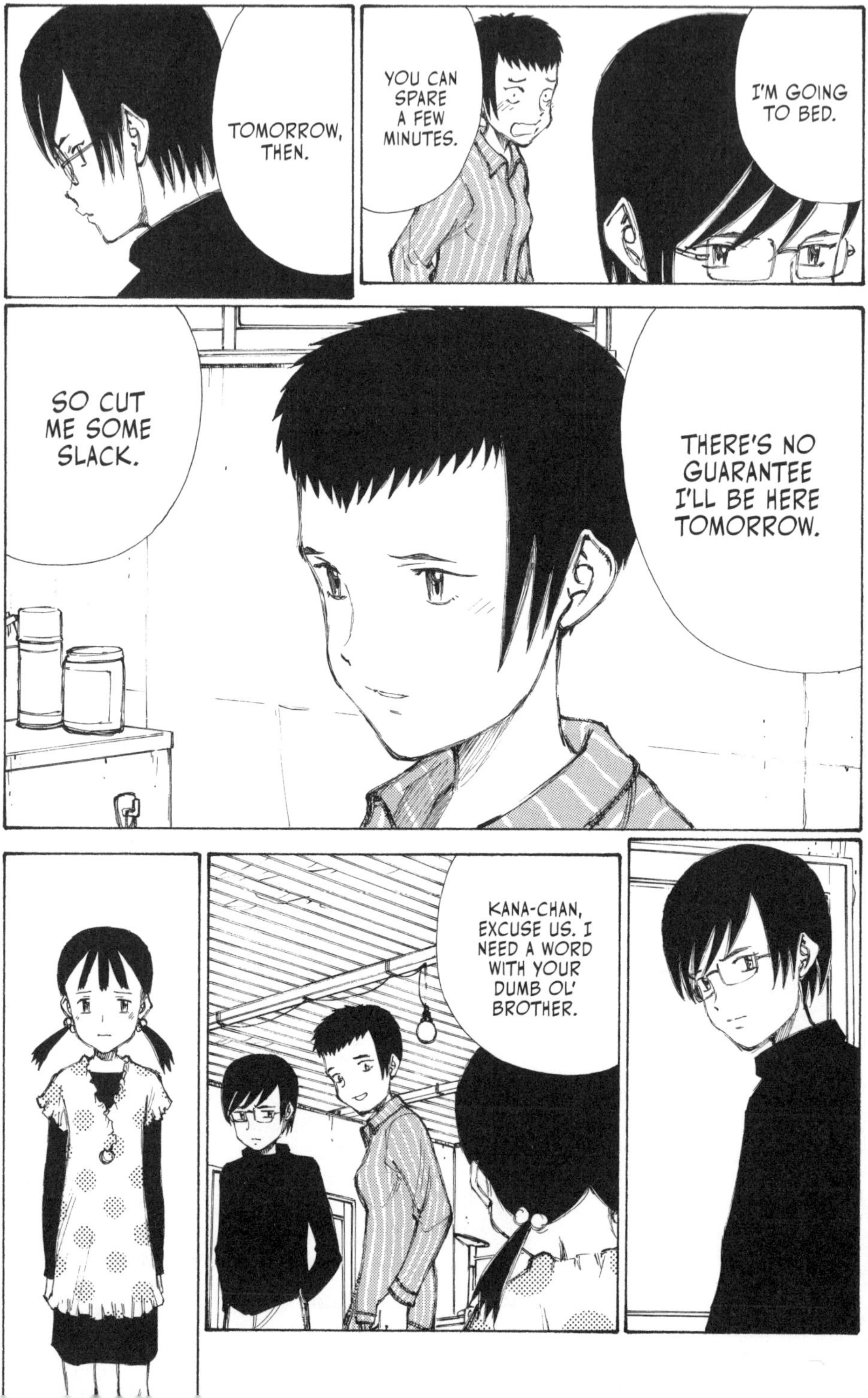
I'M GOING TO BED.
YOU CAN SPARE A FEW MINUTES.
TOMORROW, THEN.
THERE'S NO GUARANTEE I'LL BE HERE TOMORROW.
SO CUT ME SOME SLACK.
KANA-CHAN, EXCUSE US. I NEED A WORD WITH YOUR DUMB OL' BROTHER.

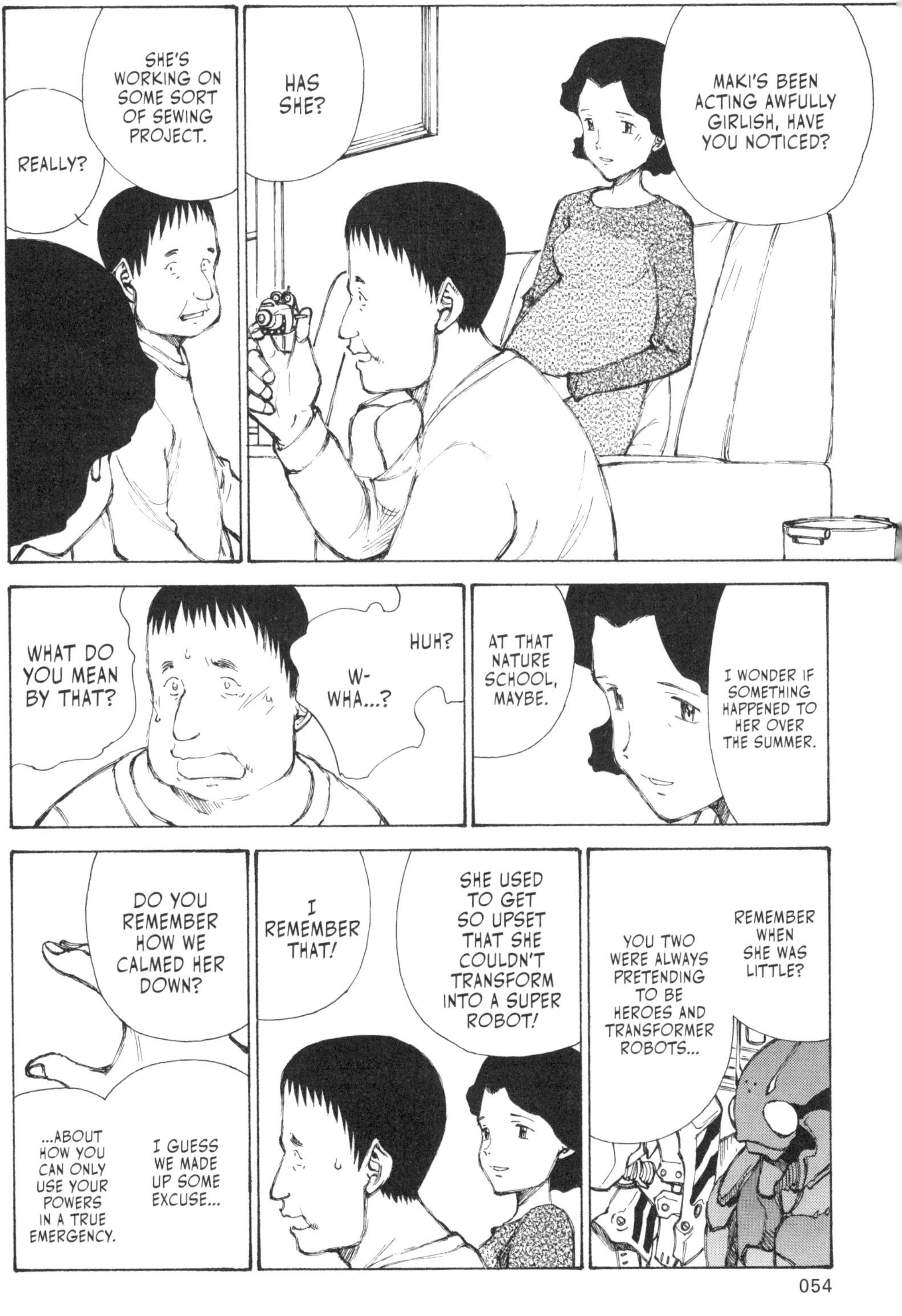
MAKI'S BEEN ACTING AWFULLY GIRLISH, HAVE YOU NOTICED?
HAS SHE?
SHE'S WORKING ON SOME SORT OF SEWING PROJECT.
REALLY?
I WONDER IF SOMETHING HAPPENED TO HER OVER THE SUMMER.
AT THAT NATURE SCHOOL, MAYBE.
HUH?
W-WHA...?
WHAT DO YOU MEAN BY THAT?
REMEMBER WHEN SHE WAS LITTLE?
YOU TWO WERE ALWAYS PRETENDING TO BE HEROES AND TRANSFORMER ROBOTS...
SHE USED TO GET SO UPSET THAT SHE COULDN'T TRANSFORM INTO A SUPER ROBOT!
I REMEMBER THAT!
DO YOU REMEMBER HOW WE CALMED HER DOWN?
I GUESS WE MADE UP SOME EXCUSE...
...ABOUT HOW YOU CAN ONLY USE YOUR POWERS IN A TRUE EMERGENCY.

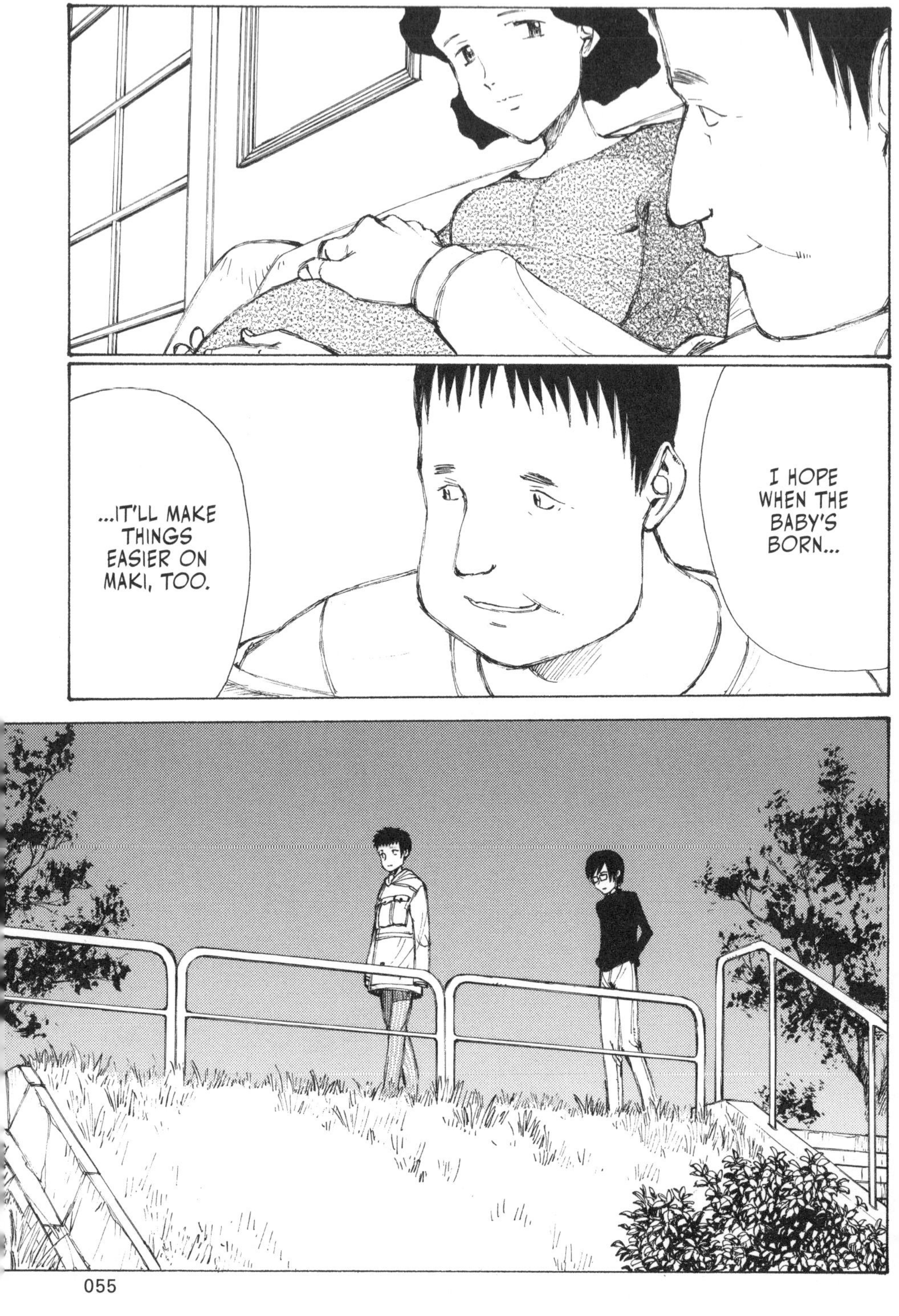
I HOPE WHEN THE BABY'S BORN...
...IT'LL MAKE THINGS EASIER ON MAKI, TOO.

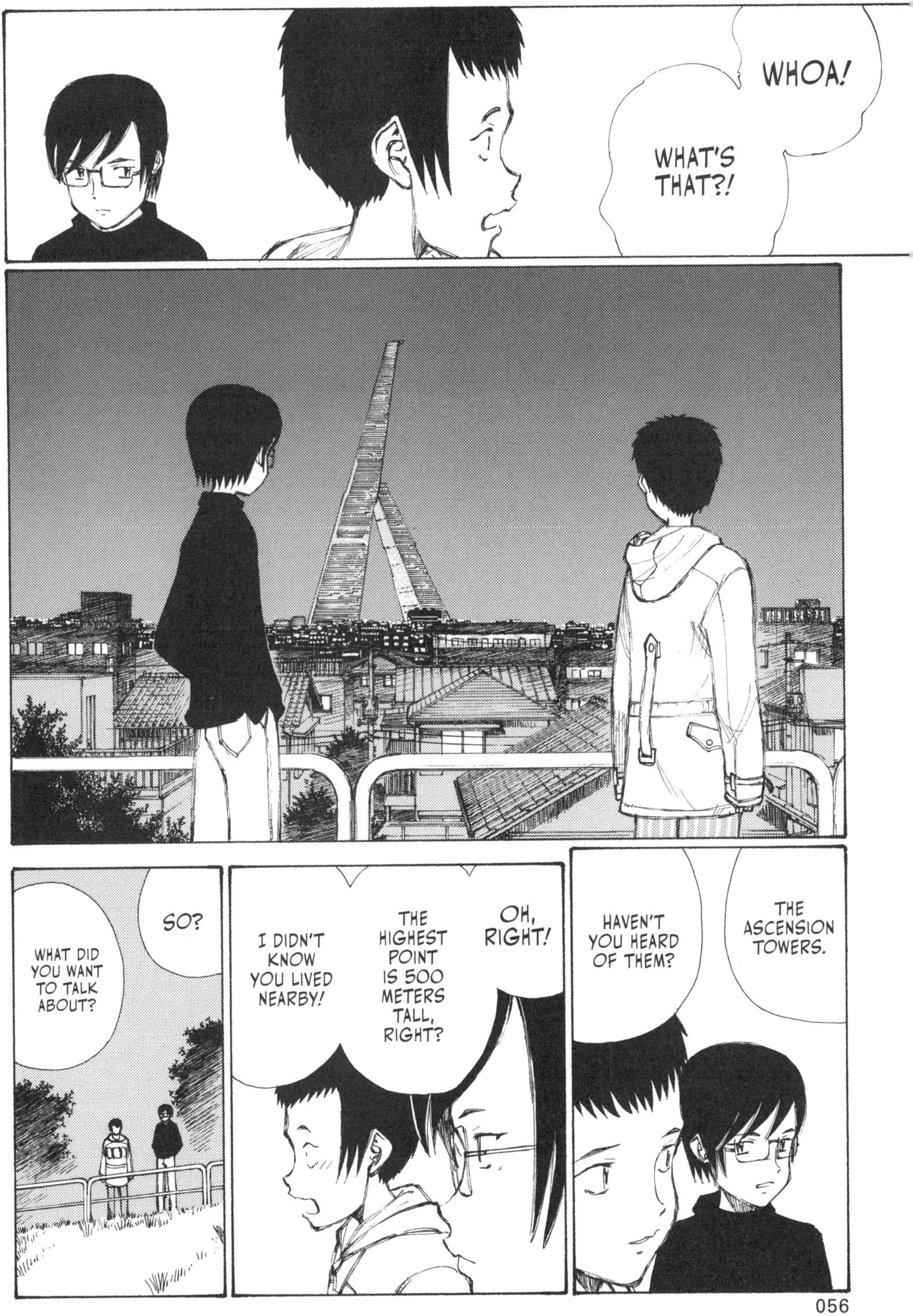
WHOA!
WHAT'S THAT?!
THE ASCENSION TOWERS.
HAVEN'T YOU HEARD OF THEM?
OH, RIGHT!
THE HIGHEST POINT IS 500 METERS TALL, RIGHT?
I DIDN'T KNOW YOU LIVED NEARBY!
SO?
WHAT DID YOU WANT TO TALK ABOUT?

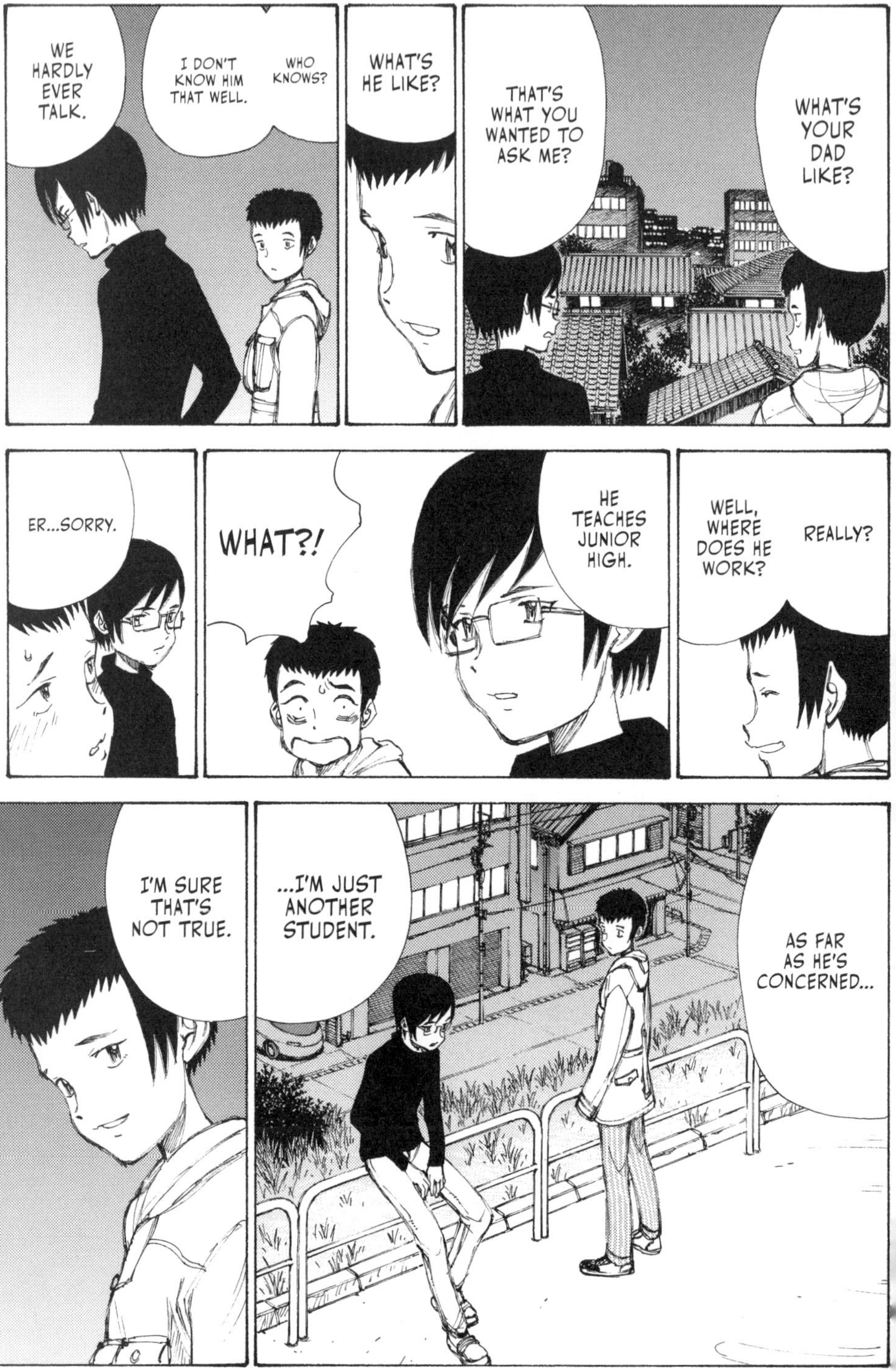
WHAT'S YOUR DAD LIKE?
THAT'S WHAT YOU WANTED TO ASK ME?
WHAT'S HE LIKE?
WHO KNOWS?
I DON'T KNOW HIM THAT WELL.
WE HARDLY EVER TALK.
REALLY?
WELL, WHERE DOES HE WORK?
HE TEACHES JUNIOR HIGH.
WHAT?!
ER...SORRY.
AS FAR AS HE'S CONCERNED...
...I'M JUST ANOTHER STUDENT.
I'M SURE THAT'S NOT TRUE.

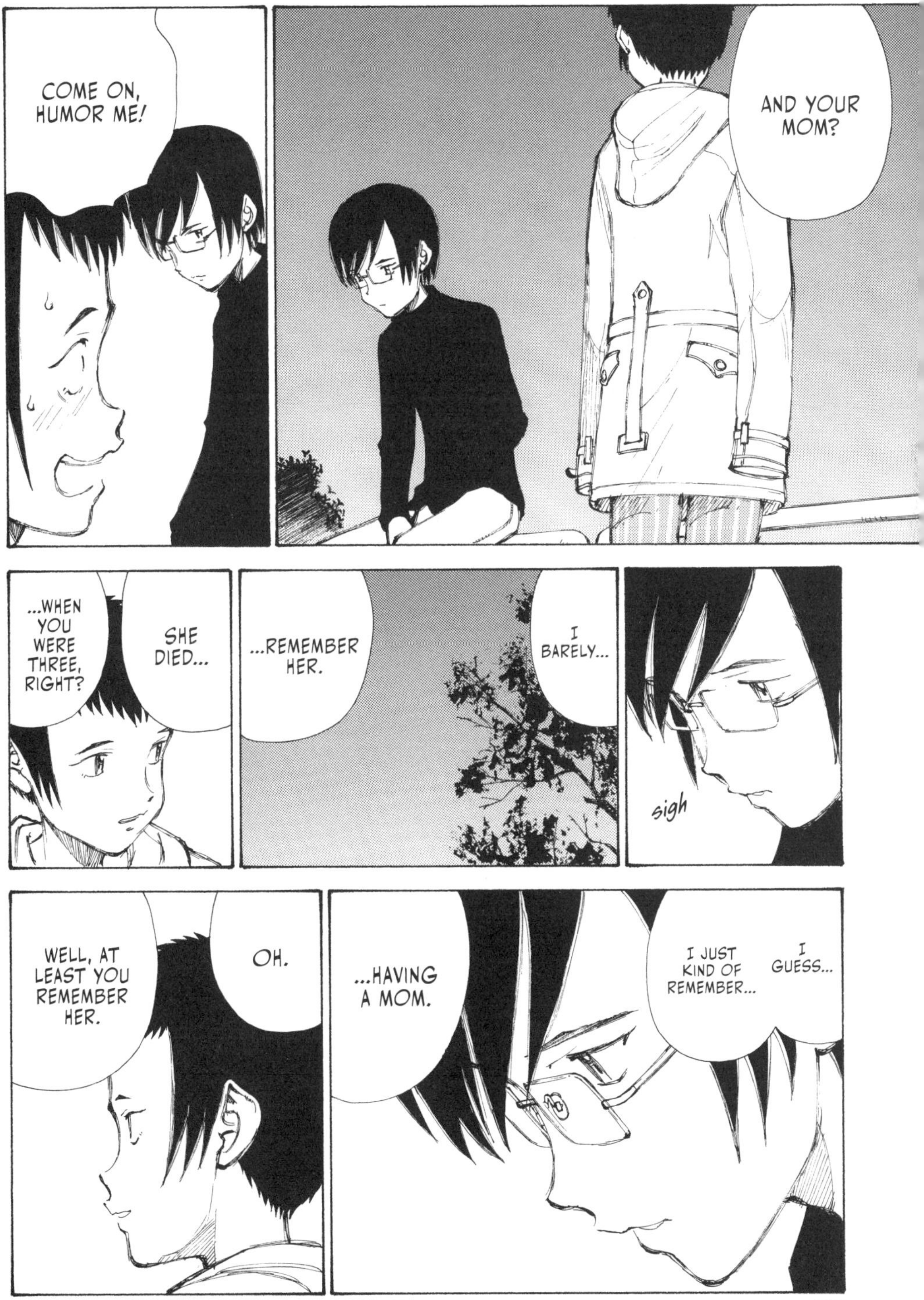
AND YOUR MOM?
COME ON, HUMOR ME!
sigh
I BARELY...
...REMEMBER HER.
SHE DIED...
...WHEN YOU WERE THREE, RIGHT?
I GUESS...
I JUST KIND OF REMEMBER...
...HAVING A MOM.
OH.
WELL, AT LEAST YOU REMEMBER HER.

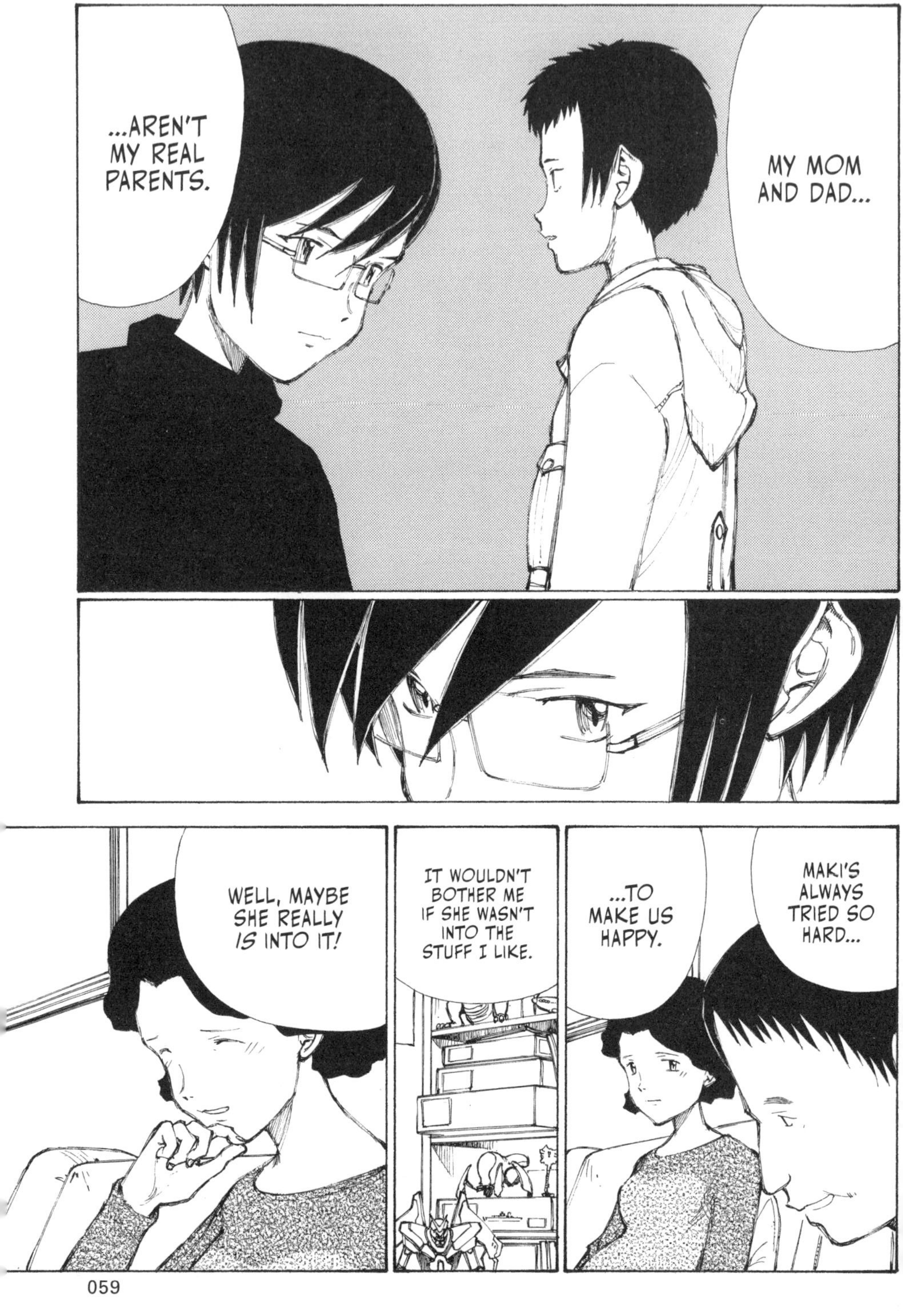
MY MOM AND DAD...
...AREN'T MY REAL PARENTS.
MAKI'S ALWAYS TRIED SO HARD...
...TO MAKE US HAPPY.
IT WOULDN'T BOTHER ME IF SHE WASN'T INTO THE STUFF I LIKE.
WELL, MAYBE SHE REALLY *IS* INTO IT!

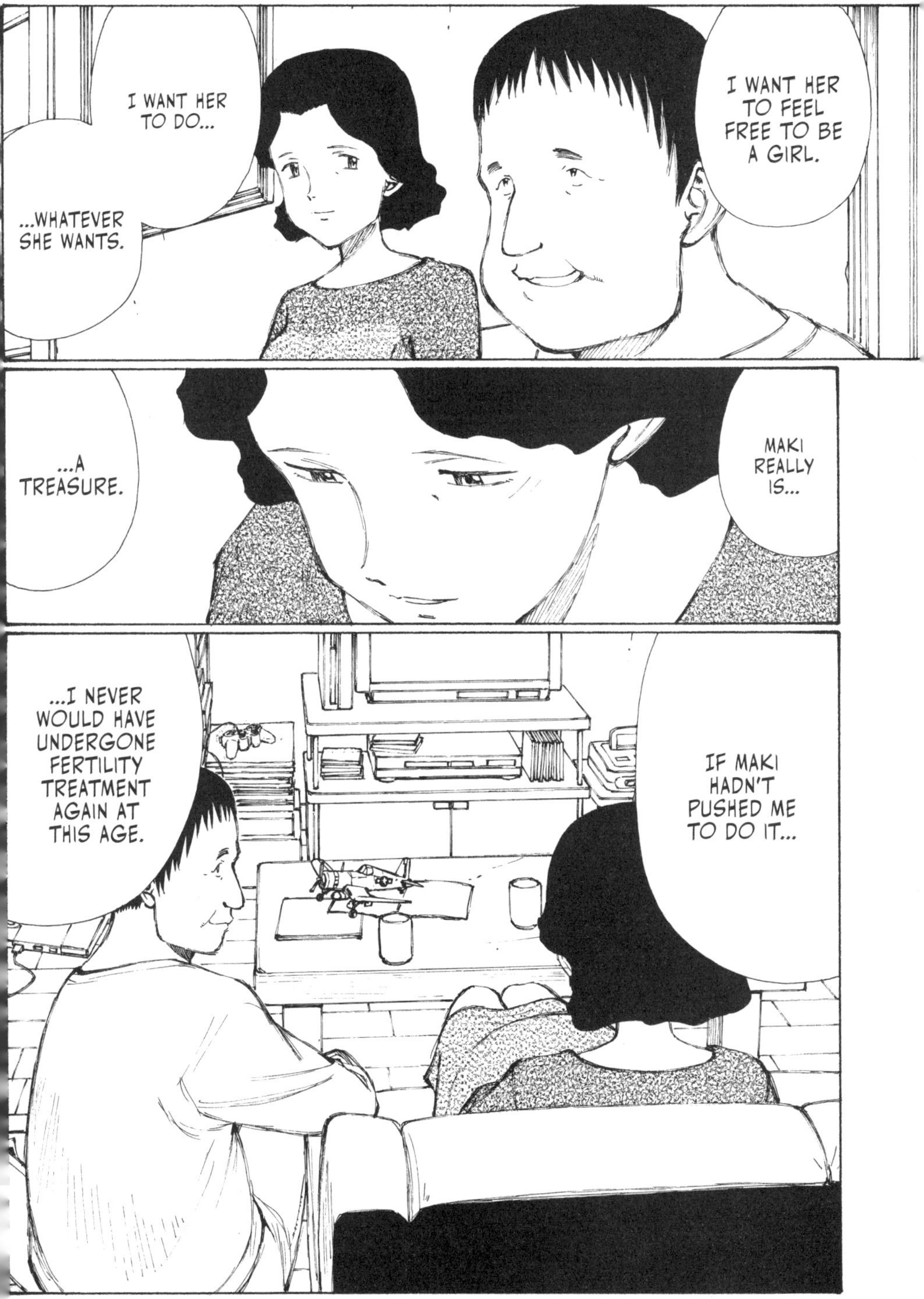
I WANT HER TO FEEL FREE TO BE A GIRL.
I WANT HER TO DO...
...WHATEVER SHE WANTS.
MAKI REALLY IS...
...A TREASURE.
IF MAKI HADN'T PUSHED ME TO DO IT...
...I NEVER WOULD HAVE UNDERGONE FERTILITY TREATMENT AGAIN AT THIS AGE.

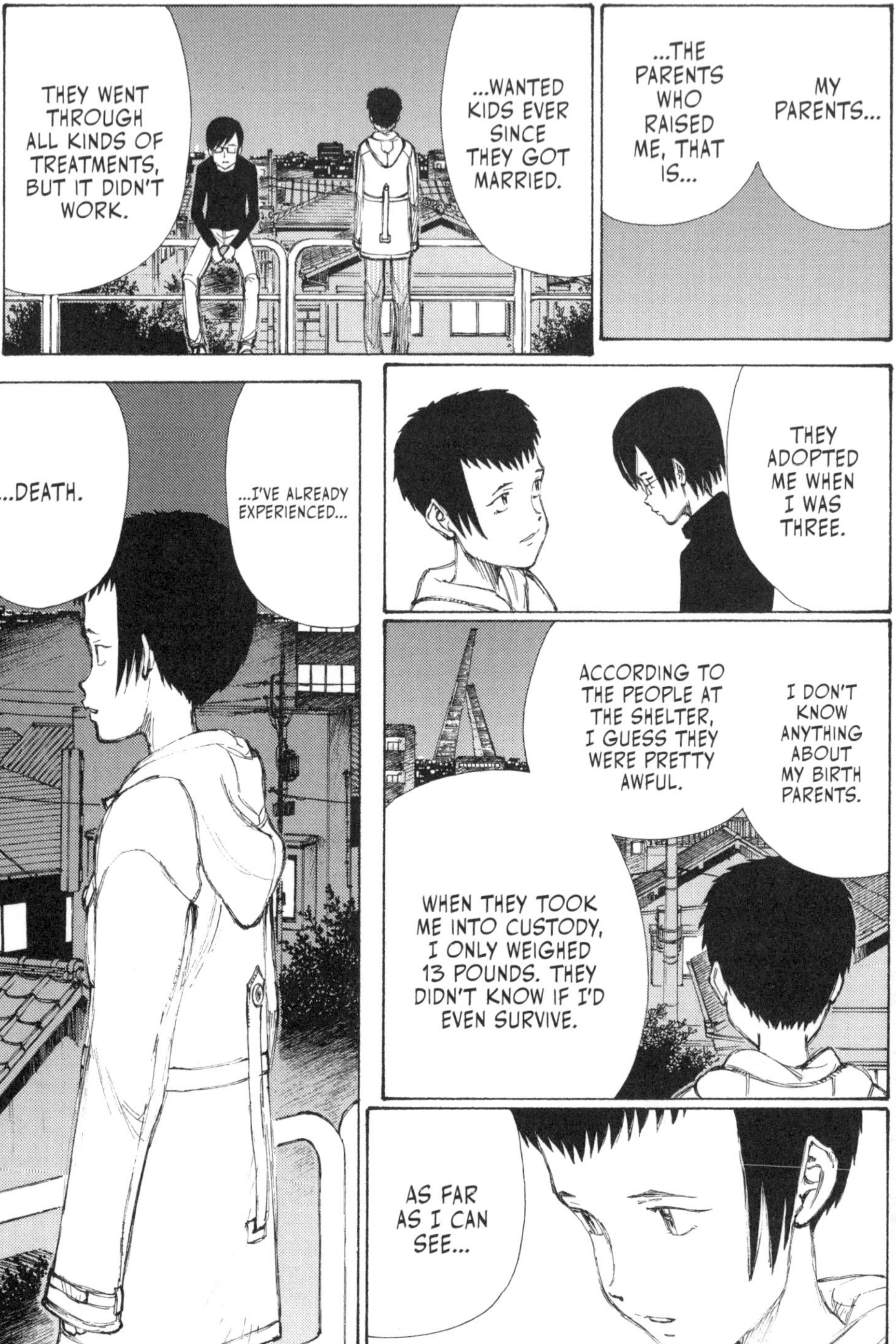
MY PARENTS...
...THE PARENTS WHO RAISED ME, THAT IS...
...WANTED KIDS EVER SINCE THEY GOT MARRIED.
THEY WENT THROUGH ALL KINDS OF TREATMENTS, BUT IT DIDN'T WORK.
THEY ADOPTED ME WHEN I WAS THREE.
I DON'T KNOW ANYTHING ABOUT MY BIRTH PARENTS.
ACCORDING TO THE PEOPLE AT THE SHELTER, I GUESS THEY WERE PRETTY AWFUL.
WHEN THEY TOOK ME INTO CUSTODY, I ONLY WEIGHED 13 POUNDS. THEY DIDN'T KNOW IF I'D EVEN SURVIVE.
AS FAR AS I CAN SEE...
...I'VE ALREADY EXPERIENCED...
...DEATH.

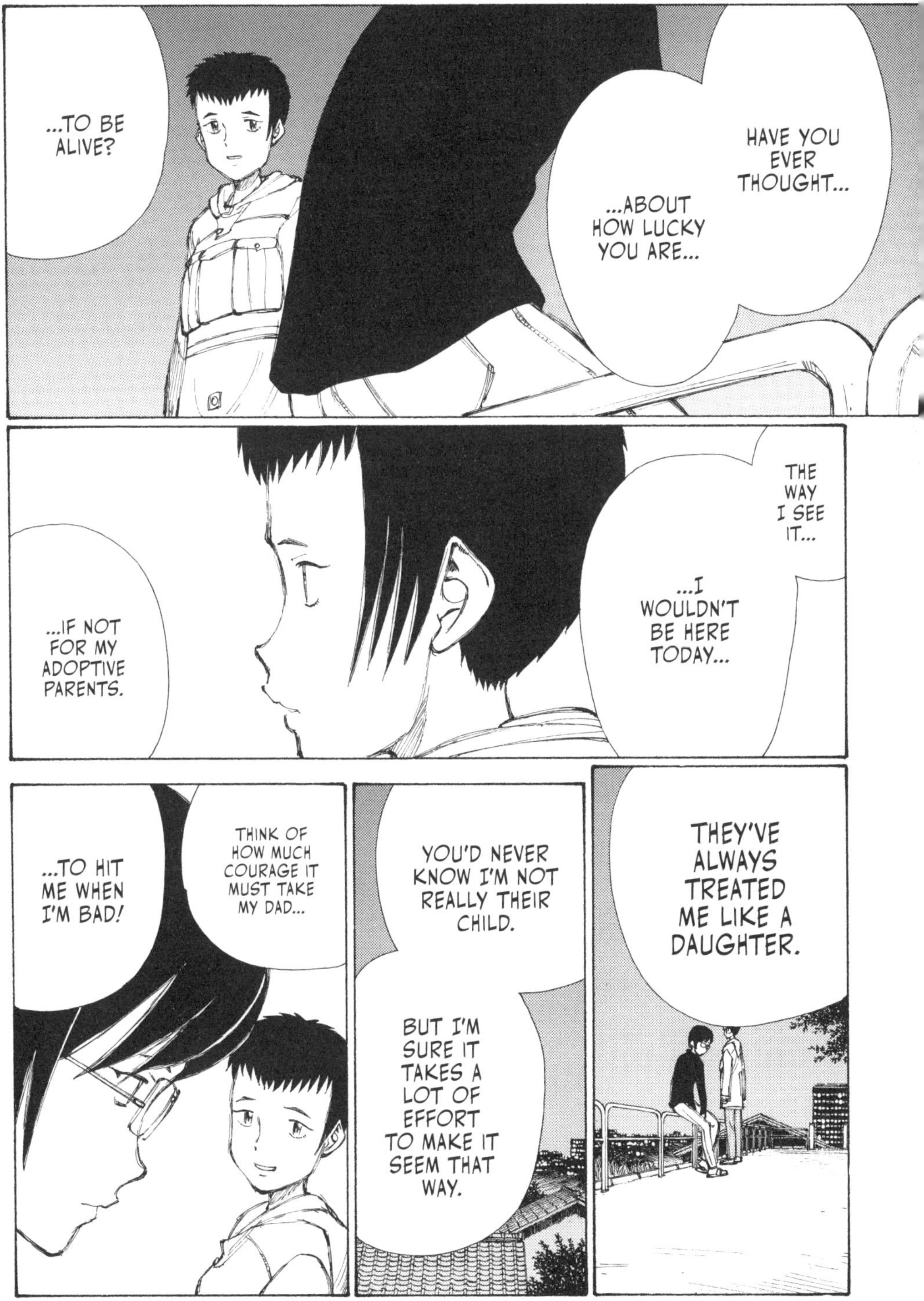
HAVE YOU EVER THOUGHT...
...ABOUT HOW LUCKY YOU ARE...
...TO BE ALIVE?
THE WAY I SEE IT...
...I WOULDN'T BE HERE TODAY...
...IF NOT FOR MY ADOPTIVE PARENTS.
THEY'VE ALWAYS TREATED ME LIKE A DAUGHTER.
YOU'D NEVER KNOW I'M NOT REALLY THEIR CHILD.
BUT I'M SURE IT TAKES A LOT OF EFFORT TO MAKE IT SEEM THAT WAY.
THINK OF HOW MUCH COURAGE IT MUST TAKE MY DAD...
...TO HIT ME WHEN I'M BAD!

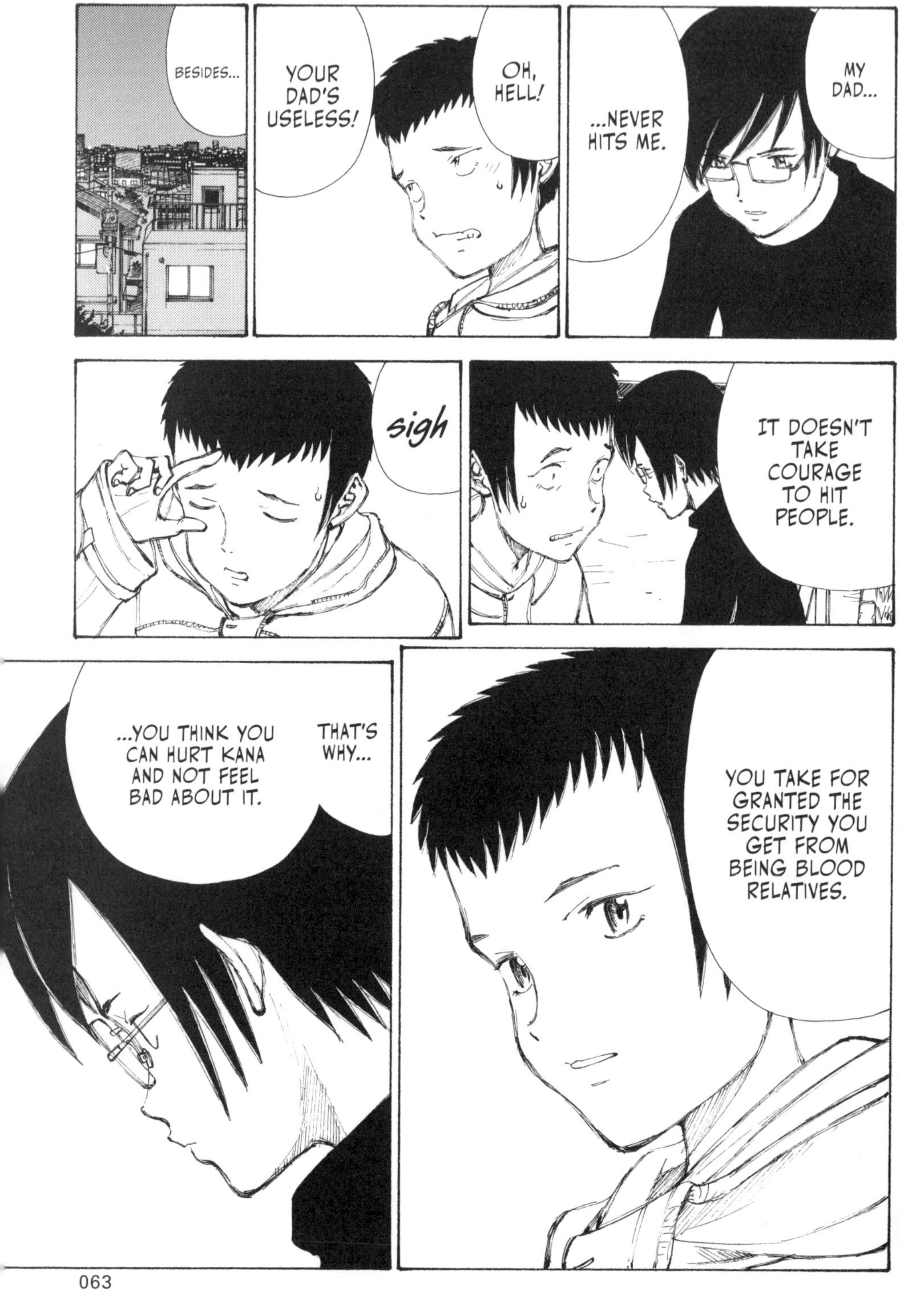
MY DAD...
...NEVER HITS ME.
OH, HELL!
YOUR DAD'S USELESS!
BESIDES...
IT DOESN'T TAKE COURAGE TO HIT PEOPLE.
sigh
YOU TAKE FOR GRANTED THE SECURITY YOU GET FROM BEING BLOOD RELATIVES.
THAT'S WHY...
...YOU THINK YOU CAN HURT KANA AND NOT FEEL BAD ABOUT IT.

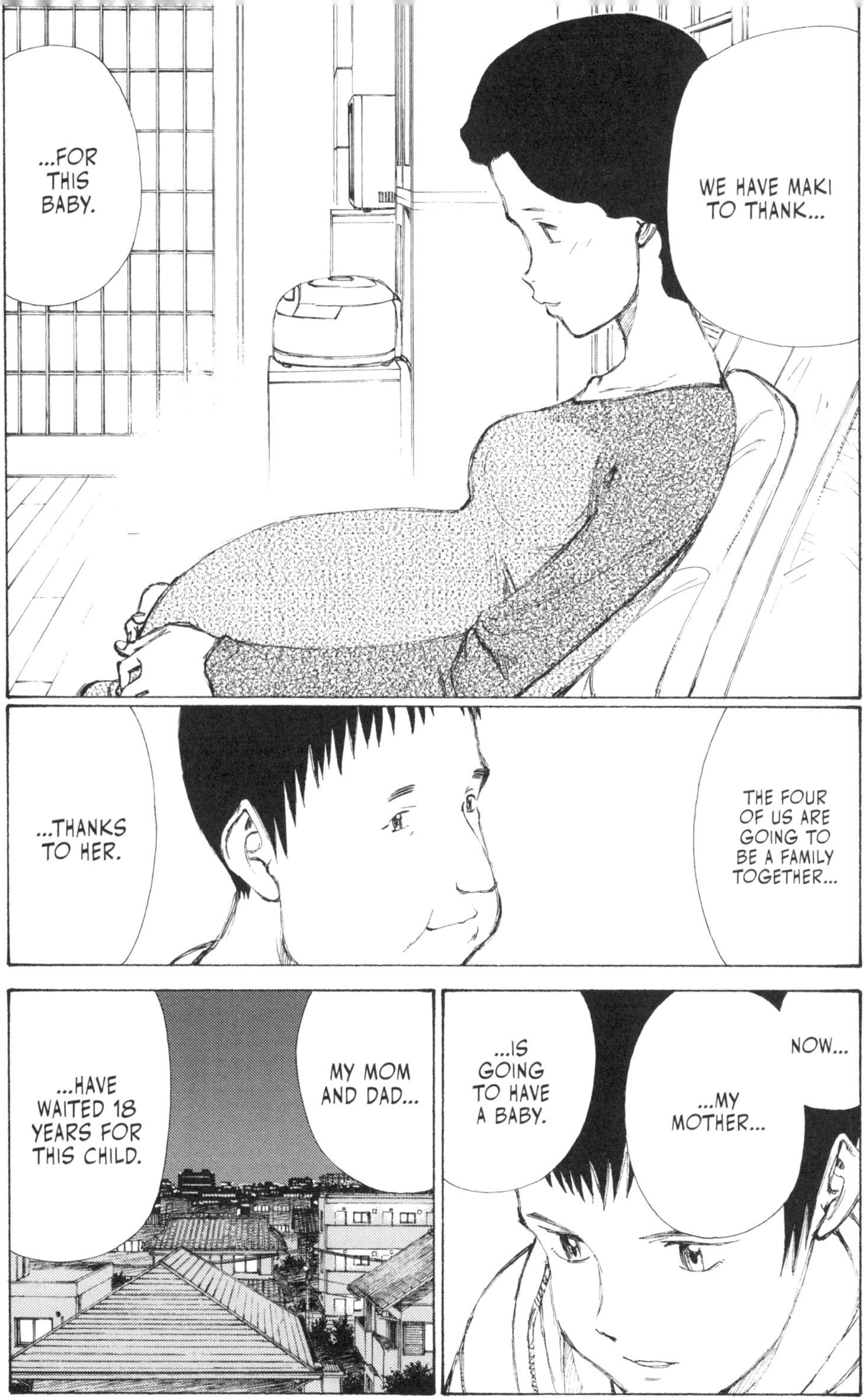
WE HAVE MAKI TO THANK...
...FOR THIS BABY.
THE FOUR OF US ARE GOING TO BE A FAMILY TOGETHER...
...THANKS TO HER.
NOW...
...MY MOTHER...
...IS GOING TO HAVE A BABY.
MY MOM AND DAD...
...HAVE WAITED 18 YEARS FOR THIS CHILD.

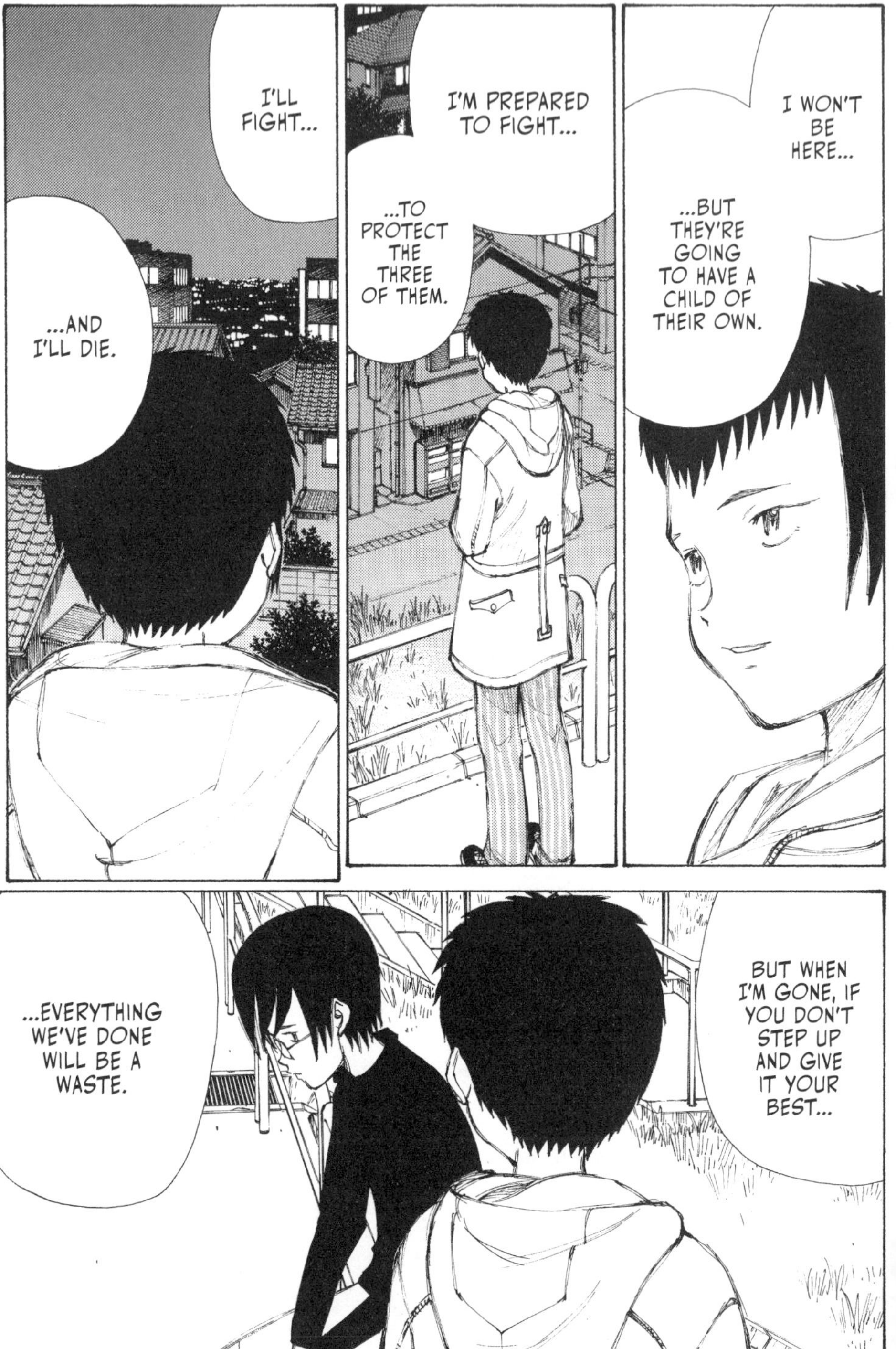

I WON'T BE HERE...
...BUT THEY'RE GOING TO HAVE A CHILD OF THEIR OWN.
I'M PREPARED TO FIGHT...
...TO PROTECT THE THREE OF THEM.
I'LL FIGHT...
...AND I'LL DIE.
BUT WHEN I'M GONE, IF YOU DON'T STEP UP AND GIVE IT YOUR BEST...
...EVERYTHING WE'VE DONE WILL BE A WASTE.

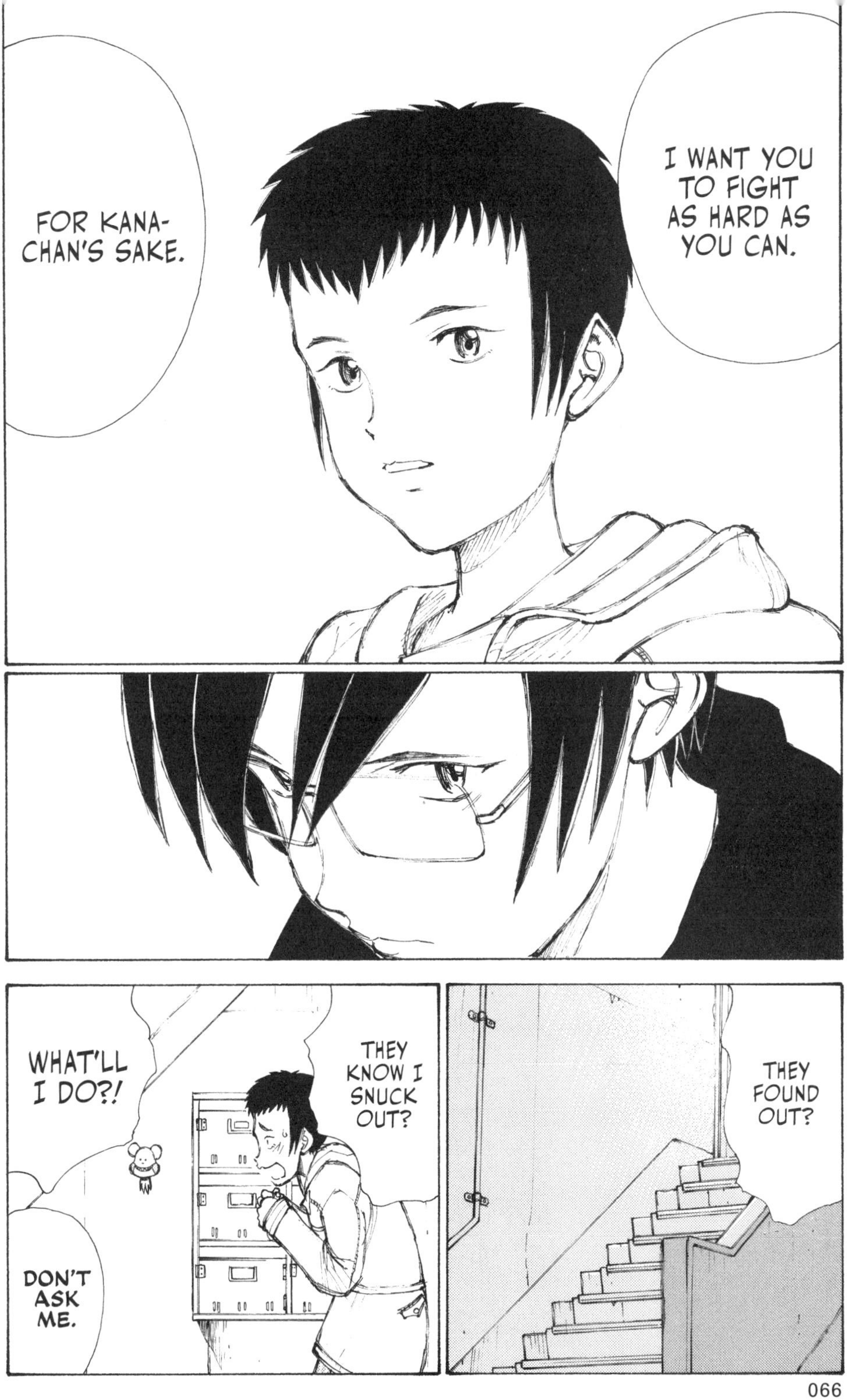
I WANT YOU TO FIGHT AS HARD AS YOU CAN.
FOR KANA-CHAN'S SAKE.
THEY FOUND OUT?
THEY KNOW I SNUCK OUT?
WHAT'LL I DO?!
DON'T ASK ME.

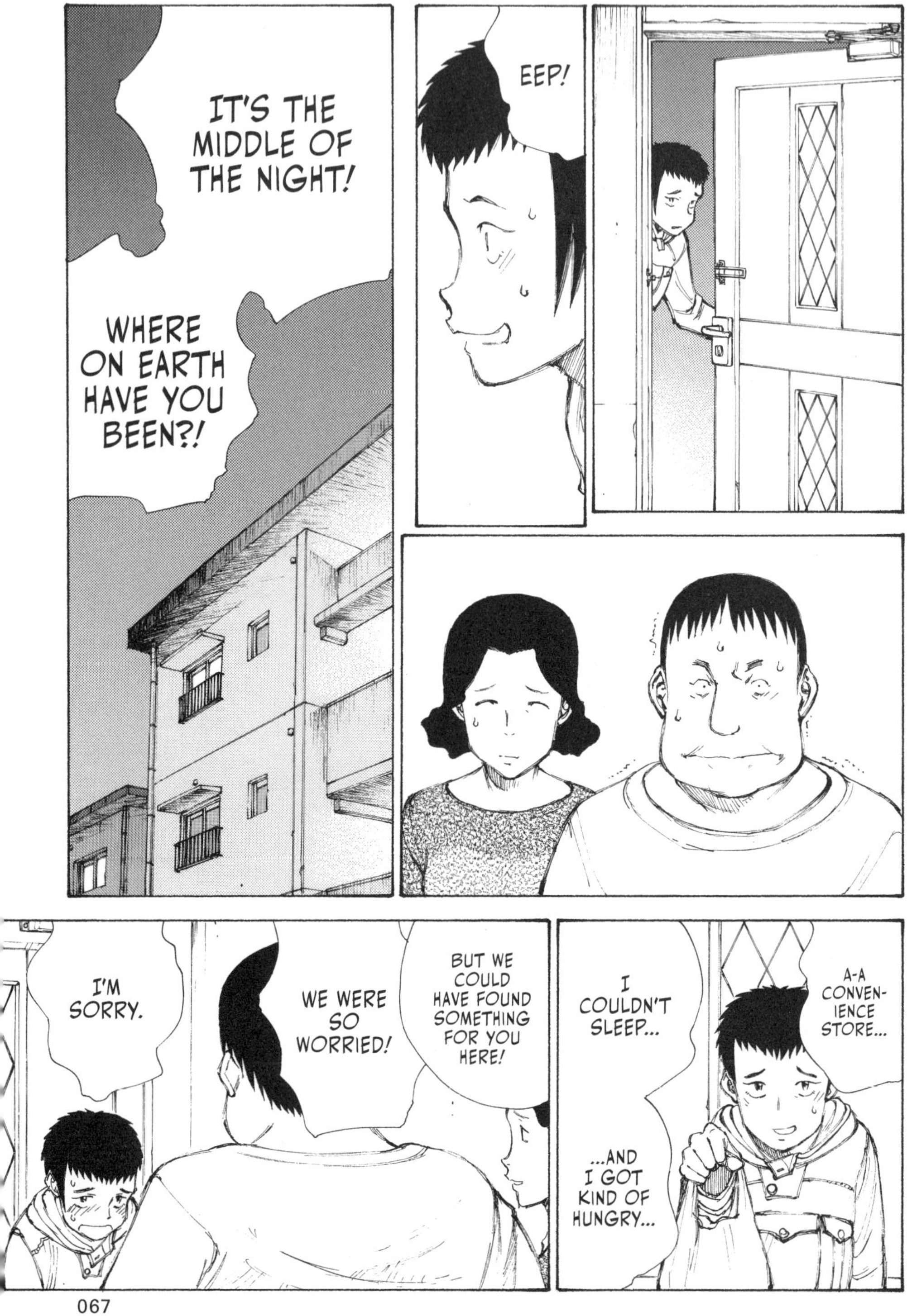
EEP!
IT'S THE MIDDLE OF THE NIGHT!
WHERE ON EARTH HAVE YOU BEEN?!
A-A CONVEN-IENCE STORE...
I COULDN'T SLEEP...
...AND I GOT KIND OF HUNGRY...
BUT WE COULD HAVE FOUND SOMETHING FOR YOU HERE!
WE WERE SO WORRIED!
I'M SORRY.

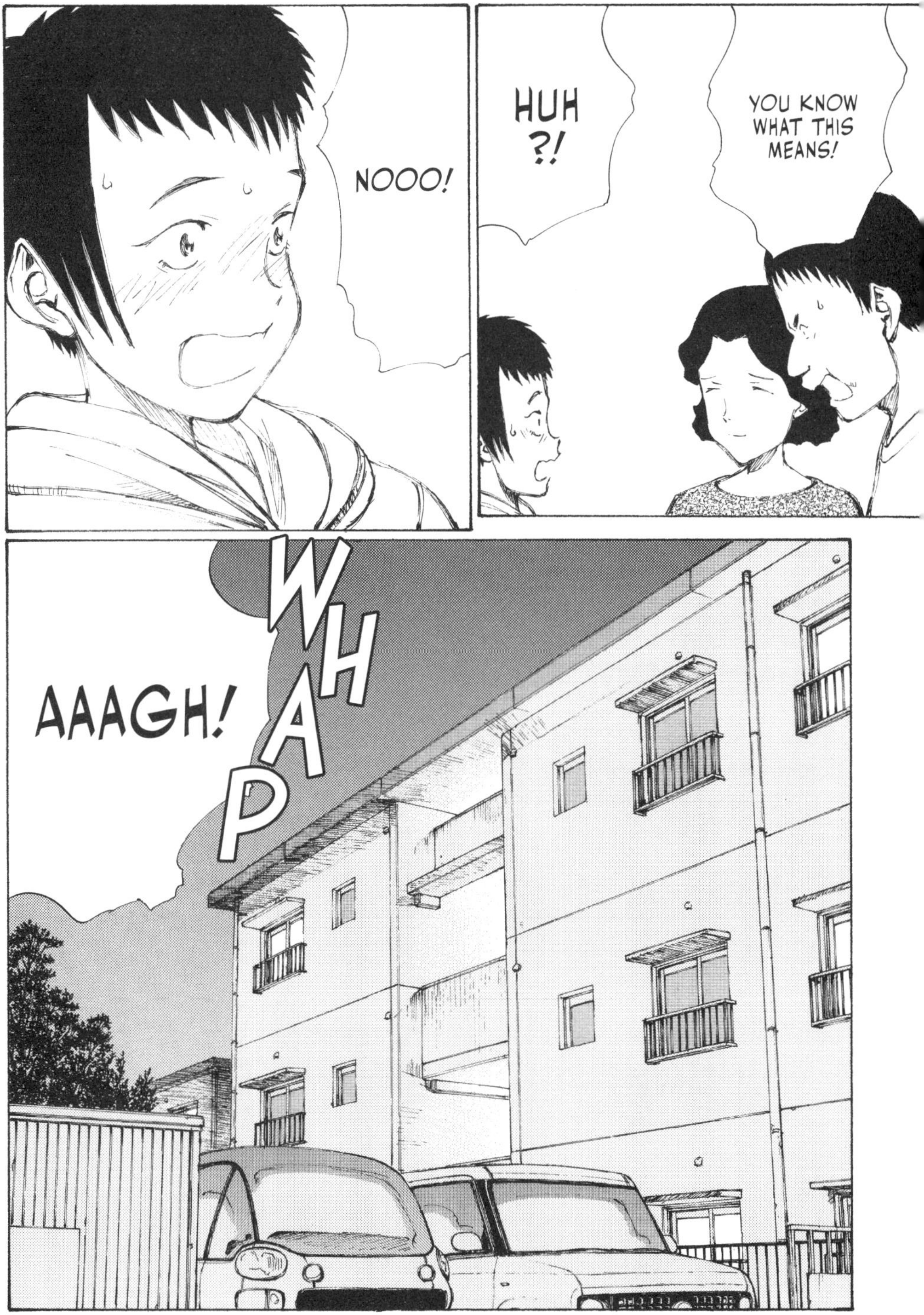
YOU KNOW WHAT THIS MEANS!
HUH ?!
NOOO!
WHAP
AAAGH!

CHAPTER 26: MAKI ANO 2

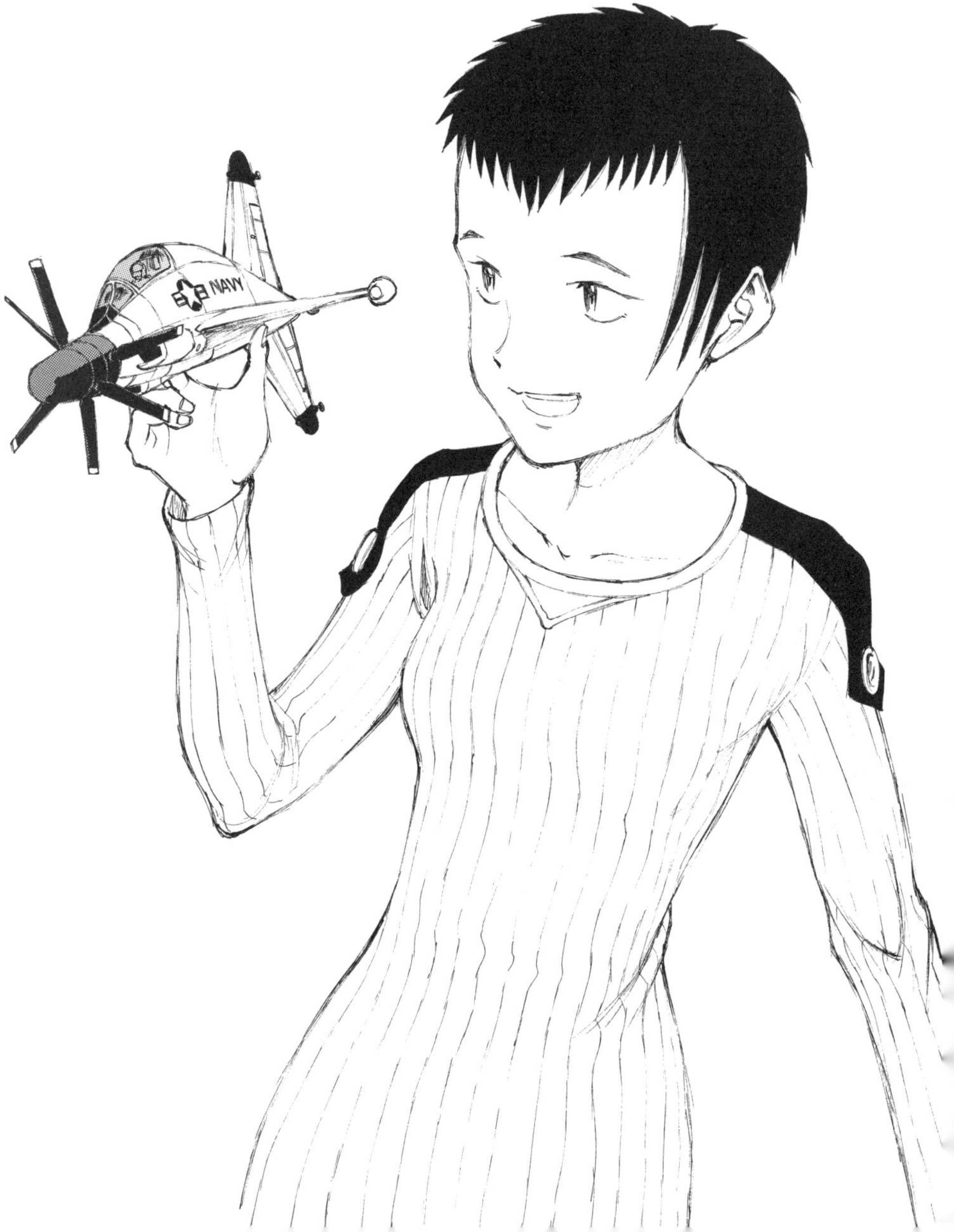
NAVY

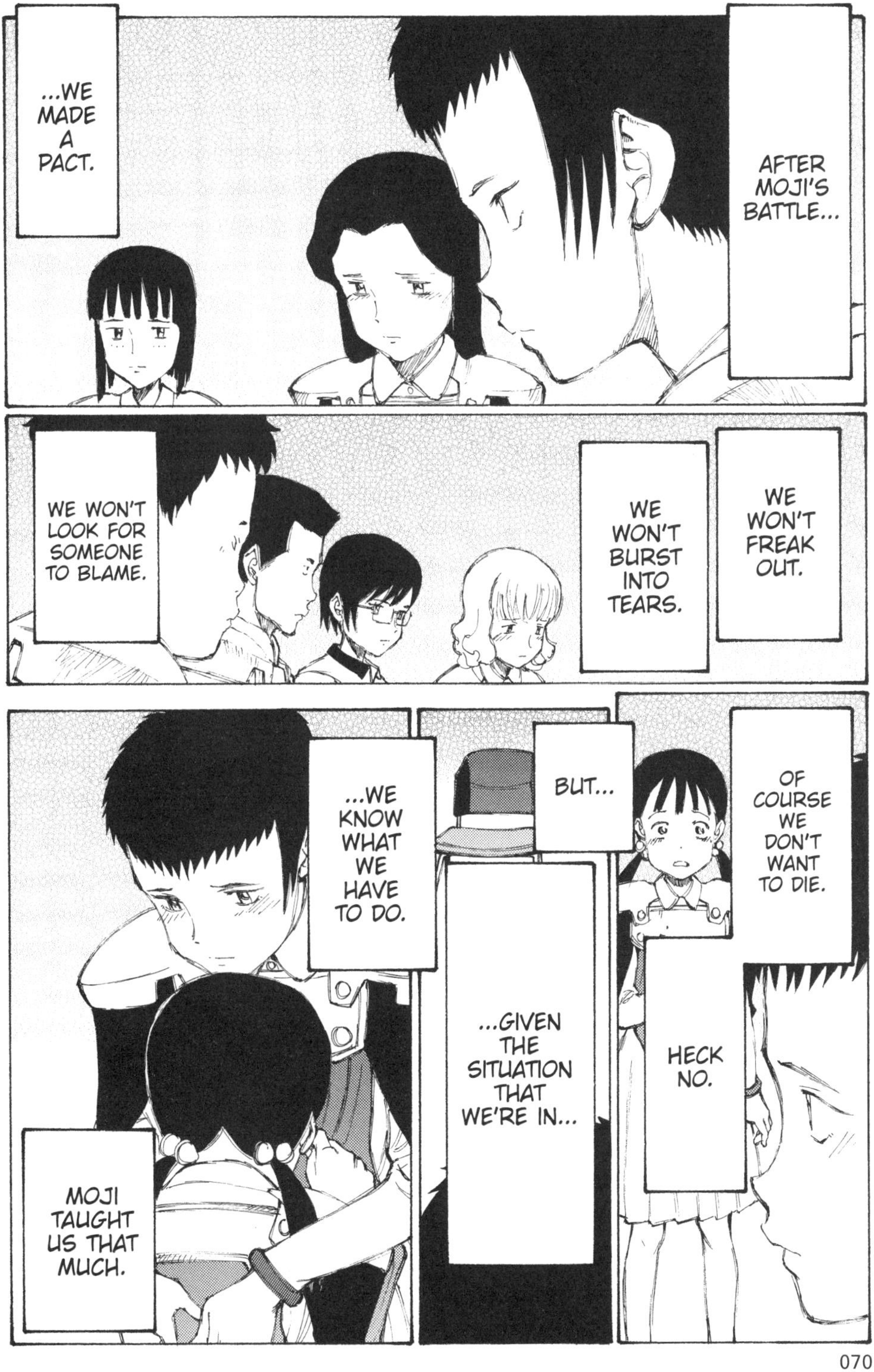
AFTER MOJI'S BATTLE...
...WE MADE A PACT.
WE WON'T FREAK OUT.
WE WON'T BURST INTO TEARS.
WE WON'T LOOK FOR SOMEONE TO BLAME.
OF COURSE WE DON'T WANT TO DIE.
HECK NO.
BUT...
...GIVEN THE SITUATION THAT WE'RE IN...
...WE KNOW WHAT WE HAVE TO DO.
MOJI TAUGHT US THAT MUCH.

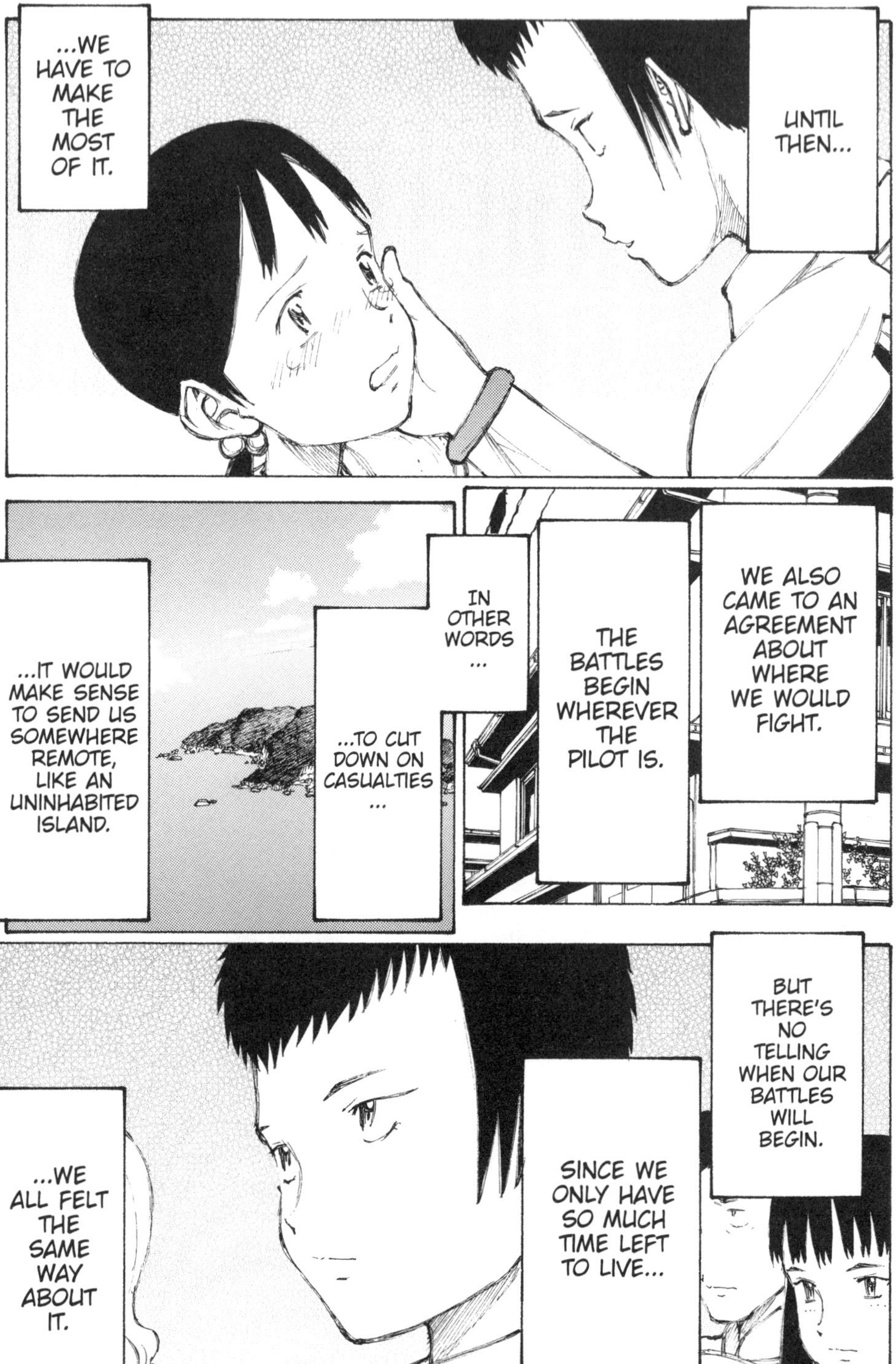
UNTIL THEN...
...WE HAVE TO MAKE THE MOST OF IT.
WE ALSO CAME TO AN AGREEMENT ABOUT WHERE WE WOULD FIGHT.
THE BATTLES BEGIN WHEREVER THE PILOT IS.
IN OTHER WORDS...
...TO CUT DOWN ON CASUALTIES...
...IT WOULD MAKE SENSE TO SEND US SOMEWHERE REMOTE, LIKE AN UNINHABITED ISLAND.
BUT THERE'S NO TELLING WHEN OUR BATTLES WILL BEGIN.
SINCE WE ONLY HAVE SO MUCH TIME LEFT TO LIVE...
...WE ALL FELT THE SAME WAY ABOUT IT.

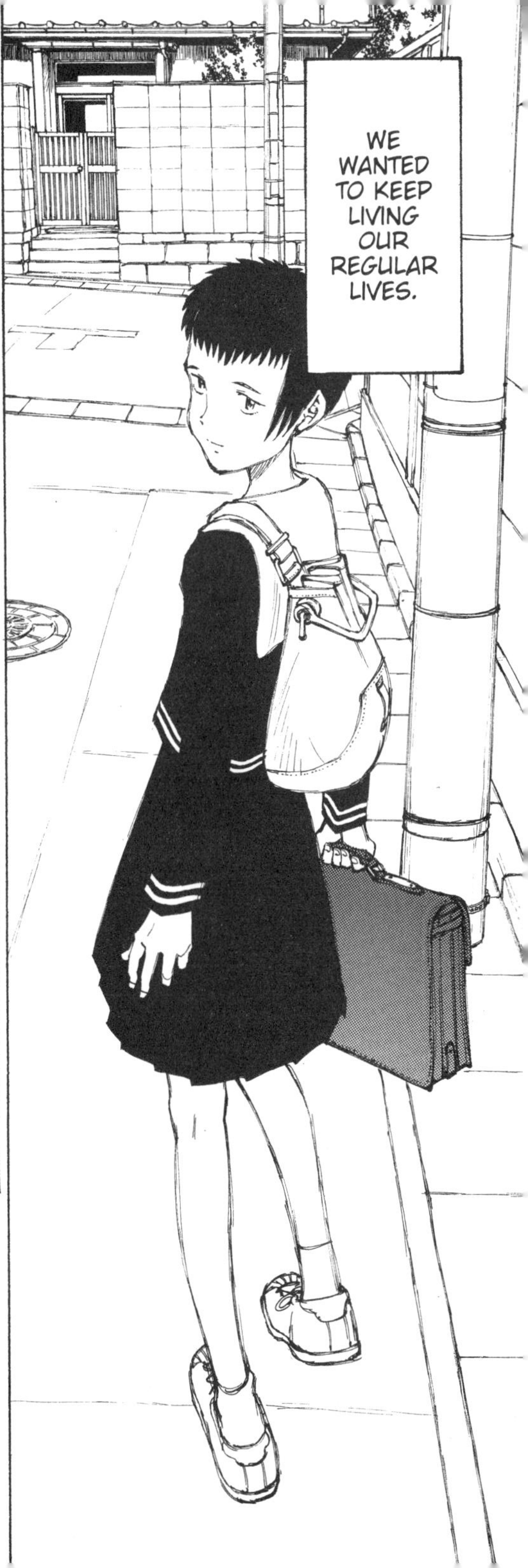
WE WANTED TO KEEP LIVING OUR REGULAR LIVES.

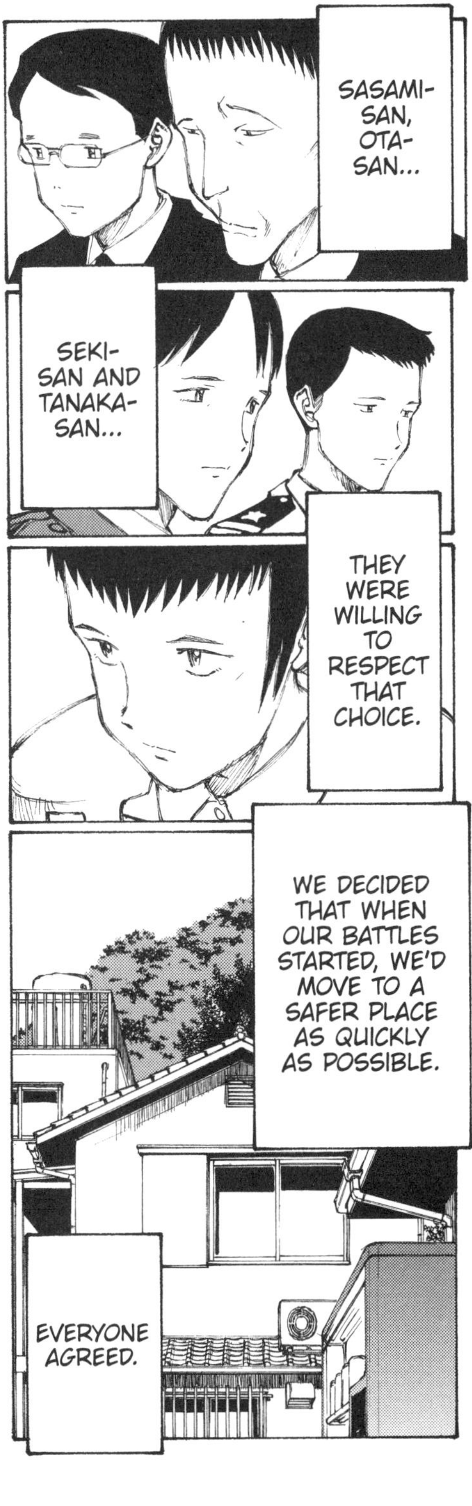
SASAMI-SAN, OTA-SAN...
SEKI-SAN AND TANAKA-SAN...
THEY WERE WILLING TO RESPECT THAT CHOICE.
WE DECIDED THAT WHEN OUR BATTLES STARTED, WE'D MOVE TO A SAFER PLACE AS QUICKLY AS POSSIBLE.
EVERYONE AGREED.

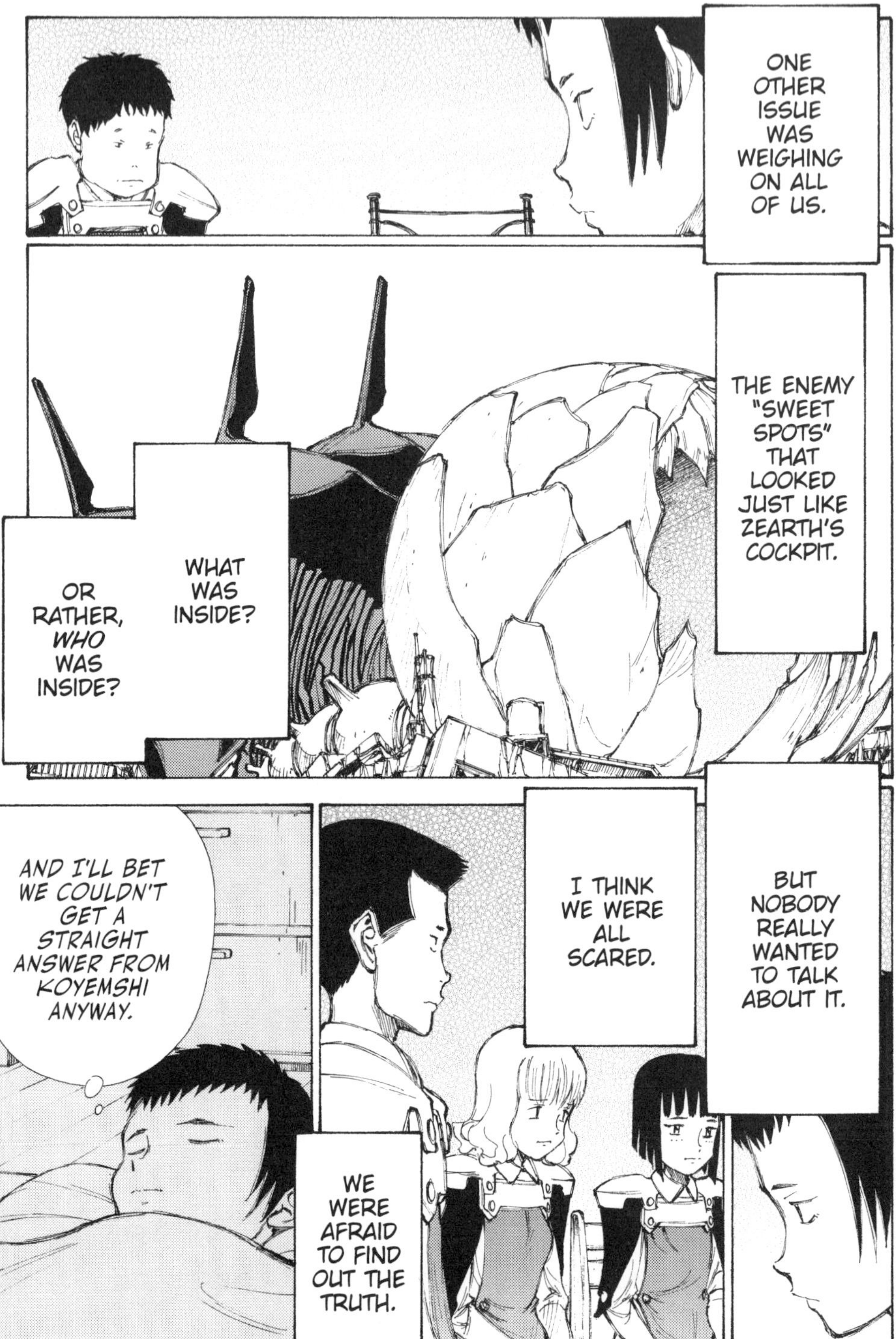
ONE OTHER ISSUE WAS WEIGHING ON ALL OF US.
THE ENEMY "SWEET SPOTS" THAT LOOKED JUST LIKE ZEARTH'S COCKPIT.
WHAT WAS INSIDE?
OR RATHER, *WHO* WAS INSIDE?
BUT NOBODY REALLY WANTED TO TALK ABOUT IT.
I THINK WE WERE ALL SCARED.
WE WERE AFRAID TO FIND OUT THE TRUTH.
AND I'LL BET WE COULDN'T GET A STRAIGHT ANSWER FROM KOYEMSHI ANYWAY.

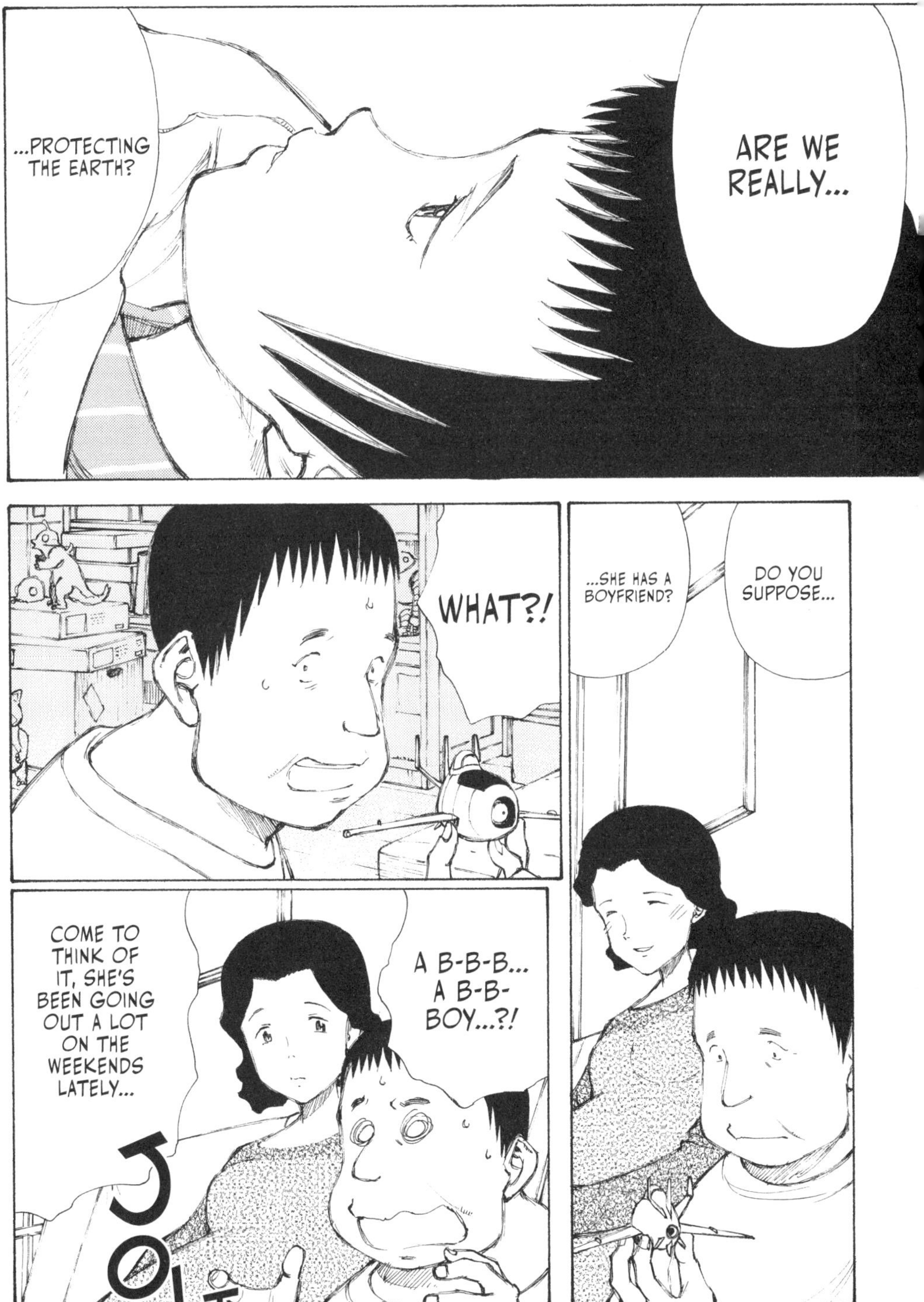
ARE WE REALLY...
...PROTECTING THE EARTH?
DO YOU SUPPOSE...
...SHE HAS A BOYFRIEND?
WHAT?!
A B-B-B... A B-B- BOY...?!
COME TO THINK OF IT, SHE'S BEEN GOING OUT A LOT ON THE WEEKENDS LATELY...
JOLT

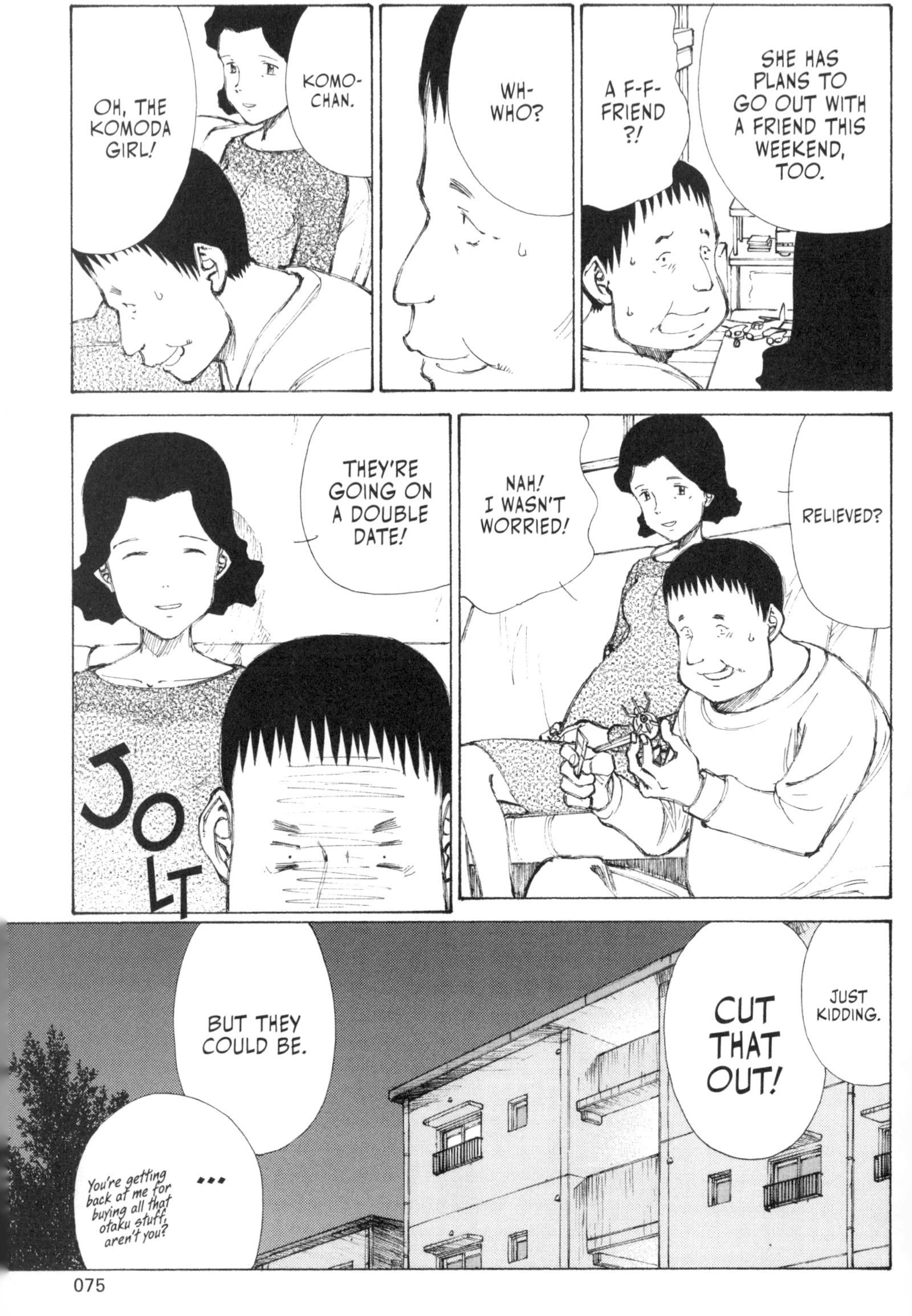
SHE HAS PLANS TO GO OUT WITH A FRIEND THIS WEEKEND, TOO.
A F-F-FRIEND ?!
WH-WHO?
KOMO-CHAN.
OH, THE KOMODA GIRL!
RELIEVED?
NAH! I WASN'T WORRIED!
THEY'RE GOING ON A DOUBLE DATE!
JOLT
JUST KIDDING.
CUT THAT OUT!
BUT THEY COULD BE.
...
You're getting back at me for buying all that otaku stuff, aren't you?

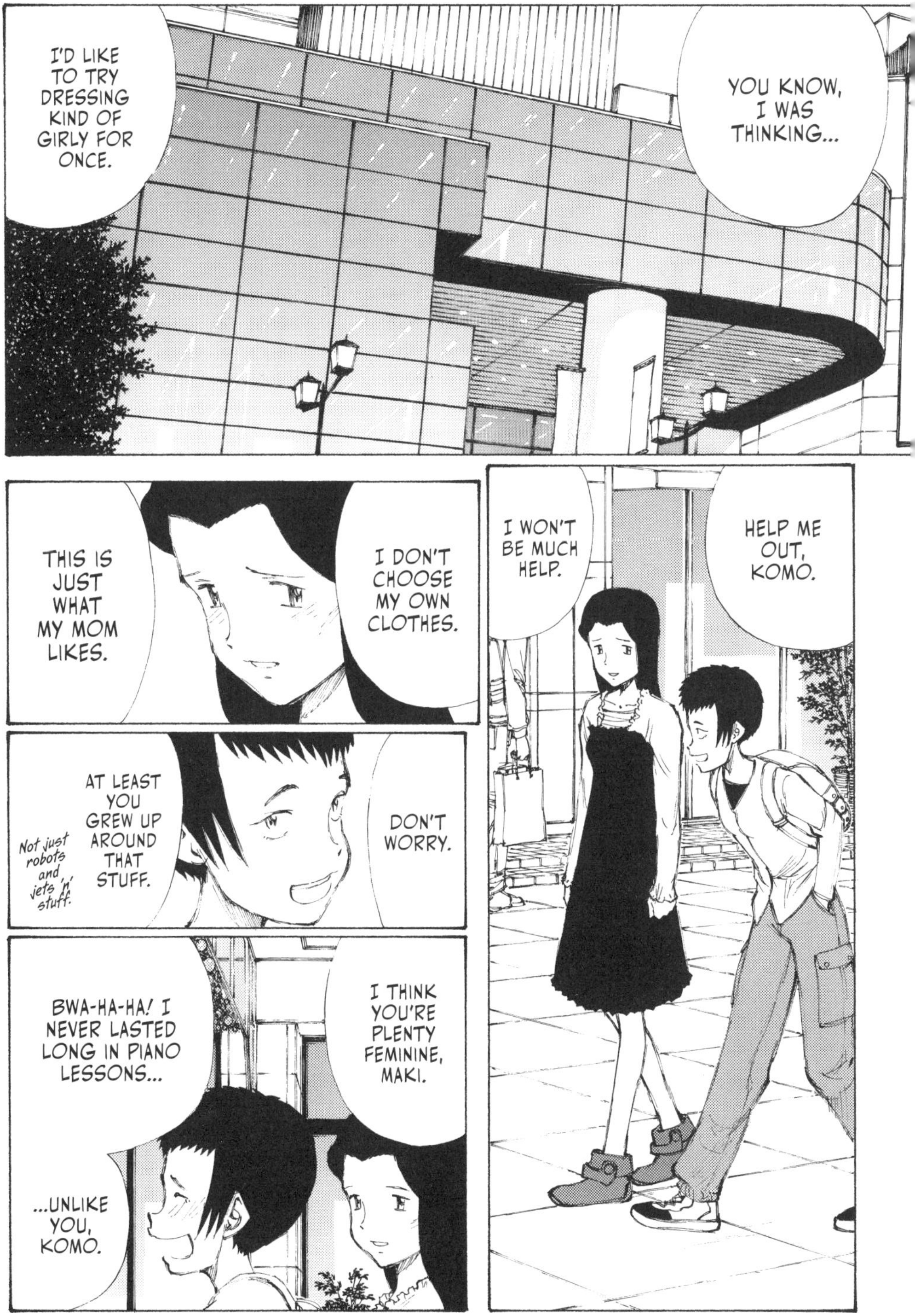
YOU KNOW, I WAS THINKING...
I'D LIKE TO TRY DRESSING KIND OF GIRLY FOR ONCE.
HELP ME OUT, KOMO.
I WON'T BE MUCH HELP.
I DON'T CHOOSE MY OWN CLOTHES.
THIS IS JUST WHAT MY MOM LIKES.
DON'T WORRY.
AT LEAST YOU GREW UP AROUND THAT STUFF.
Not just robots and jets 'n' stuff.
I THINK YOU'RE PLENTY FEMININE, MAKI.
BWA-HA-HA! I NEVER LASTED LONG IN PIANO LESSONS...
...UNLIKE YOU, KOMO.

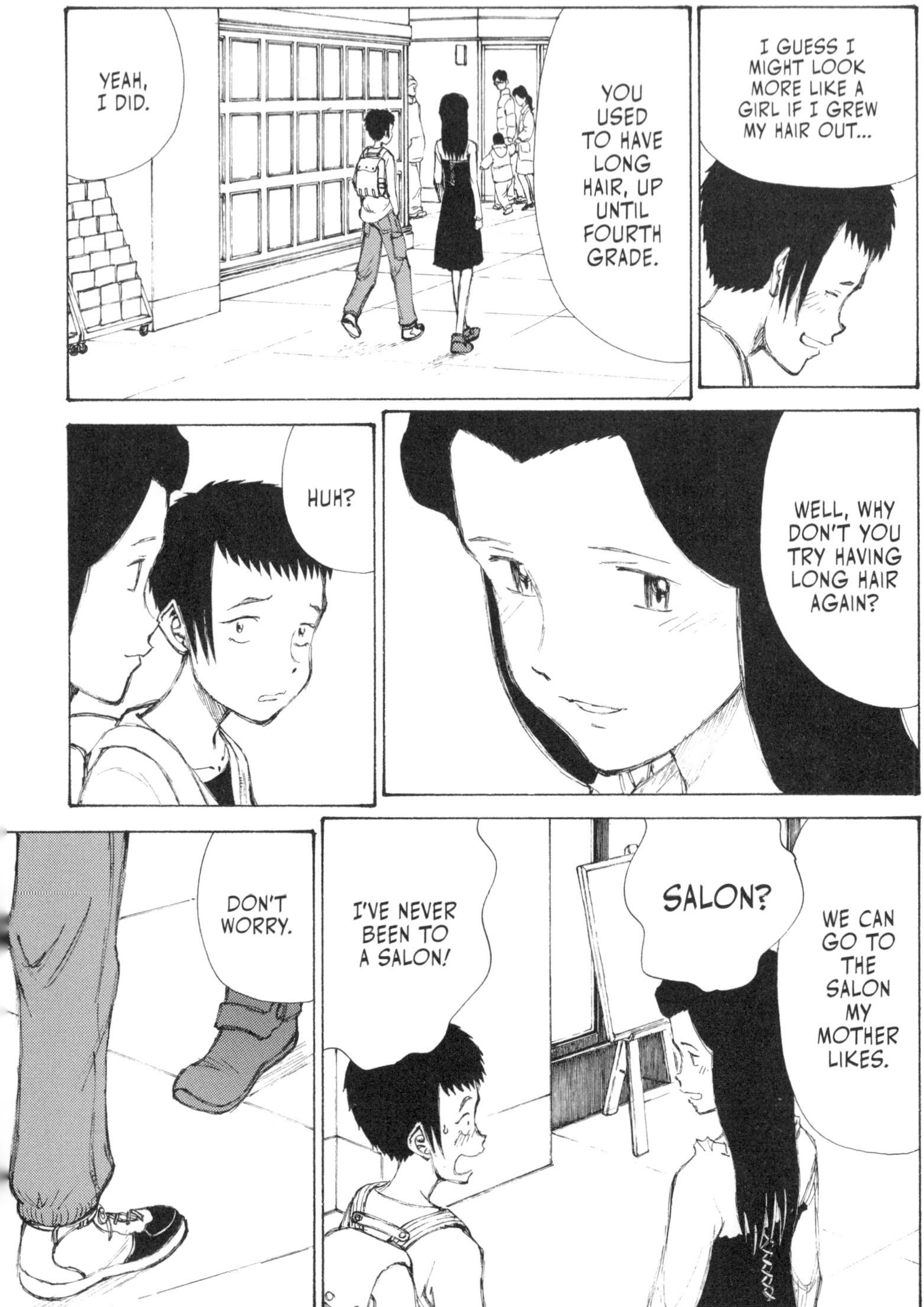
I GUESS I MIGHT LOOK MORE LIKE A GIRL IF I GREW MY HAIR OUT...
YOU USED TO HAVE LONG HAIR, UP UNTIL FOURTH GRADE.
YEAH, I DID.
WELL, WHY DON'T YOU TRY HAVING LONG HAIR AGAIN?
HUH?
WE CAN GO TO THE SALON MY MOTHER LIKES.
SALON?
I'VE NEVER BEEN TO A SALON!
DON'T WORRY.

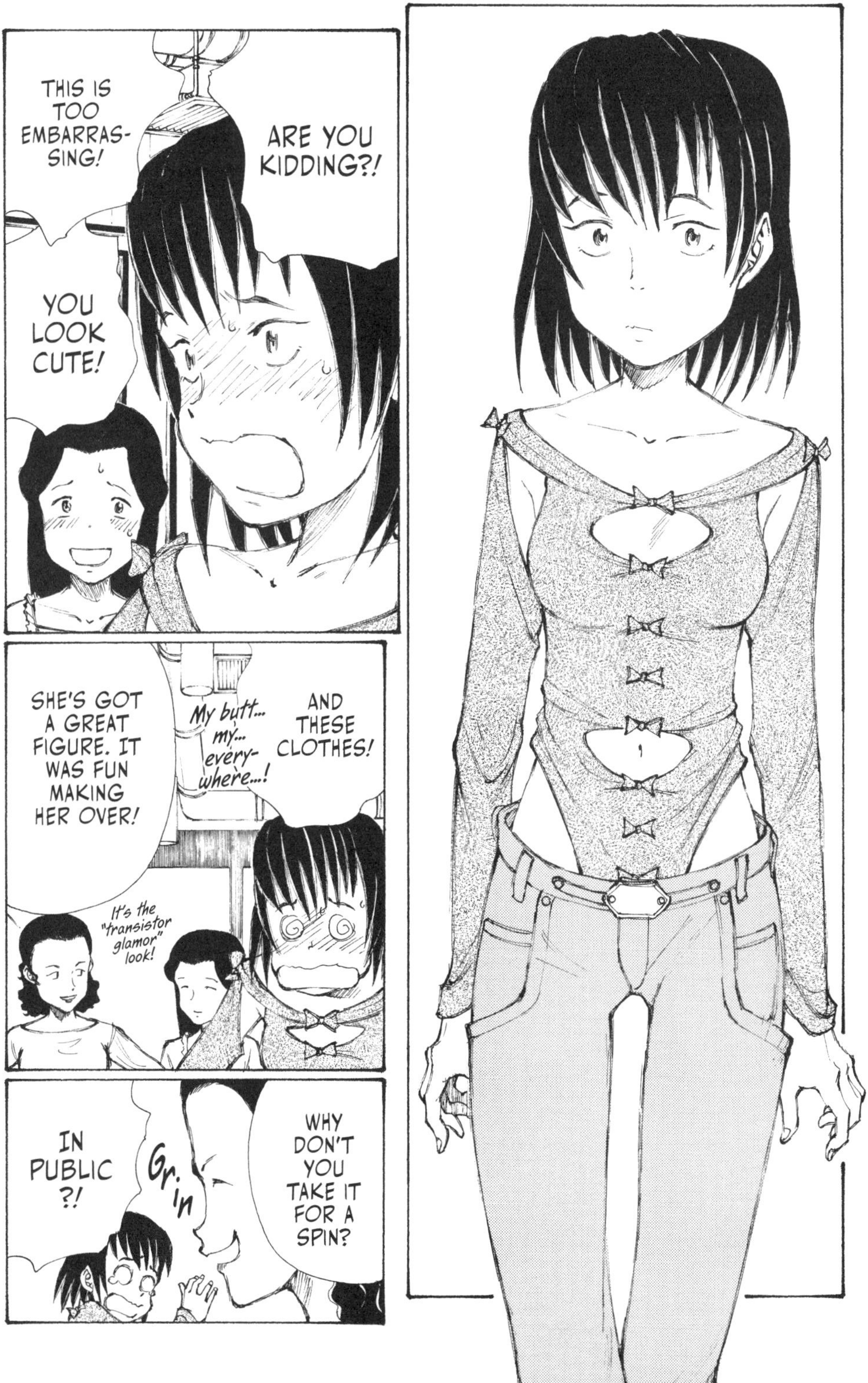
ARE YOU KIDDING?!
THIS IS TOO EMBARRAS-SING!
YOU LOOK CUTE!
AND THESE CLOTHES!
My butt... my... every-where...!
SHE'S GOT A GREAT FIGURE. IT WAS FUN MAKING HER OVER!
It's the "transistor glamor" look!
WHY DON'T YOU TAKE IT FOR A SPIN?
Grin
IN PUBLIC?!

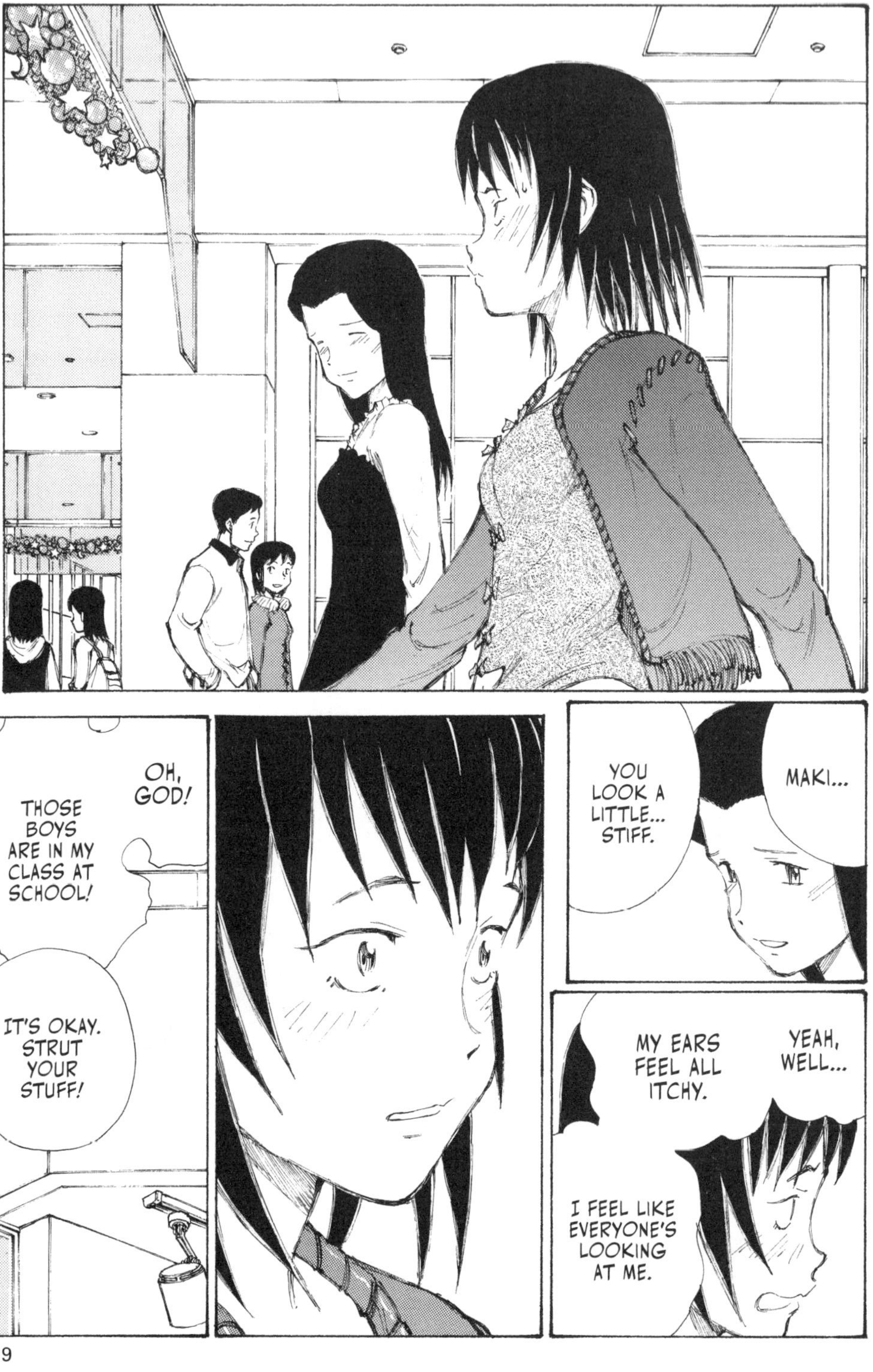
MAKI...
YOU LOOK A LITTLE... STIFF.
YEAH, WELL...
MY EARS FEEL ALL ITCHY.
I FEEL LIKE EVERYONE'S LOOKING AT ME.
OH, GOD!
THOSE BOYS ARE IN MY CLASS AT SCHOOL!
IT'S OKAY. STRUT YOUR STUFF!

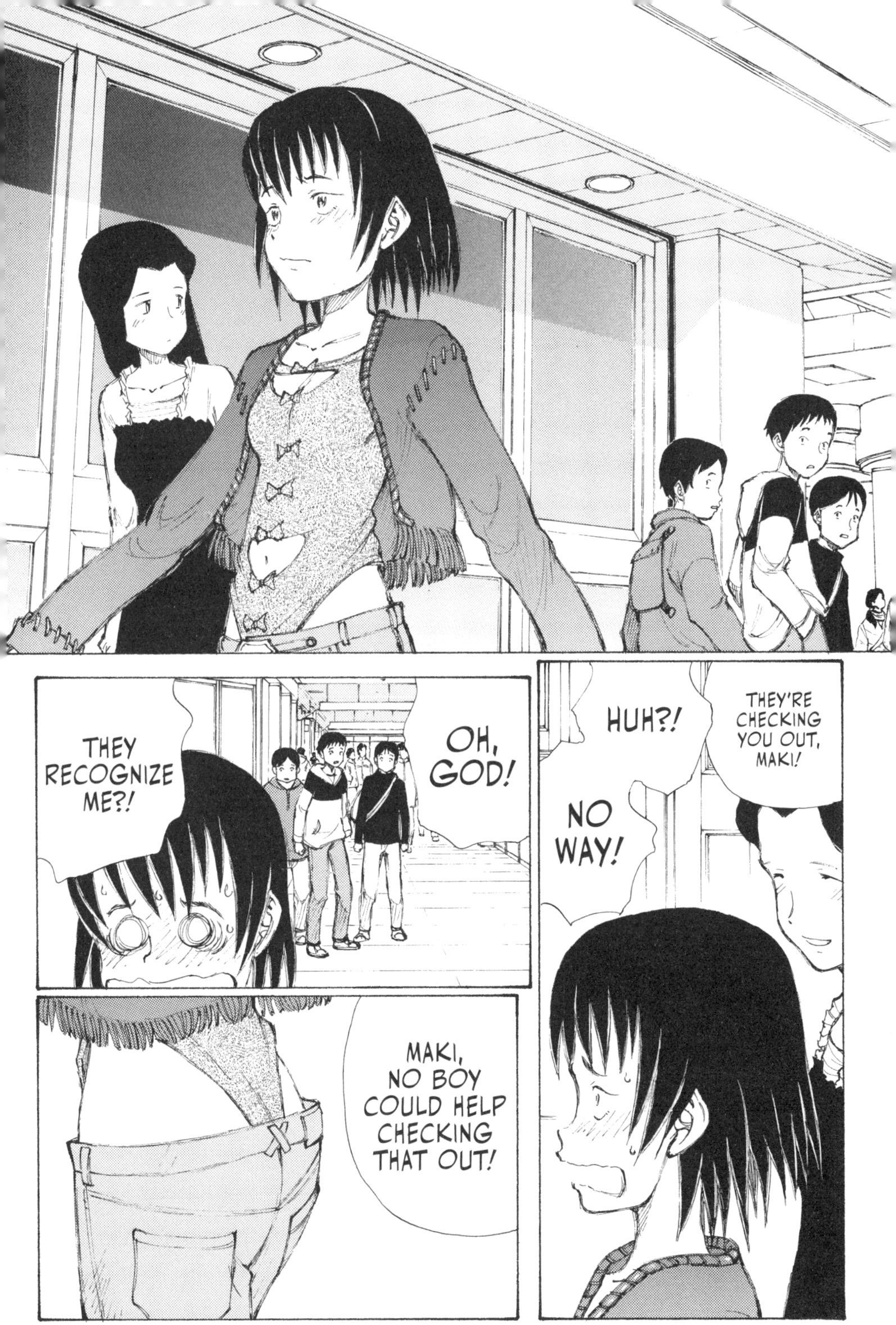
THEY'RE CHECKING YOU OUT, MAKI!
HUH?!
NO WAY!
OH, GOD!
THEY RECOGNIZE ME?!
MAKI, NO BOY COULD HELP CHECKING THAT OUT!

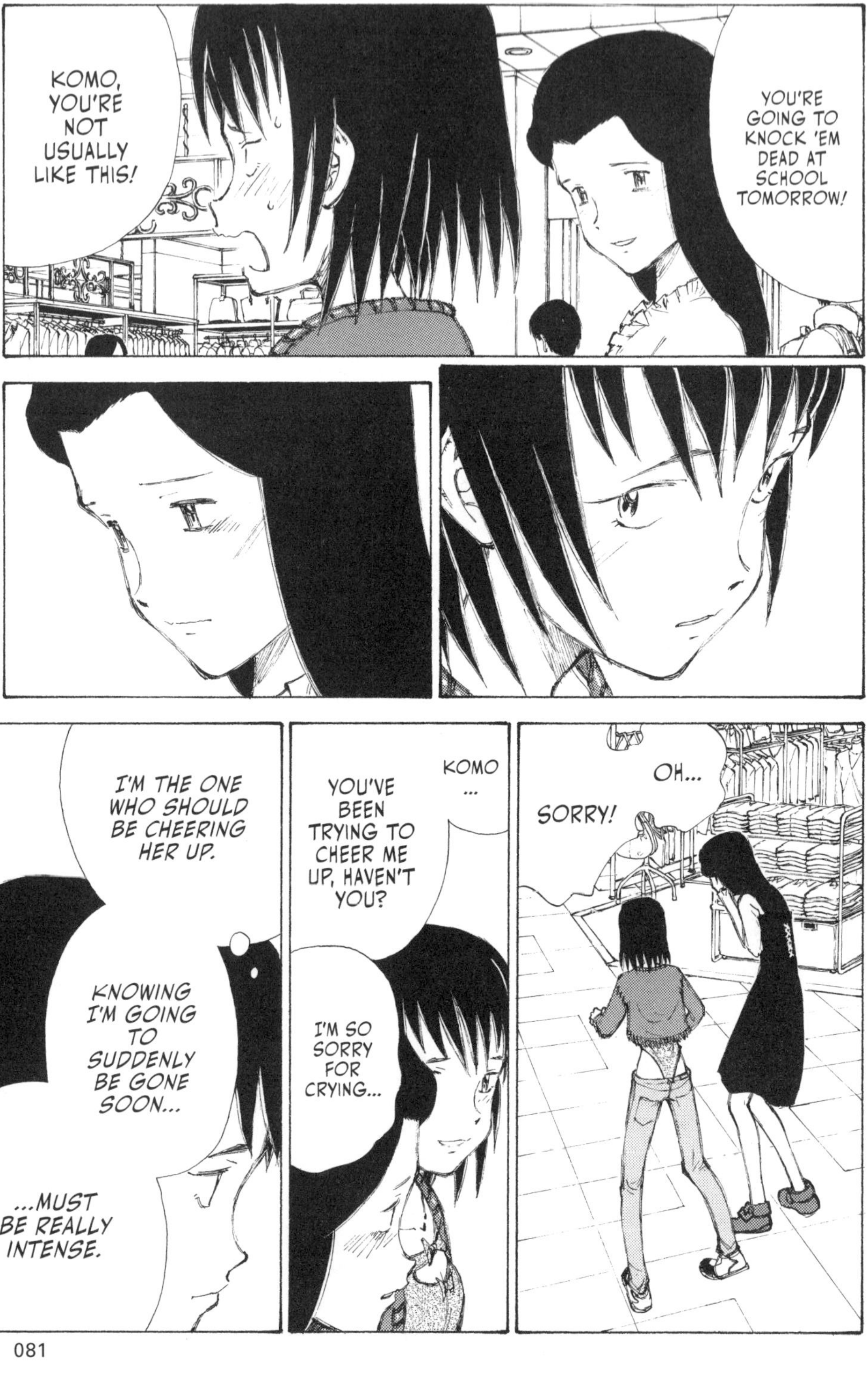
YOU'RE GOING TO KNOCK 'EM DEAD AT SCHOOL TOMORROW!
KOMO, YOU'RE NOT USUALLY LIKE THIS!
OH...
SORRY!
KOMO ...
YOU'VE BEEN TRYING TO CHEER ME UP, HAVEN'T YOU?
I'M SO SORRY FOR CRYING...
I'M THE ONE WHO SHOULD BE CHEERING HER UP.
KNOWING I'M GOING TO SUDDENLY BE GONE SOON...
...MUST BE REALLY INTENSE.

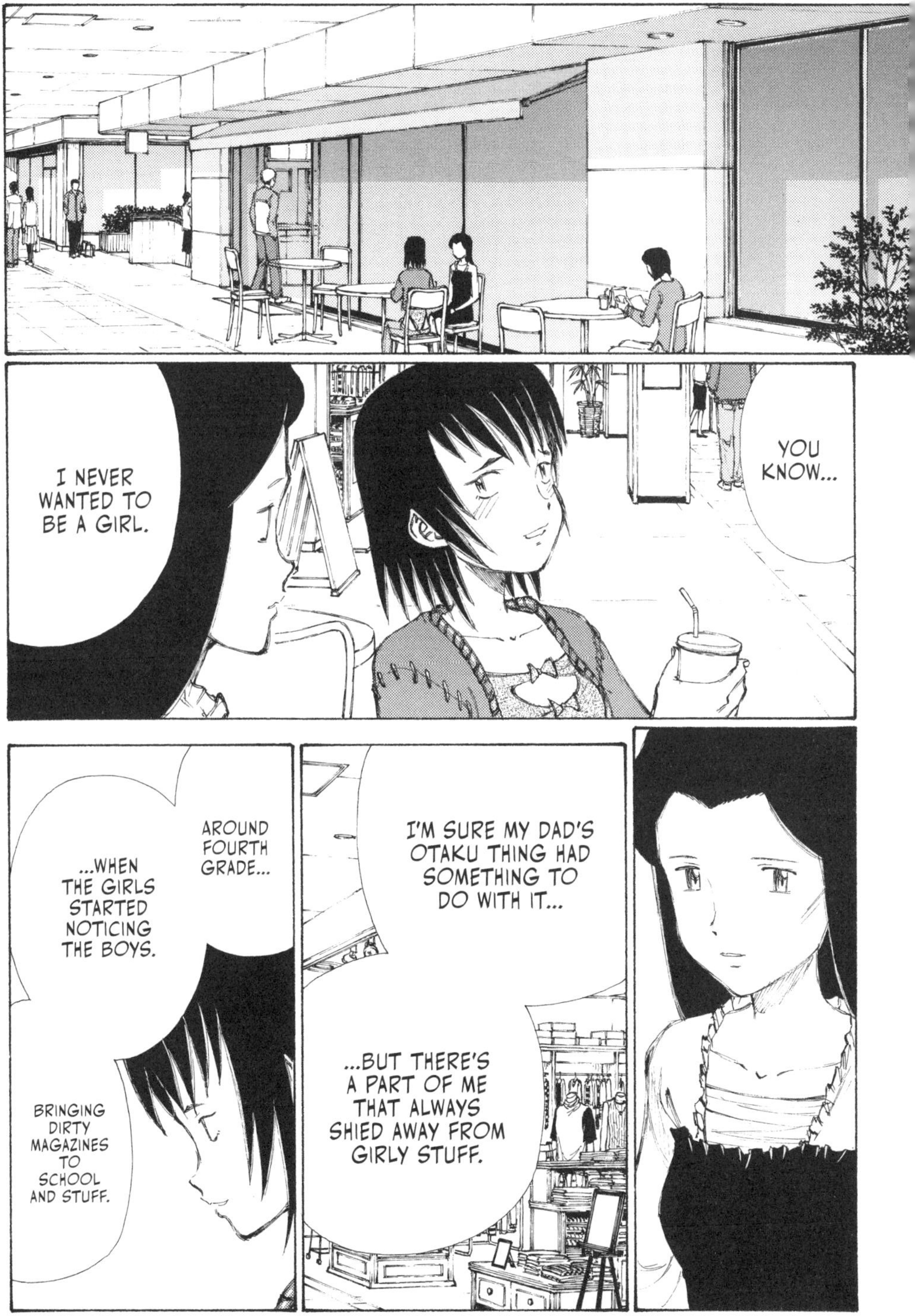
YOU KNOW...
I NEVER WANTED TO BE A GIRL.
I'M SURE MY DAD'S OTAKU THING HAD SOMETHING TO DO WITH IT...
...BUT THERE'S A PART OF ME THAT ALWAYS SHIED AWAY FROM GIRLY STUFF.
AROUND FOURTH GRADE...
...WHEN THE GIRLS STARTED NOTICING THE BOYS.
BRINGING DIRTY MAGAZINES TO SCHOOL AND STUFF.

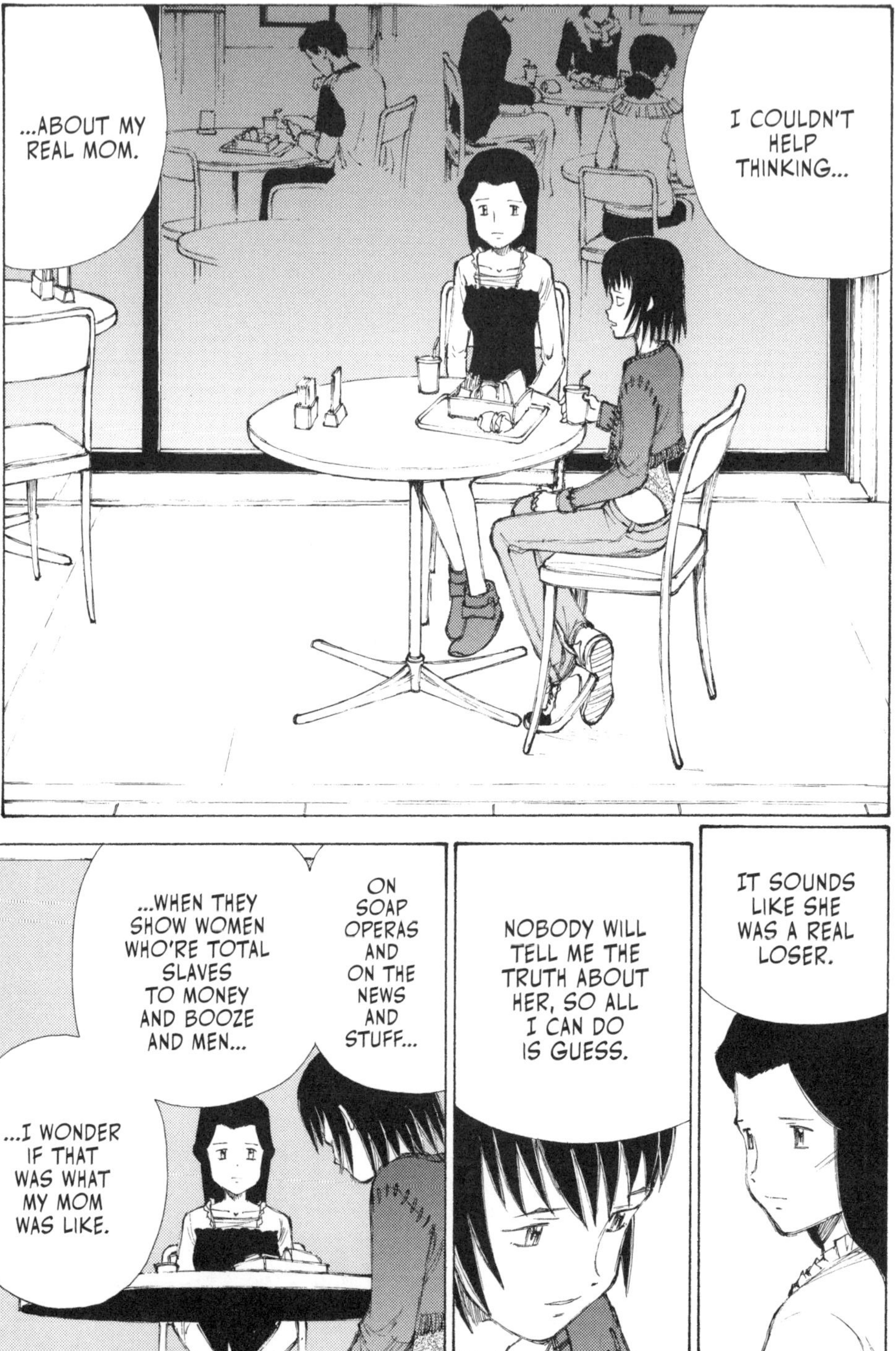
I COULDN'T HELP THINKING...
...ABOUT MY REAL MOM.
IT SOUNDS LIKE SHE WAS A REAL LOSER.
NOBODY WILL TELL ME THE TRUTH ABOUT HER, SO ALL I CAN DO IS GUESS.
ON SOAP OPERAS AND ON THE NEWS AND STUFF...
...WHEN THEY SHOW WOMEN WHO'RE TOTAL SLAVES TO MONEY AND BOOZE AND MEN...
...I WONDER IF THAT WAS WHAT MY MOM WAS LIKE.

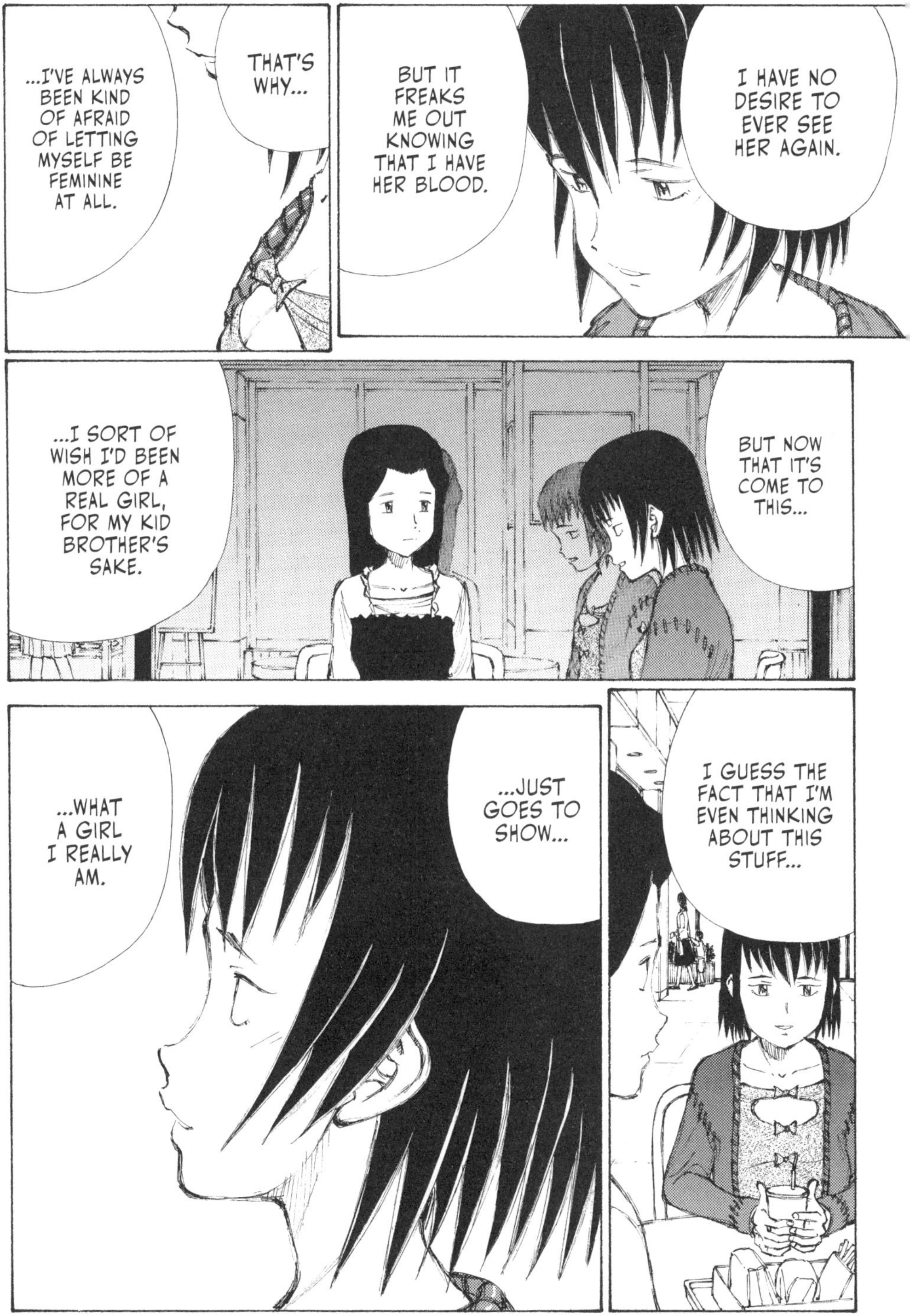
I HAVE NO DESIRE TO EVER SEE HER AGAIN.
BUT IT FREAKS ME OUT KNOWING THAT I HAVE HER BLOOD.
THAT'S WHY...
...I'VE ALWAYS BEEN KIND OF AFRAID OF LETTING MYSELF BE FEMININE AT ALL.
BUT NOW THAT IT'S COME TO THIS...
...I SORT OF WISH I'D BEEN MORE OF A REAL GIRL, FOR MY KID BROTHER'S SAKE.
I GUESS THE FACT THAT I'M EVEN THINKING ABOUT THIS STUFF...
...JUST GOES TO SHOW...
...WHAT A GIRL I REALLY AM.

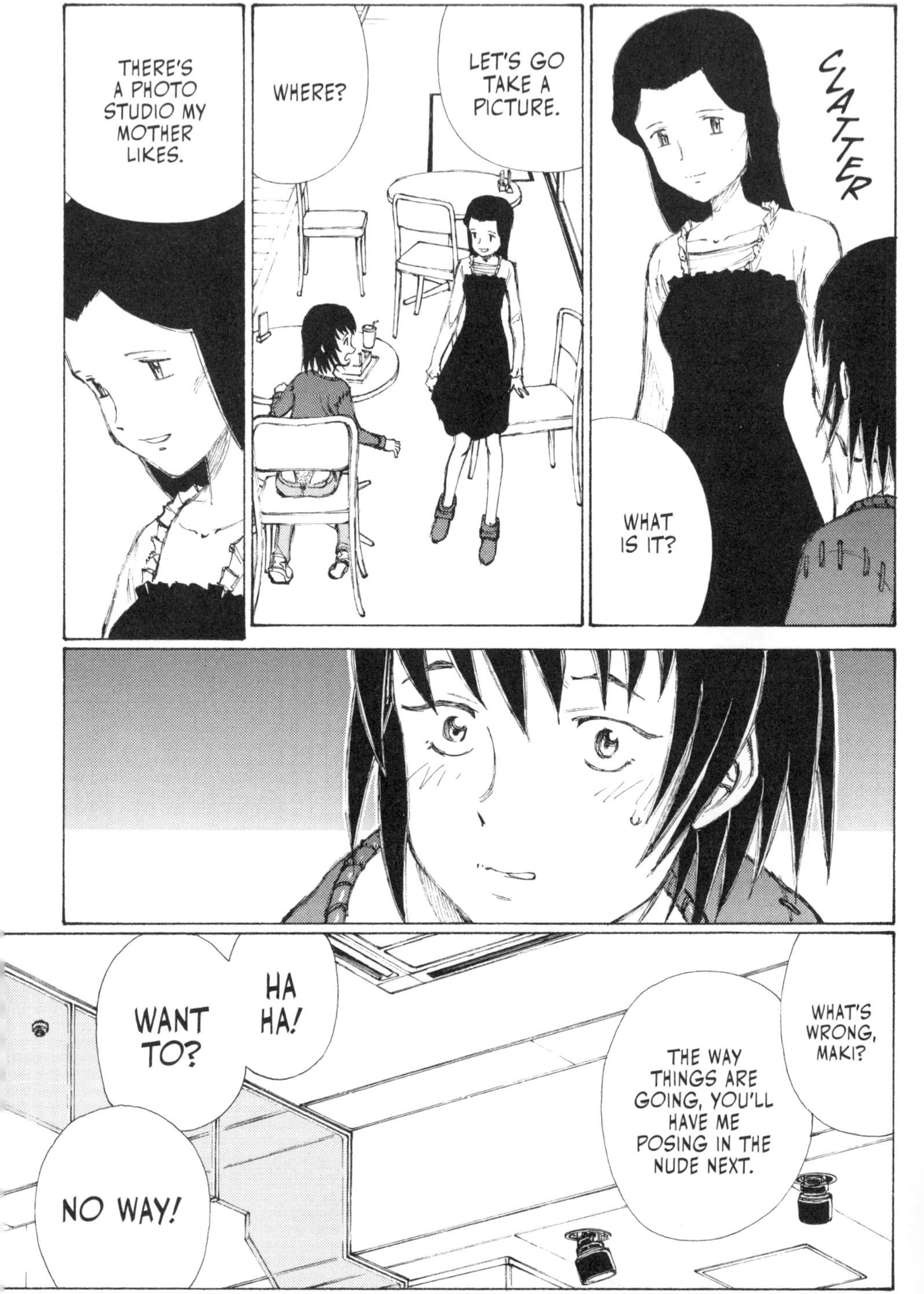
CLATTER
WHAT IS IT?
LET'S GO TAKE A PICTURE.
WHERE?
THERE'S A PHOTO STUDIO MY MOTHER LIKES.
WHAT'S WRONG, MAKI?
THE WAY THINGS ARE GOING, YOU'LL HAVE ME POSING IN THE NUDE NEXT.
HA HA!
WANT TO?
NO WAY!

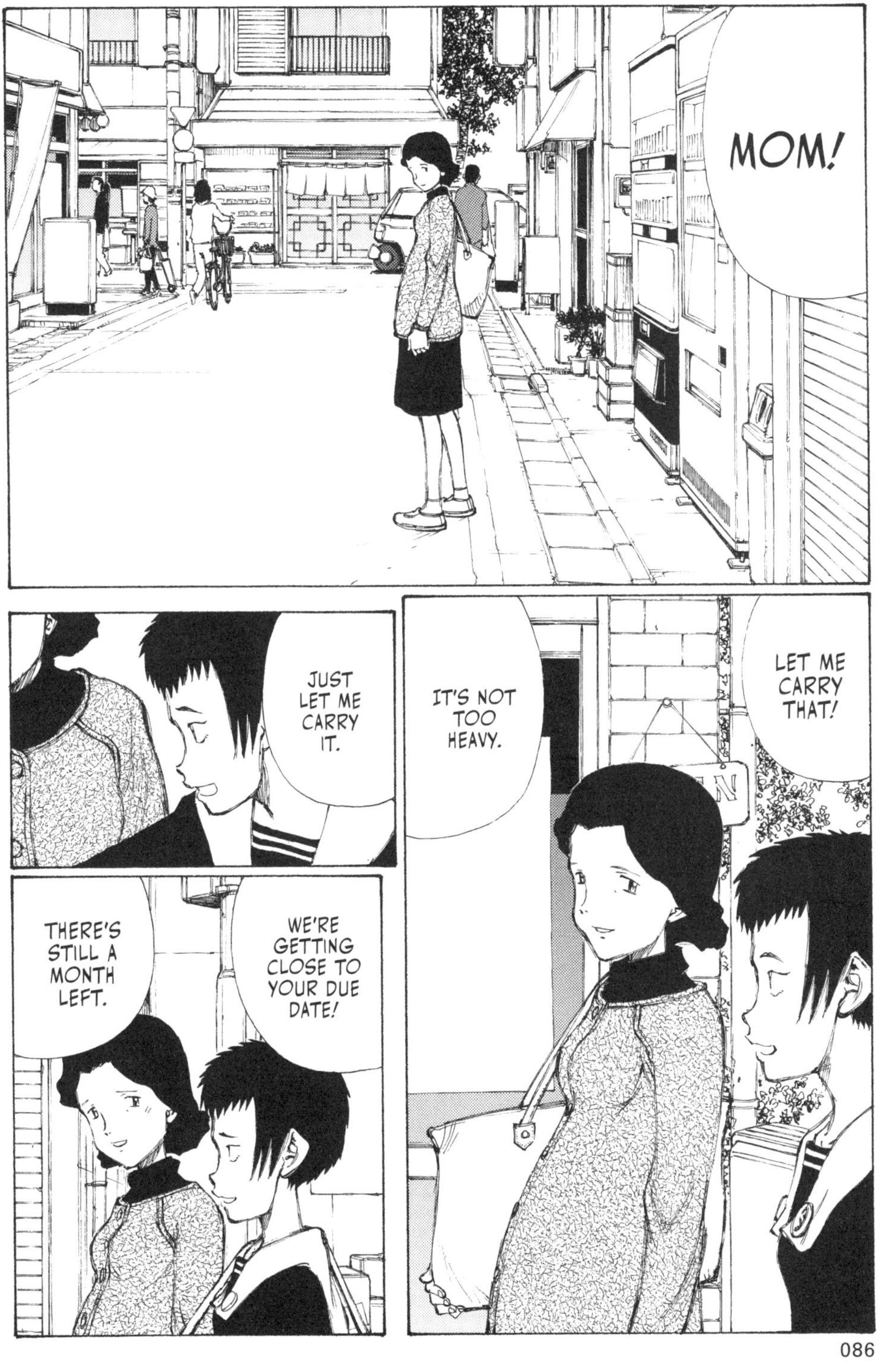
MOM!
LET ME CARRY THAT!
IT'S NOT TOO HEAVY.
JUST LET ME CARRY IT.
WE'RE GETTING CLOSE TO YOUR DUE DATE!
THERE'S STILL A MONTH LEFT.

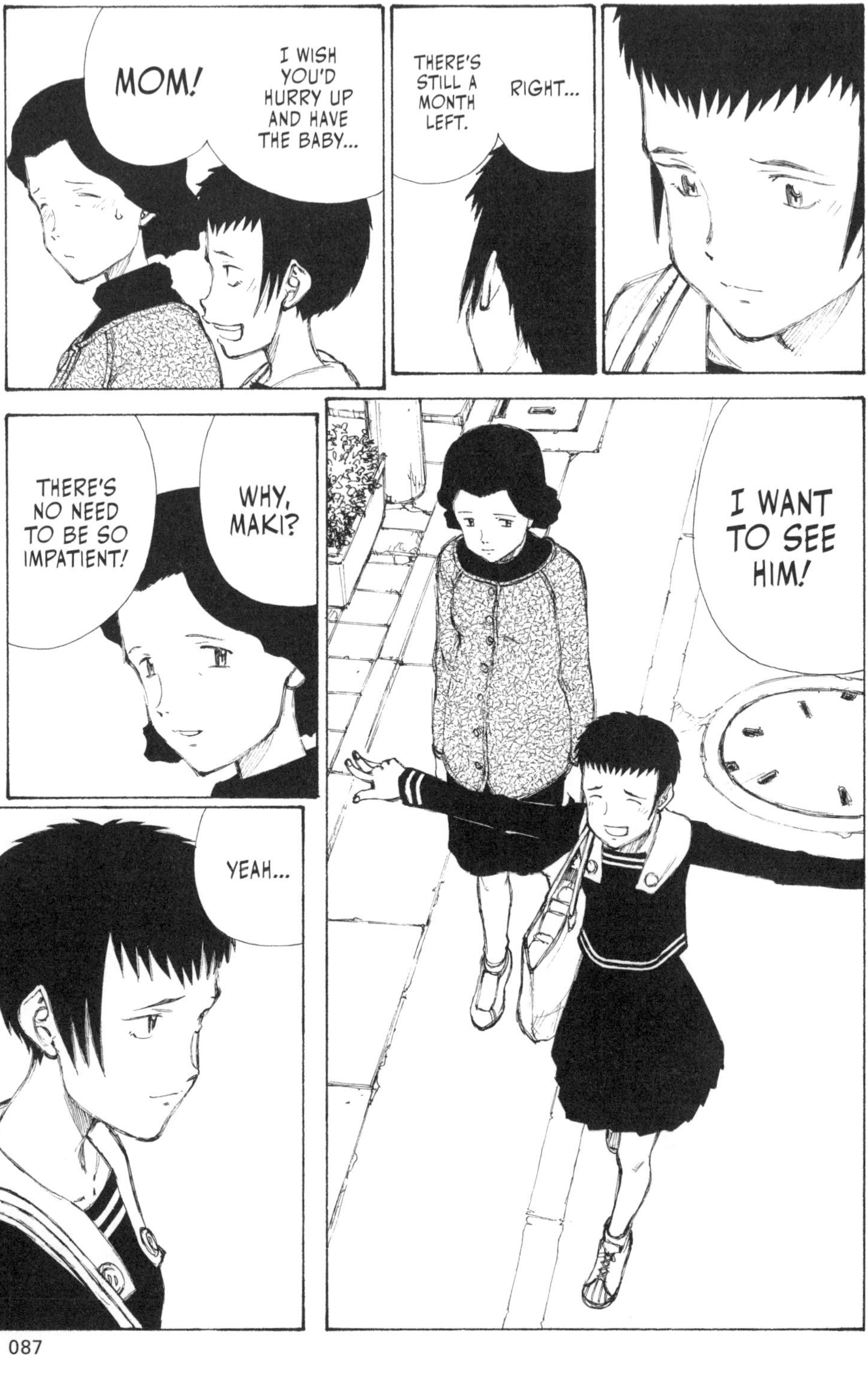
MOM!
I WISH YOU'D HURRY UP AND HAVE THE BABY...
THERE'S STILL A MONTH LEFT.
RIGHT...
THERE'S NO NEED TO BE SO IMPATIENT!
WHY, MAKI?
YEAH...
I WANT TO SEE HIM!

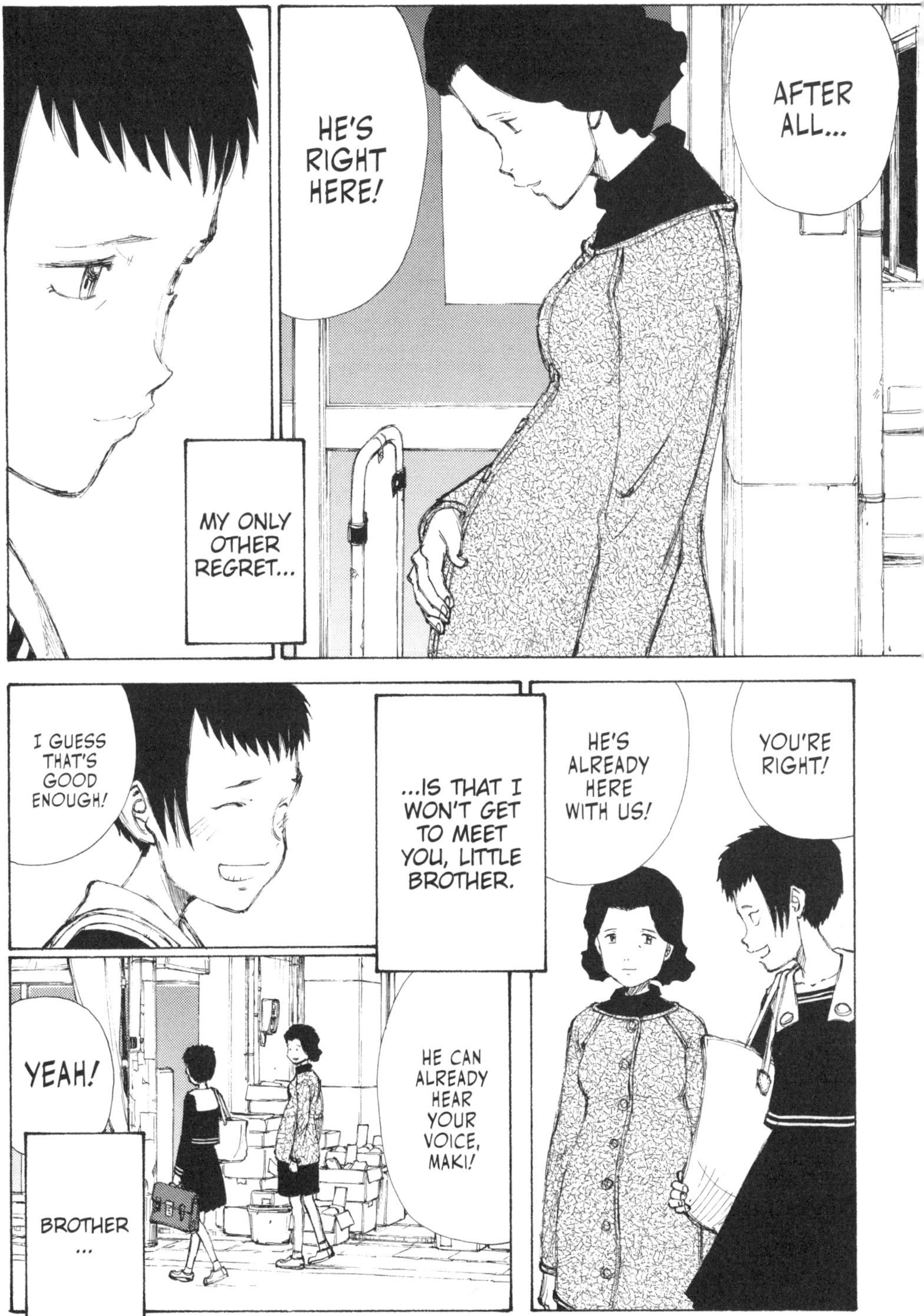
AFTER ALL...
HE'S RIGHT HERE!
MY ONLY OTHER REGRET...
YOU'RE RIGHT!
HE'S ALREADY HERE WITH US!
...IS THAT I WON'T GET TO MEET YOU, LITTLE BROTHER.
I GUESS THAT'S GOOD ENOUGH!
HE CAN ALREADY HEAR YOUR VOICE, MAKI!
YEAH!
BROTHER ...

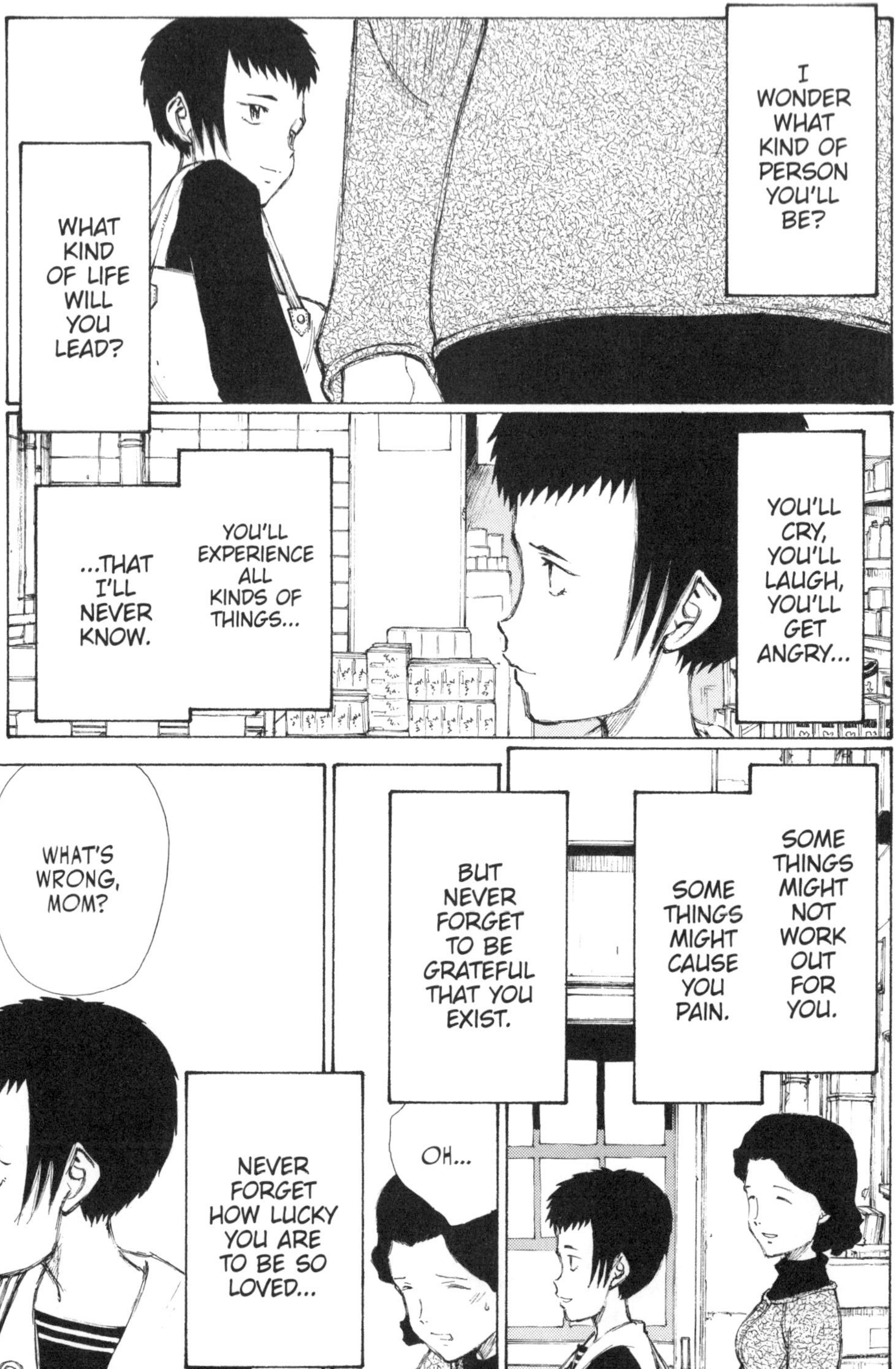
I WONDER WHAT KIND OF PERSON YOU'LL BE?
WHAT KIND OF LIFE WILL YOU LEAD?
YOU'LL CRY, YOU'LL LAUGH, YOU'LL GET ANGRY...
YOU'LL EXPERIENCE ALL KINDS OF THINGS...
...THAT I'LL NEVER KNOW.
SOME THINGS MIGHT NOT WORK OUT FOR YOU.
SOME THINGS MIGHT CAUSE YOU PAIN.
BUT NEVER FORGET TO BE GRATEFUL THAT YOU EXIST.
NEVER FORGET HOW LUCKY YOU ARE TO BE SO LOVED...
OH...
WHAT'S WRONG, MOM?

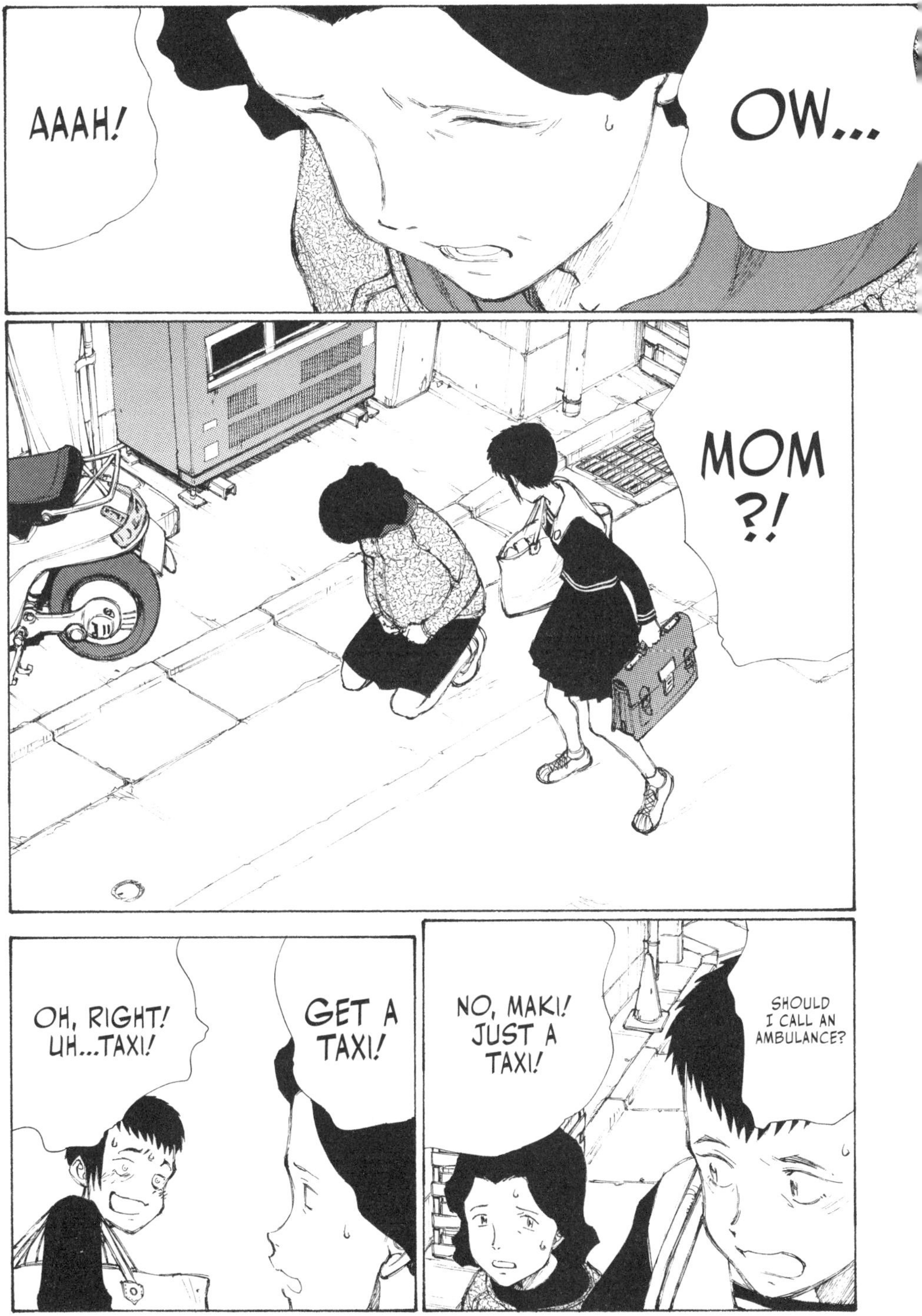
OW...
AAAH!
MOM ?!
SHOULD I CALL AN AMBULANCE?
NO, MAKI! JUST A TAXI!
GET A TAXI!
OH, RIGHT! UH...TAXI!

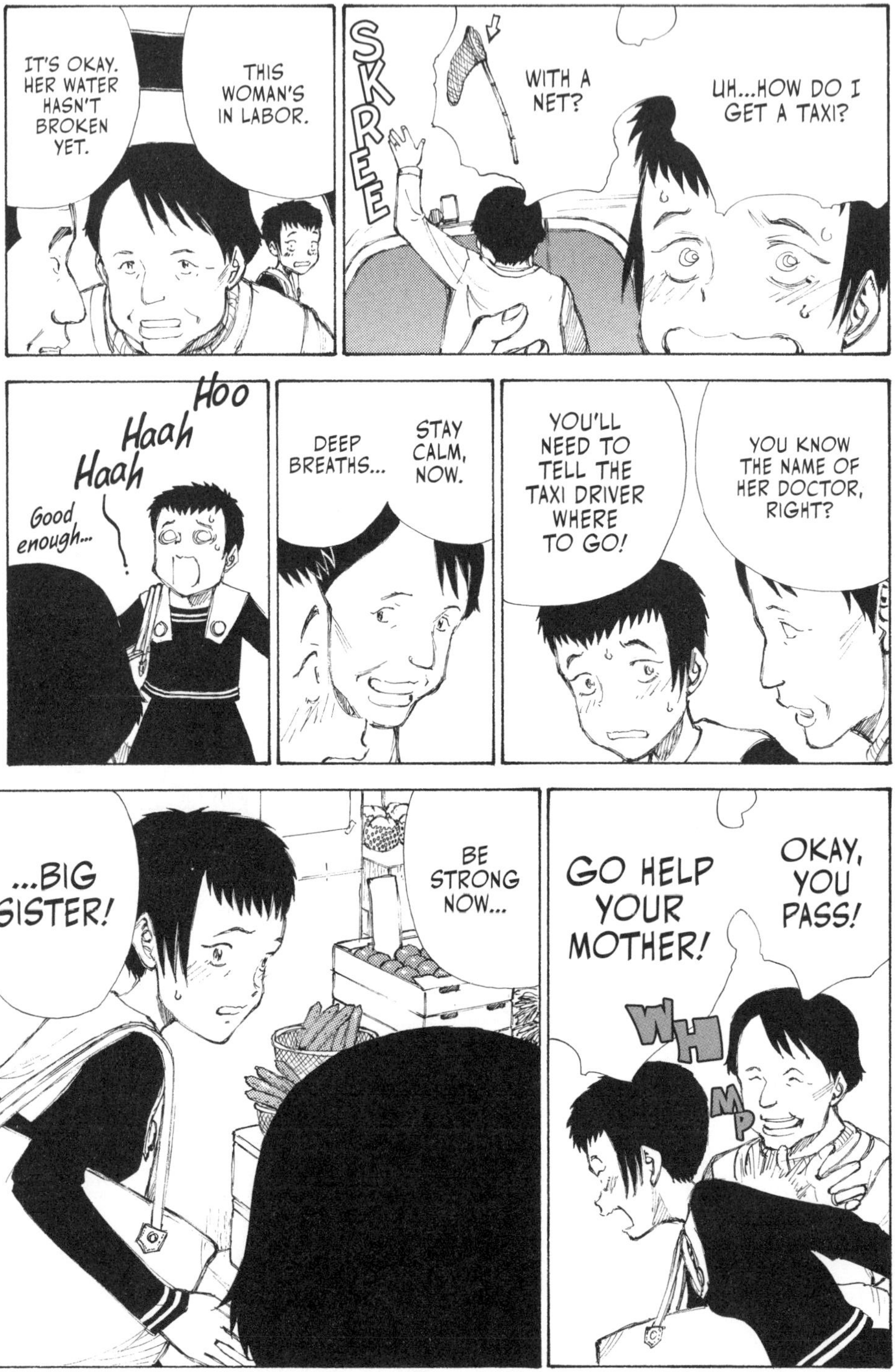
UH...HOW DO I GET A TAXI?
WITH A NET?
SKREE
THIS WOMAN'S IN LABOR.
IT'S OKAY. HER WATER HASN'T BROKEN YET.
YOU KNOW THE NAME OF HER DOCTOR, RIGHT?
YOU'LL NEED TO TELL THE TAXI DRIVER WHERE TO GO!
STAY CALM, NOW.
DEEP BREATHS...
Hoo
Haah
Haah
Good enough...
OKAY, YOU PASS!
GO HELP YOUR MOTHER!
WHMMP
BE STRONG NOW...
...BIG SISTER!

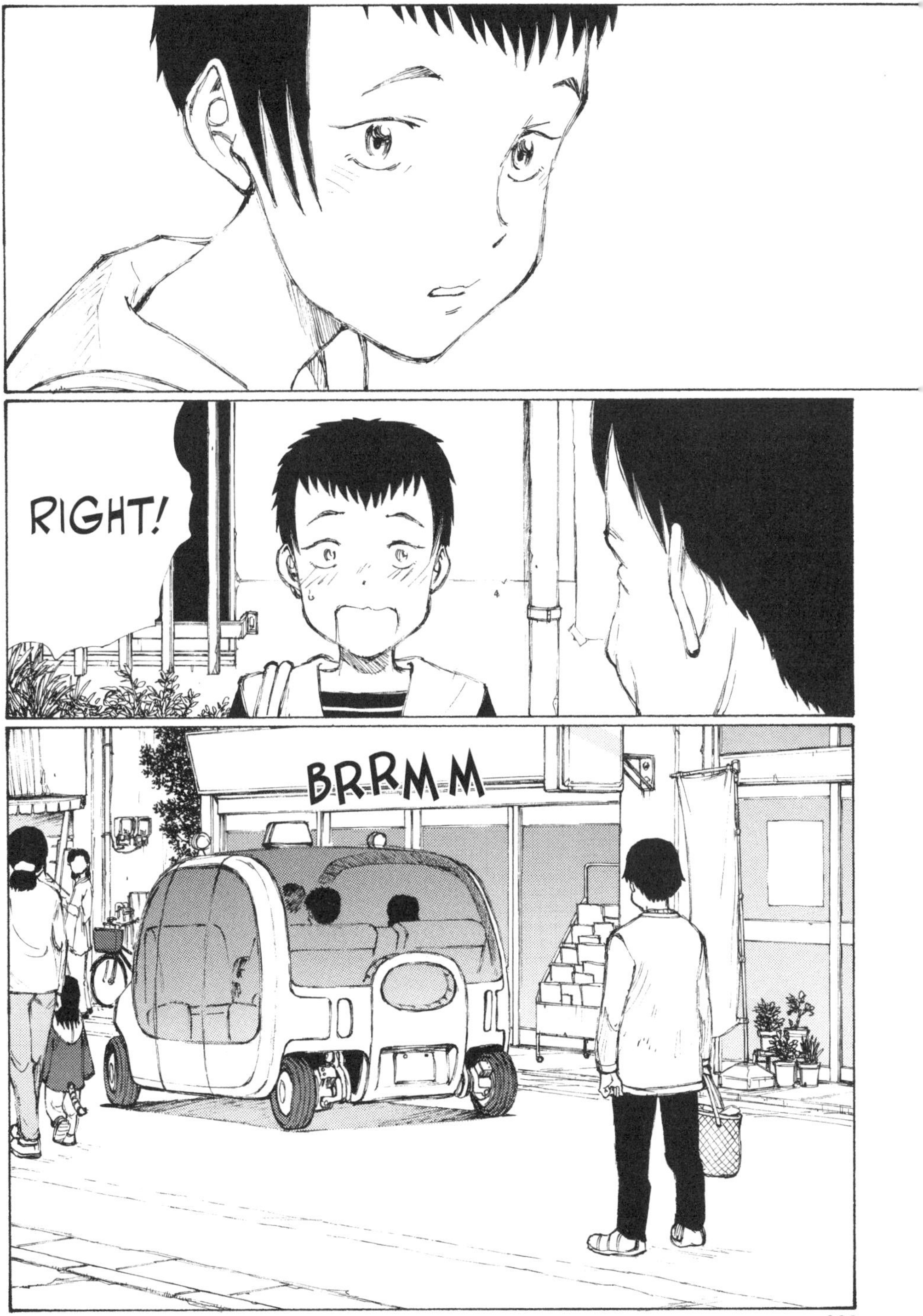
RIGHT!
BRRMM

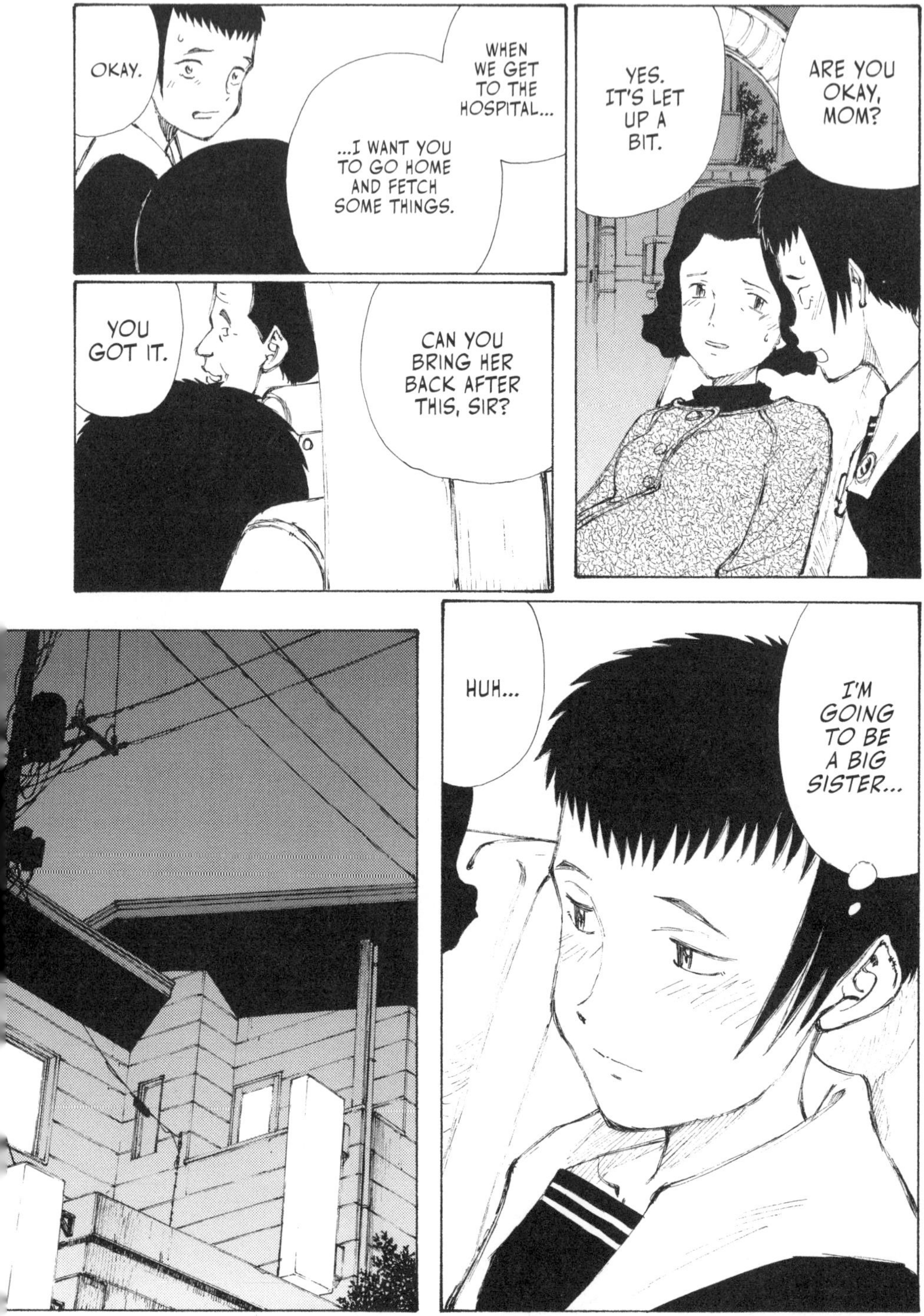
ARE YOU OKAY, MOM?
YES. IT'S LET UP A BIT.
WHEN WE GET TO THE HOSPITAL...
...I WANT YOU TO GO HOME AND FETCH SOME THINGS.
OKAY.
CAN YOU BRING HER BACK AFTER THIS, SIR?
YOU GOT IT.
I'M GOING TO BE A BIG SISTER...
HUH...

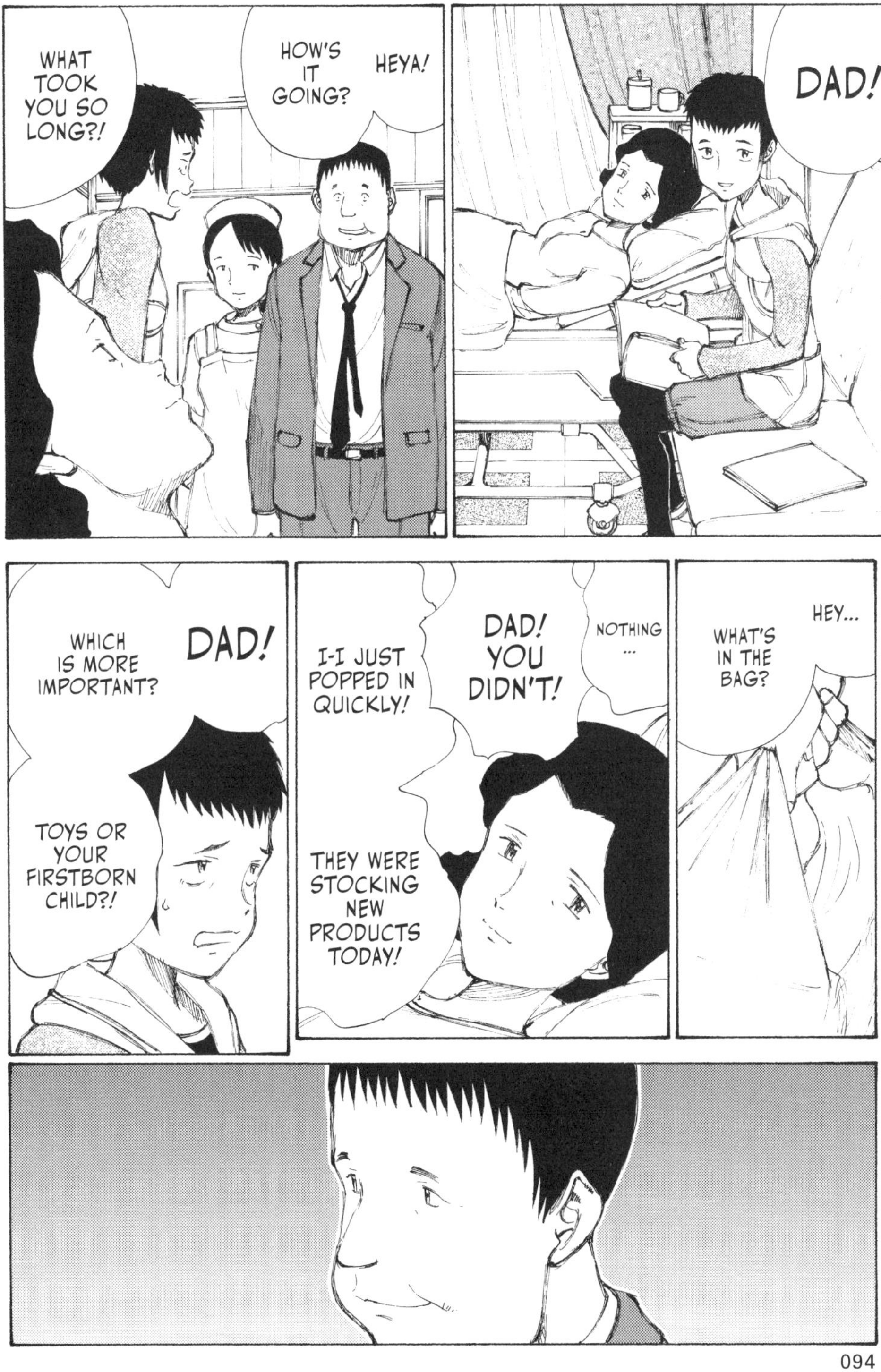
DAD!
HEYA!
HOW'S IT GOING?
WHAT TOOK YOU SO LONG?!
HEY...
WHAT'S IN THE BAG?
NOTHING ...
DAD! YOU DIDN'T!
I-I JUST POPPED IN QUICKLY!
THEY WERE STOCKING NEW PRODUCTS TODAY!
DAD!
WHICH IS MORE IMPORTANT?
TOYS OR YOUR FIRSTBORN CHILD?!

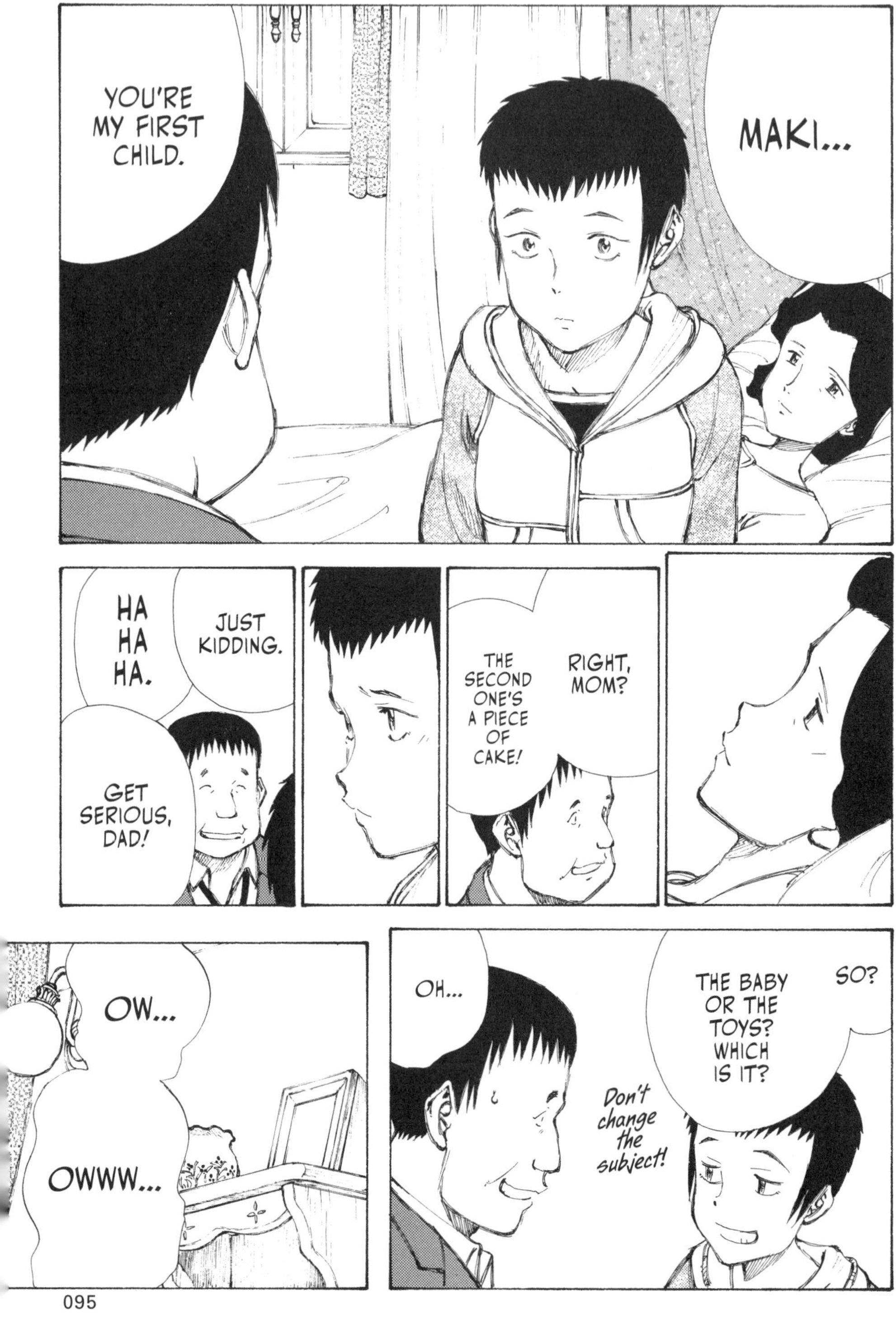
MAKI...
YOU'RE MY FIRST CHILD.
RIGHT, MOM?
THE SECOND ONE'S A PIECE OF CAKE!
JUST KIDDING.
HA HA HA.
GET SERIOUS, DAD!
SO?
THE BABY OR THE TOYS? WHICH IS IT?
Don't change the subject!
OH...
OW...
OWWW...

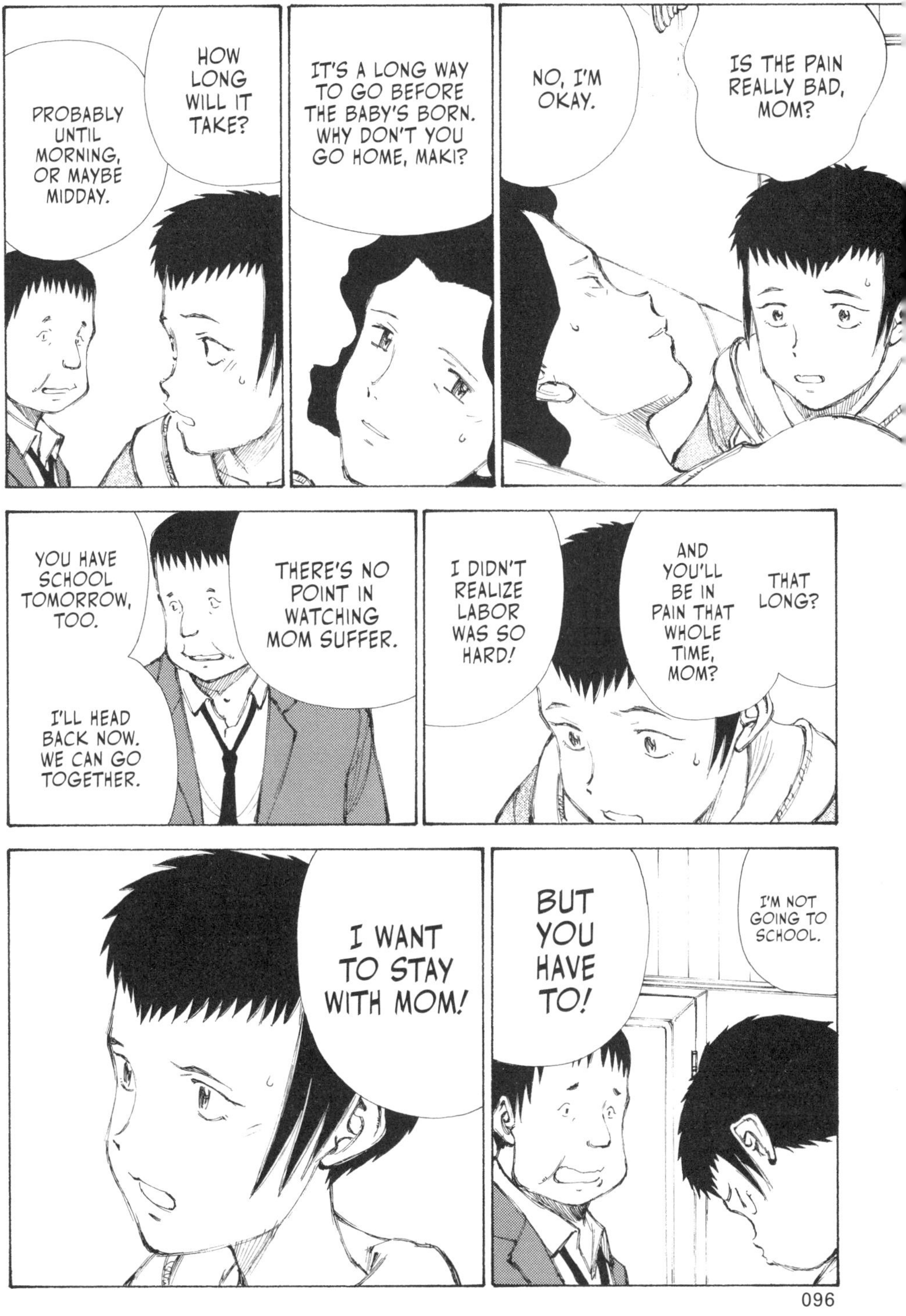
IS THE PAIN REALLY BAD, MOM?
NO, I'M OKAY.
IT'S A LONG WAY TO GO BEFORE THE BABY'S BORN. WHY DON'T YOU GO HOME, MAKI?
HOW LONG WILL IT TAKE?
PROBABLY UNTIL MORNING, OR MAYBE MIDDAY.
THAT LONG?
AND YOU'LL BE IN PAIN THAT WHOLE TIME, MOM?
I DIDN'T REALIZE LABOR WAS SO HARD!
THERE'S NO POINT IN WATCHING MOM SUFFER.
YOU HAVE SCHOOL TOMORROW, TOO.
I'LL HEAD BACK NOW. WE CAN GO TOGETHER.
I'M NOT GOING TO SCHOOL.
BUT YOU HAVE TO!
I WANT TO STAY WITH MOM!

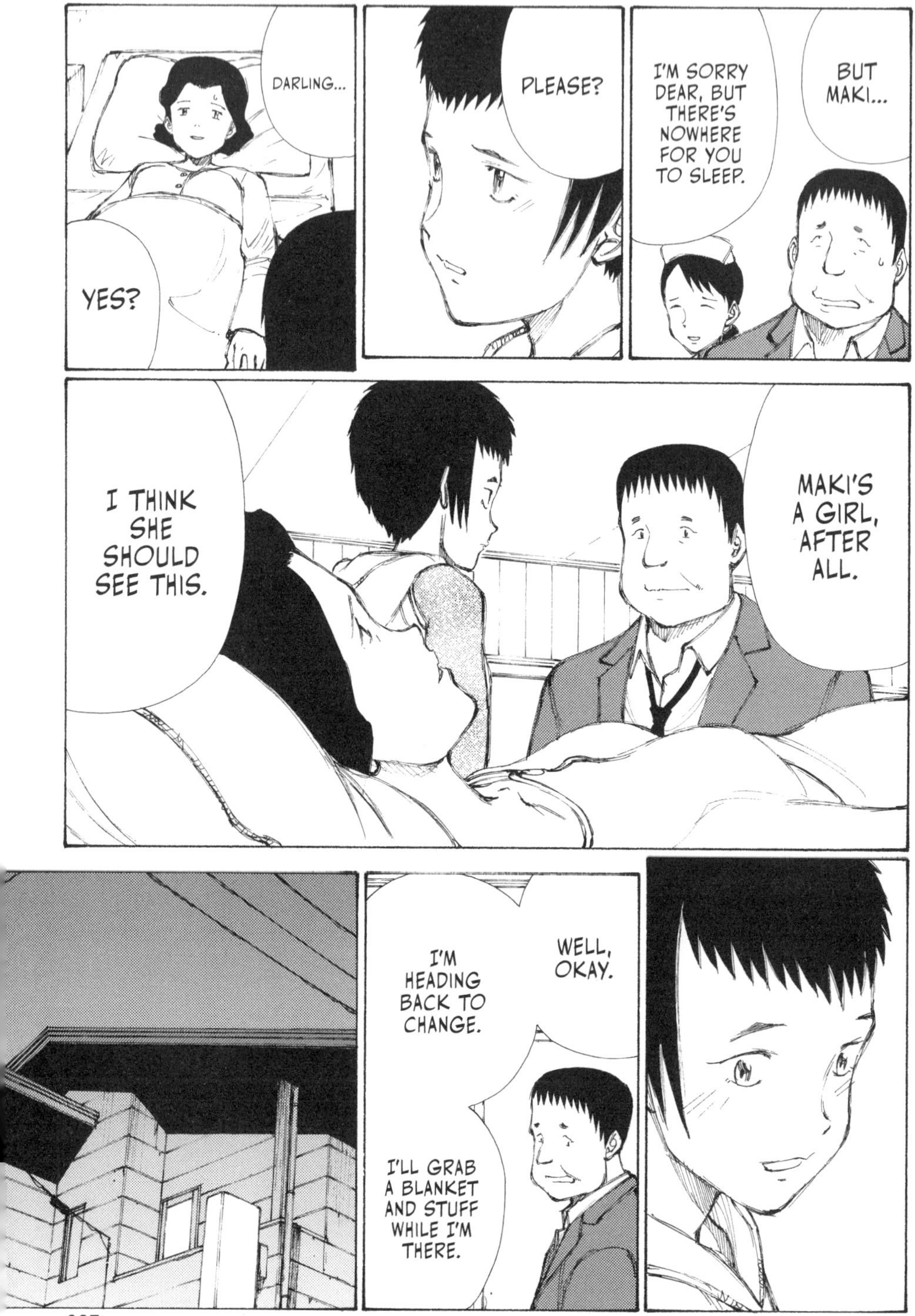
BUT MAKI...
I'M SORRY DEAR, BUT THERE'S NOWHERE FOR YOU TO SLEEP.
PLEASE?
DARLING...
YES?
MAKI'S A GIRL, AFTER ALL.
I THINK SHE SHOULD SEE THIS.
WELL, OKAY.
I'M HEADING BACK TO CHANGE.
I'LL GRAB A BLANKET AND STUFF WHILE I'M THERE.

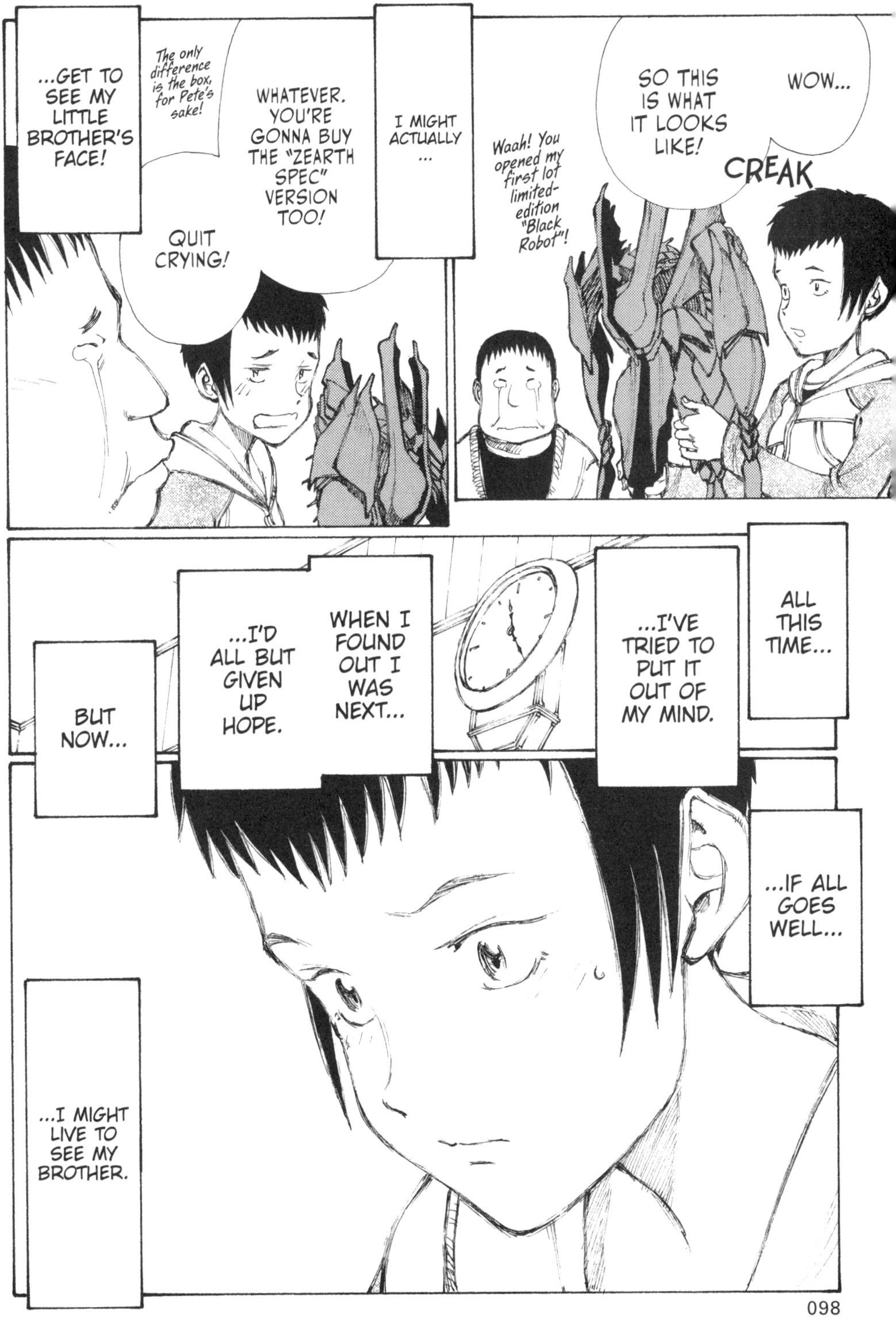
WOW...
SO THIS IS WHAT IT LOOKS LIKE!
CREAK
Waah! You opened my first lot limited-edition "Black Robot"!
I MIGHT ACTUALLY ...
WHATEVER. YOU'RE GONNA BUY THE "ZEARTH SPEC" VERSION TOO!
The only difference is the box, for Pete's sake!
QUIT CRYING!
...GET TO SEE MY LITTLE BROTHER'S FACE!
ALL THIS TIME...
...I'VE TRIED TO PUT IT OUT OF MY MIND.
WHEN I FOUND OUT I WAS NEXT...
...I'D ALL BUT GIVEN UP HOPE.
BUT NOW...
...IF ALL GOES WELL...
...I MIGHT LIVE TO SEE MY BROTHER.

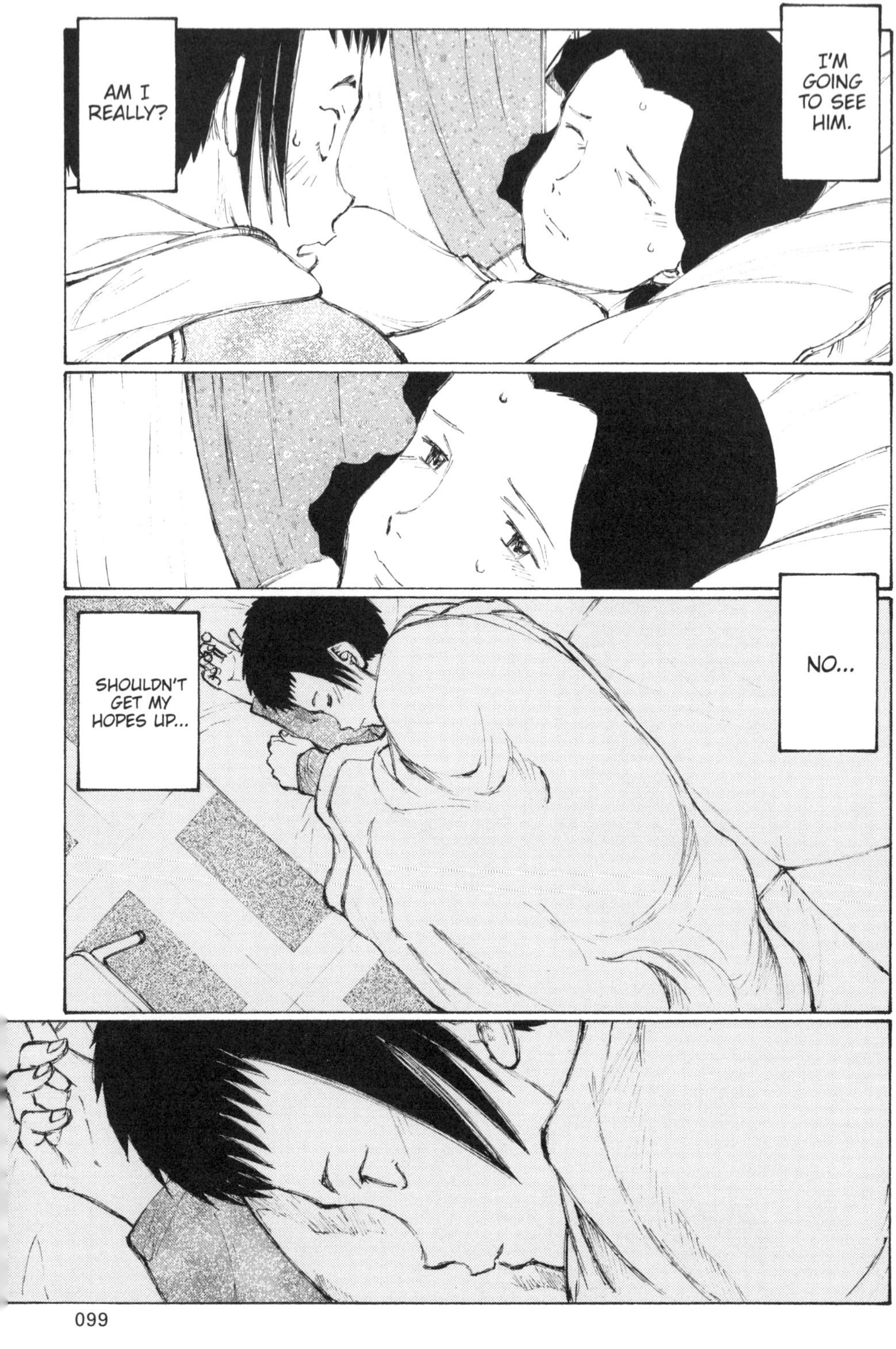
I'M GOING TO SEE HIM.
AM I REALLY?
NO...
SHOULDN'T GET MY HOPES UP...

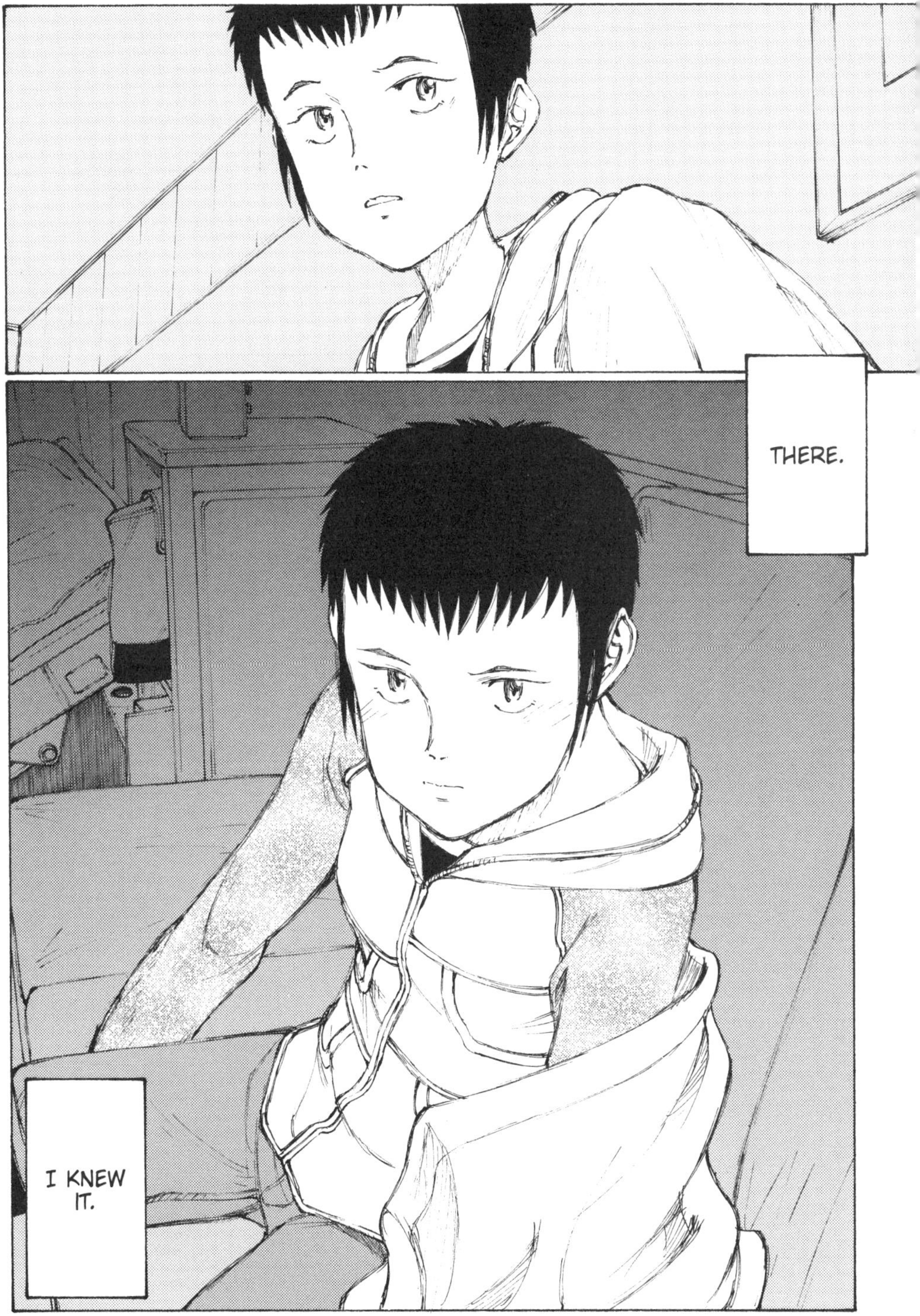
THERE.
I KNEW IT.

CHAPTER 27: MAKI ANO 3

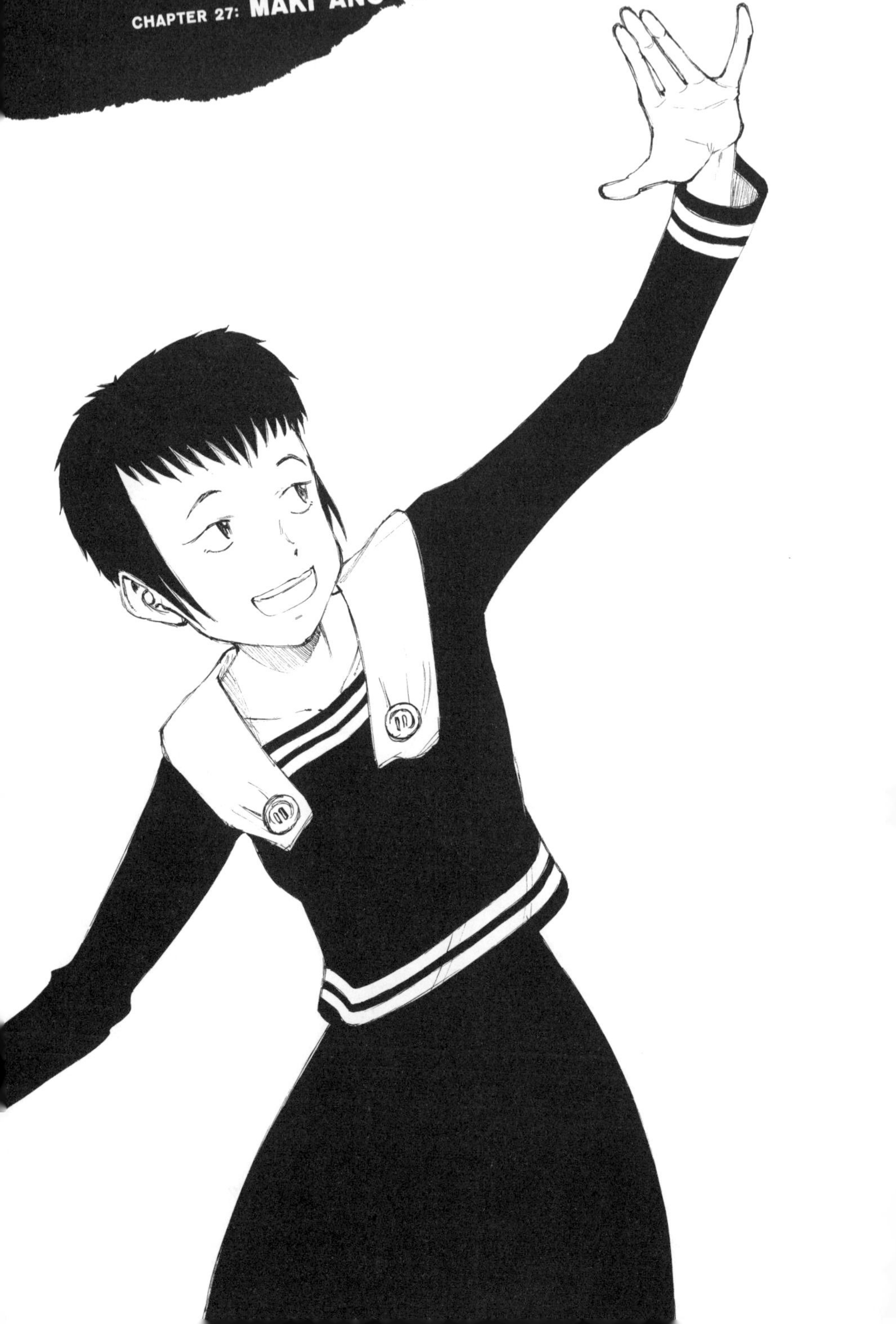

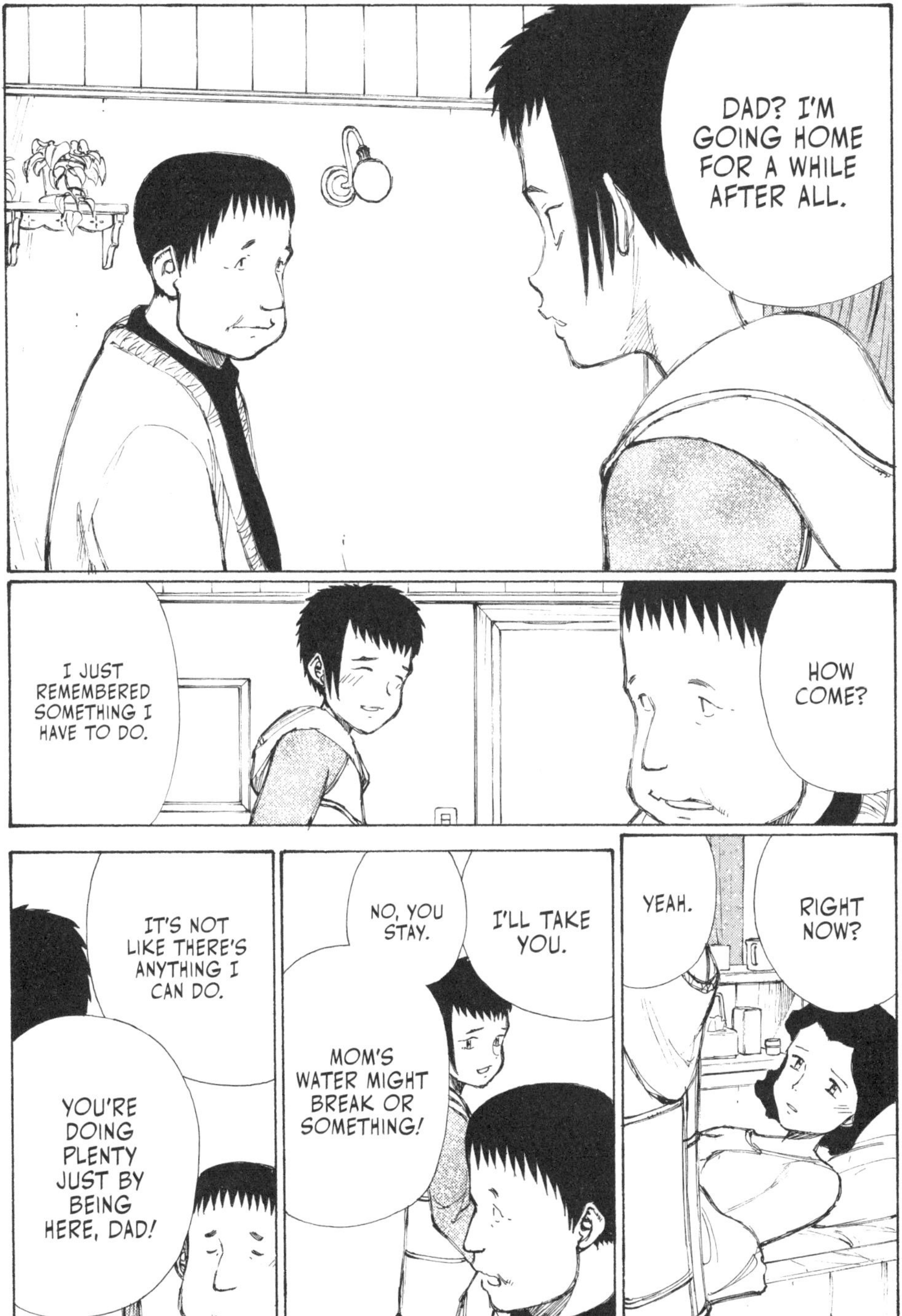
DAD? I'M GOING HOME FOR A WHILE AFTER ALL.
HOW COME?
I JUST REMEMBERED SOMETHING I HAVE TO DO.
RIGHT NOW?
YEAH.
I'LL TAKE YOU.
NO, YOU STAY.
MOM'S WATER MIGHT BREAK OR SOMETHING!
IT'S NOT LIKE THERE'S ANYTHING I CAN DO.
YOU'RE DOING PLENTY JUST BY BEING HERE, DAD!

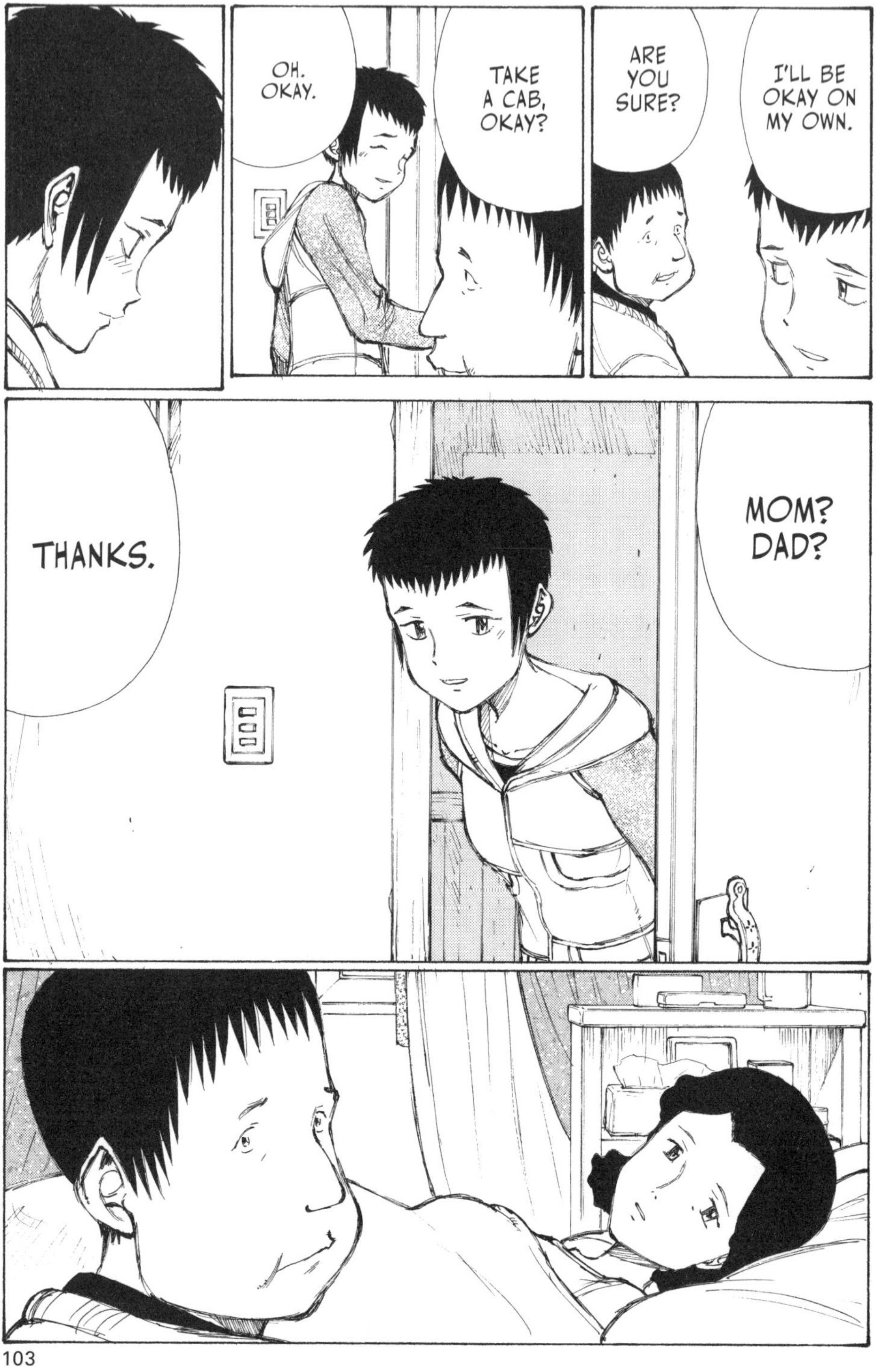
I'LL BE OKAY ON MY OWN.
ARE YOU SURE?
TAKE A CAB, OKAY?
OH. OKAY.
MOM? DAD?
THANKS.

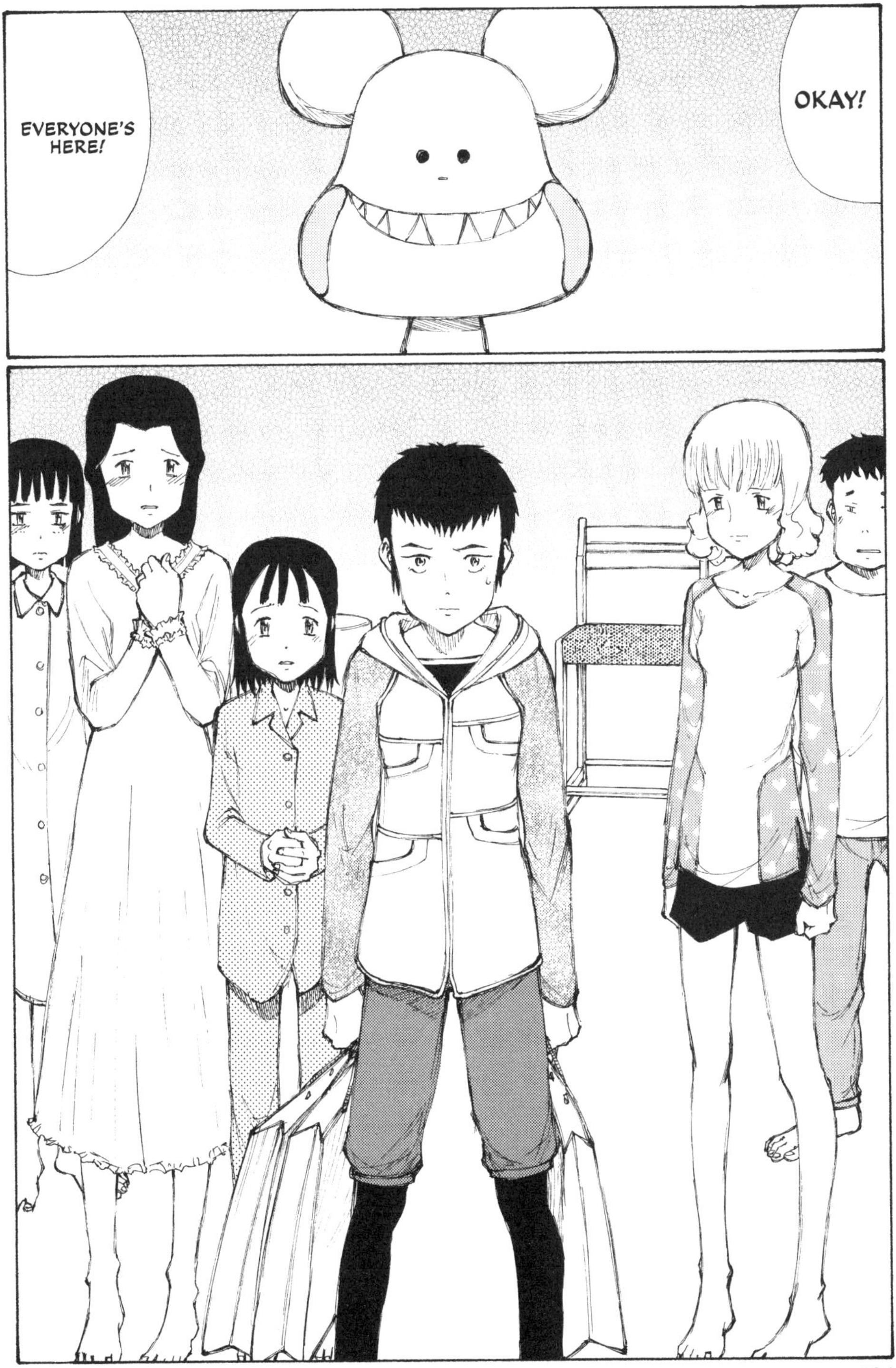
OKAY!
EVERYONE'S HERE!

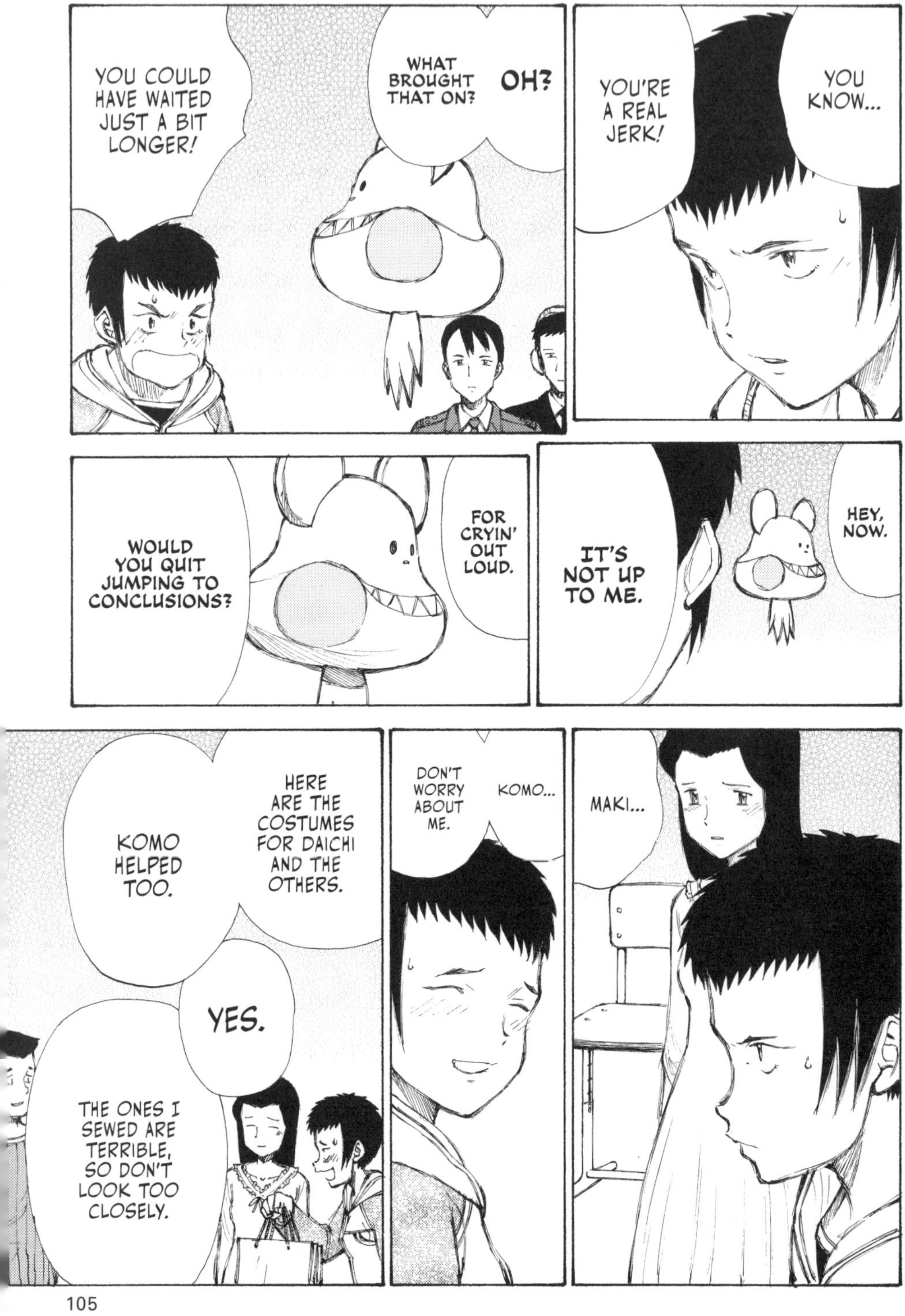
YOU KNOW...
YOU'RE A REAL JERK!
OH?
WHAT BROUGHT THAT ON?
YOU COULD HAVE WAITED JUST A BIT LONGER!
HEY, NOW.
IT'S NOT UP TO ME.
FOR CRYIN' OUT LOUD.
WOULD YOU QUIT JUMPING TO CONCLUSIONS?
MAKI...
KOMO...
DON'T WORRY ABOUT ME.
HERE ARE THE COSTUMES FOR DAICHI AND THE OTHERS.
KOMO HELPED TOO.
YES.
THE ONES I SEWED ARE TERRIBLE, SO DON'T LOOK TOO CLOSELY.

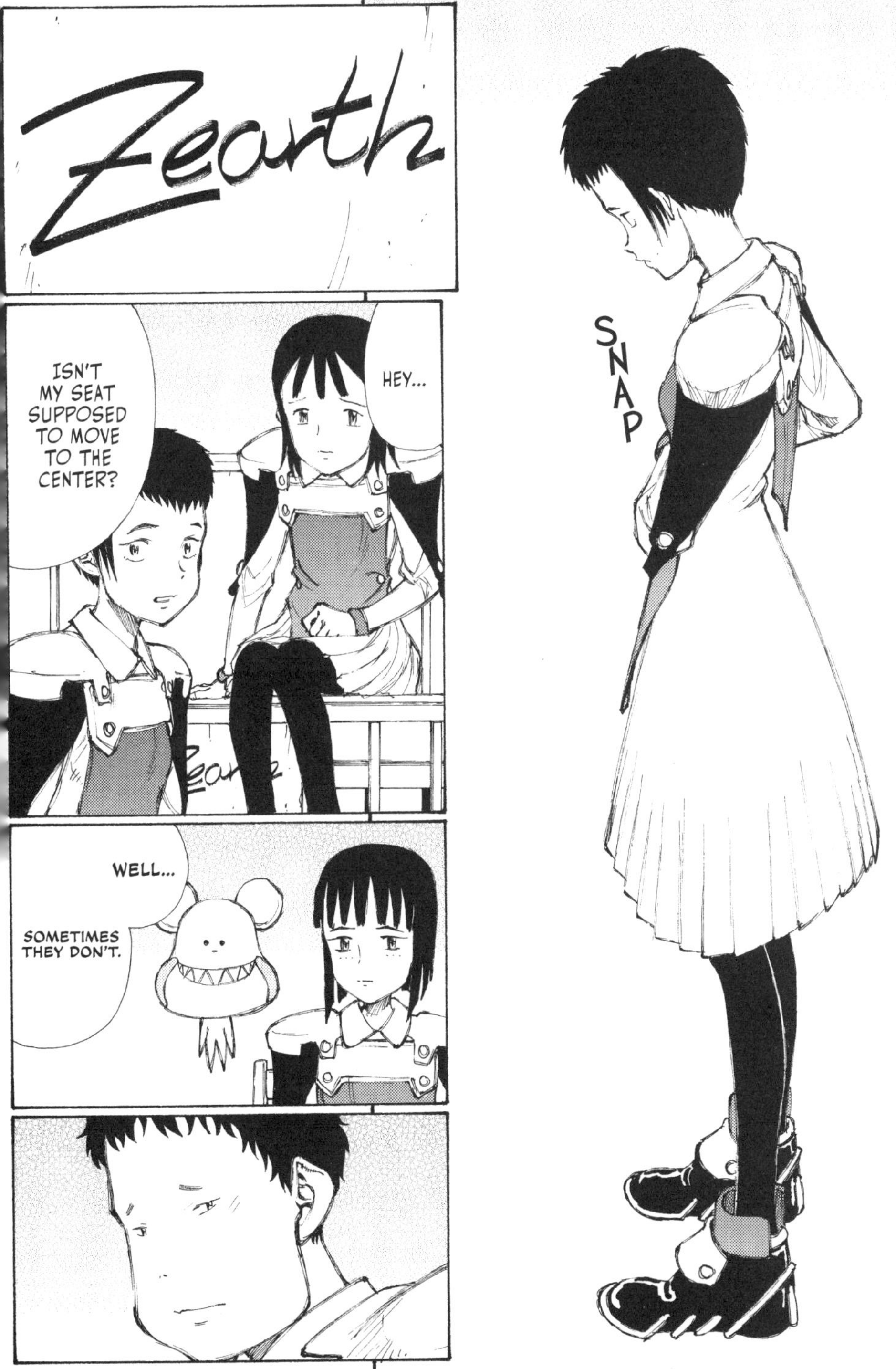
SNAP
Zearth
HEY...
ISN'T MY SEAT SUPPOSED TO MOVE TO THE CENTER?
WELL...
SOMETIMES THEY DON'T.

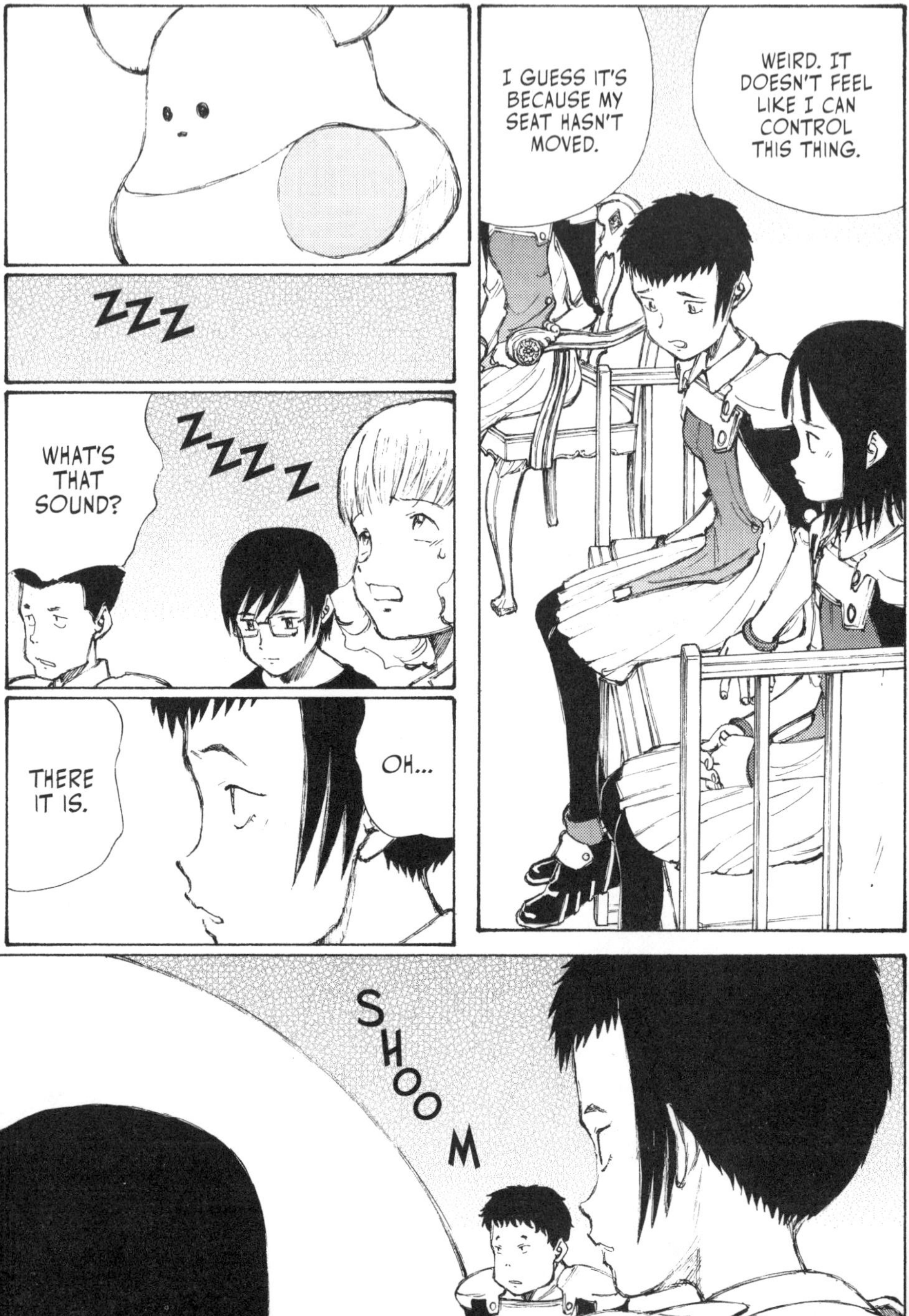
WEIRD. IT DOESN'T FEEL LIKE I CAN CONTROL THIS THING.
I GUESS IT'S BECAUSE MY SEAT HASN'T MOVED.
ZZZ
ZZZZ
WHAT'S THAT SOUND?
OH...
THERE IT IS.
SHOOM

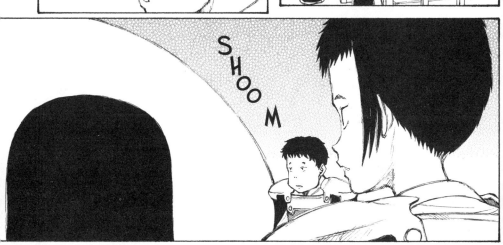

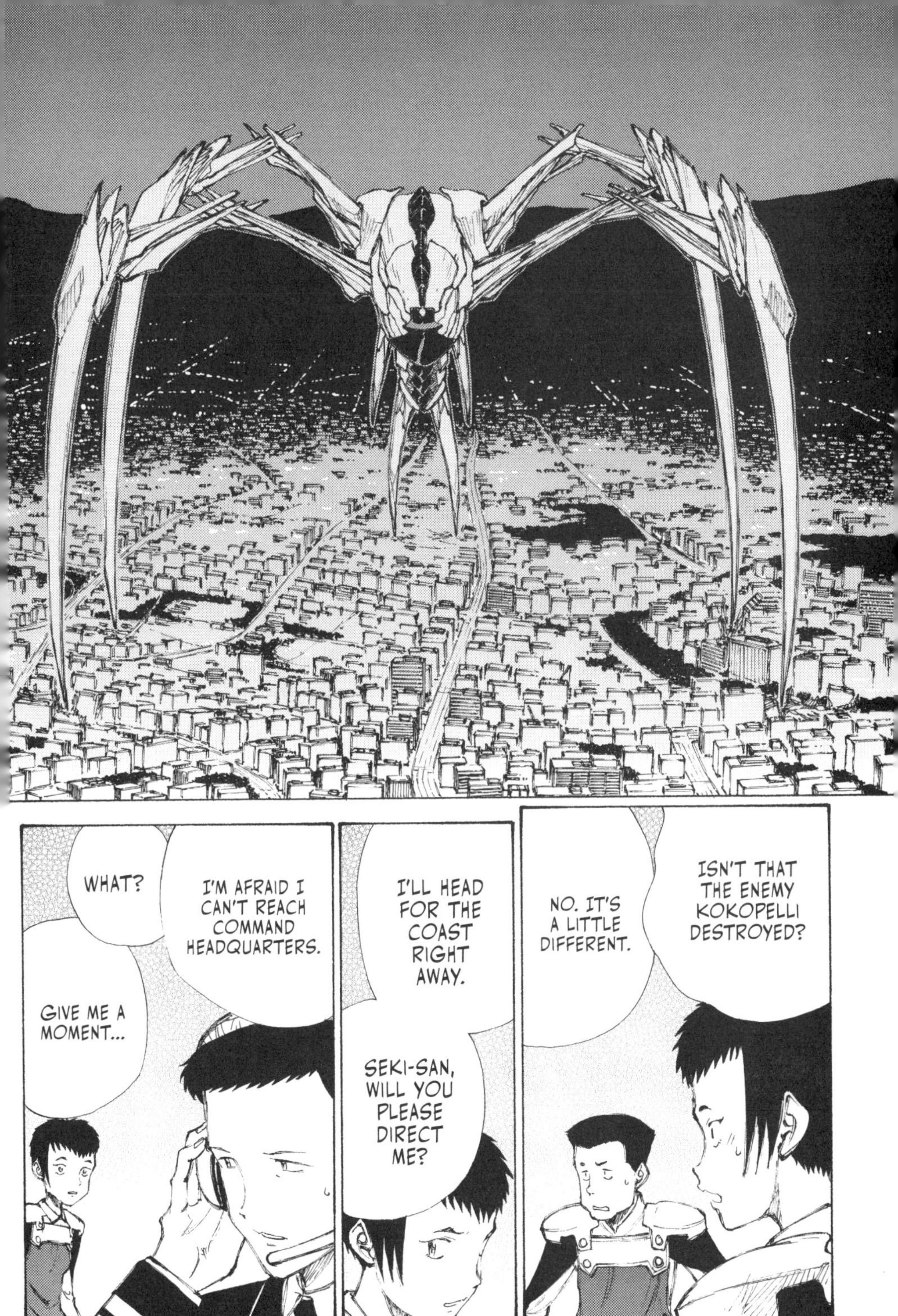
ISN'T THAT THE ENEMY KOKOPELLI DESTROYED?
NO. IT'S A LITTLE DIFFERENT.
I'LL HEAD FOR THE COAST RIGHT AWAY.
SEKI-SAN, WILL YOU PLEASE DIRECT ME?
I'M AFRAID I CAN'T REACH COMMAND HEADQUARTERS.
WHAT?
GIVE ME A MOMENT...

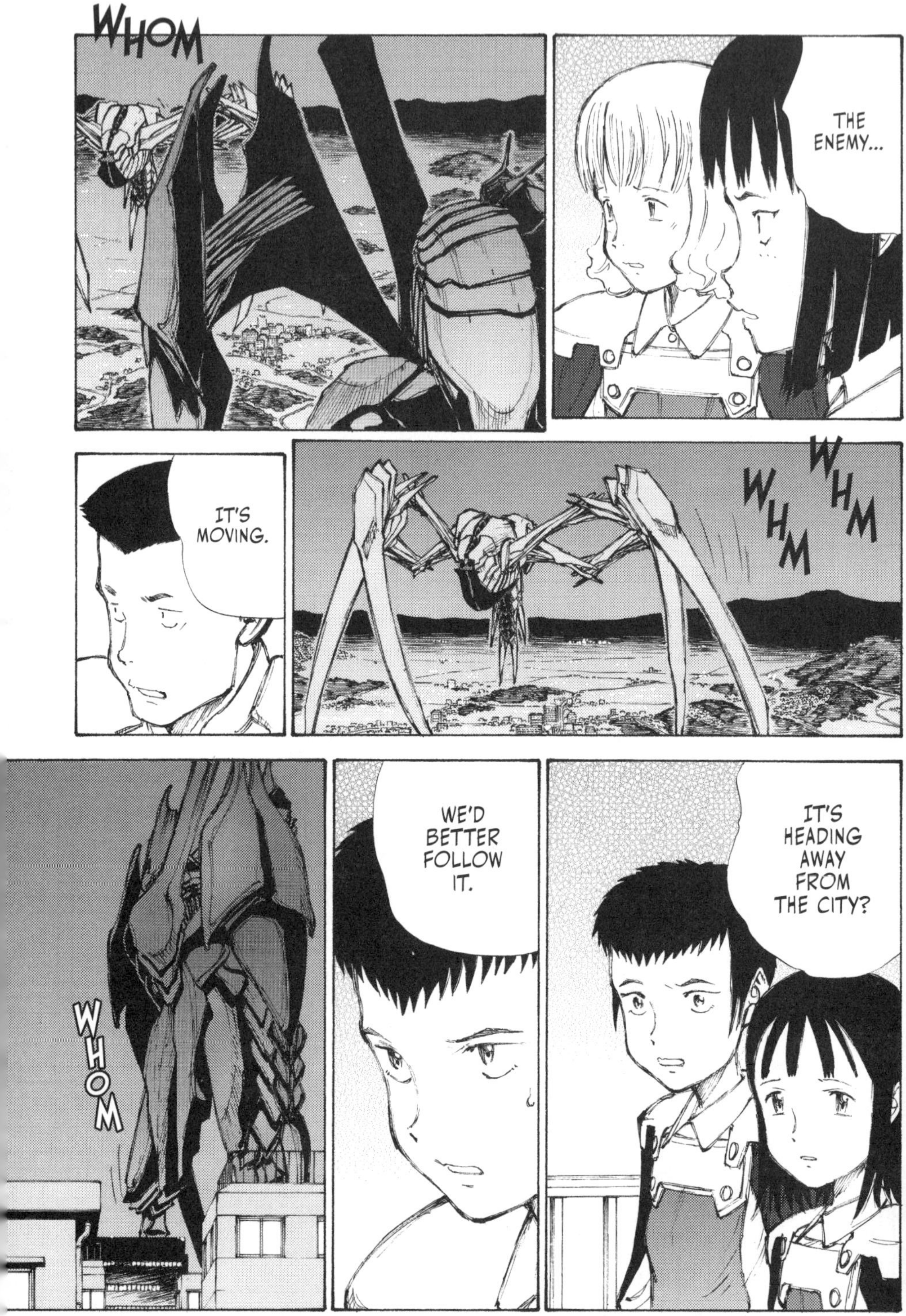
THE ENEMY...
WHOM
WHM WHM WHM
IT'S MOVING.
IT'S HEADING AWAY FROM THE CITY?
WE'D BETTER FOLLOW IT.
WHOM

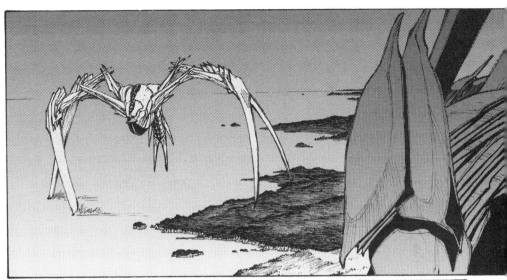

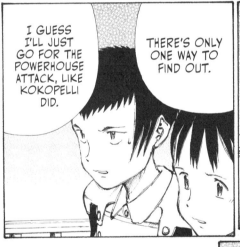

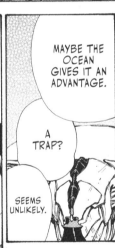

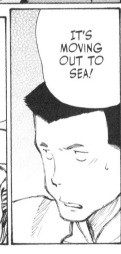

IT'S MOVING OUT TO SEA!
MAYBE THE OCEAN GIVES IT AN ADVANTAGE.
A TRAP?
SEEMS UNLIKELY.
THERE'S ONLY ONE WAY TO FIND OUT.
I GUESS I'LL JUST GO FOR THE POWERHOUSE ATTACK, LIKE KOKOPELLI DID.
THE DEFENSE BUREAU'S FIGHTER PLANES ARE HERE!

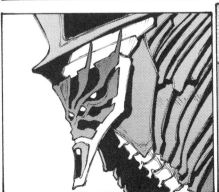

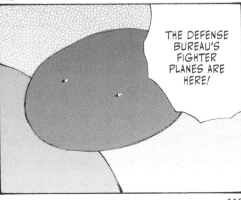

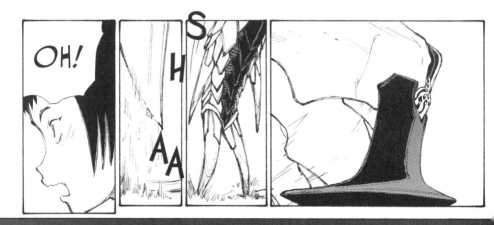

OH!

SHAA

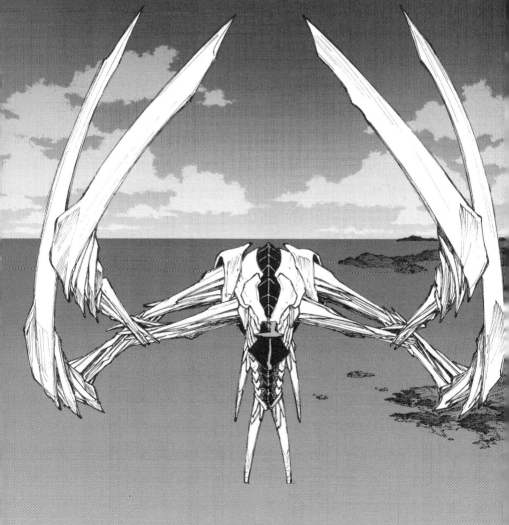

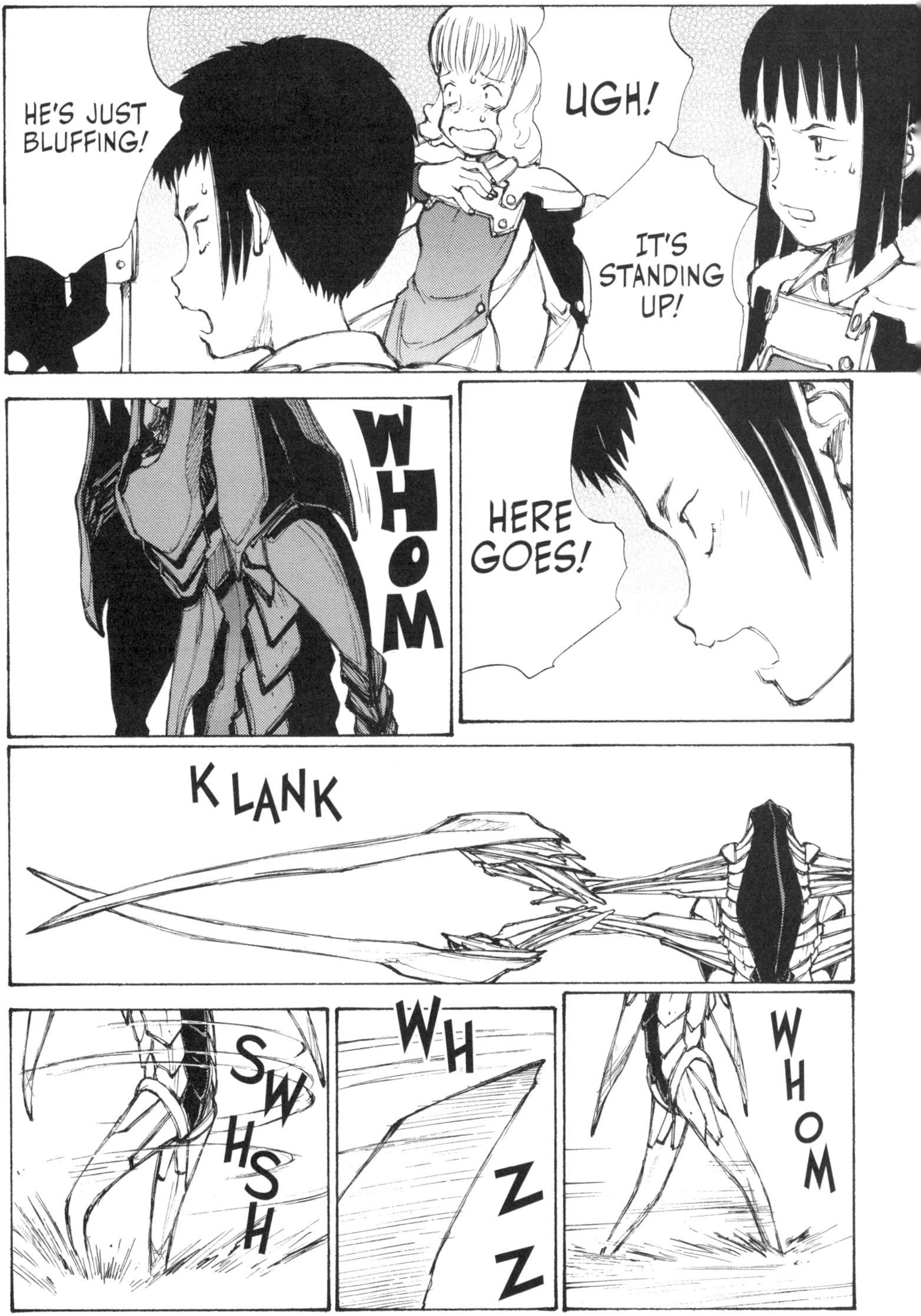
UGH!
IT'S STANDING UP!
HE'S JUST BLUFFING!
HERE GOES!
WHOM
KLANK
WHOM
WHZZ
SWHSH

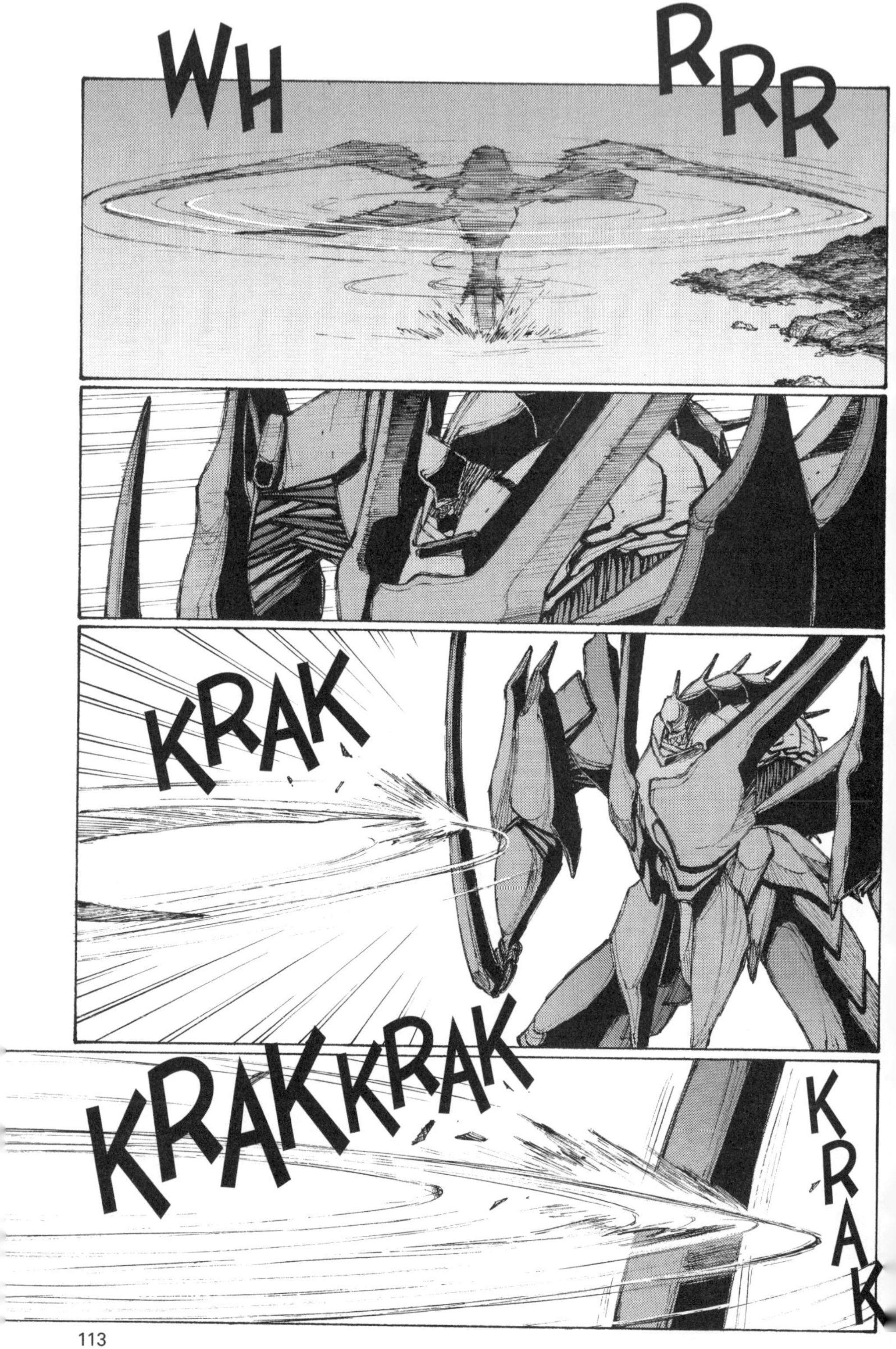
WHRRR
KRAK
KRAK
KRAKKRAK

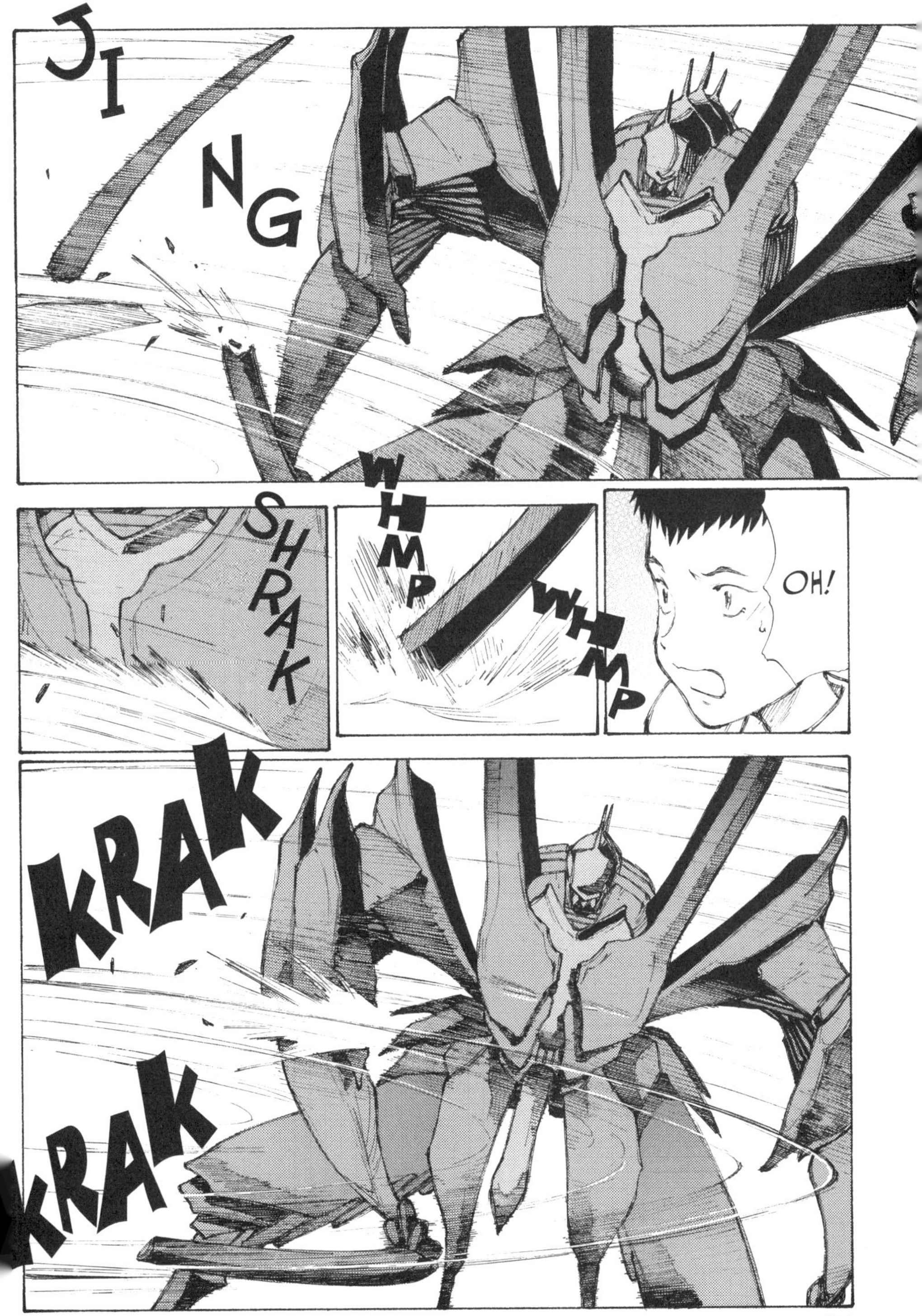
JING
OH!
WHMP
WHMP
SHRAK
KRAK
KRAK

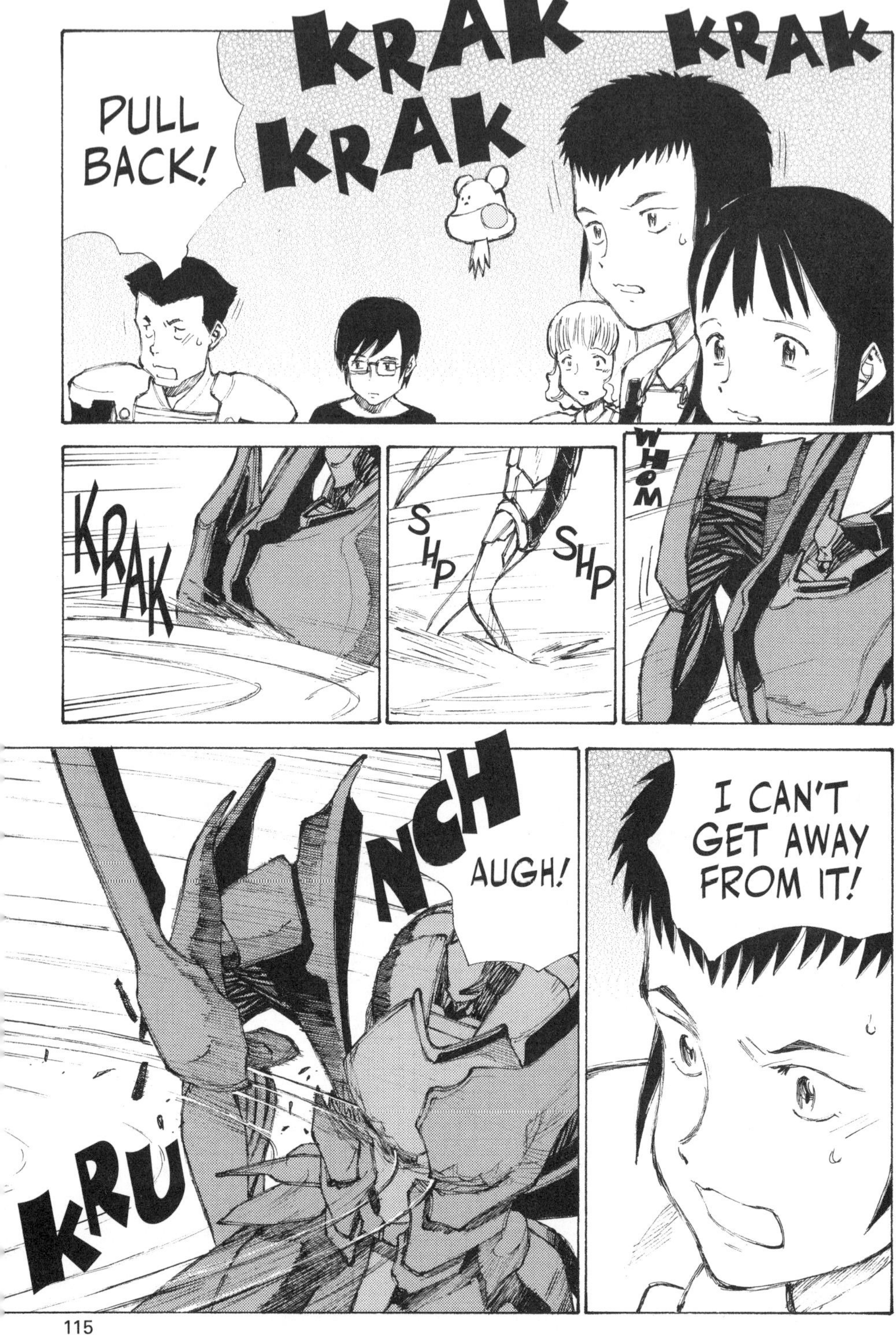
KRAK
KRAK
KRAK
PULL BACK!
WHOM
SHP
SHP
KRAK
I CAN'T GET AWAY FROM IT!
KRUNCH
AUGH!

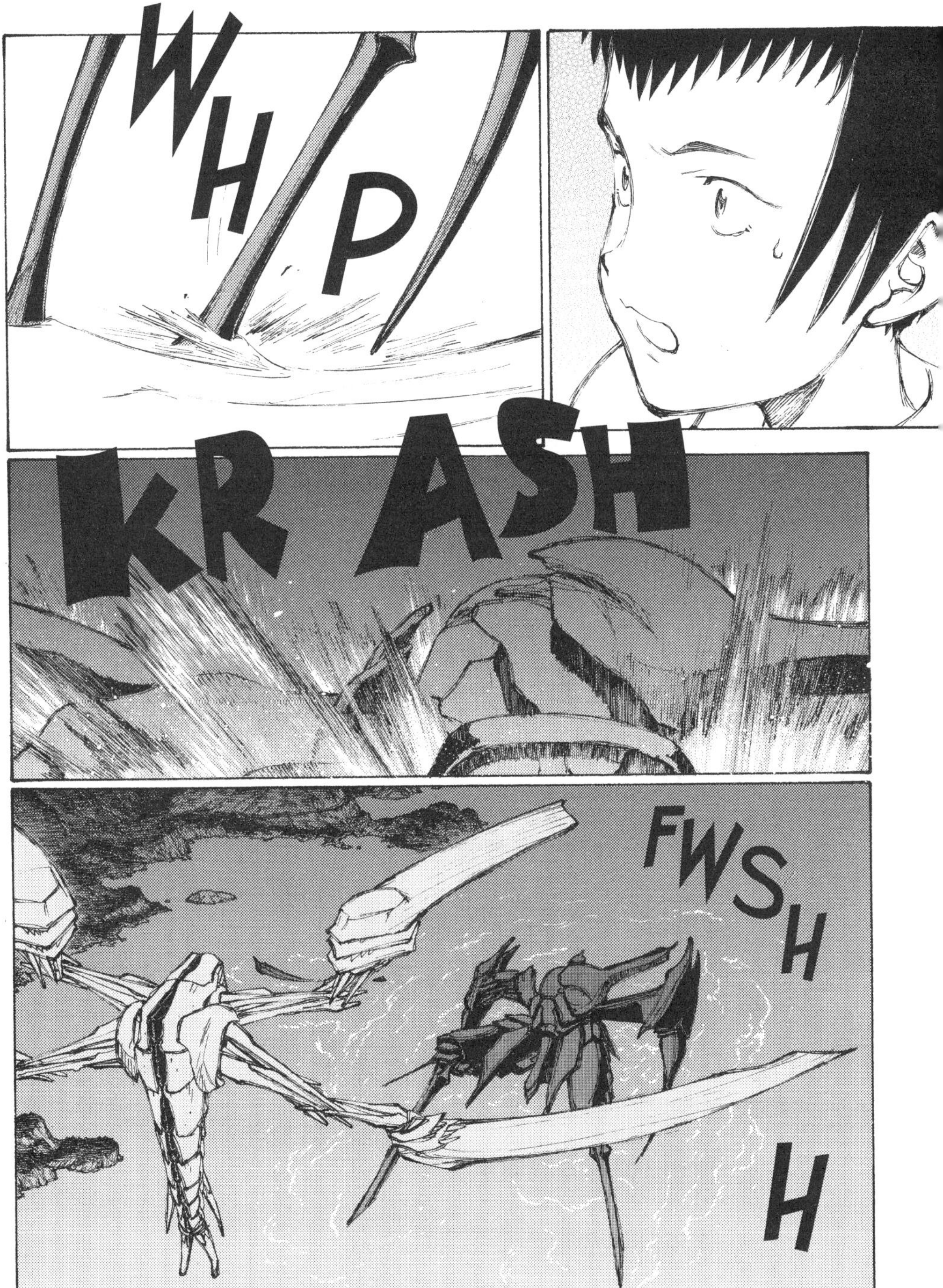
WHP
KRASH
FWSHH

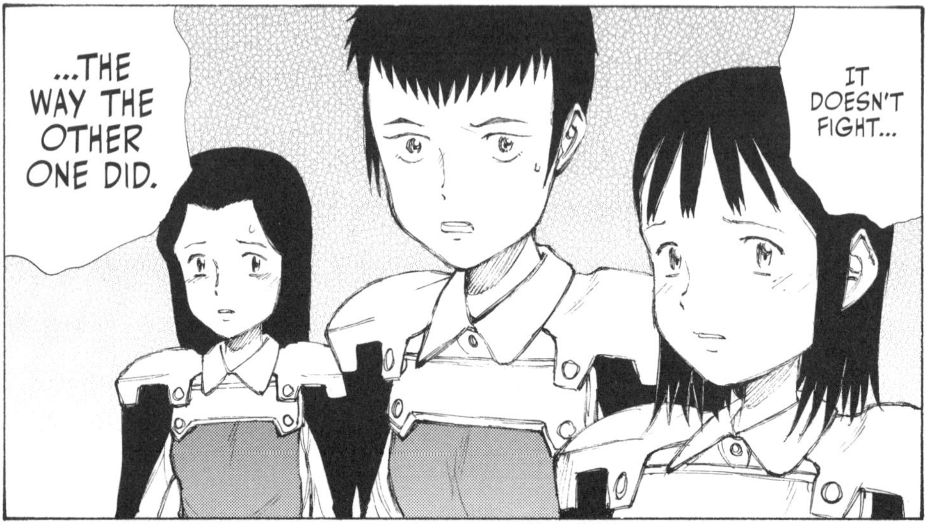
IT DOESN'T FIGHT...
...THE WAY THE OTHER ONE DID.

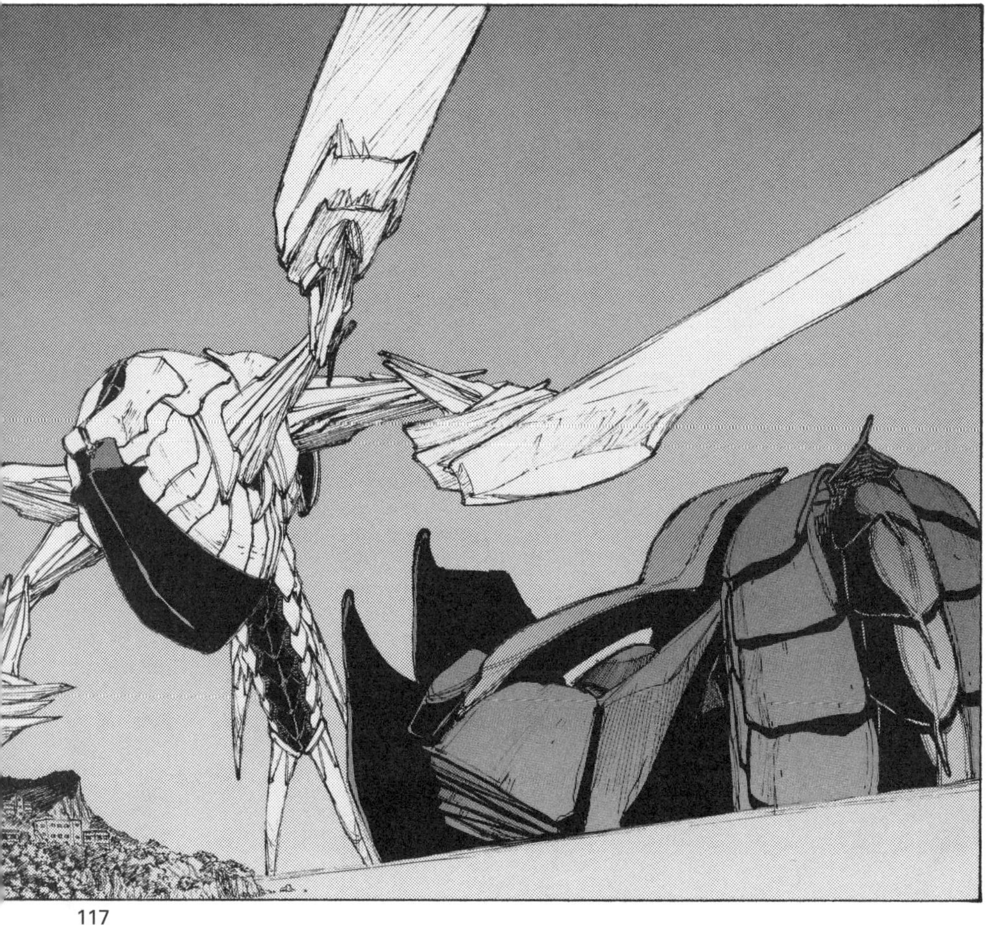

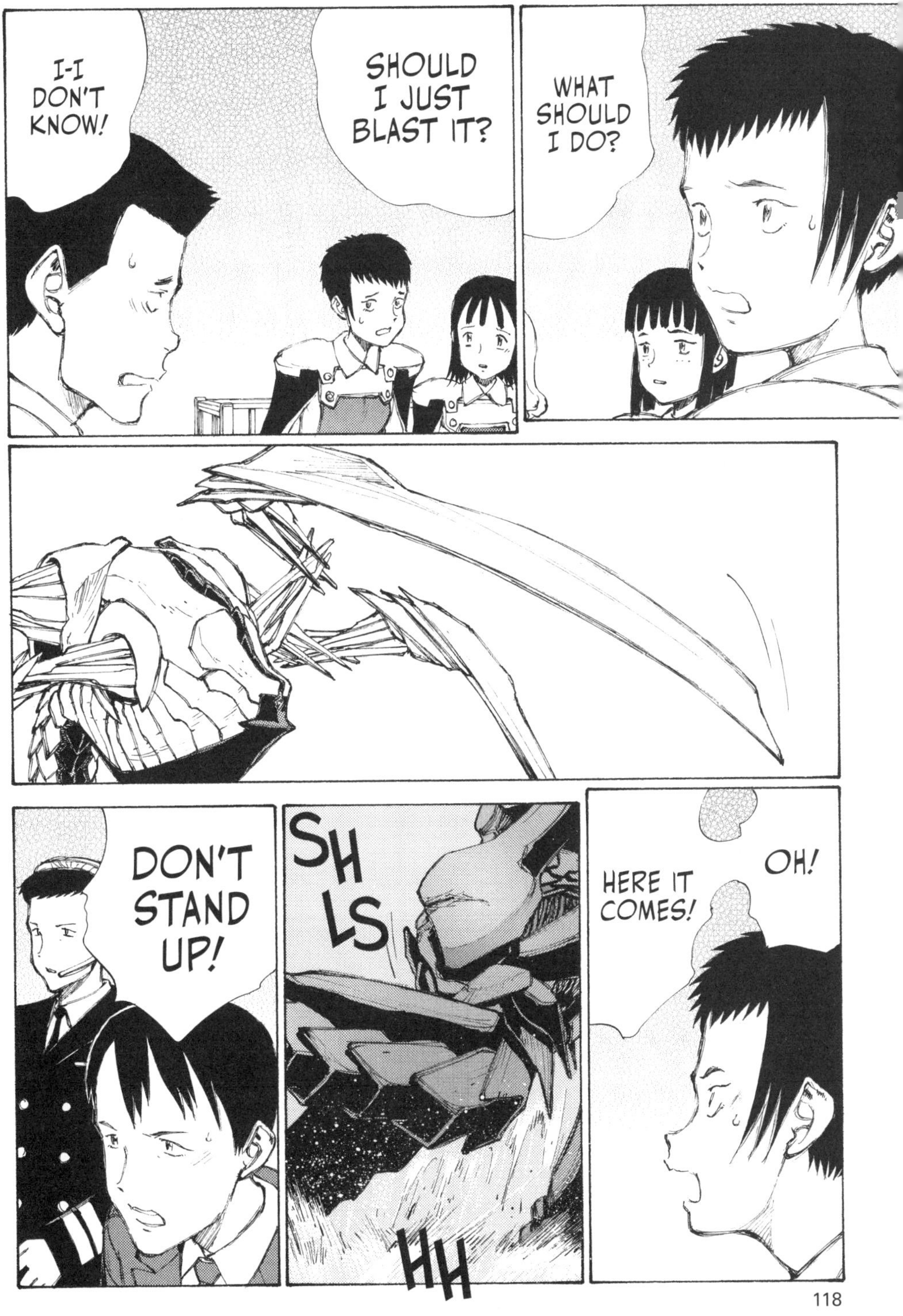
WHAT SHOULD I DO?
SHOULD I JUST BLAST IT?
I-I DON'T KNOW!
OH!
HERE IT COMES!
SH LS
HH
DON'T STAND UP!

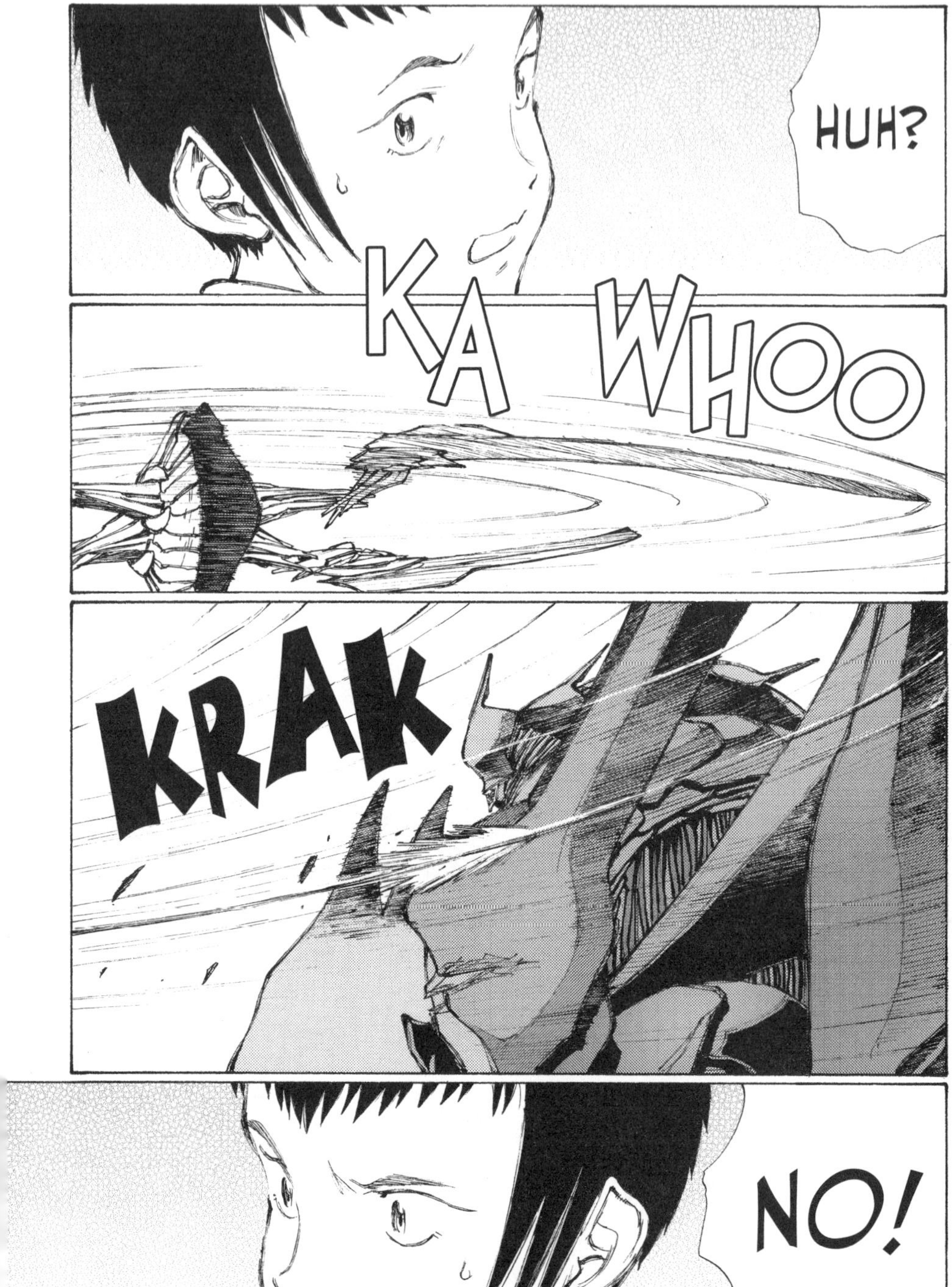
HUH?
KA WHOO
KRAK
NO!

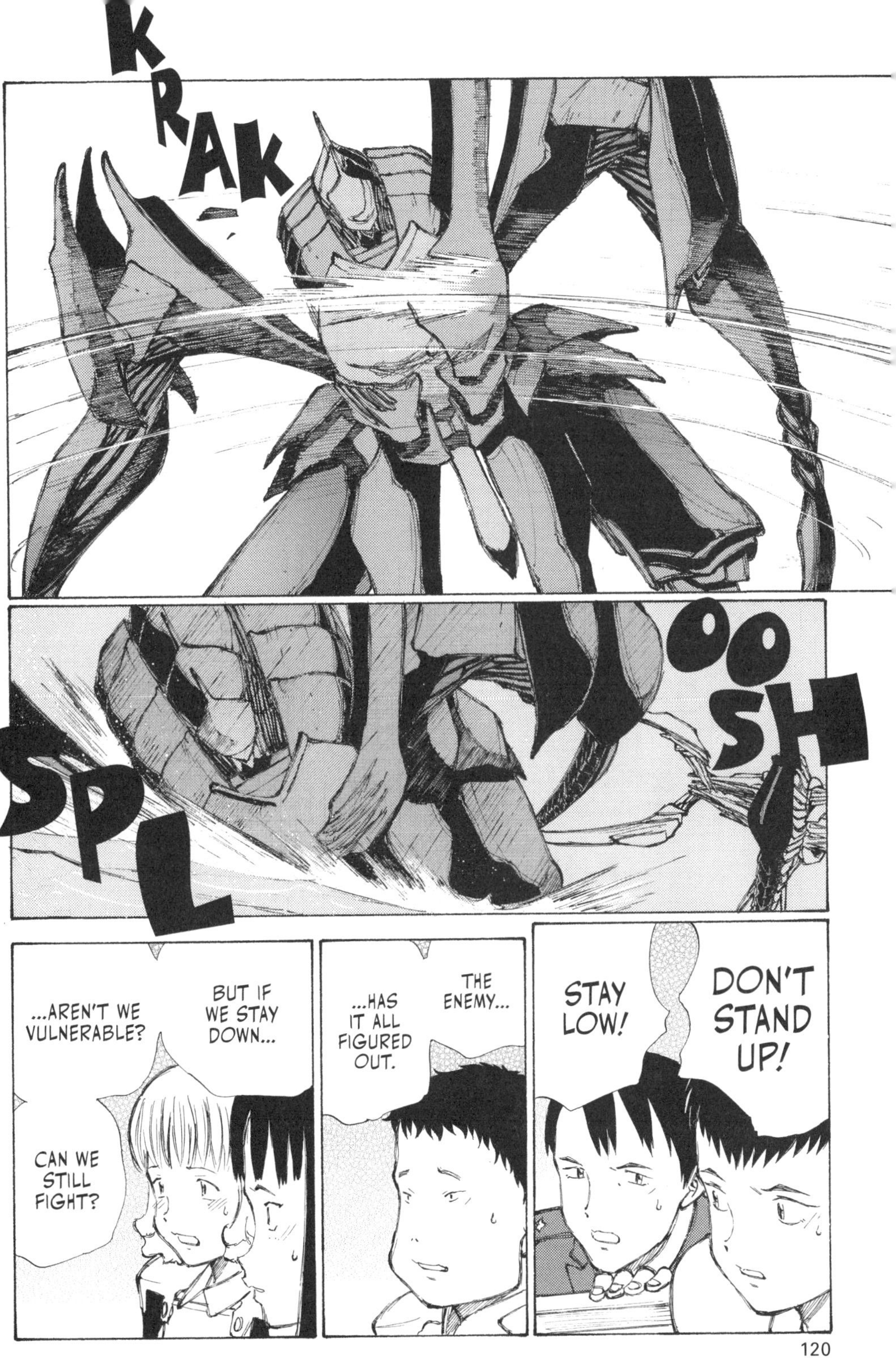
KRAK
SPLOOSH
DON'T STAND UP!
STAY LOW!
THE ENEMY...
...HAS IT ALL FIGURED OUT.
BUT IF WE STAY DOWN...
...AREN'T WE VULNERABLE?
CAN WE STILL FIGHT?

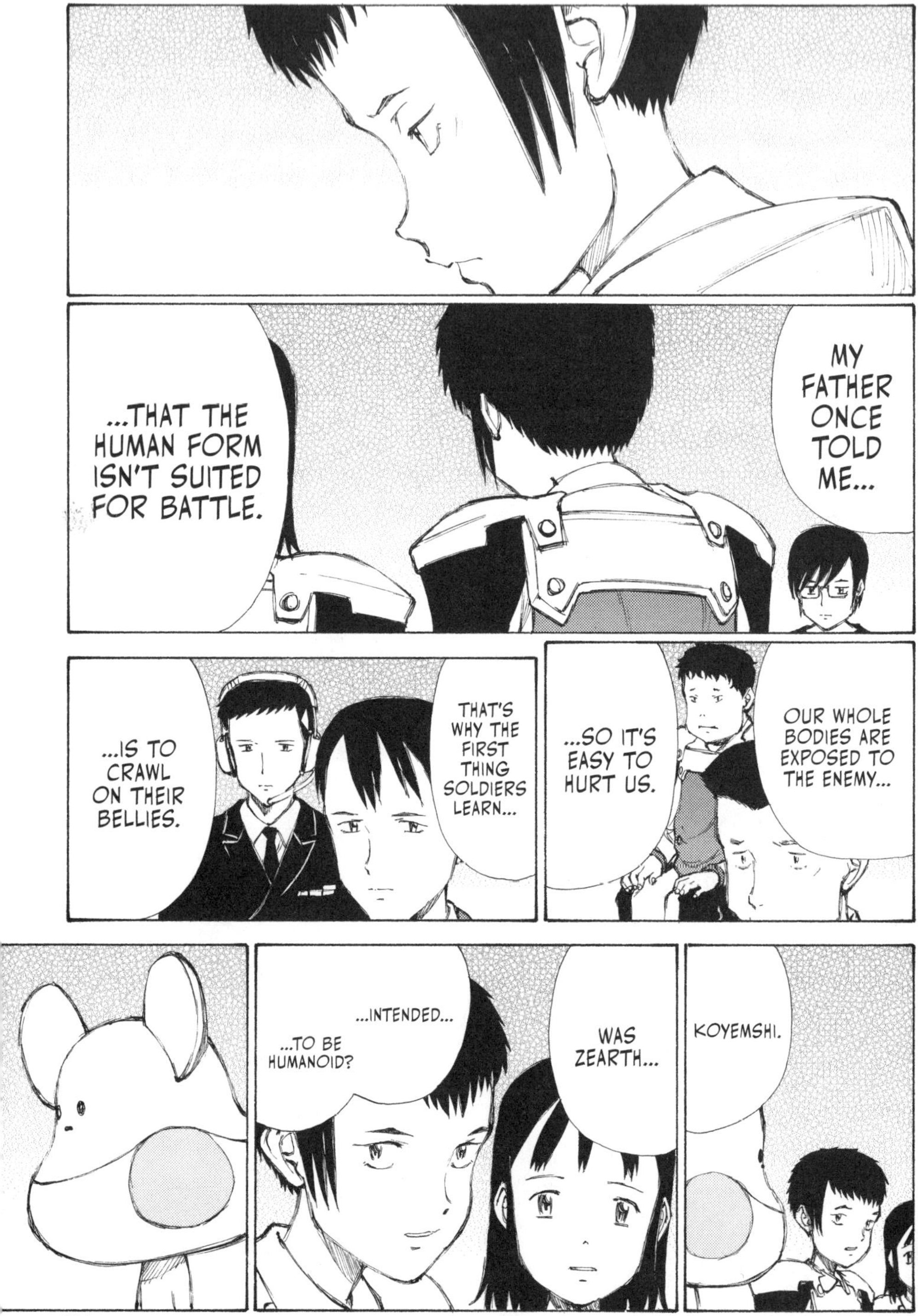
MY FATHER ONCE TOLD ME...
...THAT THE HUMAN FORM ISN'T SUITED FOR BATTLE.
OUR WHOLE BODIES ARE EXPOSED TO THE ENEMY...
...SO IT'S EASY TO HURT US.
THAT'S WHY THE FIRST THING SOLDIERS LEARN...
...IS TO CRAWL ON THEIR BELLIES.
KOYEMSHI.
WAS ZEARTH...
...INTENDED...
...TO BE HUMANOID?

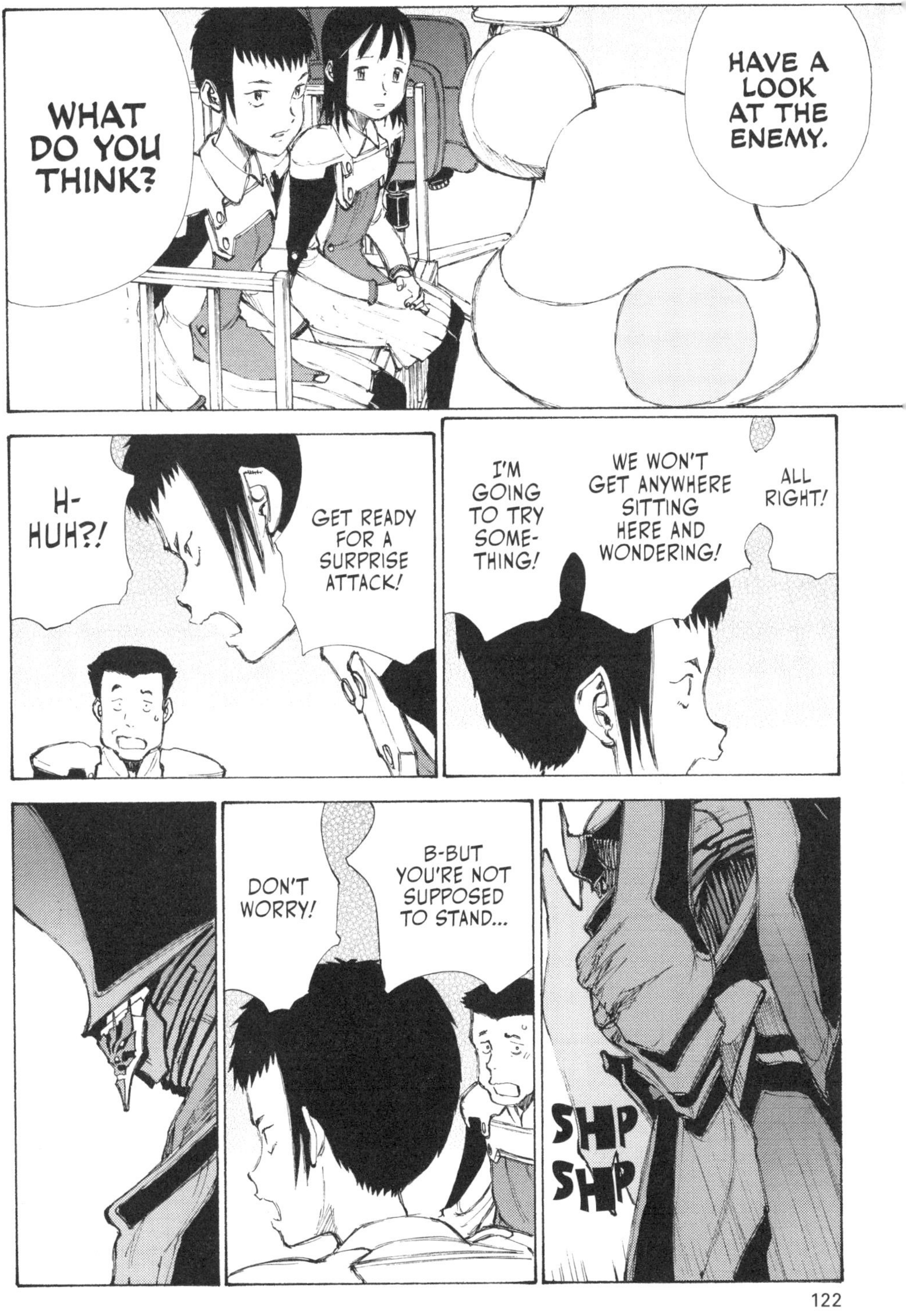
HAVE A LOOK AT THE ENEMY.
WHAT DO YOU THINK?
ALL RIGHT!
WE WON'T GET ANYWHERE SITTING HERE AND WONDERING!
I'M GOING TO TRY SOME-THING!
GET READY FOR A SURPRISE ATTACK!
H-HUH?!
SHP SHP
B-BUT YOU'RE NOT SUPPOSED TO STAND...
DON'T WORRY!

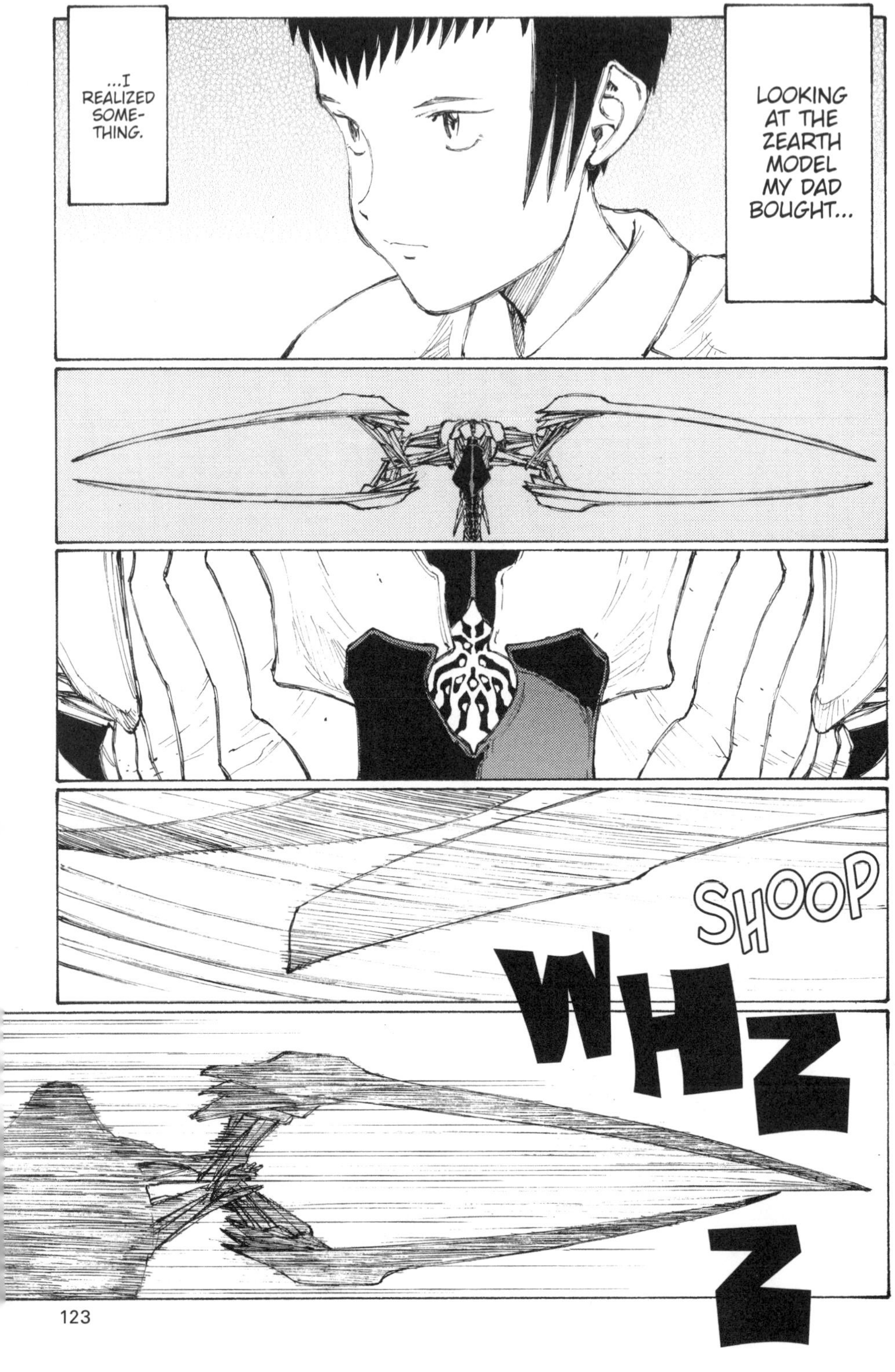
LOOKING AT THE ZEARTH MODEL MY DAD BOUGHT...
...I REALIZED SOME-THING.
SHOOP
WHZZ

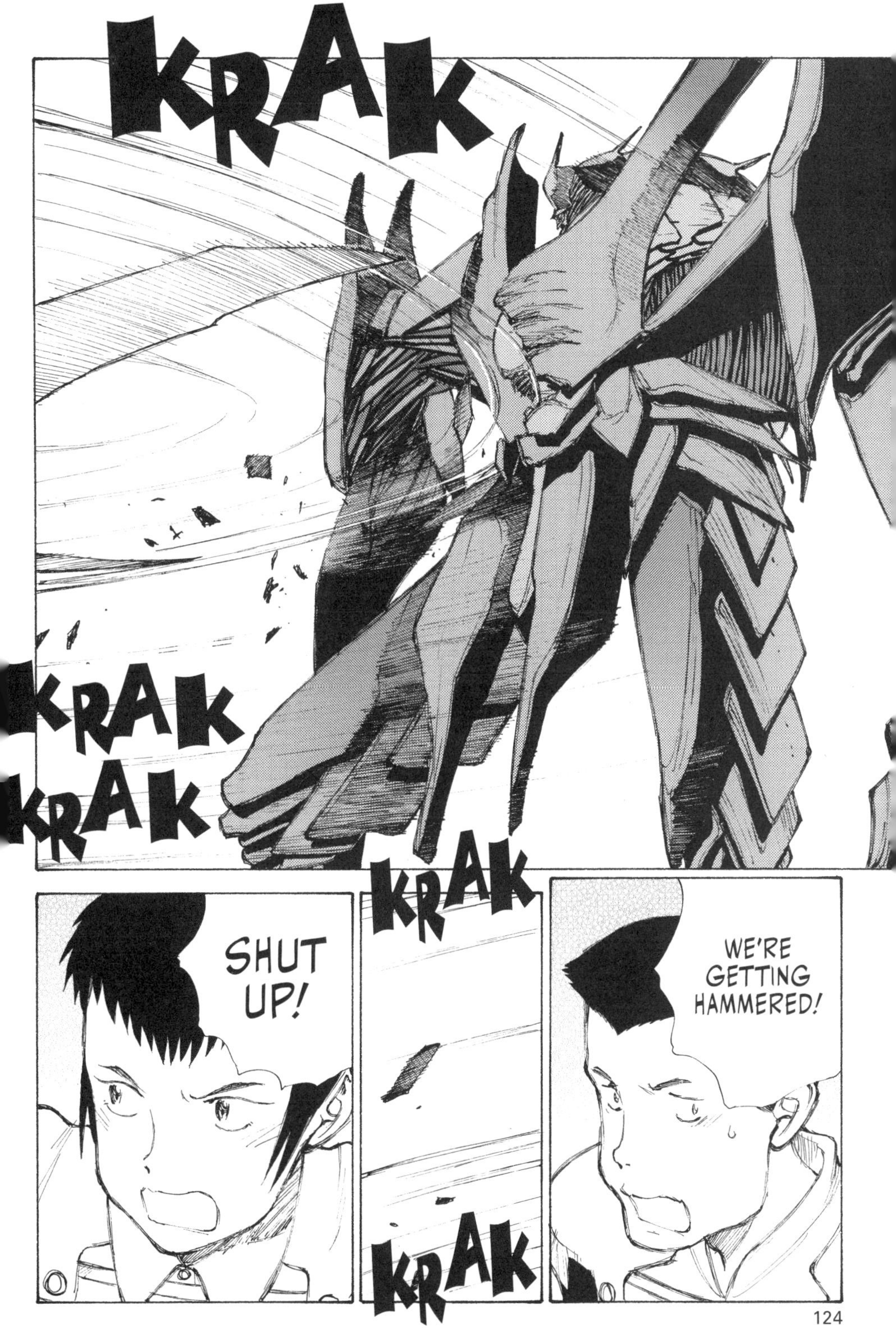
KRAK
KRAK
KRAK
KRAK
WE'RE GETTING HAMMERED!
KRAK
SHUT UP!

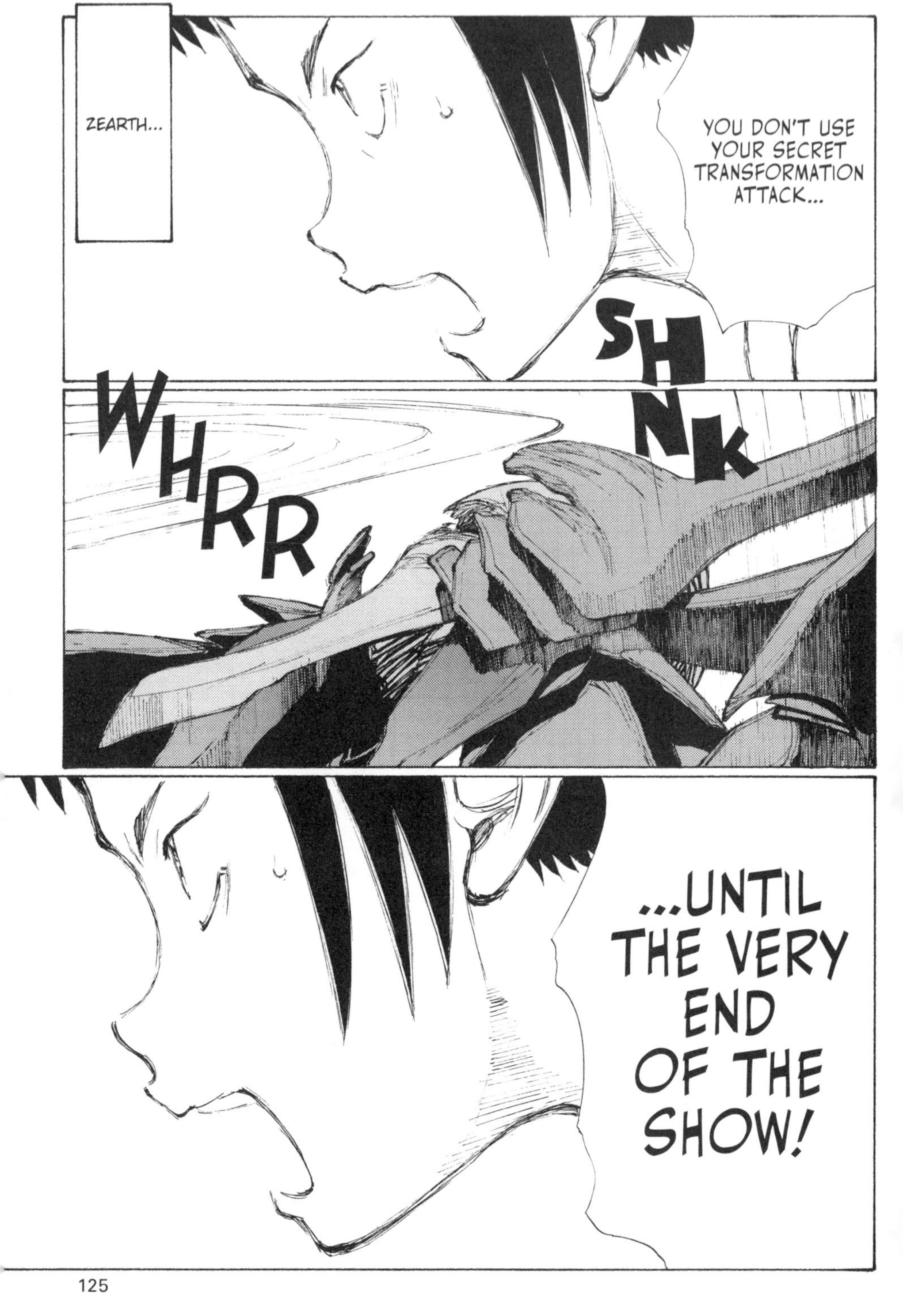
YOU DON'T USE YOUR SECRET TRANSFORMATION ATTACK...
ZEARTH...
SHNK
WHRRR
...UNTIL THE VERY END OF THE SHOW!

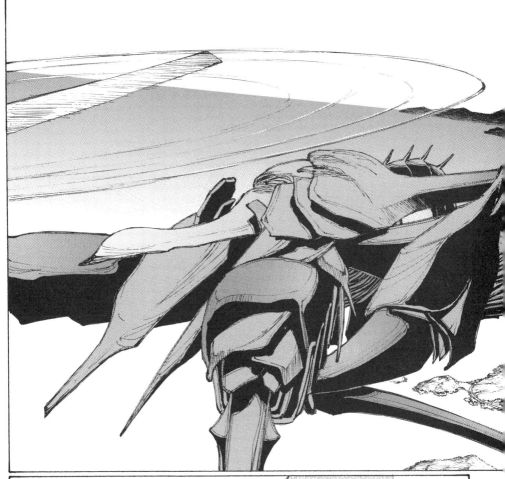

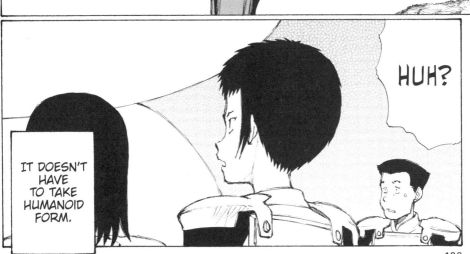

HUH?

IT DOESN'T
HAVE
TO TAKE
HUMANOID
FORM.

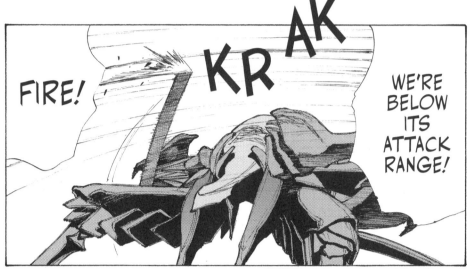

FIRE!

WE'RE BELOW ITS ATTACK RANGE!

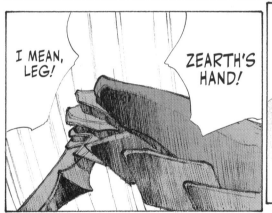

I MEAN, LEG!

ZEARTH'S HAND!

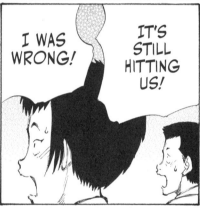

I WAS WRONG!

IT'S STILL HITTING US!

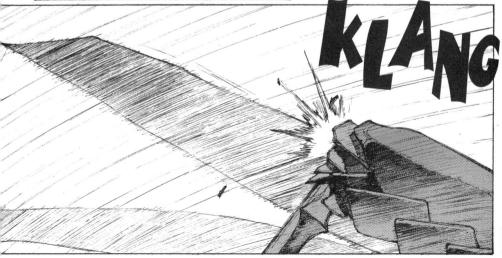

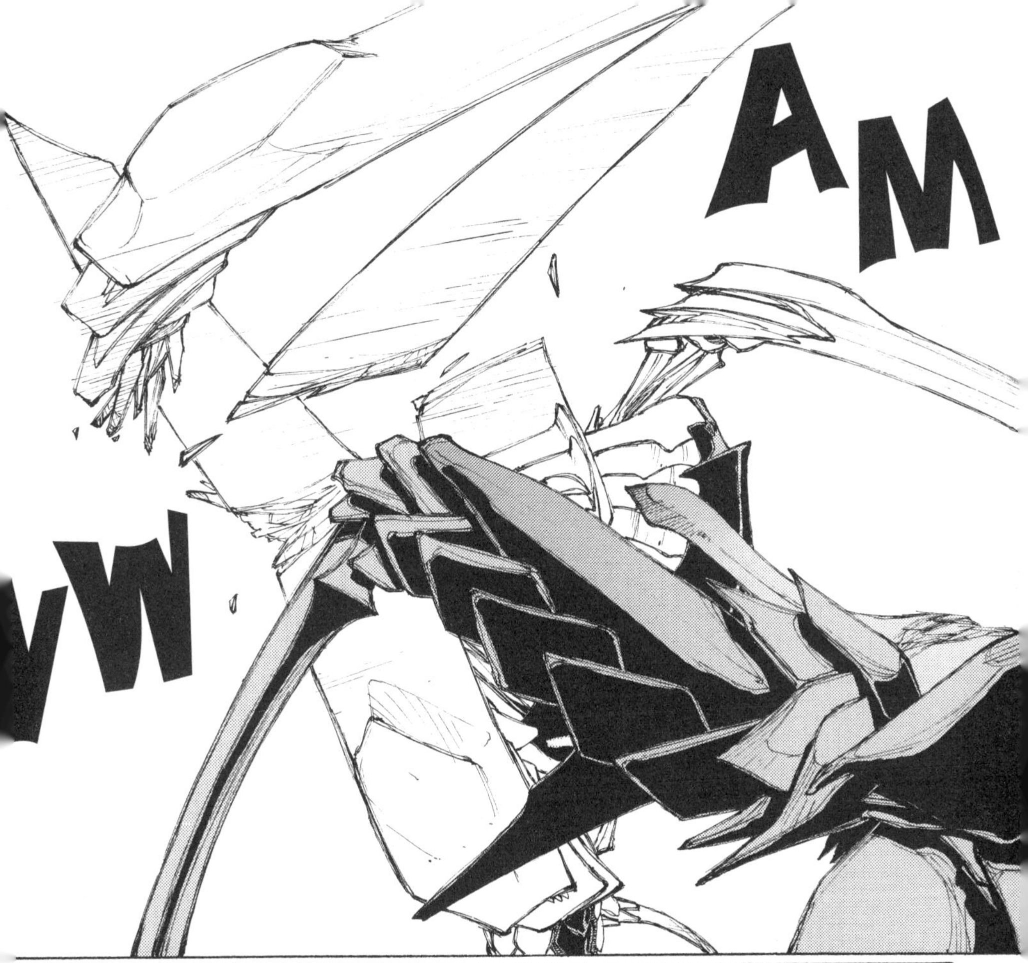
VW
AM
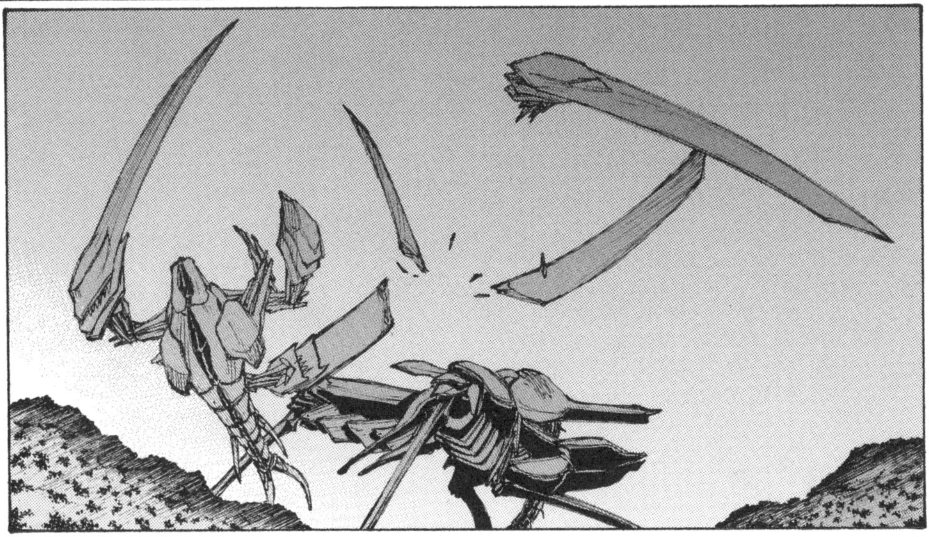

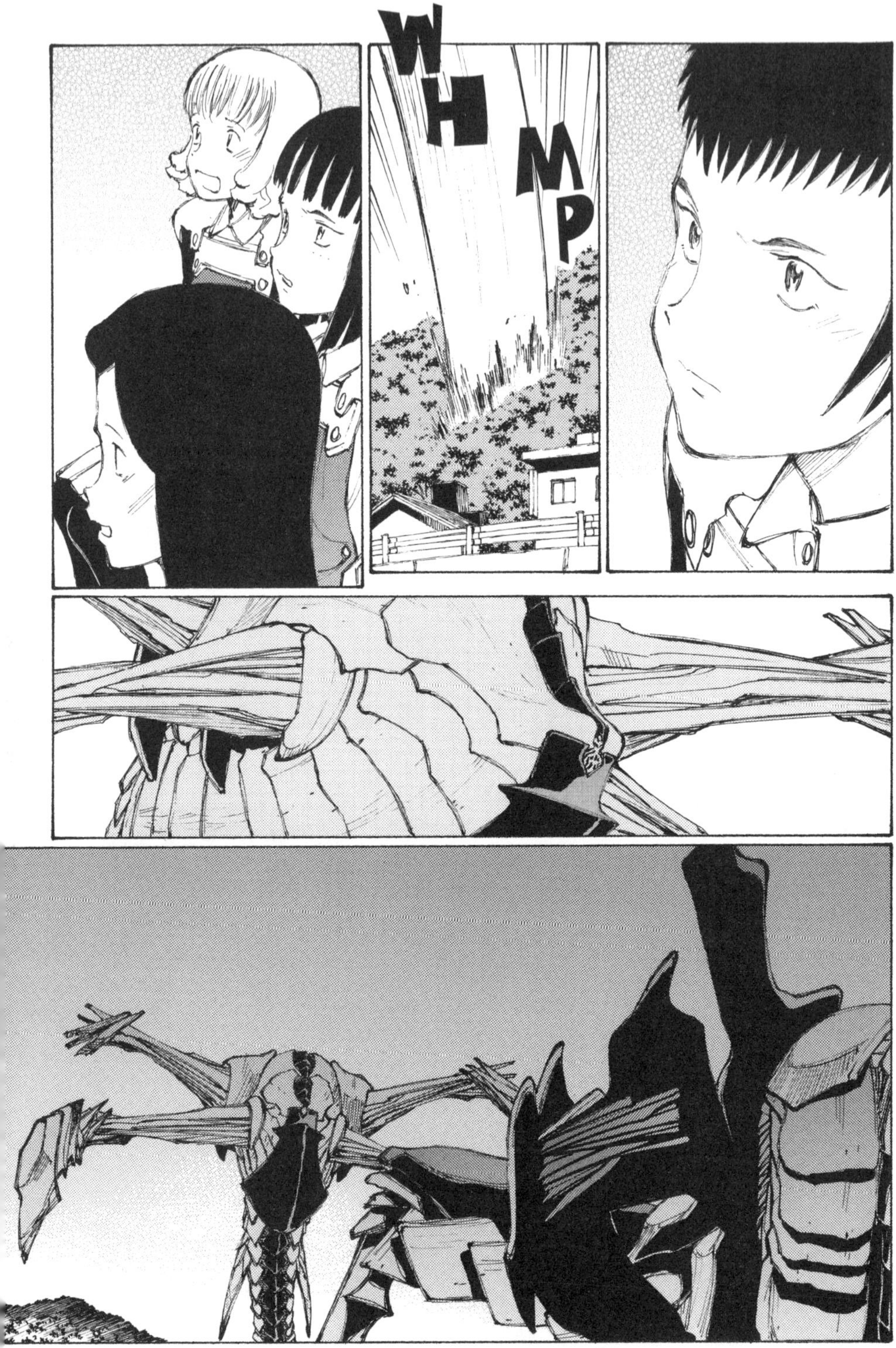
WHMP

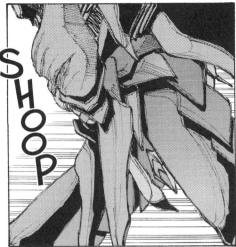

SHOOP

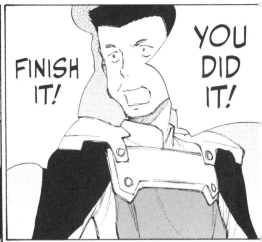

FINISH IT!

YOU DID IT!

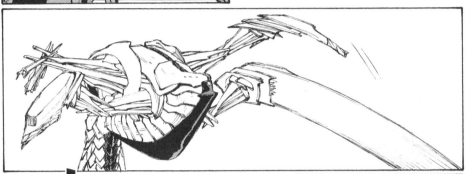

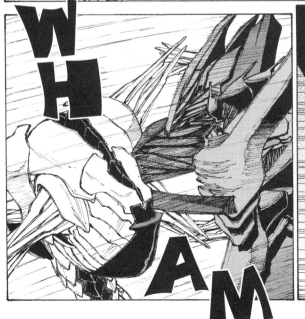

WH

AM

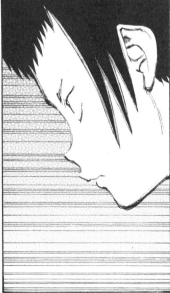

130

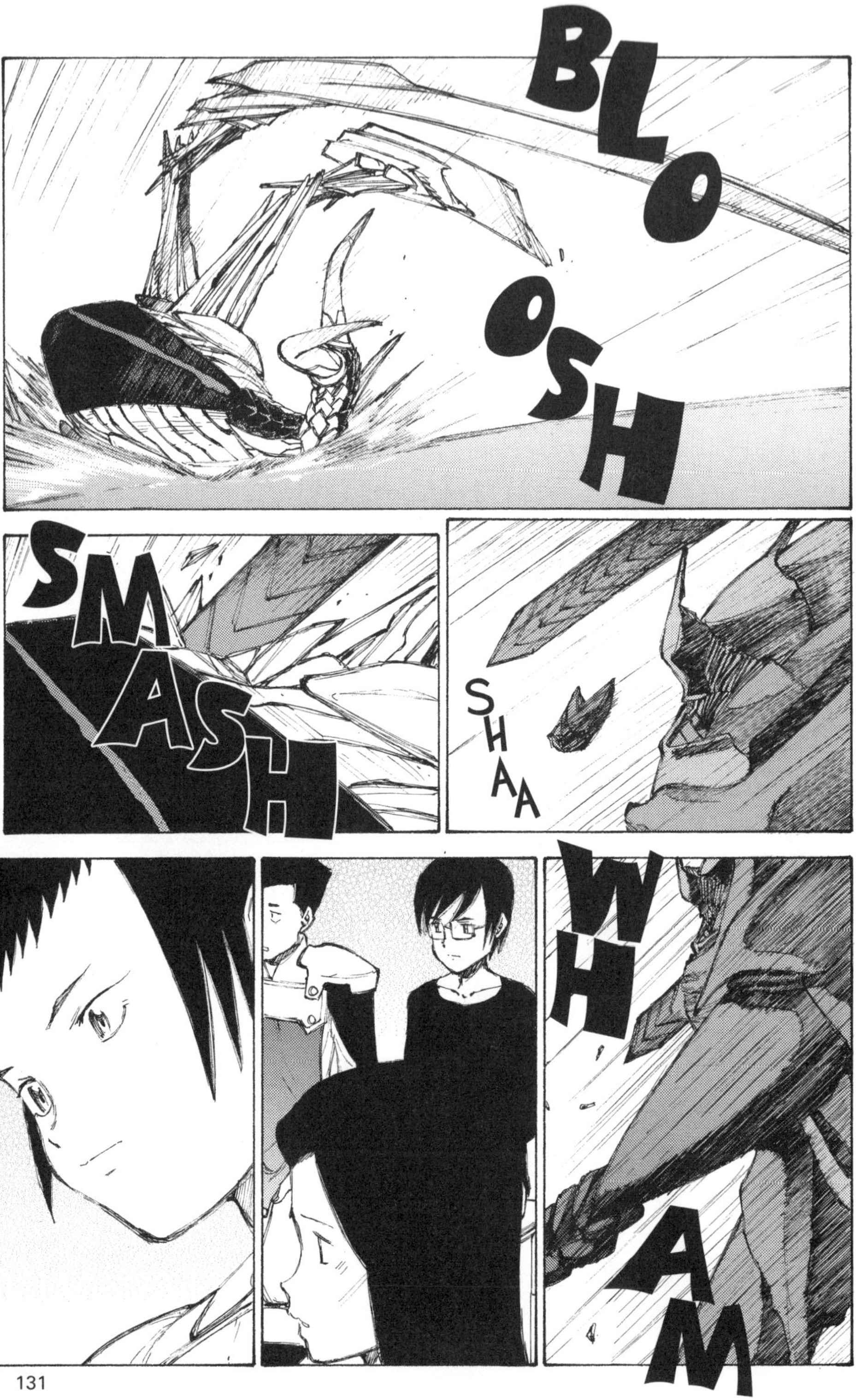
BLOOSH
SHAAA
SMASH
WHAM

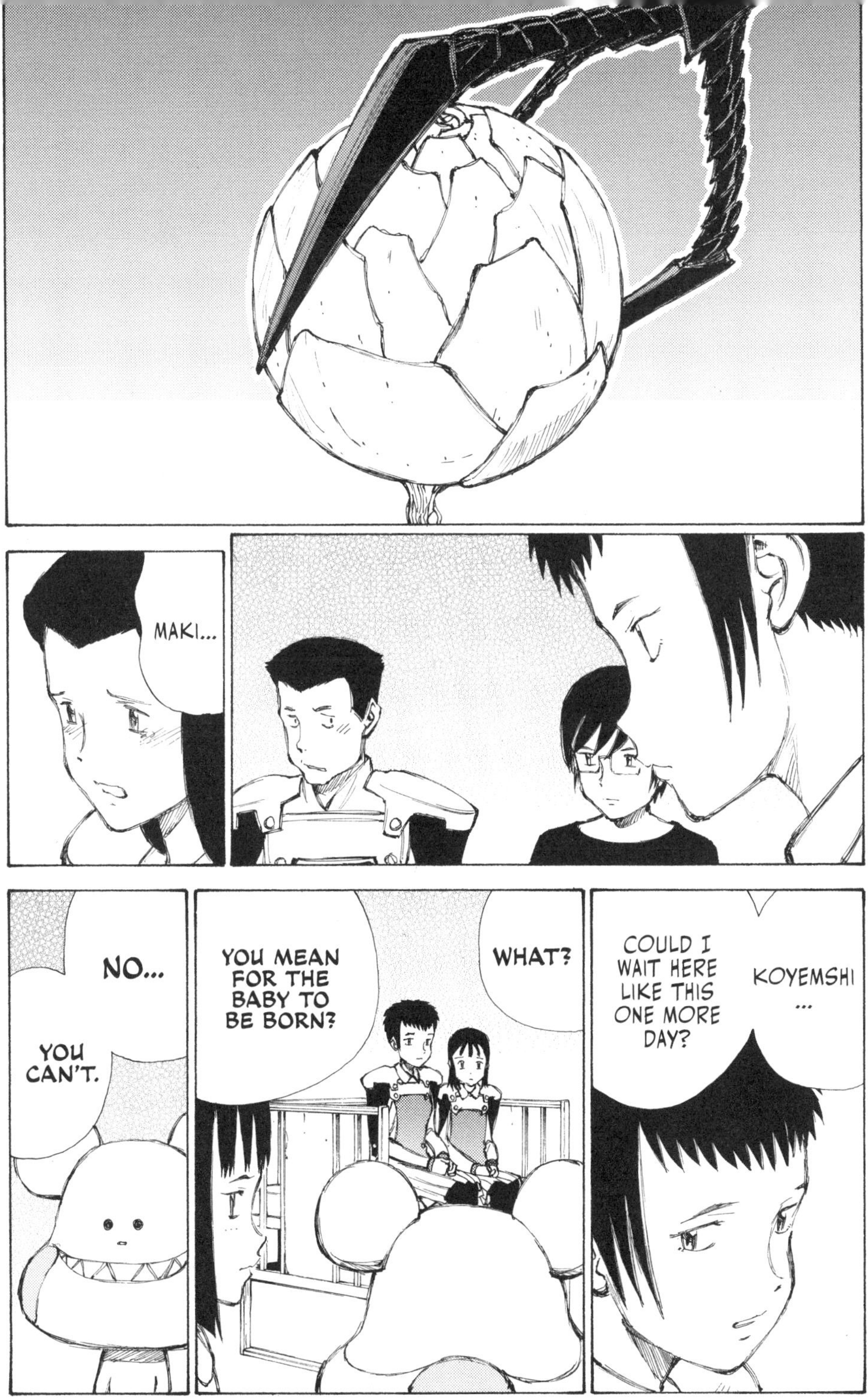
MAKI...
KOYEMSHI ...
COULD I WAIT HERE LIKE THIS ONE MORE DAY?
WHAT?
YOU MEAN FOR THE BABY TO BE BORN?
NO...
YOU CAN'T.

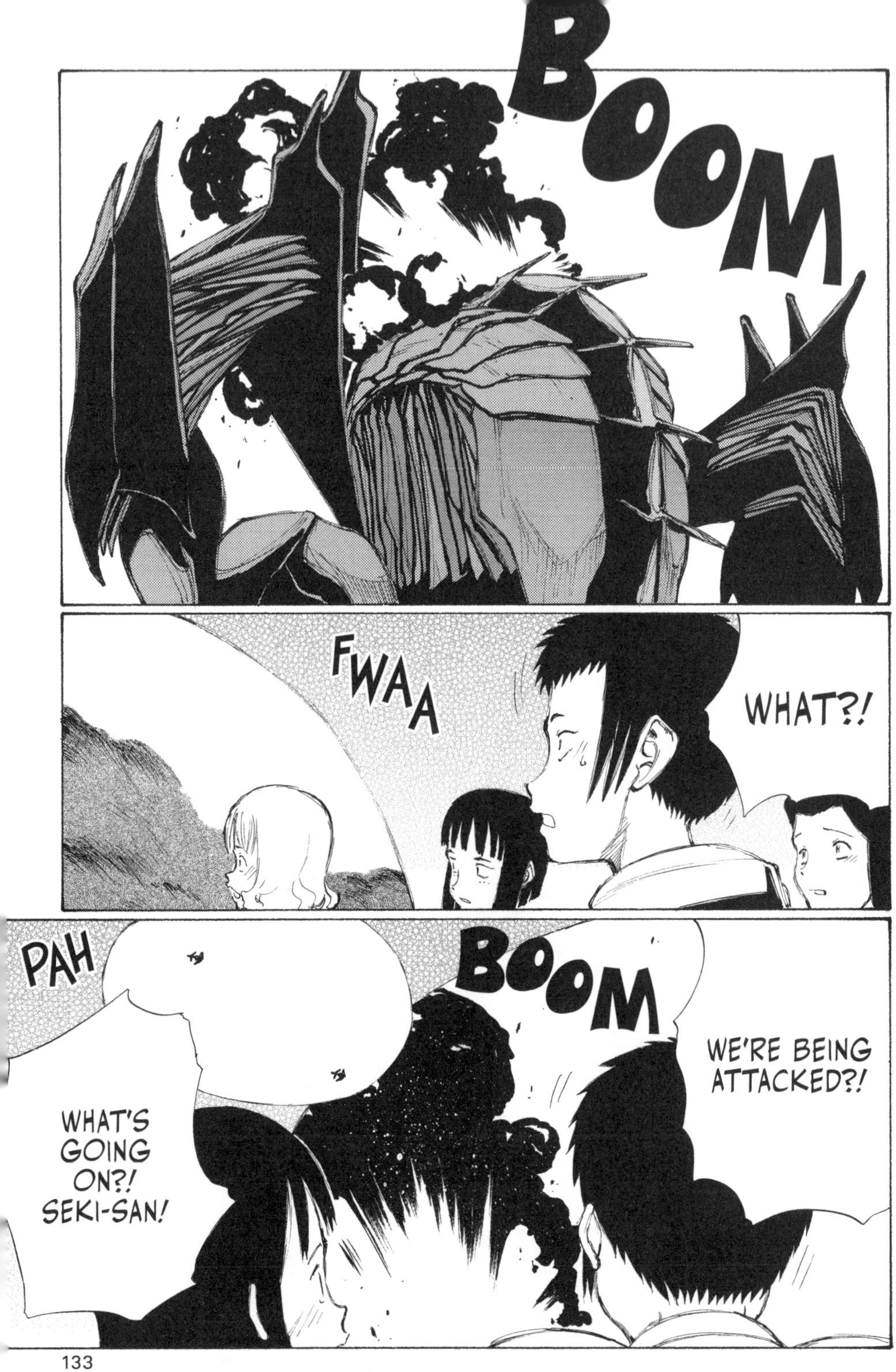
BOOM
WHAT?!
FWAA
WE'RE BEING ATTACKED?!
BOOM
PAH
WHAT'S GOING ON?! SEKI-SAN!

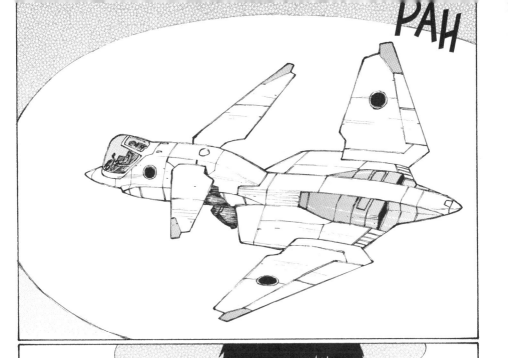

PAH

I'VE NEVER SEEN IT BEFORE!

WHAT...

THAT'S...

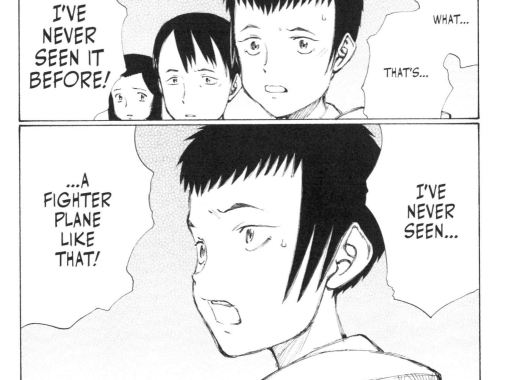

...A FIGHTER PLANE LIKE THAT!

I'VE NEVER SEEN...

134

CHAPTER 28: MAKI ANO 4

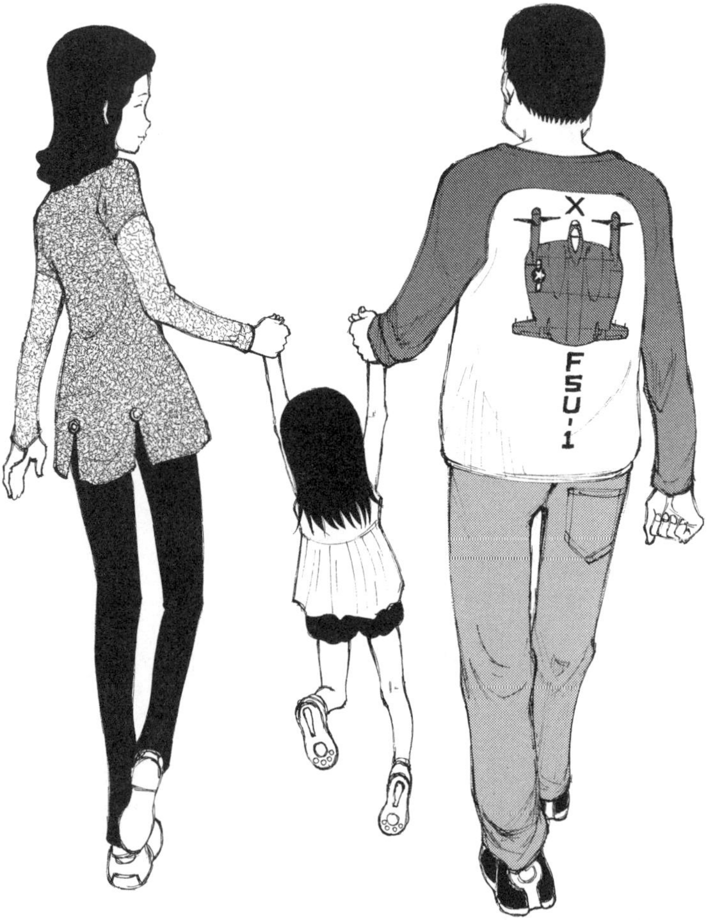
FSU-1

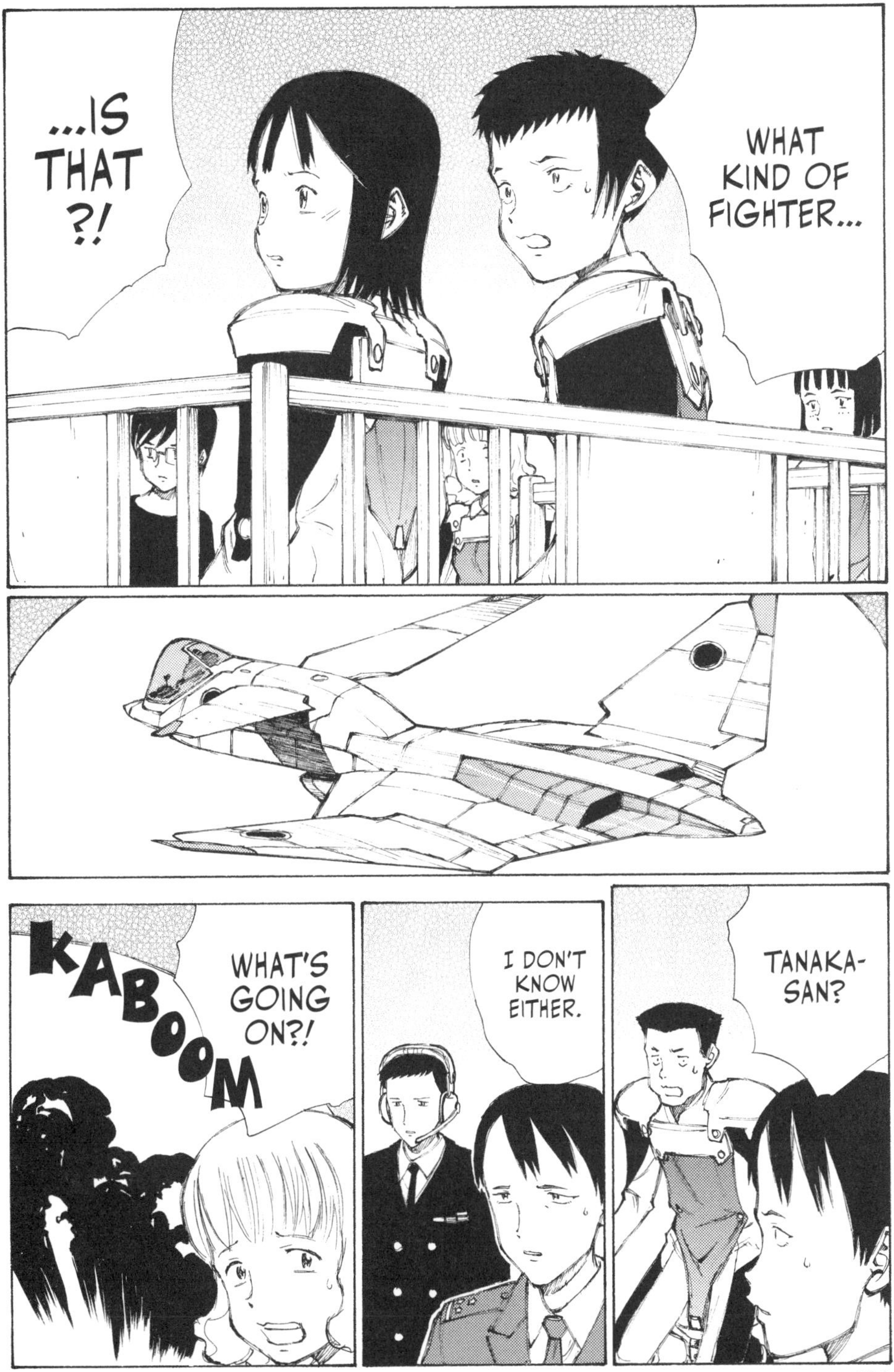
WHAT KIND OF FIGHTER...
...IS THAT?!
TANAKA-SAN?
I DON'T KNOW EITHER.
WHAT'S GOING ON?!
KABOOM

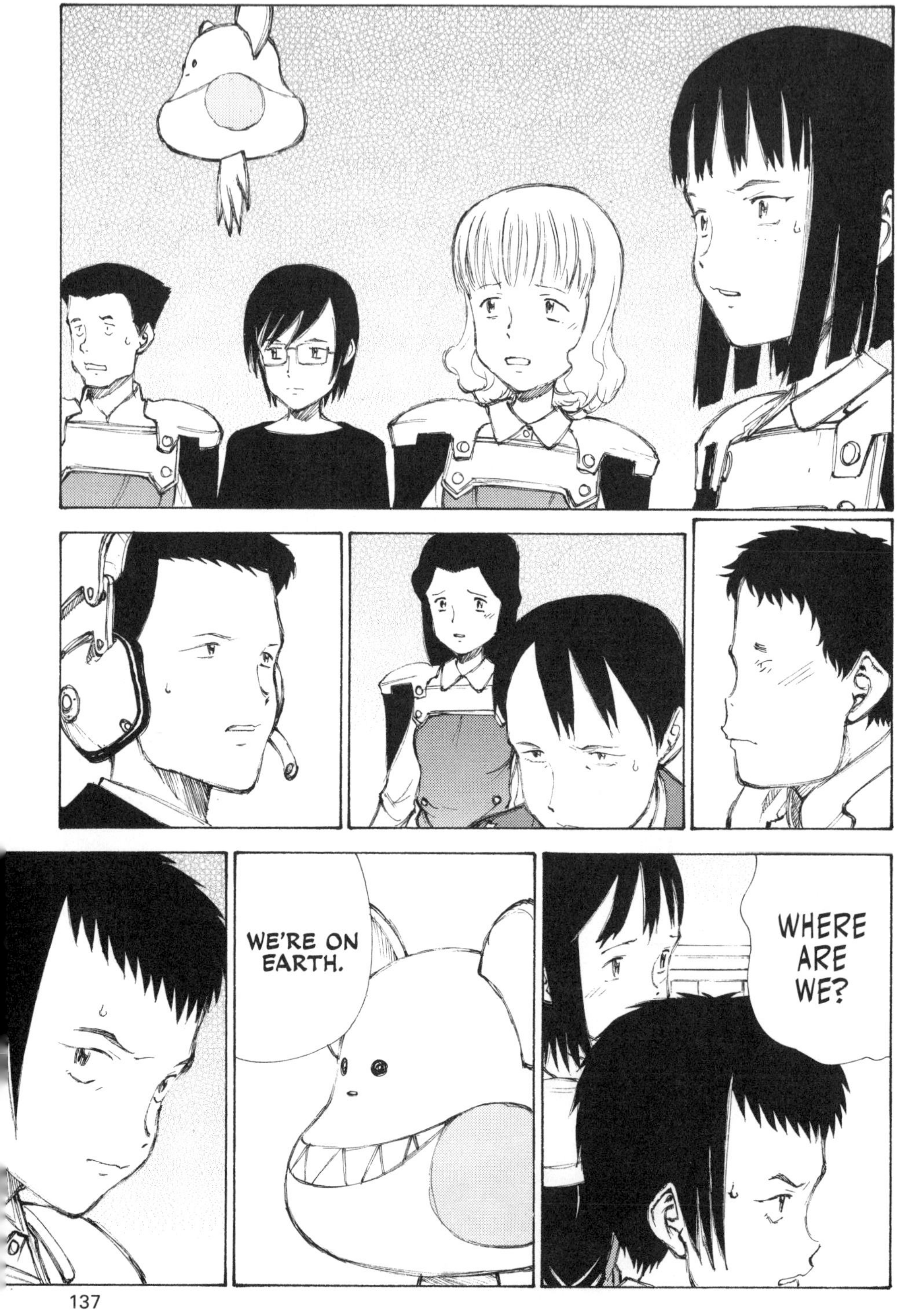
WHERE ARE WE?
WE'RE ON EARTH.

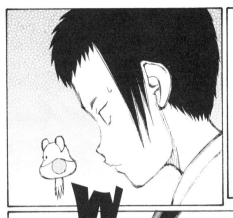

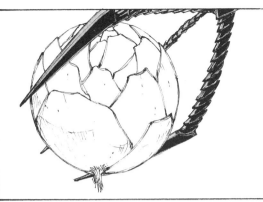

WH

MP

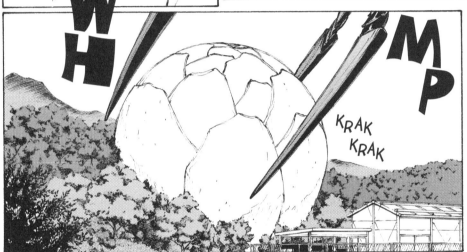

KRAK
KRAK

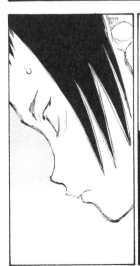

WHAT
ARE YOU
GOING
TO DO?!

W-
WHAT?

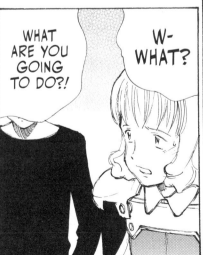

MAKI,
DON'T...

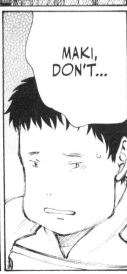

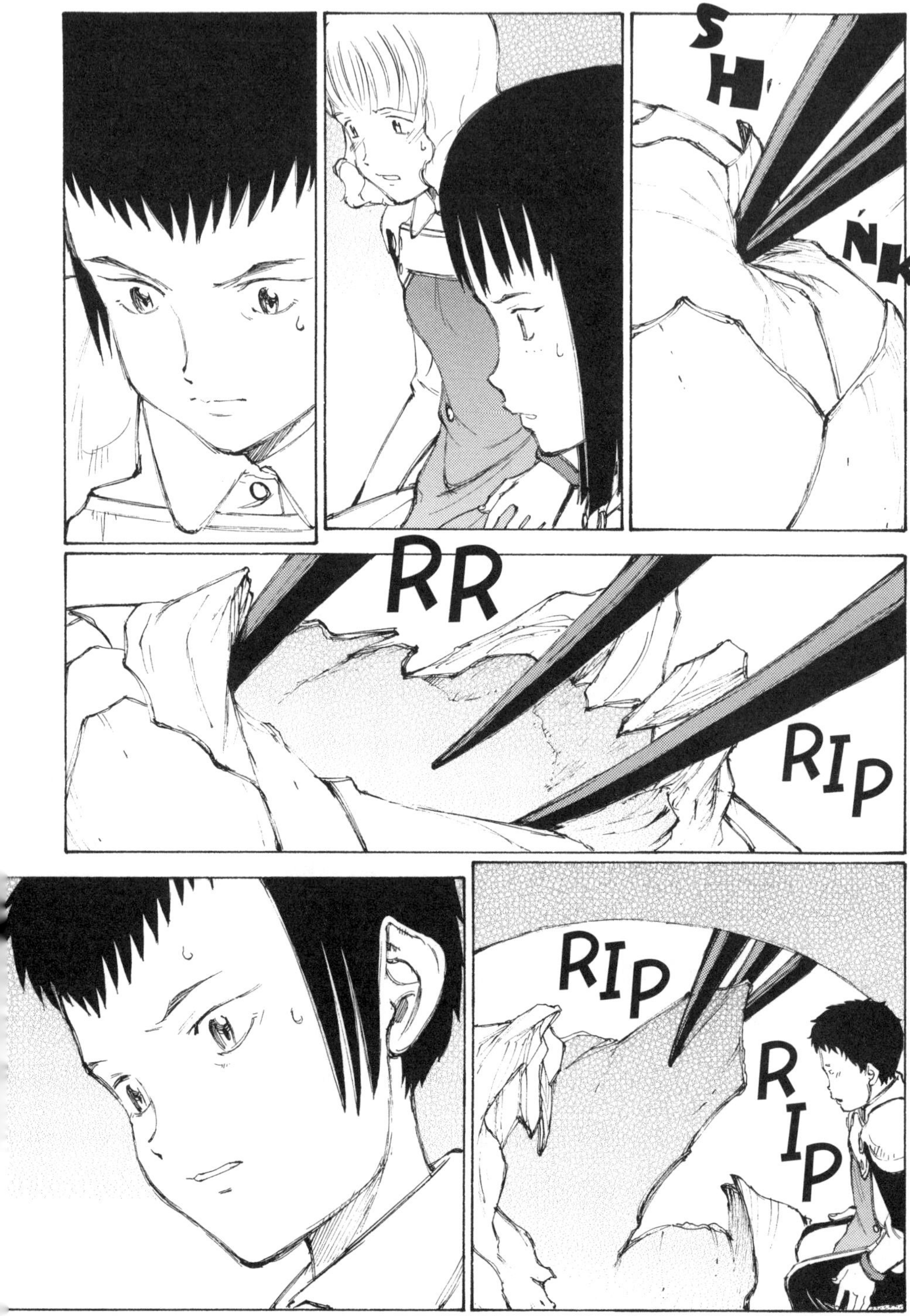
SH
NK
RR
RIP
RIP
RIP

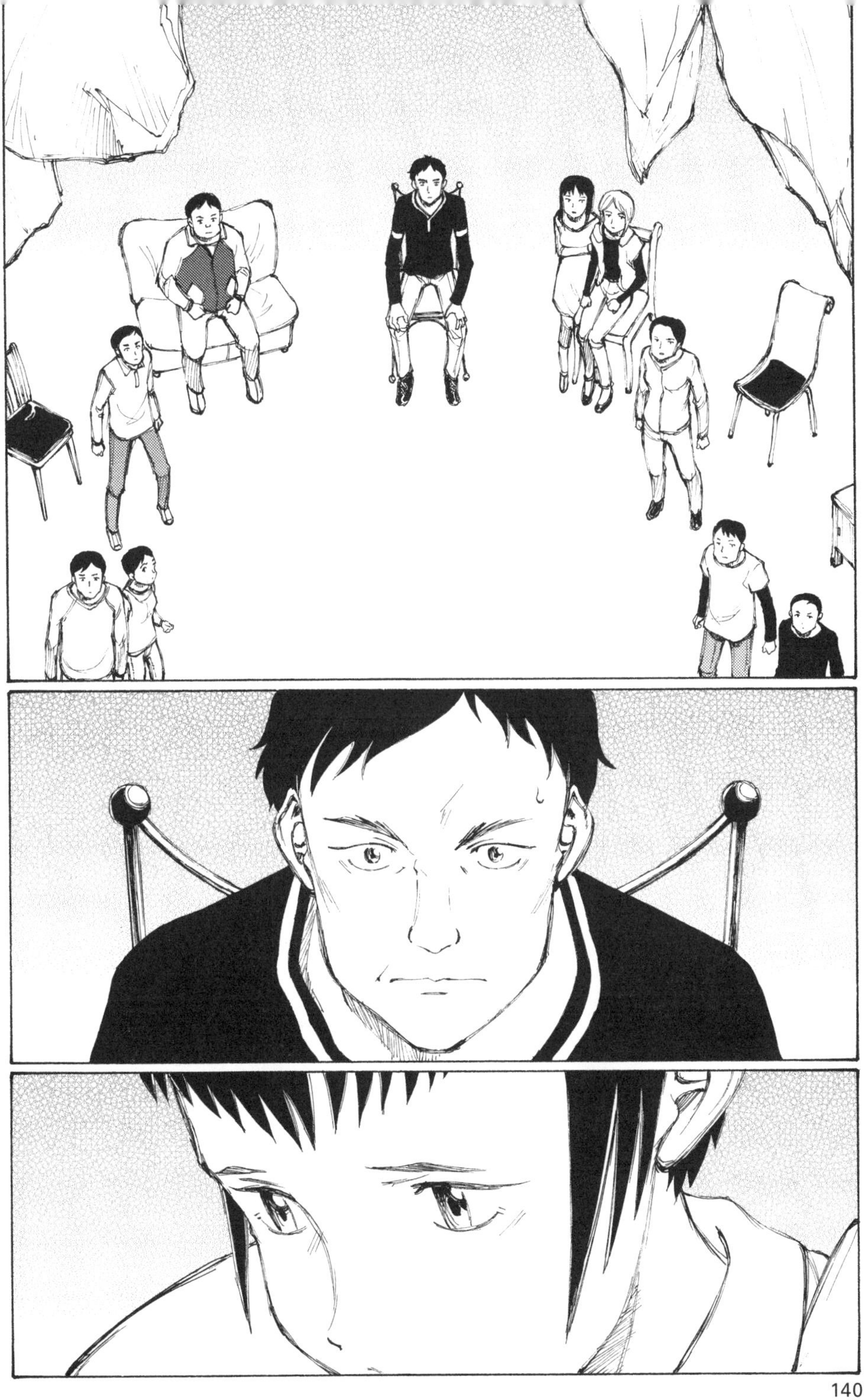

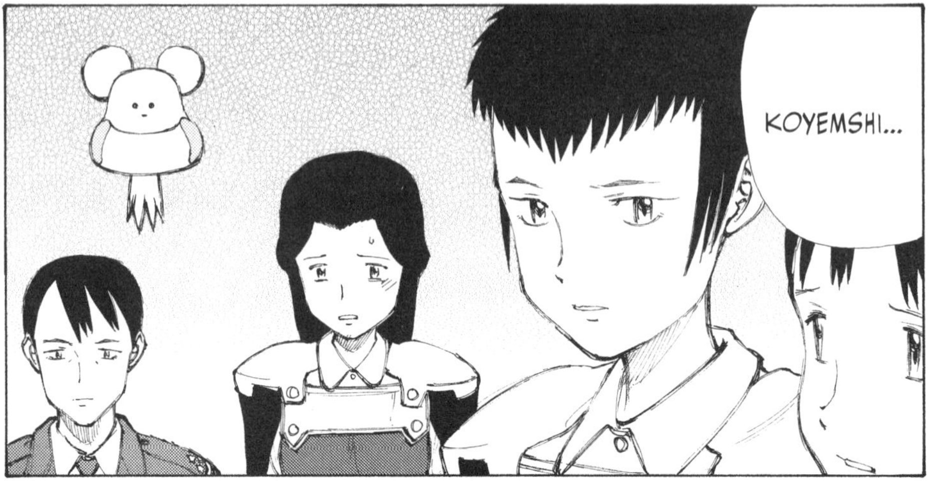
KOYEMSHI...

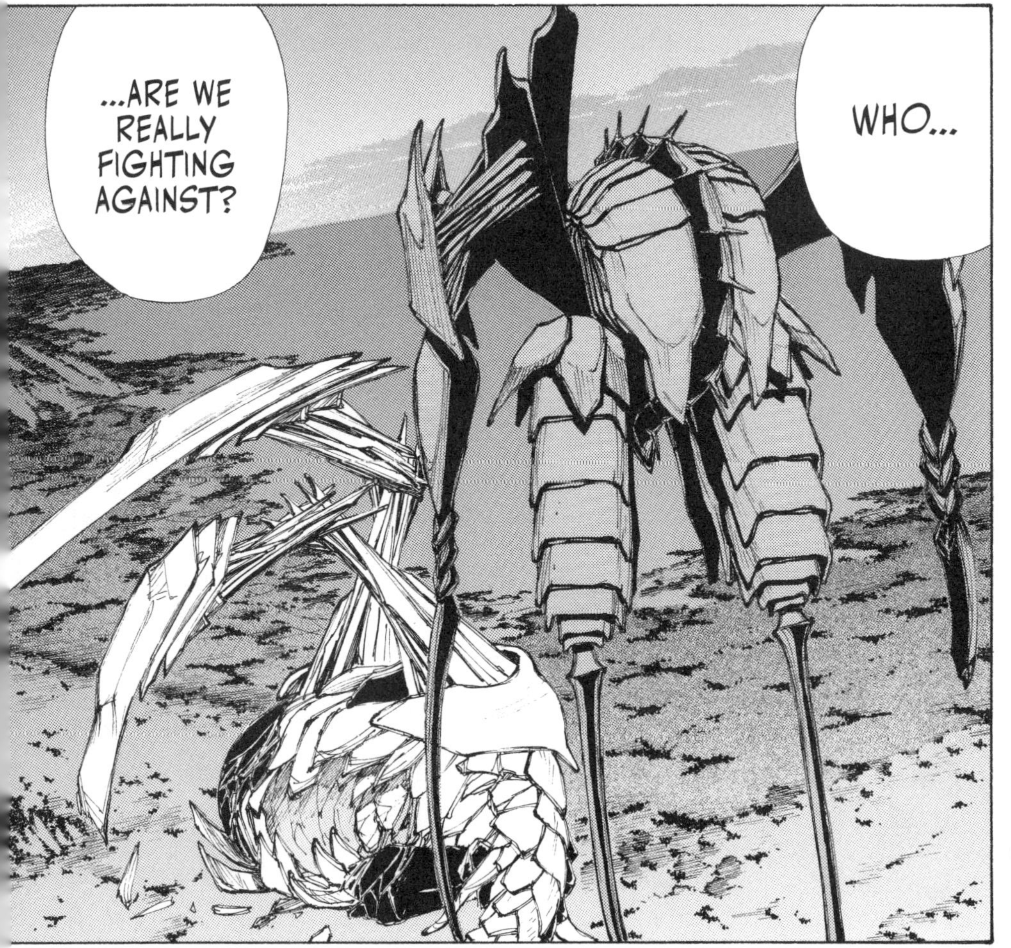
WHO...
...ARE WE REALLY FIGHTING AGAINST?

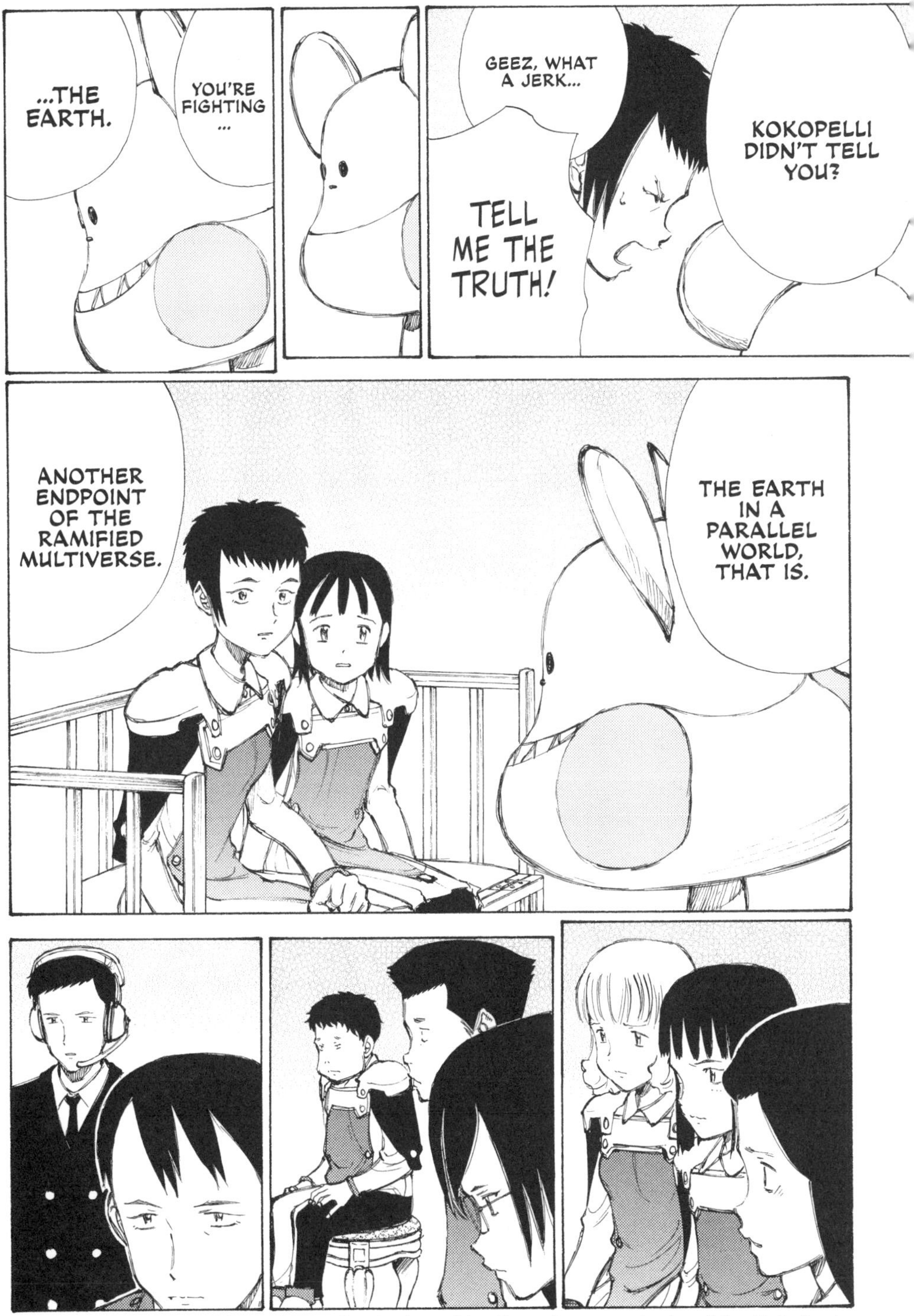
KOKOPELLI DIDN'T TELL YOU?
GEEZ, WHAT A JERK...
TELL ME THE TRUTH!
YOU'RE FIGHTING ...
...THE EARTH.
THE EARTH IN A PARALLEL WORLD, THAT IS.
ANOTHER ENDPOINT OF THE RAMIFIED MULTIVERSE.

* Endpoints of the ramified multiverse – A concept based on the parallel world cosmology common in science fiction. The Earth and the universe itself are split into a complex system of branches, in which infinite universes exist simultaneously. Universes on nearby branches of the system contain Earths similar to our own, while the Earths of increasingly distant branches would be increasingly divergent. The characters for the word "universe" in Japanese, 宇宙, stand for space (宇) and time (宙).

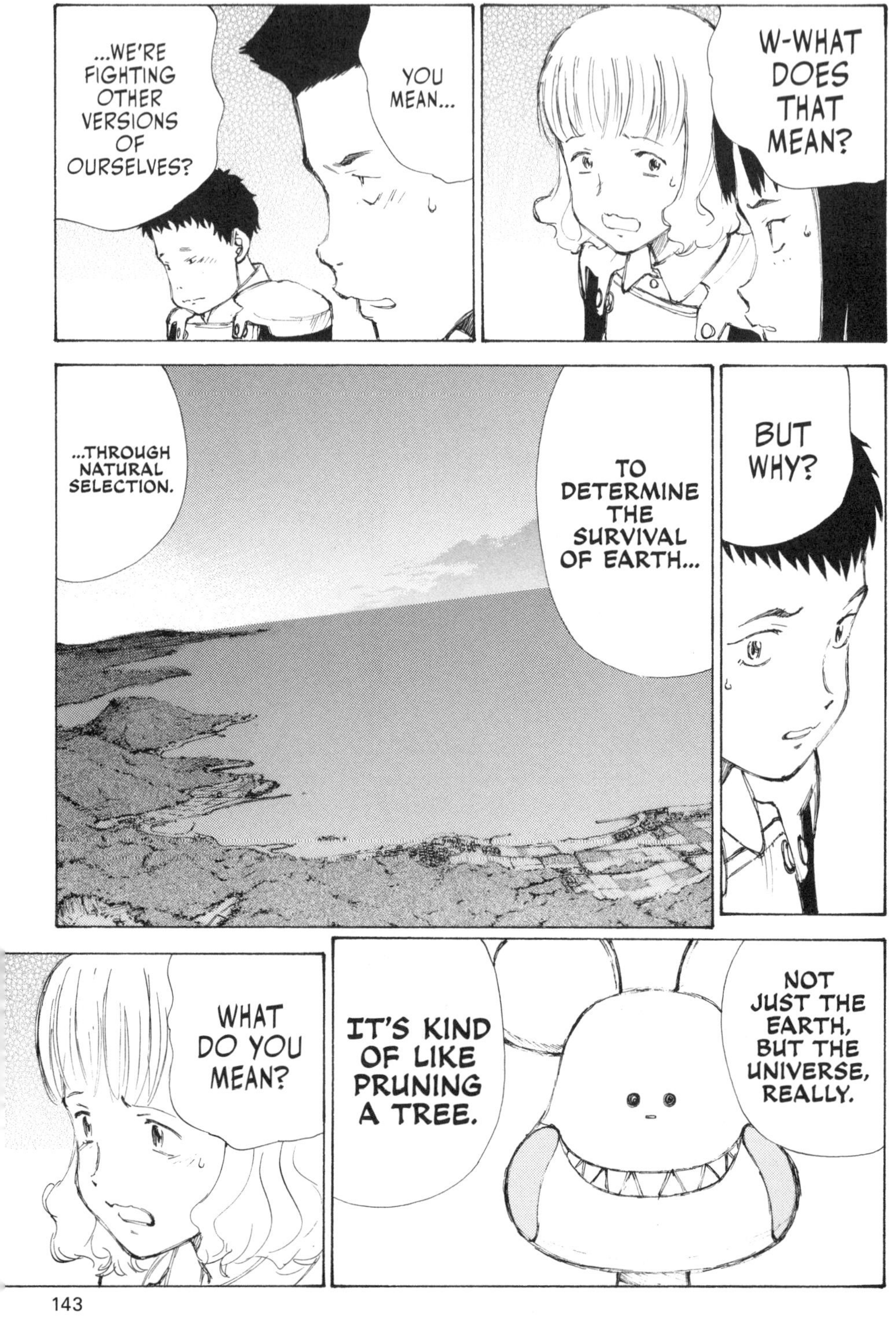
W-WHAT DOES THAT MEAN?
YOU MEAN...
...WE'RE FIGHTING OTHER VERSIONS OF OURSELVES?
BUT WHY?
TO DETERMINE THE SURVIVAL OF EARTH...
...THROUGH NATURAL SELECTION.
NOT JUST THE EARTH, BUT THE UNIVERSE, REALLY.
IT'S KIND OF LIKE PRUNING A TREE.
WHAT DO YOU MEAN?

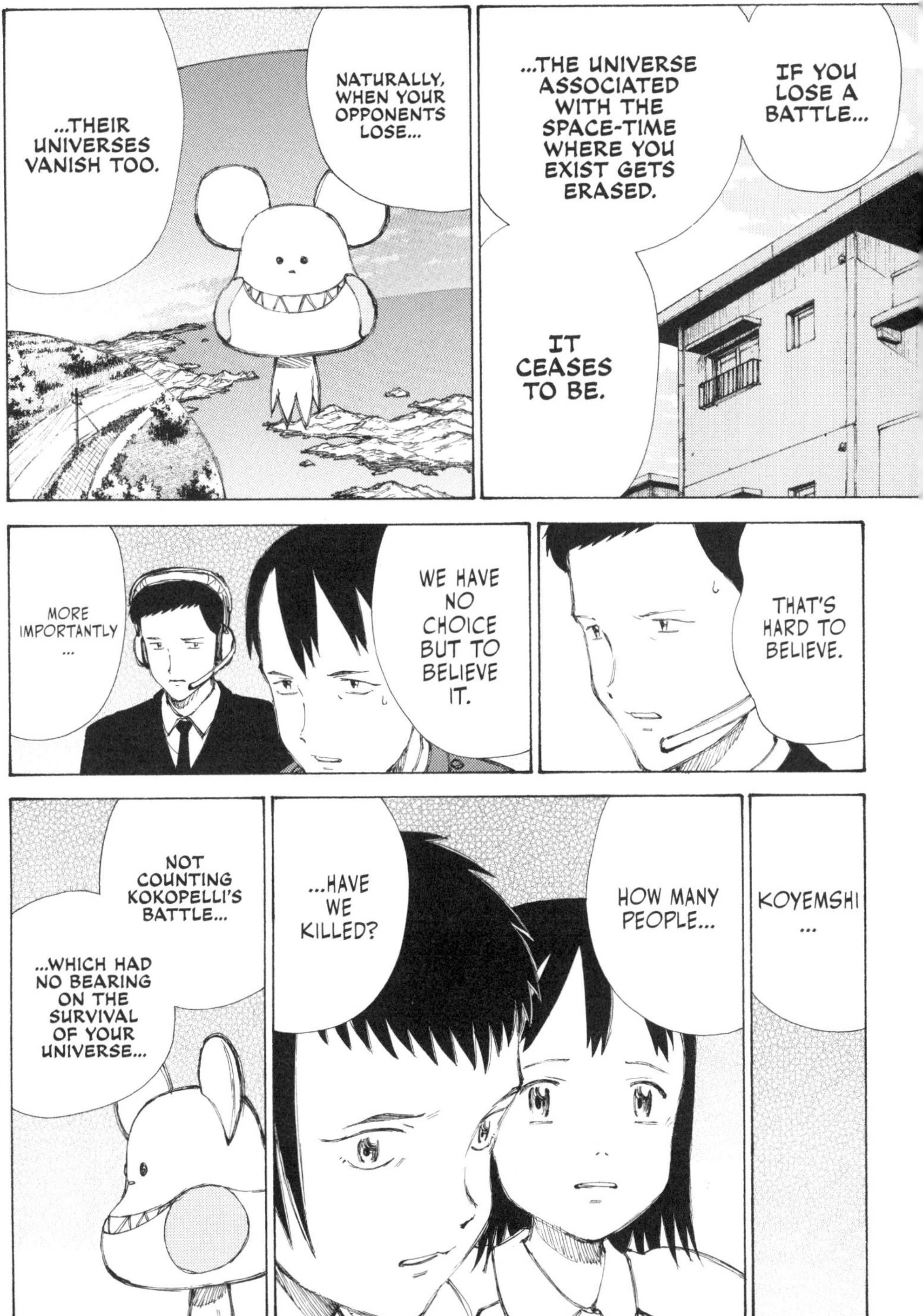
IF YOU LOSE A BATTLE...
...THE UNIVERSE ASSOCIATED WITH THE SPACE-TIME WHERE YOU EXIST GETS ERASED.
IT CEASES TO BE.
NATURALLY, WHEN YOUR OPPONENTS LOSE...
...THEIR UNIVERSES VANISH TOO.
THAT'S HARD TO BELIEVE.
WE HAVE NO CHOICE BUT TO BELIEVE IT.
MORE IMPORTANTLY ...
KOYEMSHI ...
HOW MANY PEOPLE...
...HAVE WE KILLED?
NOT COUNTING KOKOPELLI'S BATTLE...
...WHICH HAD NO BEARING ON THE SURVIVAL OF YOUR UNIVERSE...

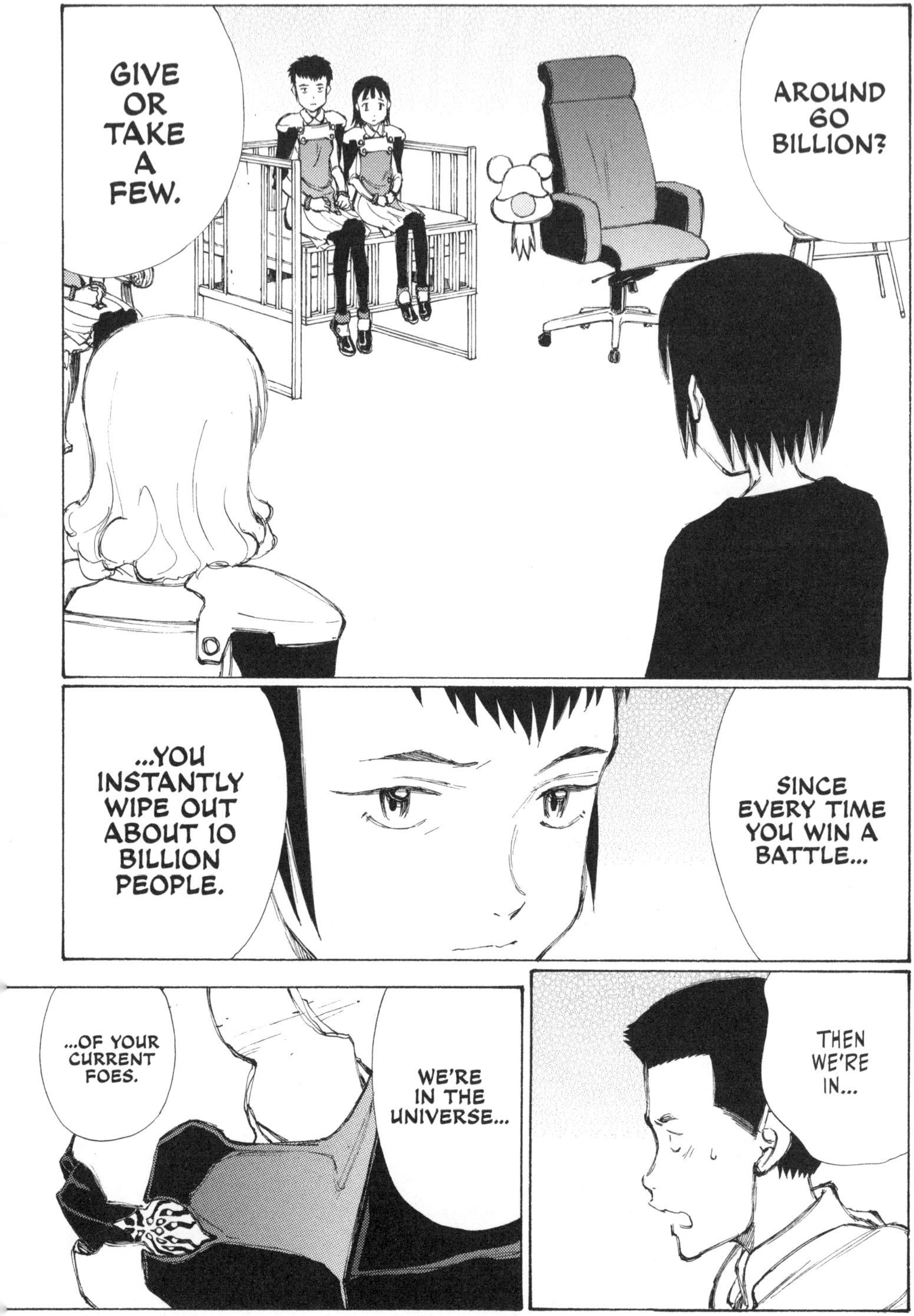
AROUND 60 BILLION?
GIVE OR TAKE A FEW.
SINCE EVERY TIME YOU WIN A BATTLE...
...YOU INSTANTLY WIPE OUT ABOUT 10 BILLION PEOPLE.
THEN WE'RE IN...
WE'RE IN THE UNIVERSE...
...OF YOUR CURRENT FOES.

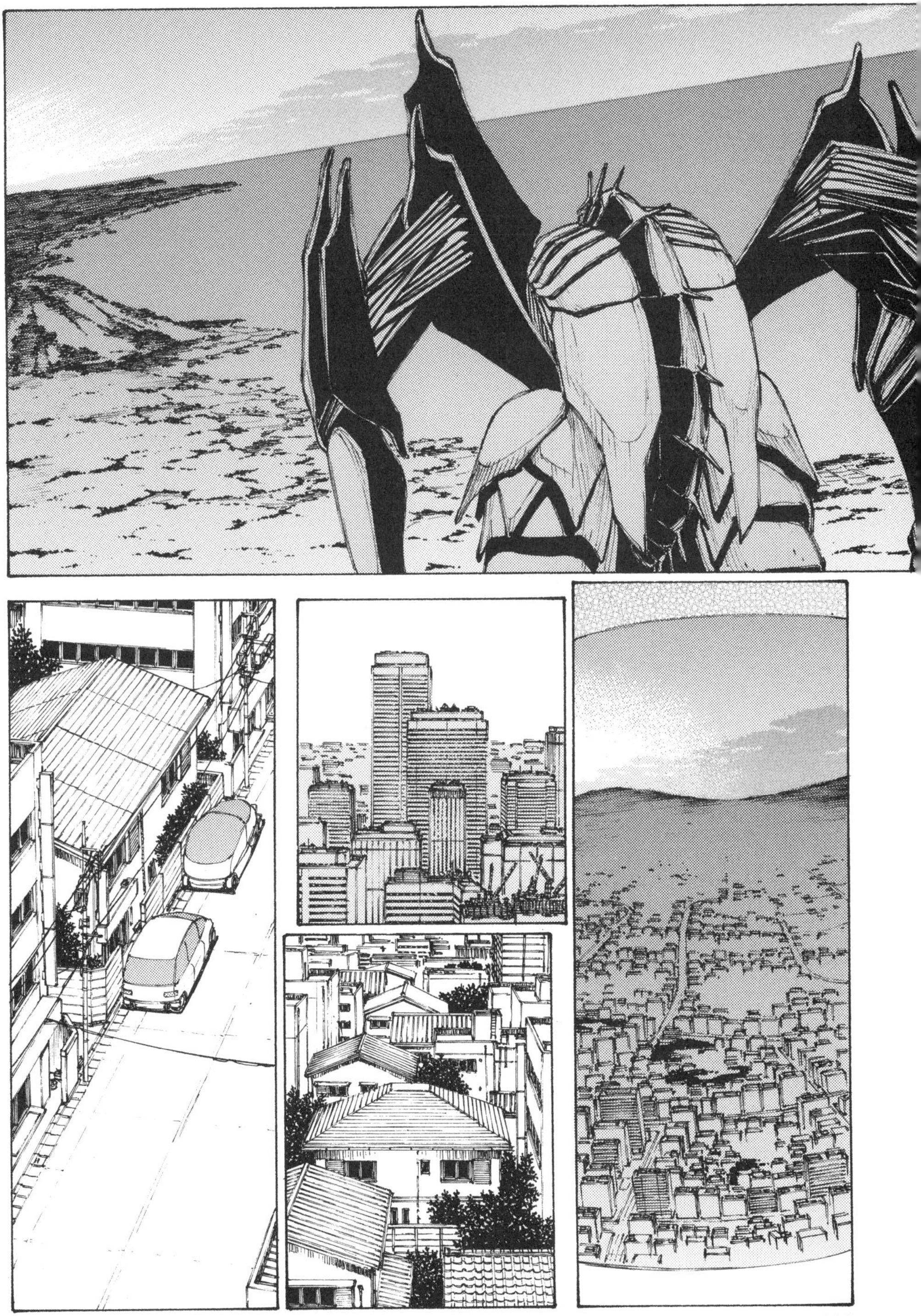

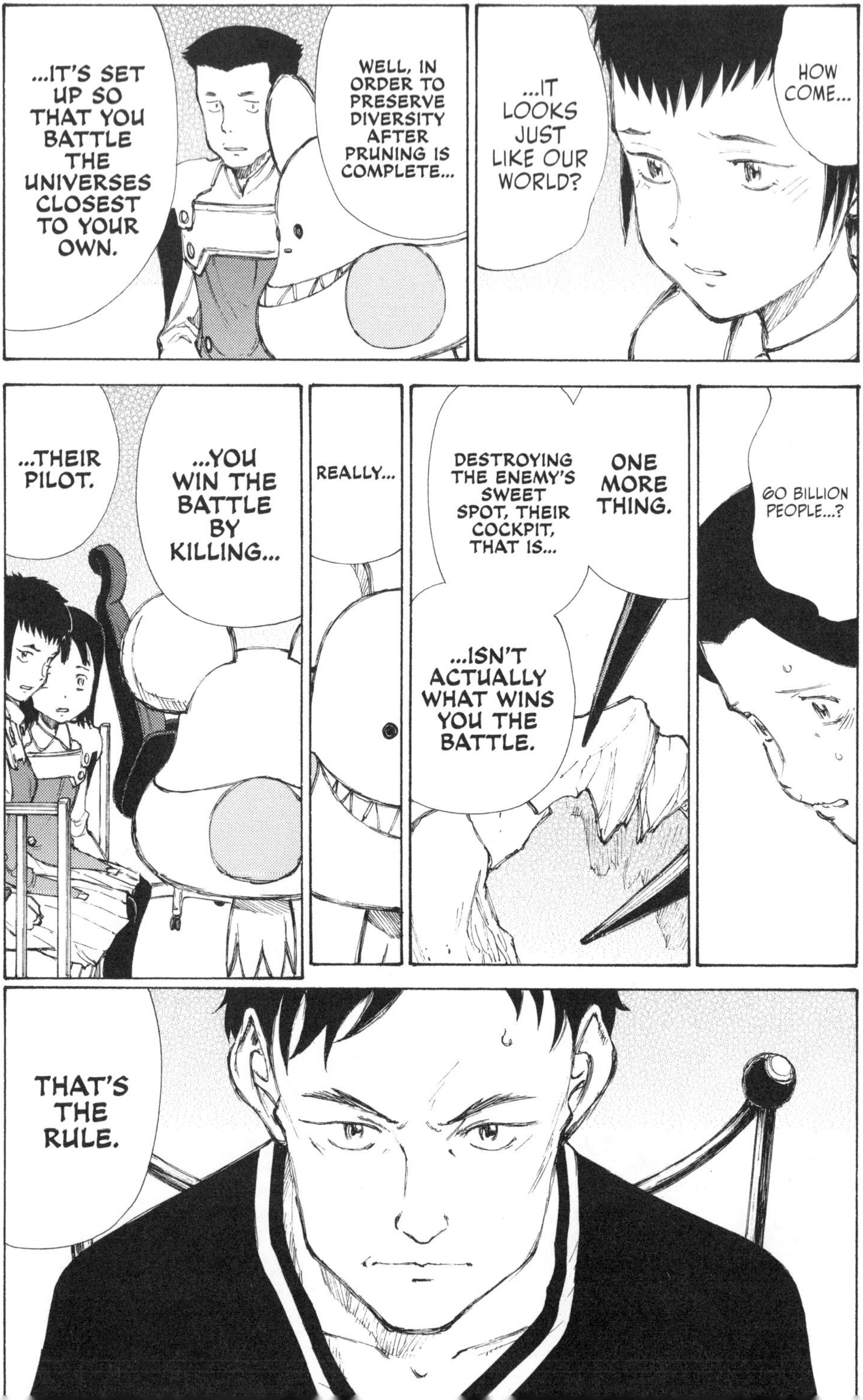
HOW COME...
...IT LOOKS JUST LIKE OUR WORLD?
WELL, IN ORDER TO PRESERVE DIVERSITY AFTER PRUNING IS COMPLETE...
...IT'S SET UP SO THAT YOU BATTLE THE UNIVERSES CLOSEST TO YOUR OWN.
60 BILLION PEOPLE...?
ONE MORE THING.
DESTROYING THE ENEMY'S SWEET SPOT, THEIR COCKPIT, THAT IS...
...ISN'T ACTUALLY WHAT WINS YOU THE BATTLE.
REALLY...
...YOU WIN THE BATTLE BY KILLING...
...THEIR PILOT.
THAT'S THE RULE.

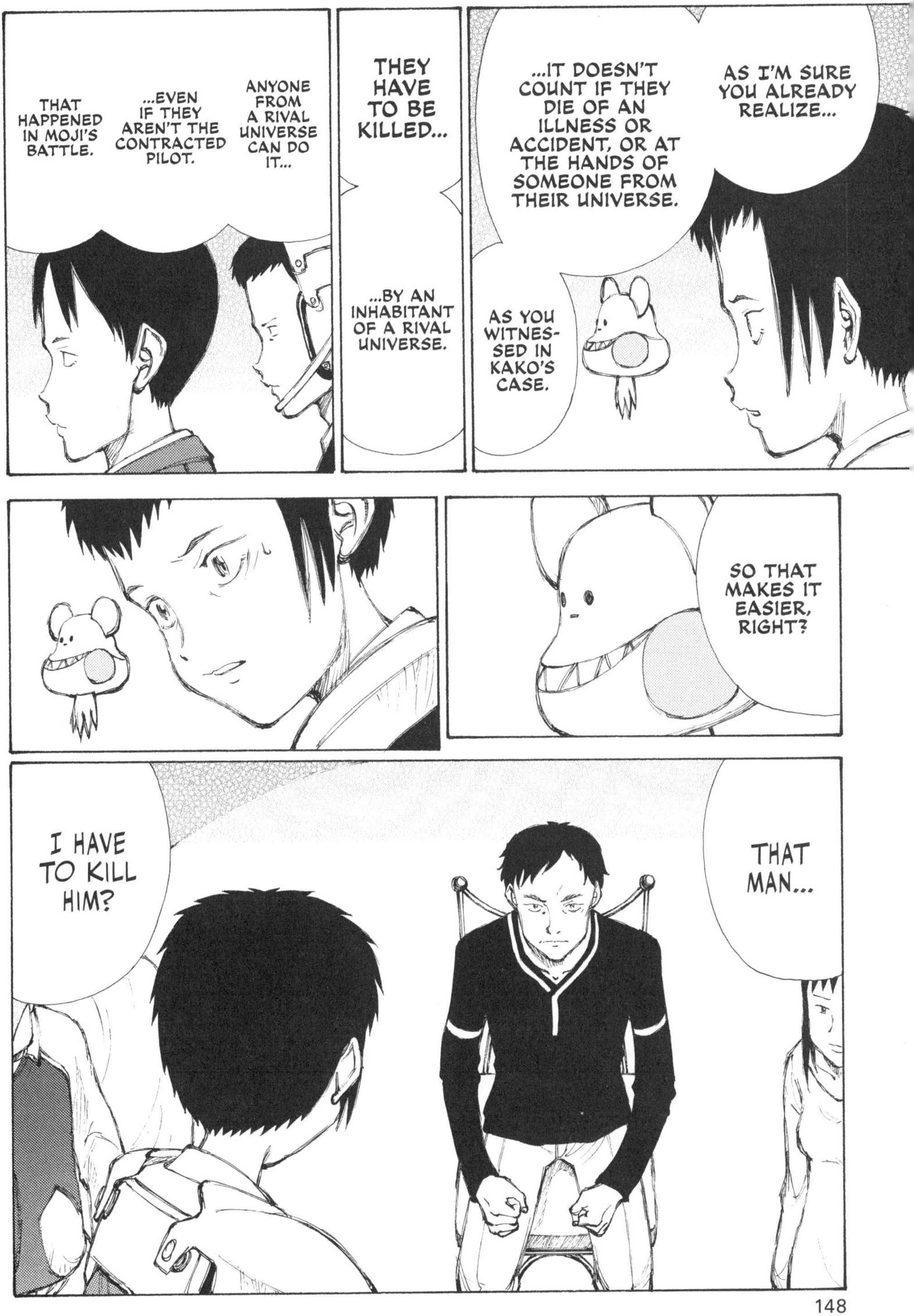
AS I'M SURE YOU ALREADY REALIZE...
...IT DOESN'T COUNT IF THEY DIE OF AN ILLNESS OR ACCIDENT, OR AT THE HANDS OF SOMEONE FROM THEIR UNIVERSE.
AS YOU WITNES-SED IN KAKO'S CASE.
THEY HAVE TO BE KILLED...
...BY AN INHABITANT OF A RIVAL UNIVERSE.
ANYONE FROM A RIVAL UNIVERSE CAN DO IT...
...EVEN IF THEY AREN'T THE CONTRACTED PILOT.
THAT HAPPENED IN MOJI'S BATTLE.
SO THAT MAKES IT EASIER, RIGHT?
THAT MAN...
I HAVE TO KILL HIM?

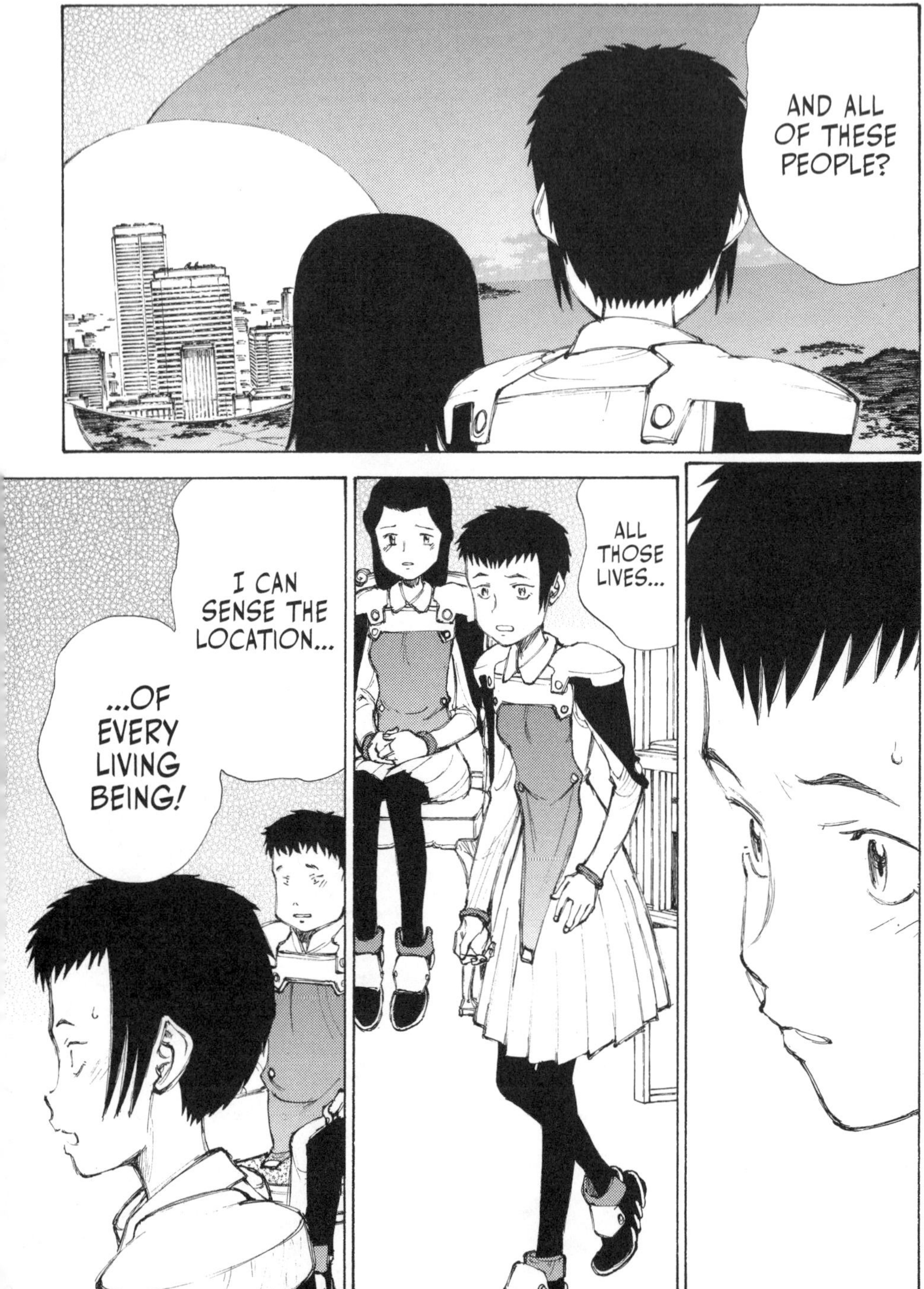
AND ALL OF THESE PEOPLE?
ALL THOSE LIVES...
I CAN SENSE THE LOCATION...
...OF EVERY LIVING BEING!

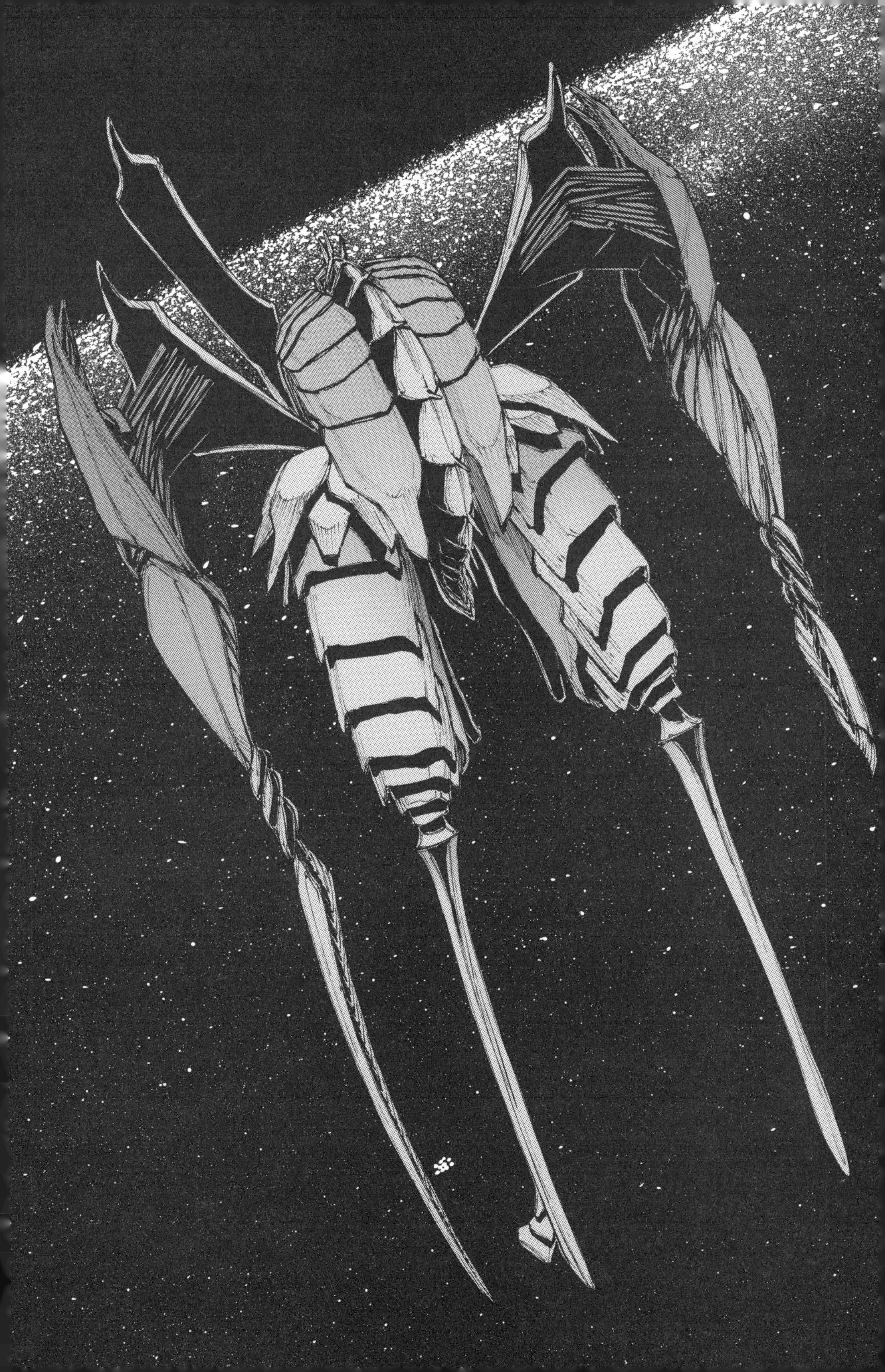

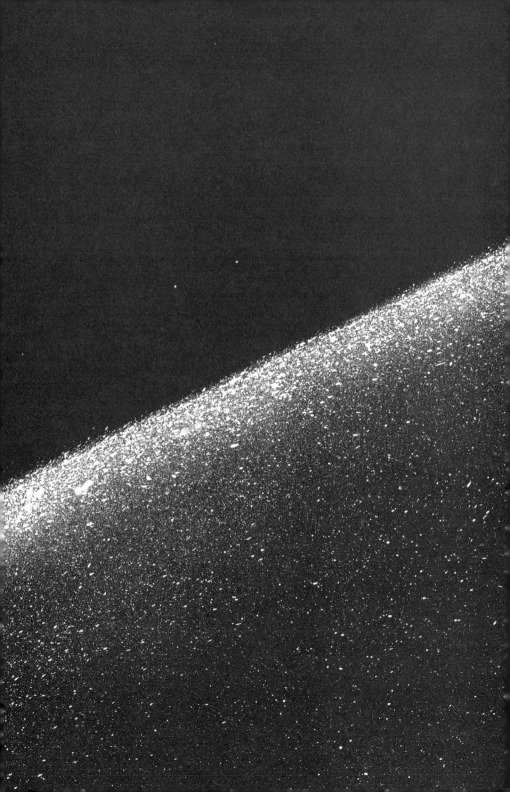

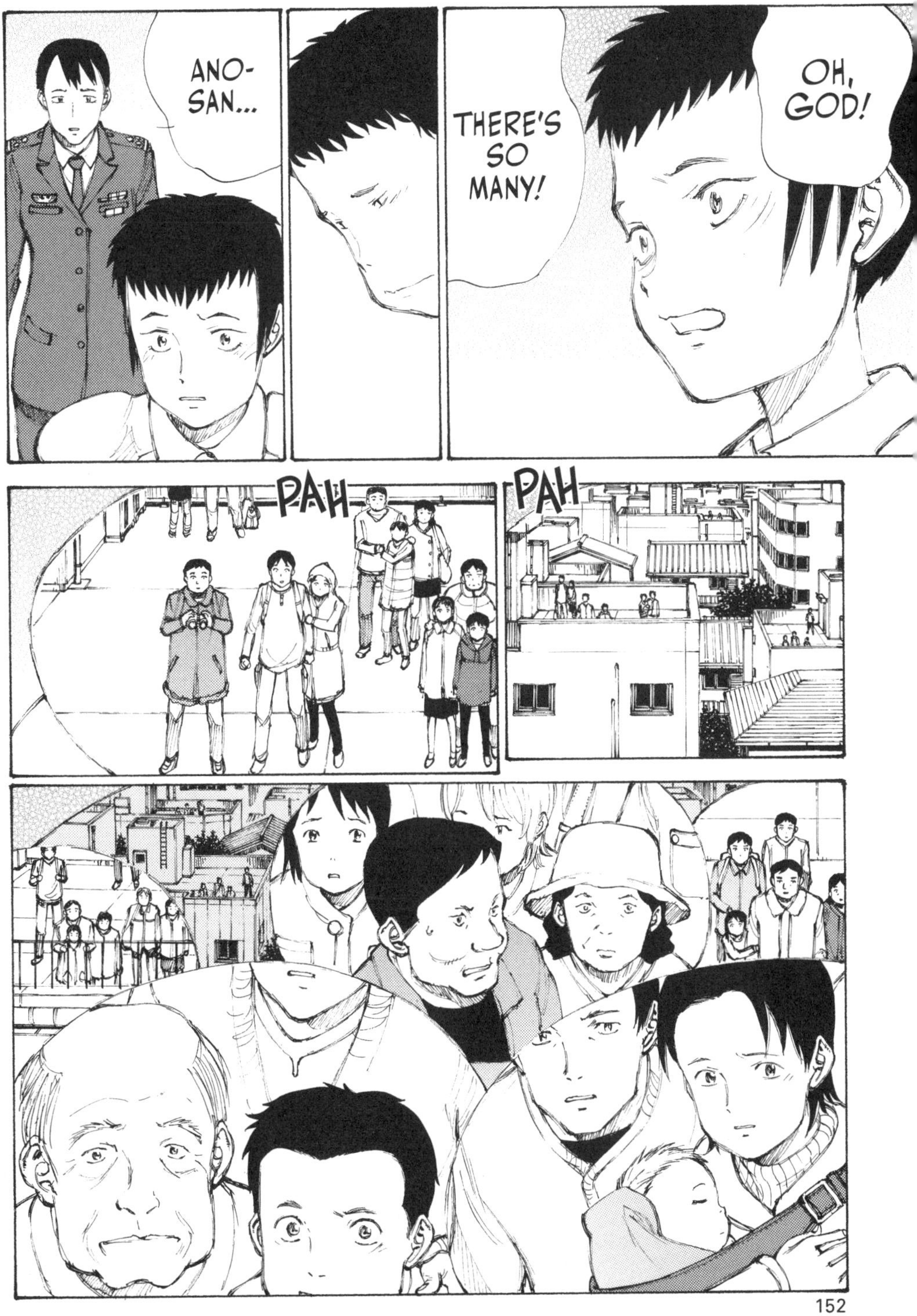
OH, GOD!
THERE'S SO MANY!
ANO-SAN...
PAH
PAH

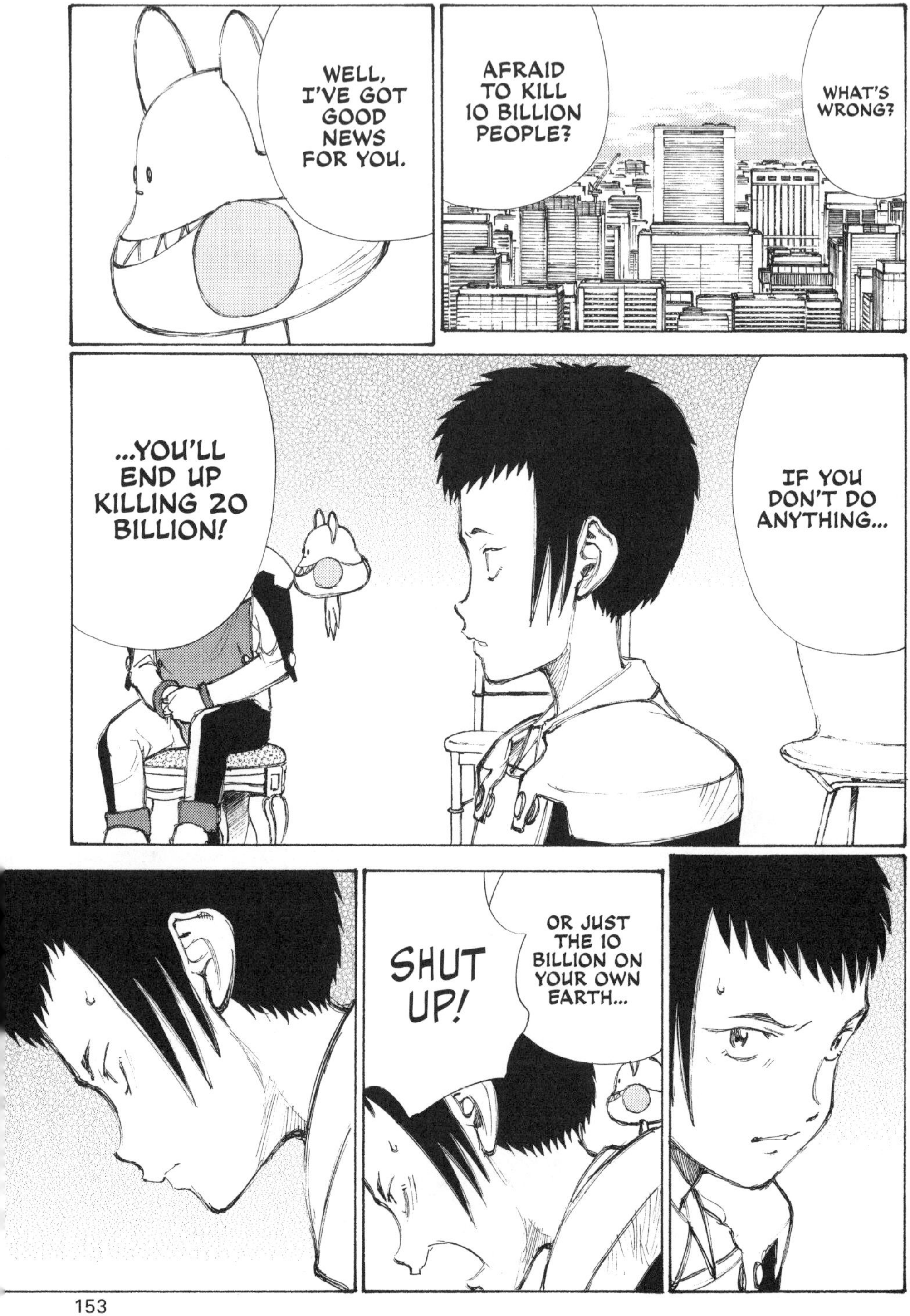
WHAT'S WRONG?
AFRAID TO KILL 10 BILLION PEOPLE?
WELL, I'VE GOT GOOD NEWS FOR YOU.
IF YOU DON'T DO ANYTHING...
...YOU'LL END UP KILLING 20 BILLION!
OR JUST THE 10 BILLION ON YOUR OWN EARTH...
SHUT UP!

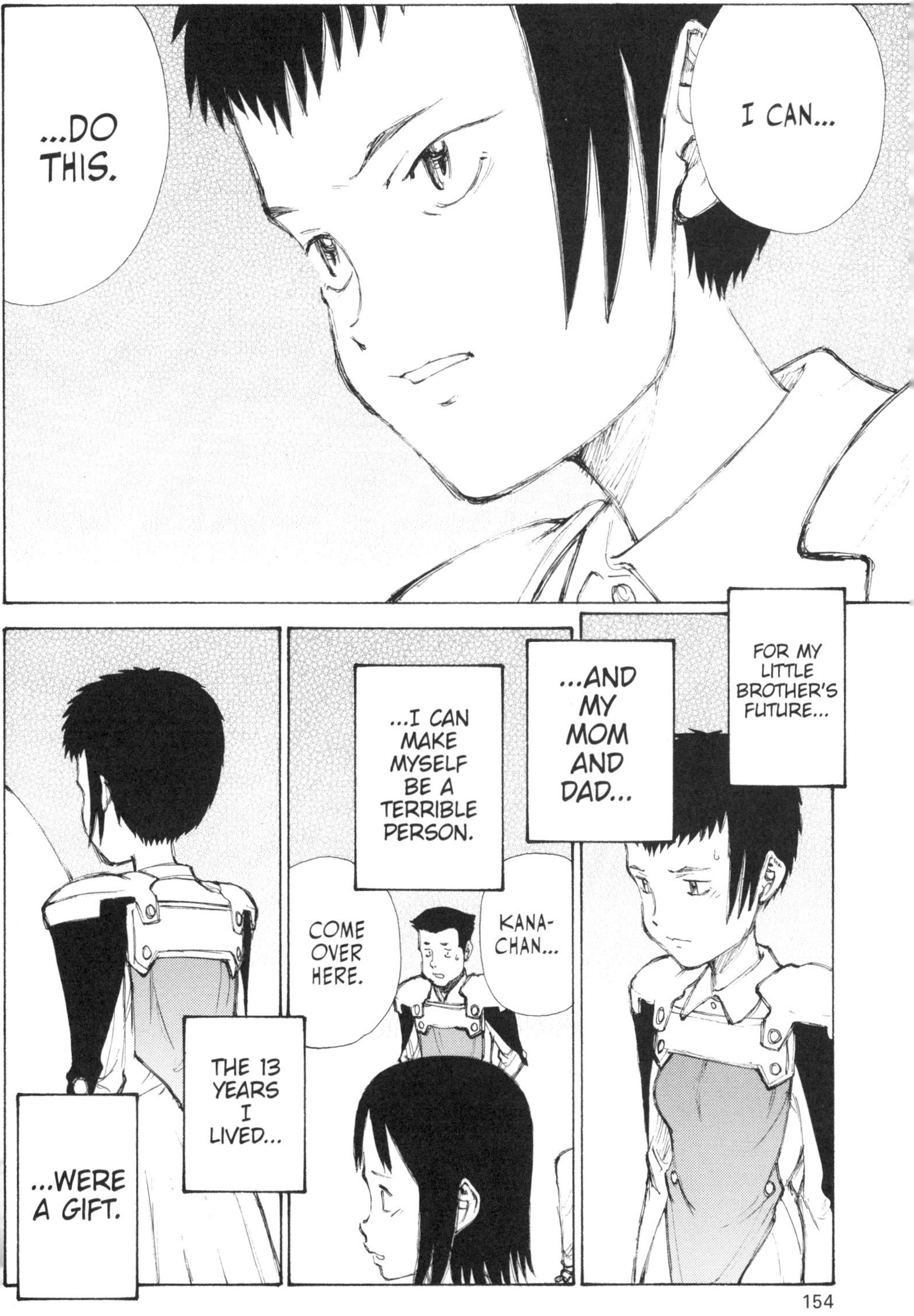
I CAN...
...DO THIS.
FOR MY LITTLE BROTHER'S FUTURE...
...AND MY MOM AND DAD...
...I CAN MAKE MYSELF BE A TERRIBLE PERSON.
KANA-CHAN...
COME OVER HERE.
THE 13 YEARS I LIVED...
...WERE A GIFT.

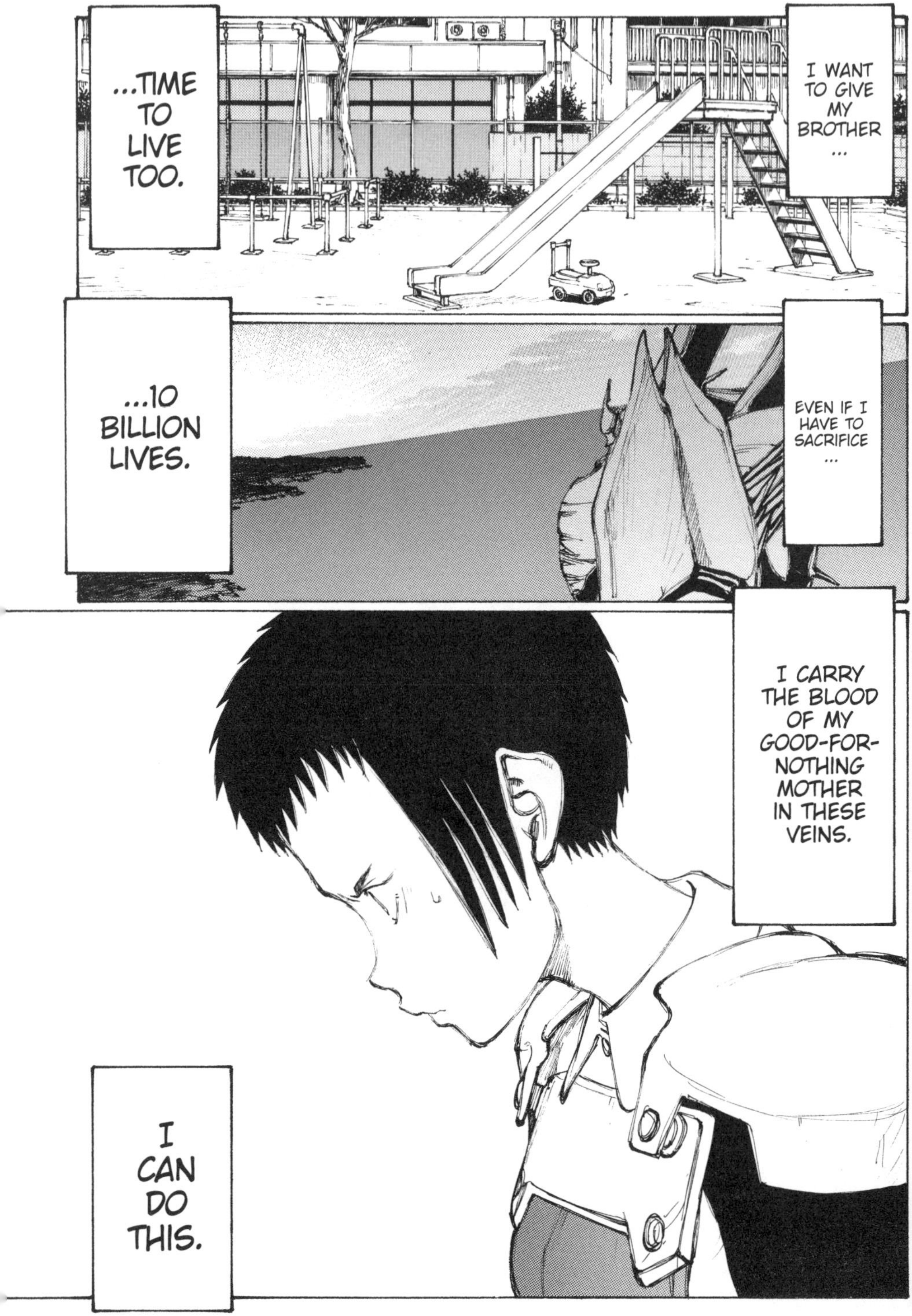
I WANT TO GIVE MY BROTHER ...
...TIME TO LIVE TOO.
EVEN IF I HAVE TO SACRIFICE ...
...10 BILLION LIVES.
I CARRY THE BLOOD OF MY GOOD-FOR-NOTHING MOTHER IN THESE VEINS.
I CAN DO THIS.

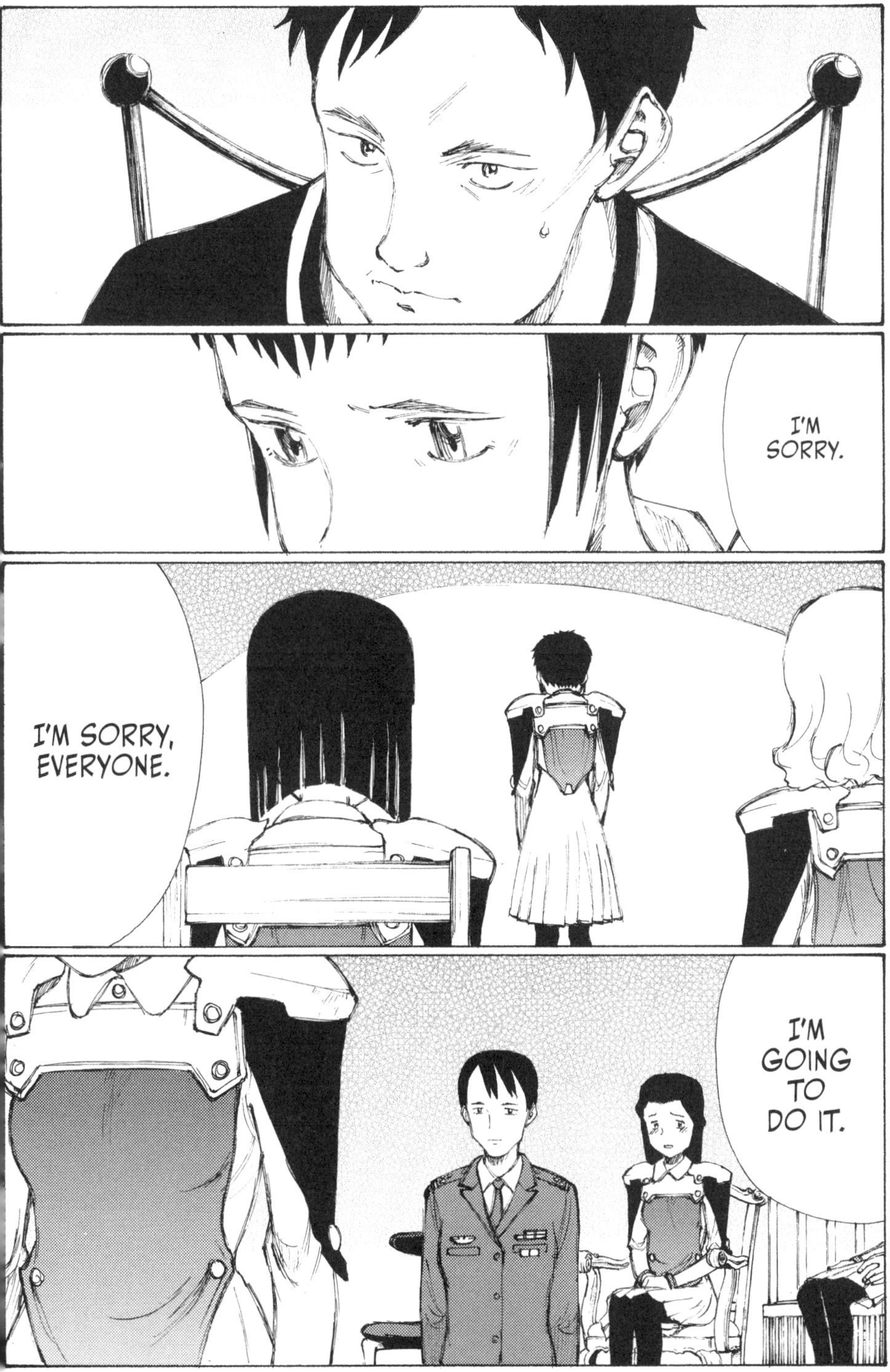
I'M SORRY.
I'M SORRY, EVERYONE.
I'M GOING TO DO IT.

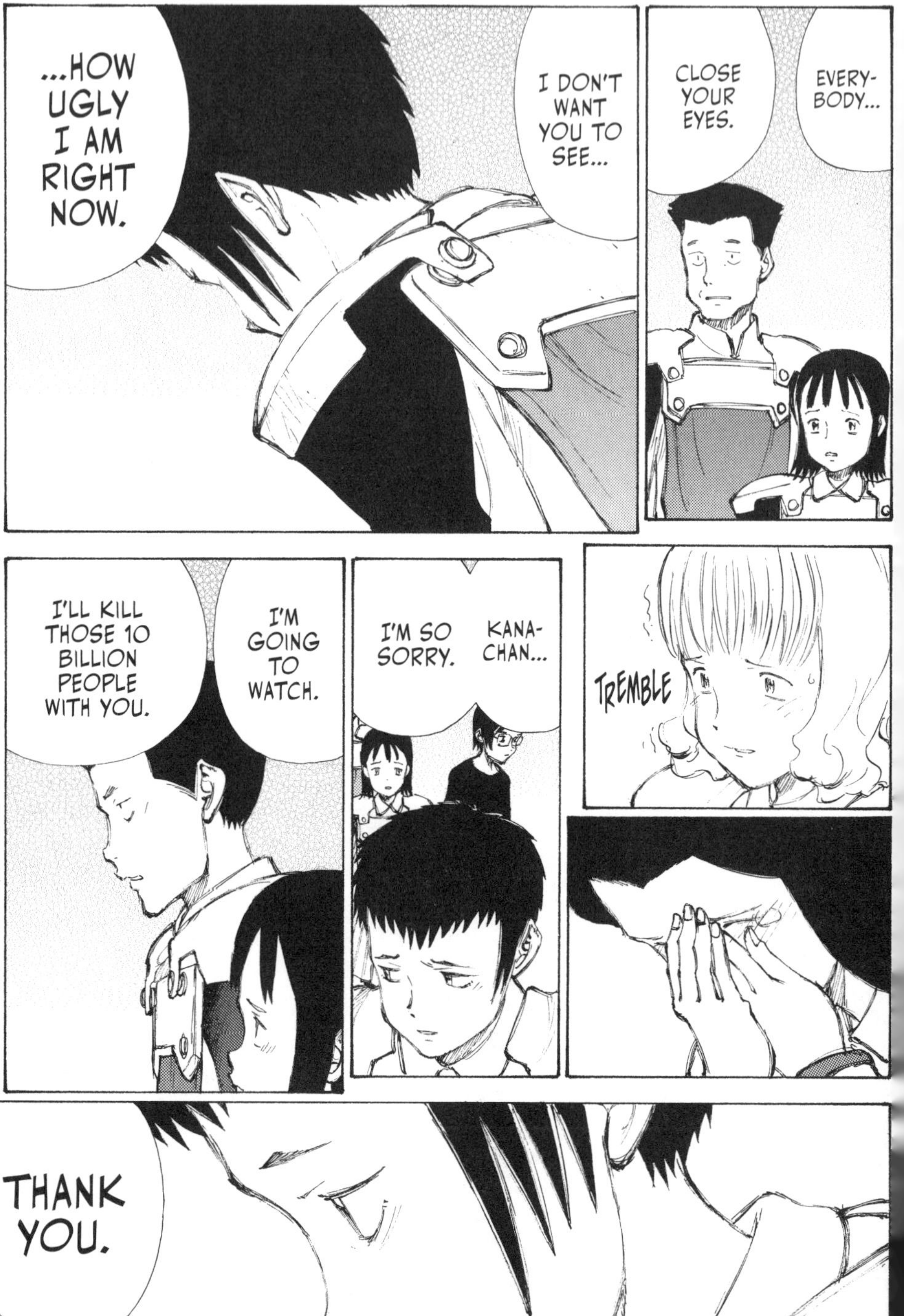
EVERY-BODY...
CLOSE YOUR EYES.
I DON'T WANT YOU TO SEE...
...HOW UGLY I AM RIGHT NOW.
TREMBLE
KANA-CHAN...
I'M SO SORRY.
I'M GOING TO WATCH.
I'LL KILL THOSE 10 BILLION PEOPLE WITH YOU.
THANK YOU.

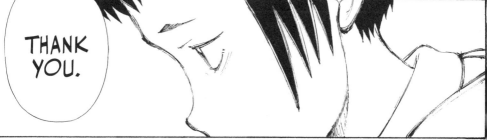

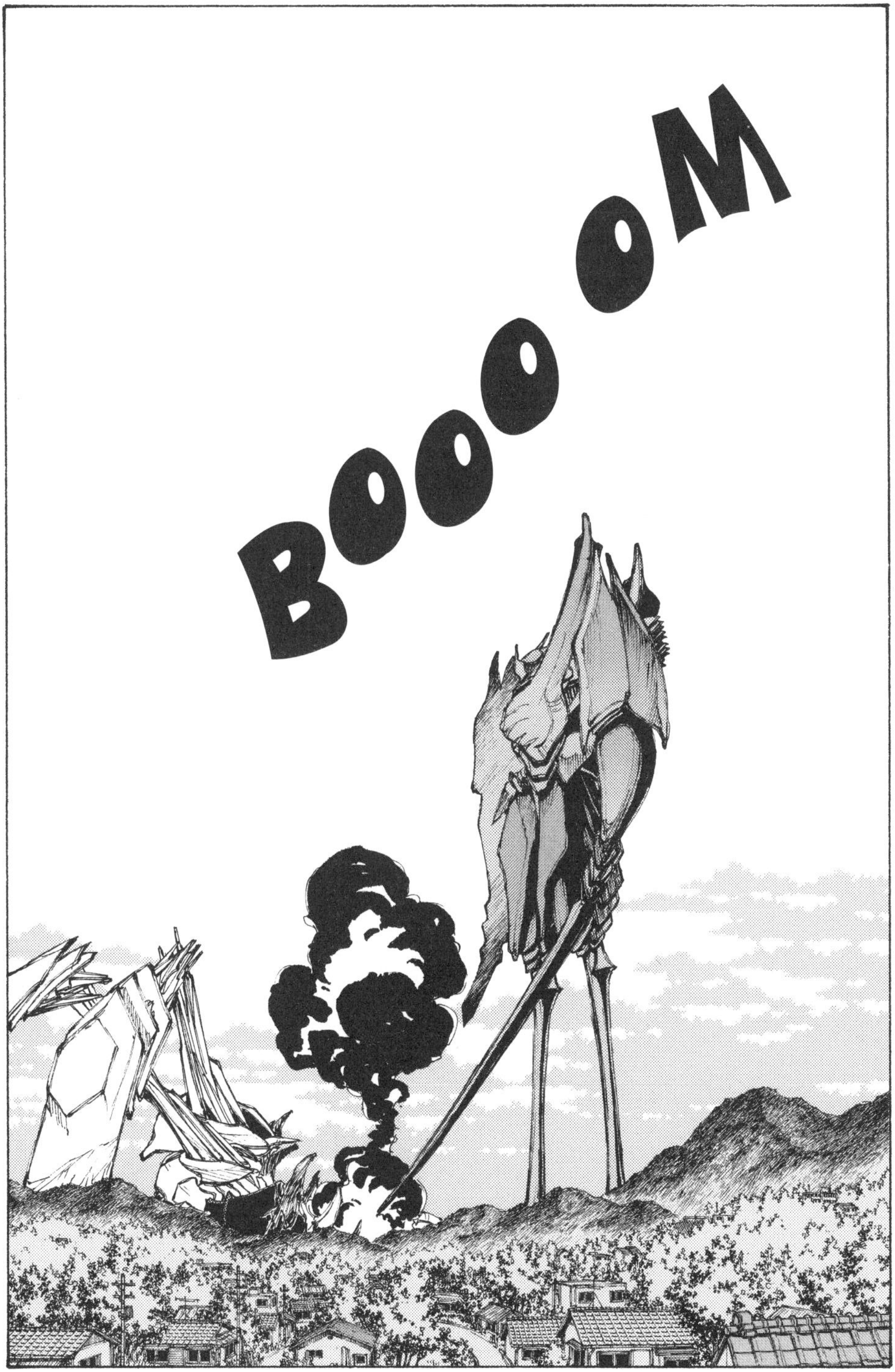
BOOOOM

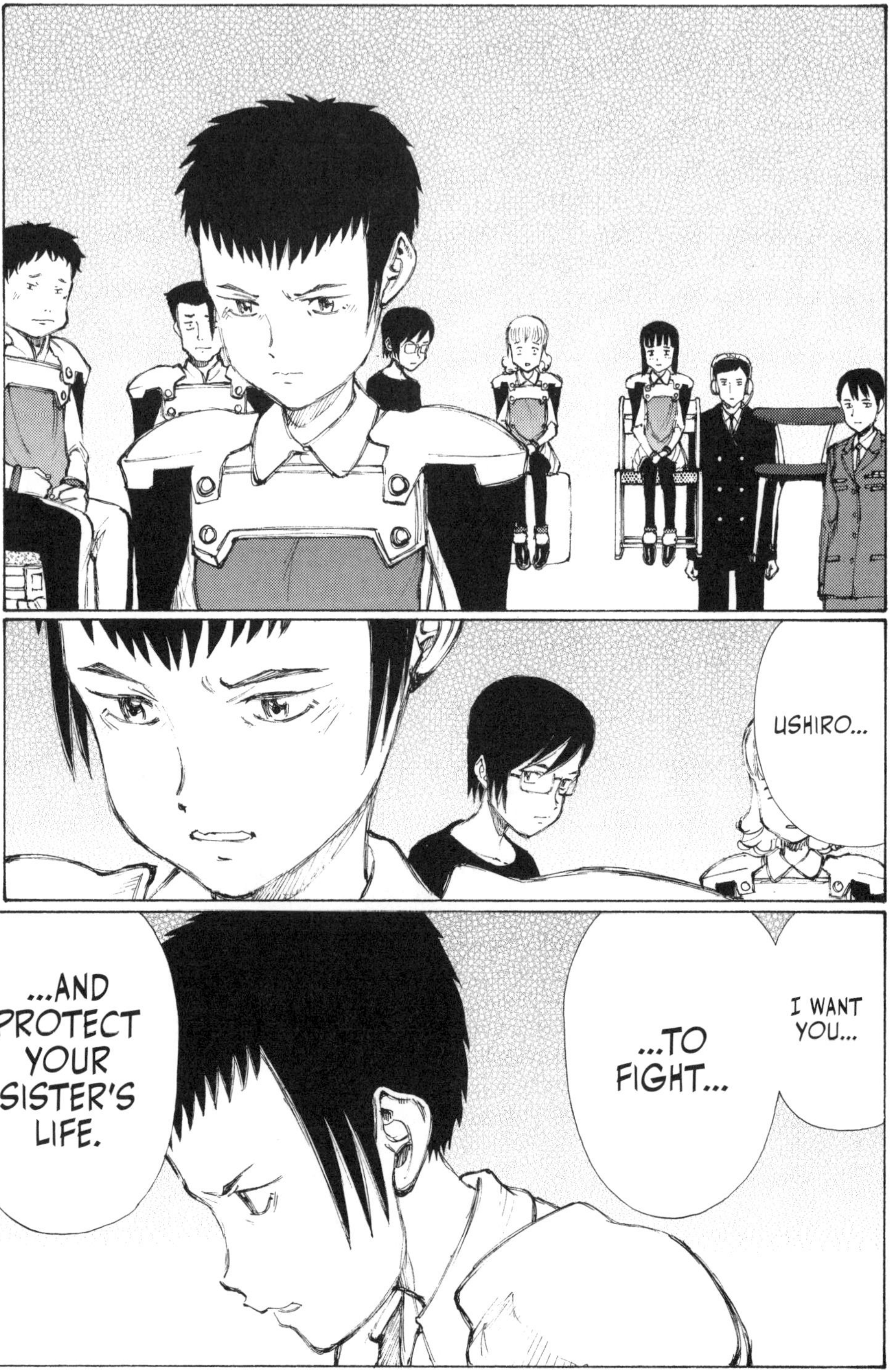
USHIRO...
I WANT YOU...
...TO FIGHT...
...AND PROTECT YOUR SISTER'S LIFE.

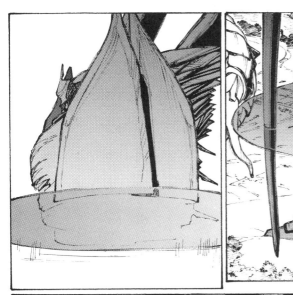

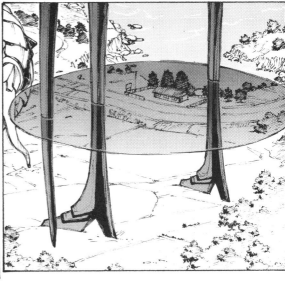

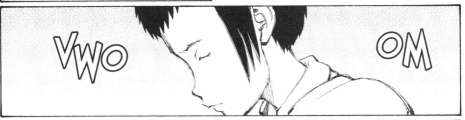

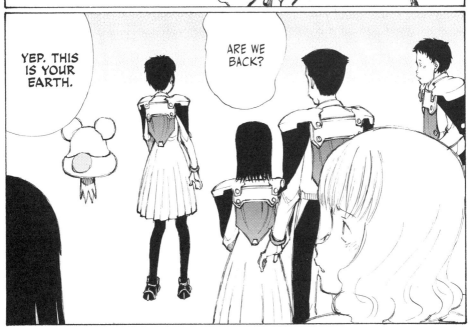

YEP. THIS IS YOUR EARTH.

ARE WE BACK?

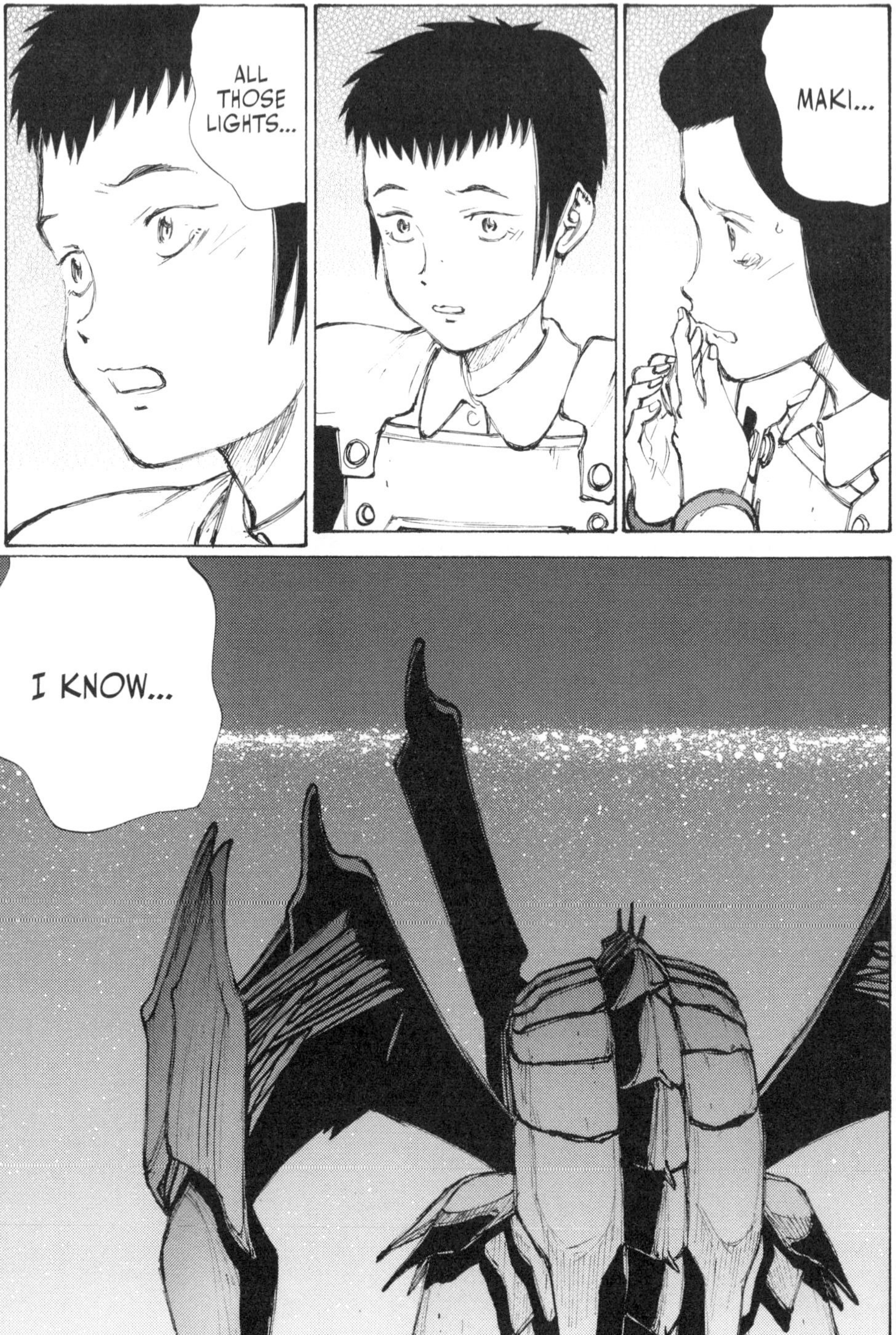
MAKI...
ALL THOSE LIGHTS...
I KNOW...

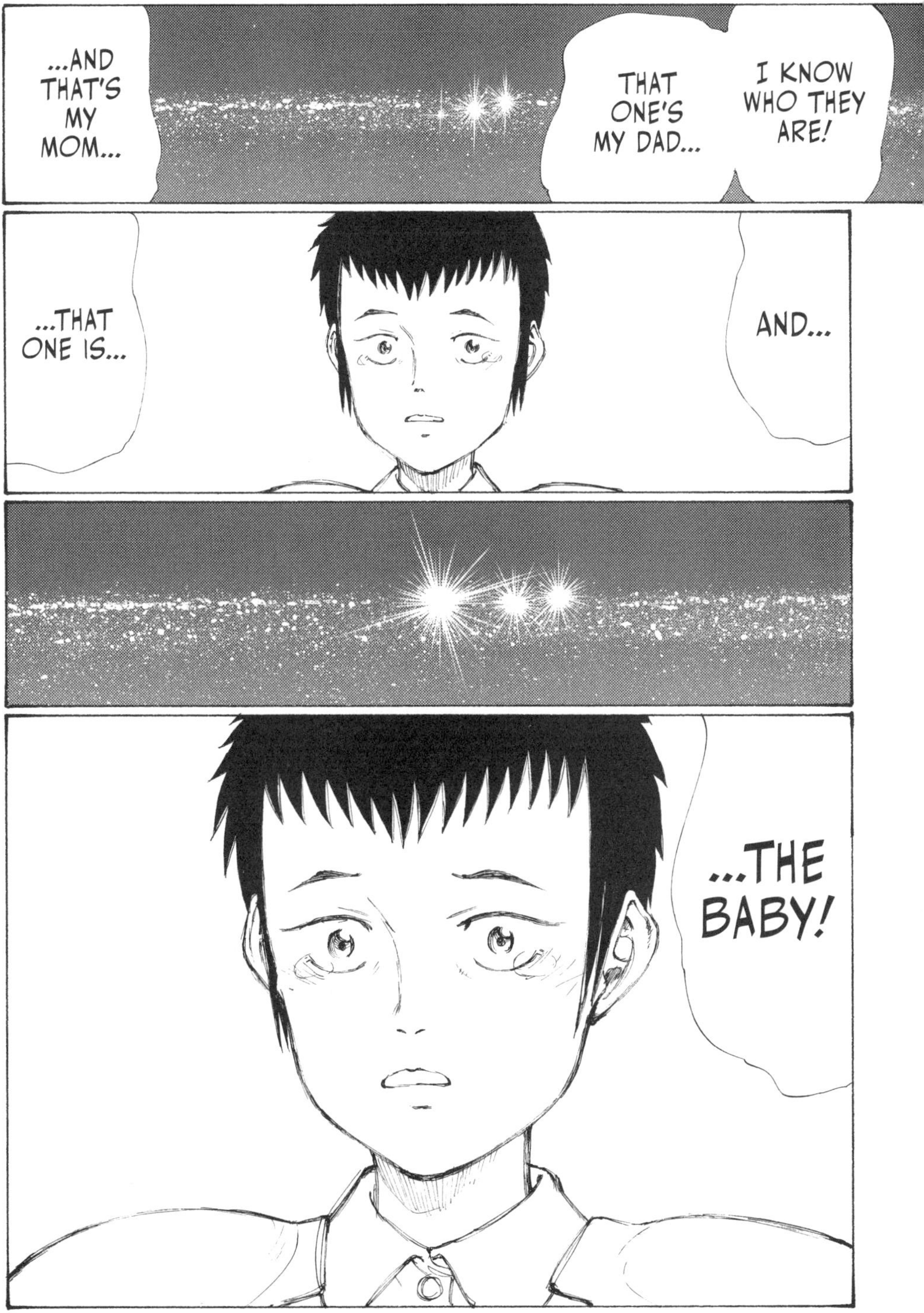
I KNOW WHO THEY ARE!
THAT ONE'S MY DAD...
...AND THAT'S MY MOM...
AND...
...THAT ONE IS...
...THE BABY!

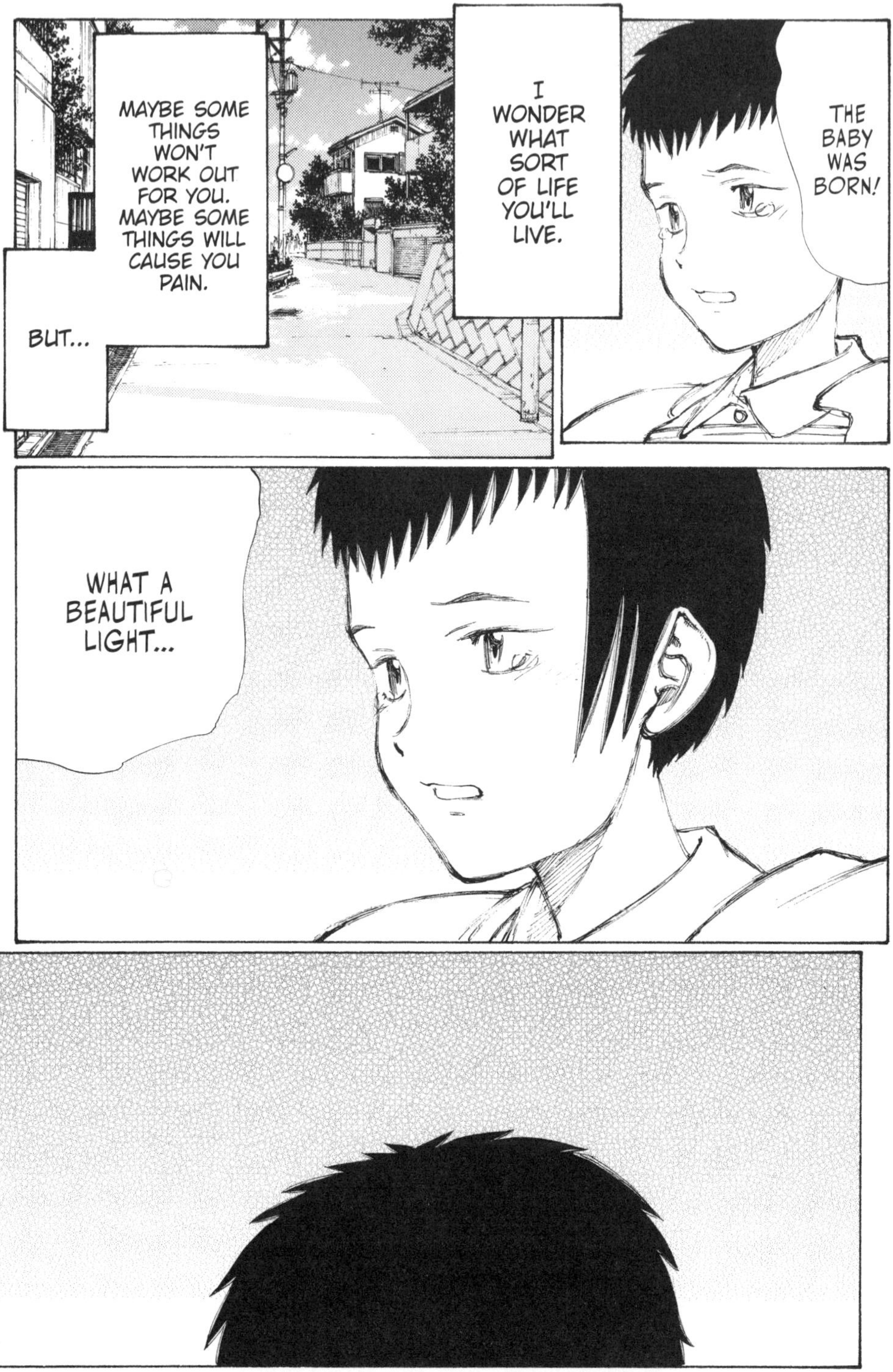
THE BABY WAS BORN!
I WONDER WHAT SORT OF LIFE YOU'LL LIVE.
MAYBE SOME THINGS WON'T WORK OUT FOR YOU. MAYBE SOME THINGS WILL CAUSE YOU PAIN.
BUT...
WHAT A BEAUTIFUL LIGHT...

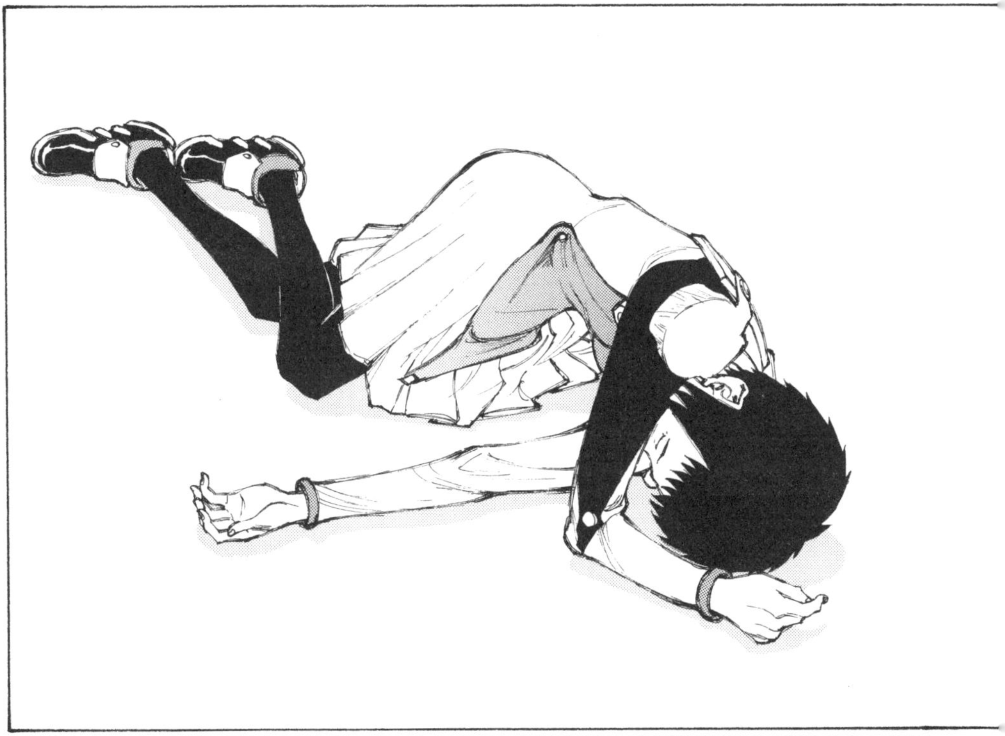

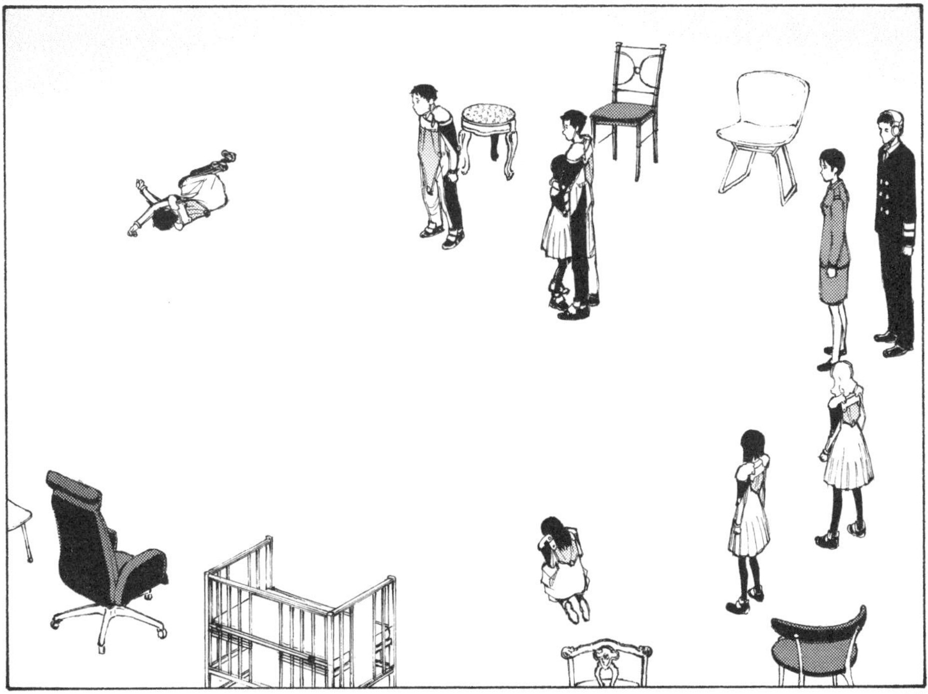

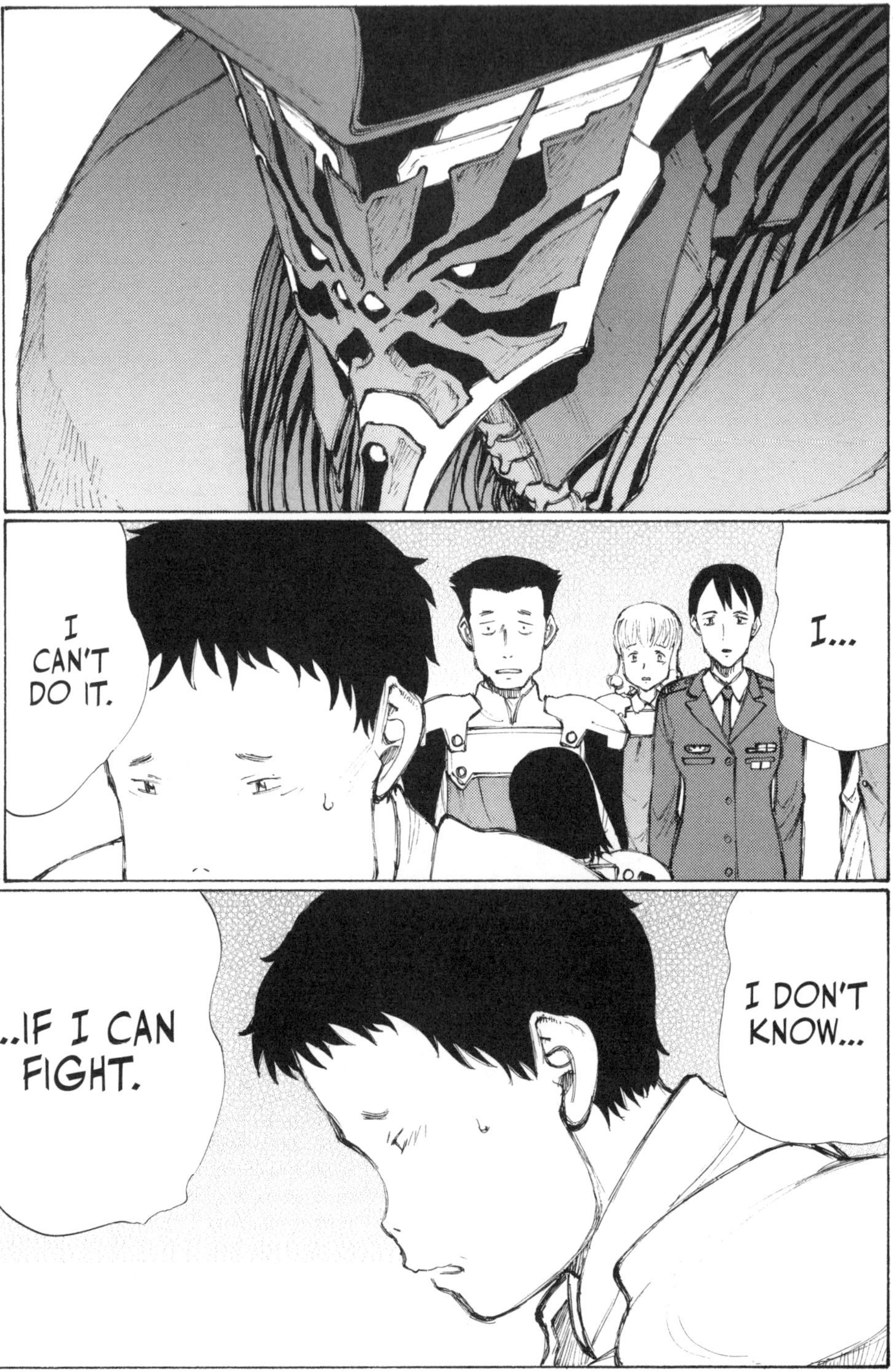
I...
I CAN'T DO IT.
I DON'T KNOW...
...IF I CAN FIGHT.

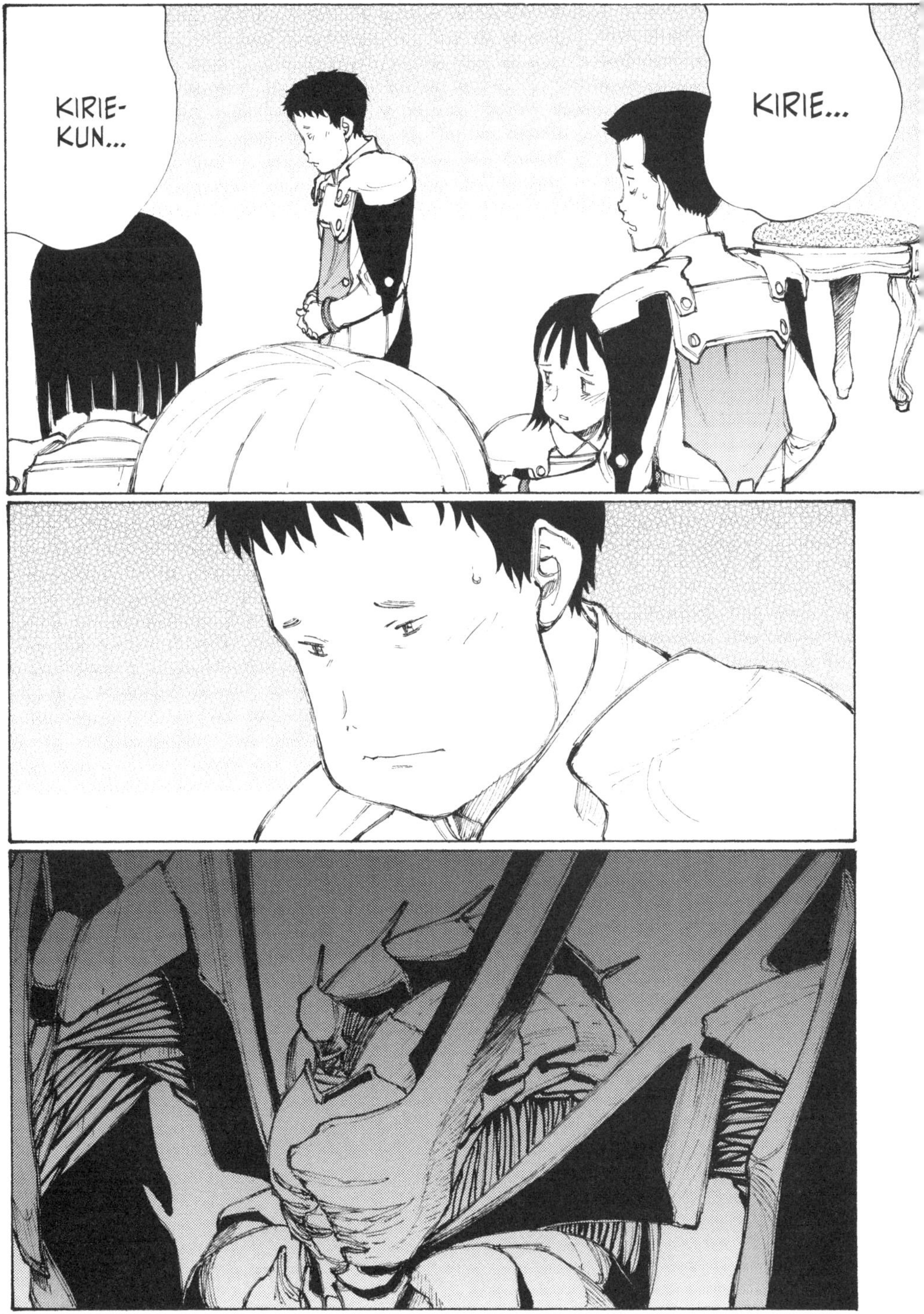
KIRIE...
KIRIE-KUN...

CHAPTER 29: YOSUKE KIRIE 1

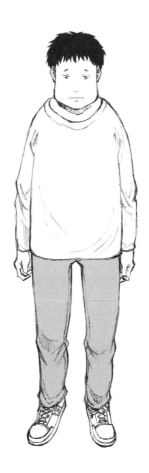

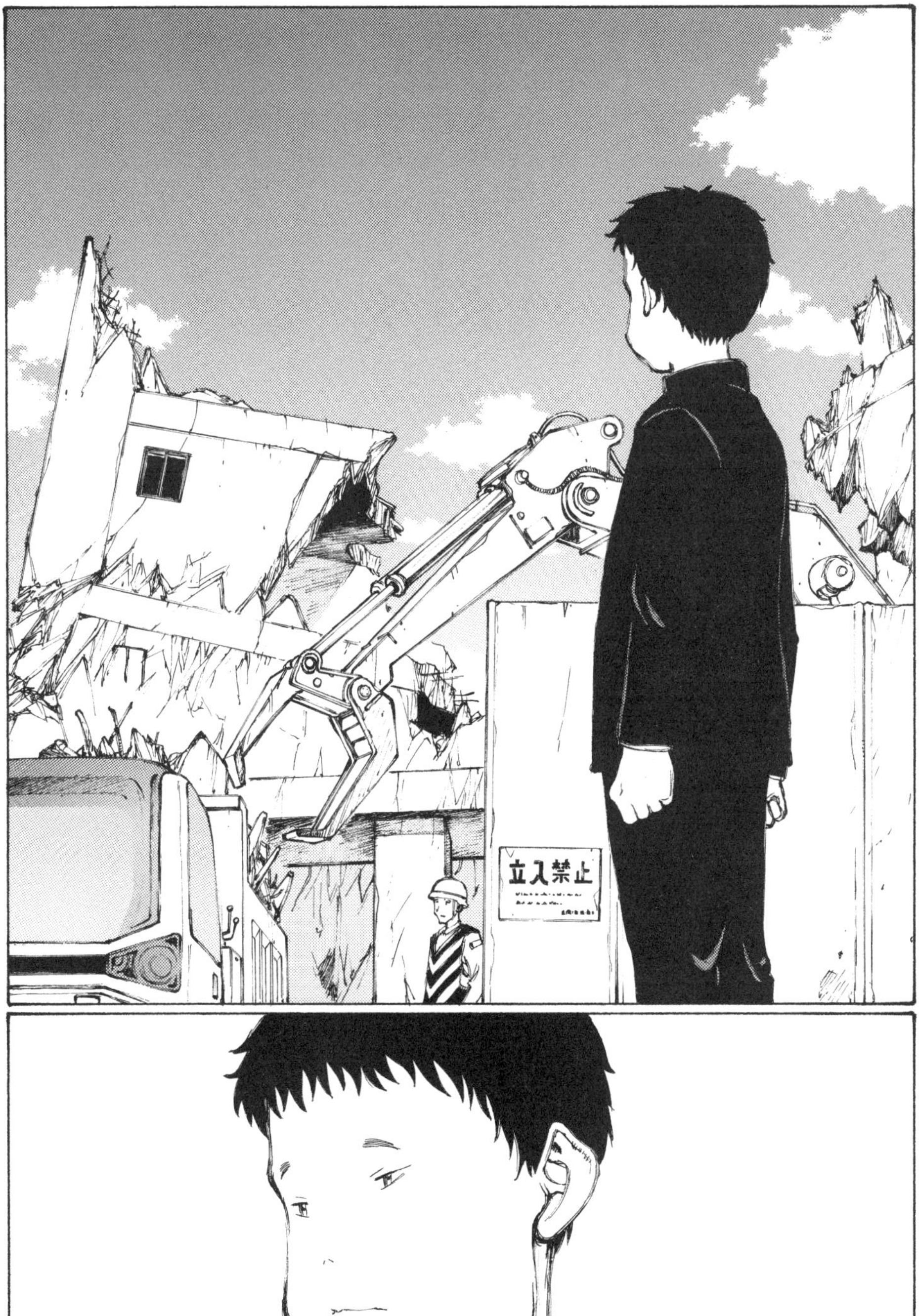
立入禁止

Sign: No Entry

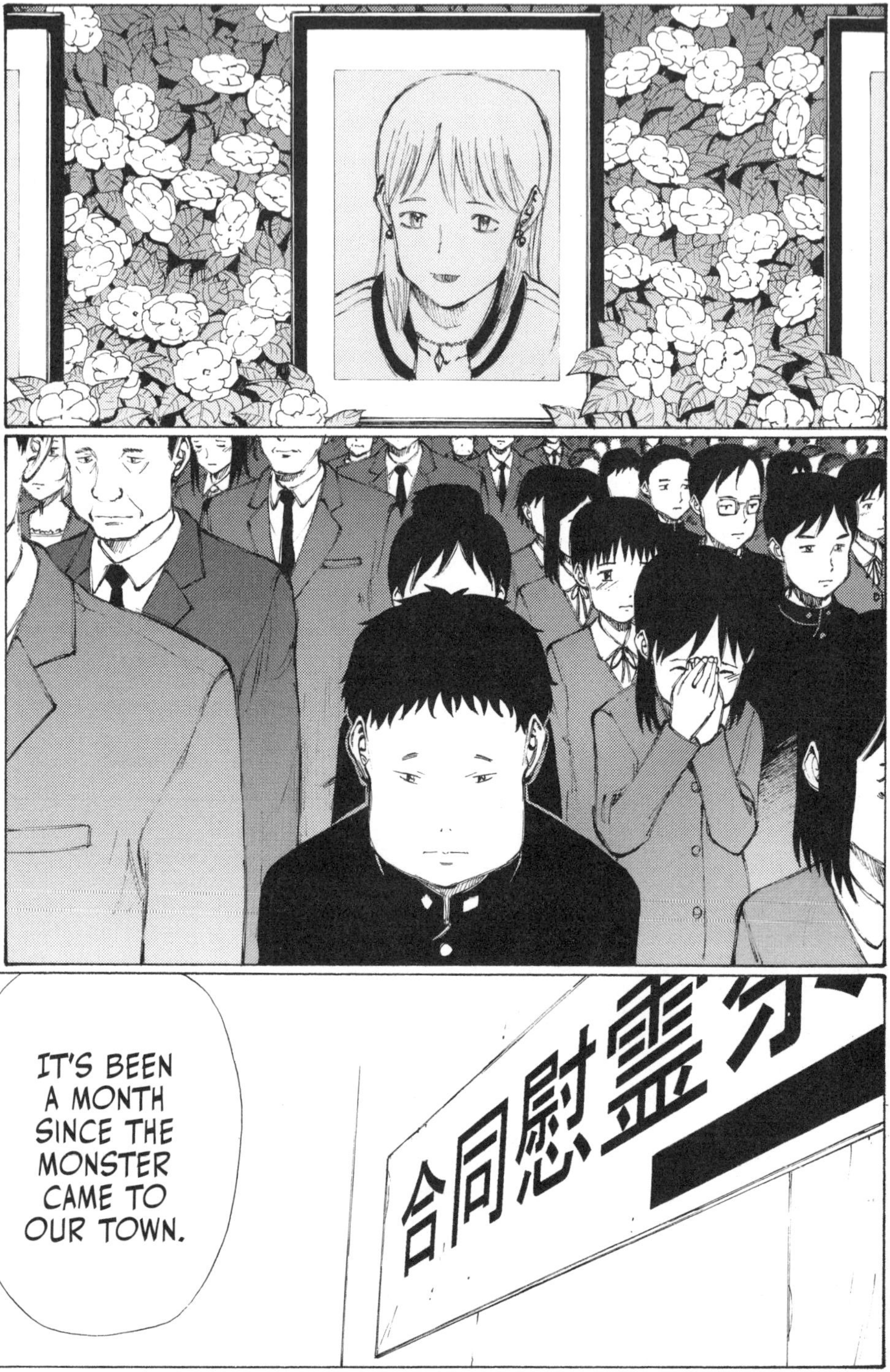
合同慰霊
IT'S BEEN A MONTH SINCE THE MONSTER CAME TO OUR TOWN.

Sign: Group Memorial Service

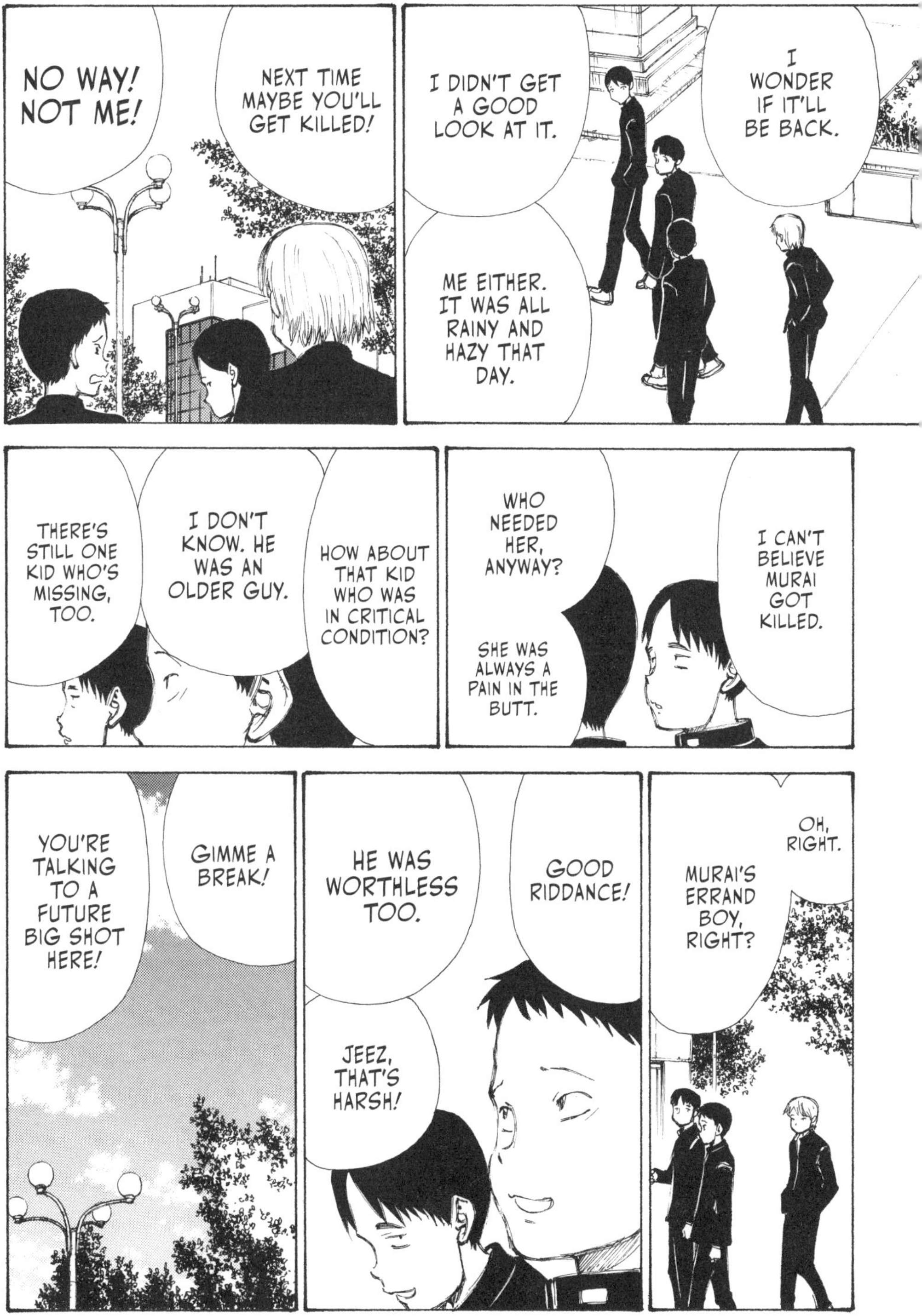
I WONDER IF IT'LL BE BACK.
I DIDN'T GET A GOOD LOOK AT IT.
ME EITHER. IT WAS ALL RAINY AND HAZY THAT DAY.
NEXT TIME MAYBE YOU'LL GET KILLED!
NO WAY! NOT ME!
I CAN'T BELIEVE MURAI GOT KILLED.
WHO NEEDED HER, ANYWAY?
SHE WAS ALWAYS A PAIN IN THE BUTT.
HOW ABOUT THAT KID WHO WAS IN CRITICAL CONDITION?
I DON'T KNOW. HE WAS AN OLDER GUY.
THERE'S STILL ONE KID WHO'S MISSING, TOO.
OH, RIGHT.
MURAI'S ERRAND BOY, RIGHT?
GOOD RIDDANCE!
HE WAS WORTHLESS TOO.
JEEZ, THAT'S HARSH!
GIMME A BREAK!
YOU'RE TALKING TO A FUTURE BIG SHOT HERE!

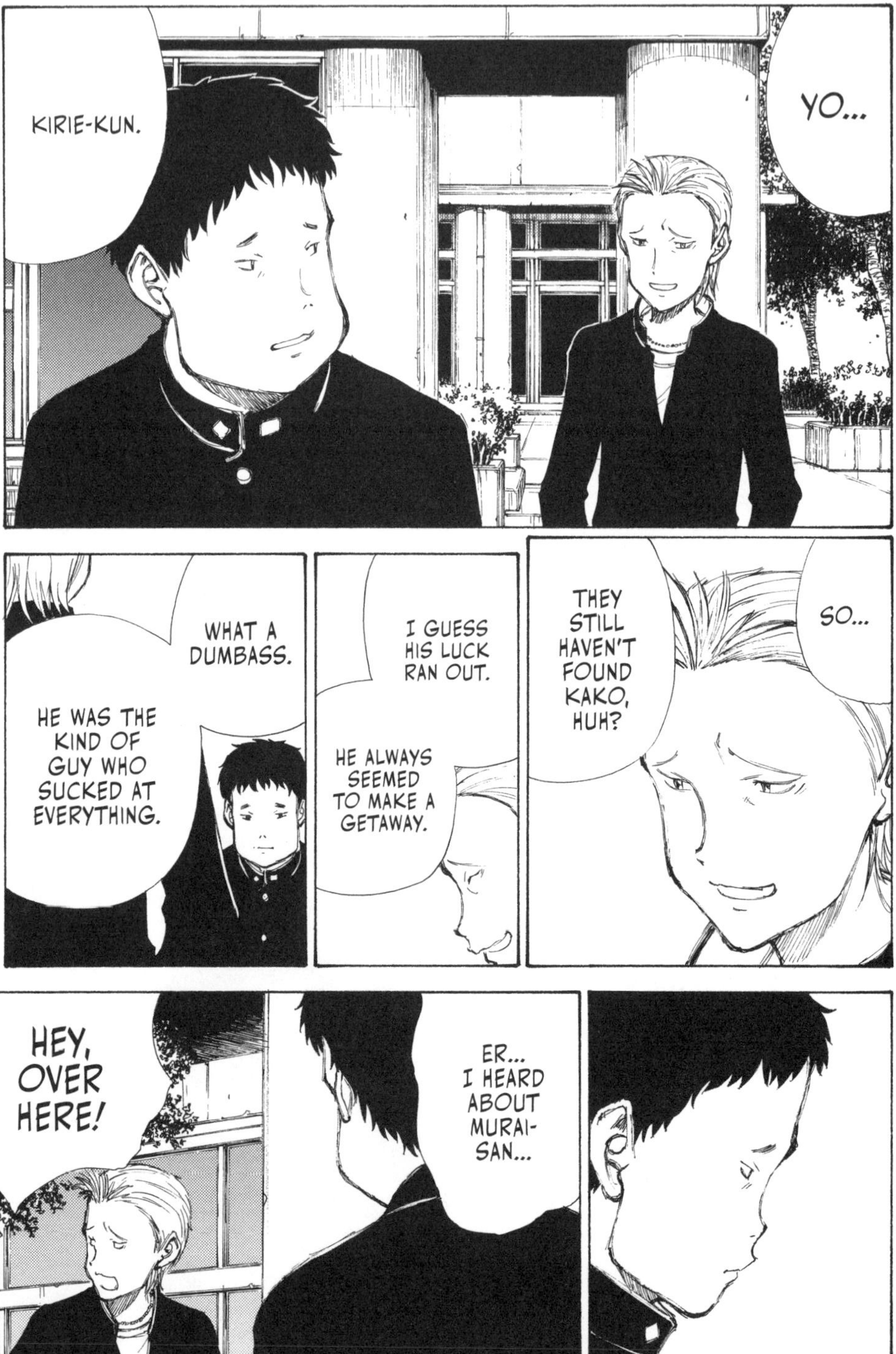
YO...
KIRIE-KUN.
SO...
THEY STILL HAVEN'T FOUND KAKO, HUH?
I GUESS HIS LUCK RAN OUT.
HE ALWAYS SEEMED TO MAKE A GETAWAY.
WHAT A DUMBASS.
HE WAS THE KIND OF GUY WHO SUCKED AT EVERYTHING.
ER... I HEARD ABOUT MURAI-SAN...
HEY, OVER HERE!

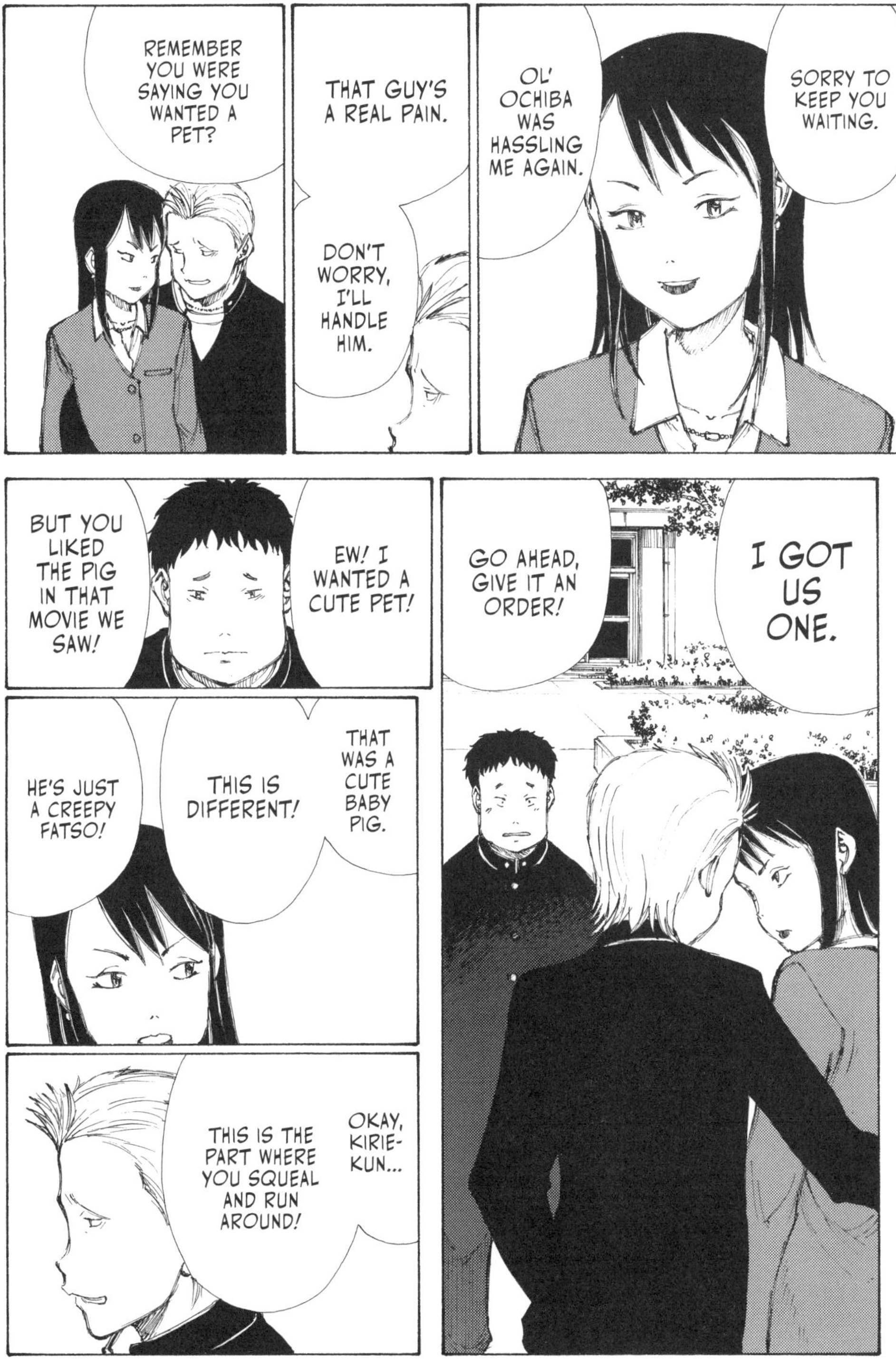
SORRY TO KEEP YOU WAITING.
OL' OCHIBA WAS HASSLING ME AGAIN.
THAT GUY'S A REAL PAIN.
DON'T WORRY, I'LL HANDLE HIM.
REMEMBER YOU WERE SAYING YOU WANTED A PET?
I GOT US ONE.
GO AHEAD, GIVE IT AN ORDER!
EW! I WANTED A CUTE PET!
BUT YOU LIKED THE PIG IN THAT MOVIE WE SAW!
THAT WAS A CUTE BABY PIG.
THIS IS DIFFERENT!
HE'S JUST A CREEPY FATSO!
OKAY, KIRIE-KUN...
THIS IS THE PART WHERE YOU SQUEAL AND RUN AROUND!

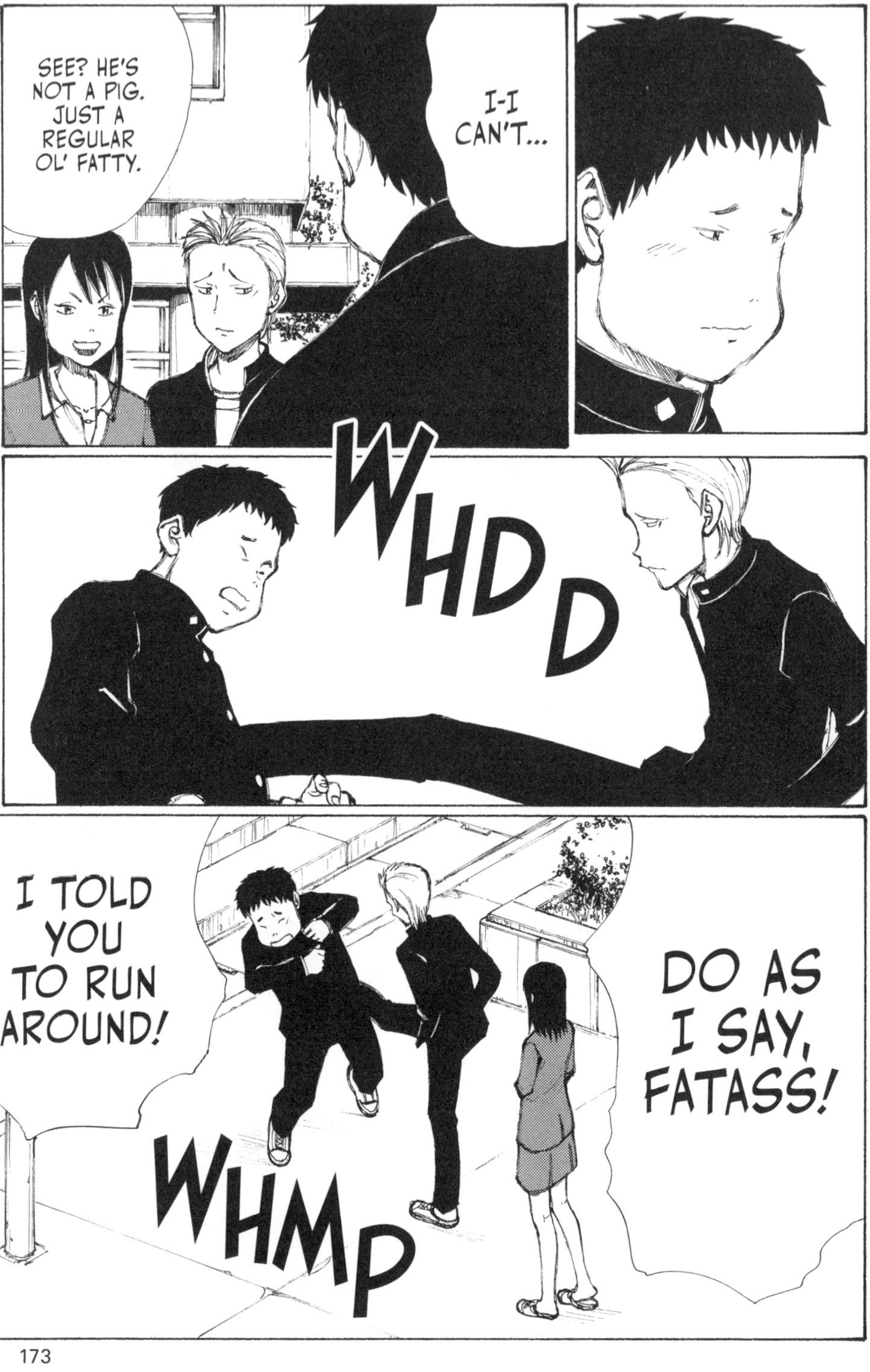
I-I CAN'T...
SEE? HE'S NOT A PIG. JUST A REGULAR OL' FATTY.
WHDD
DO AS I SAY, FATASS!
I TOLD YOU TO RUN AROUND!
WHMP

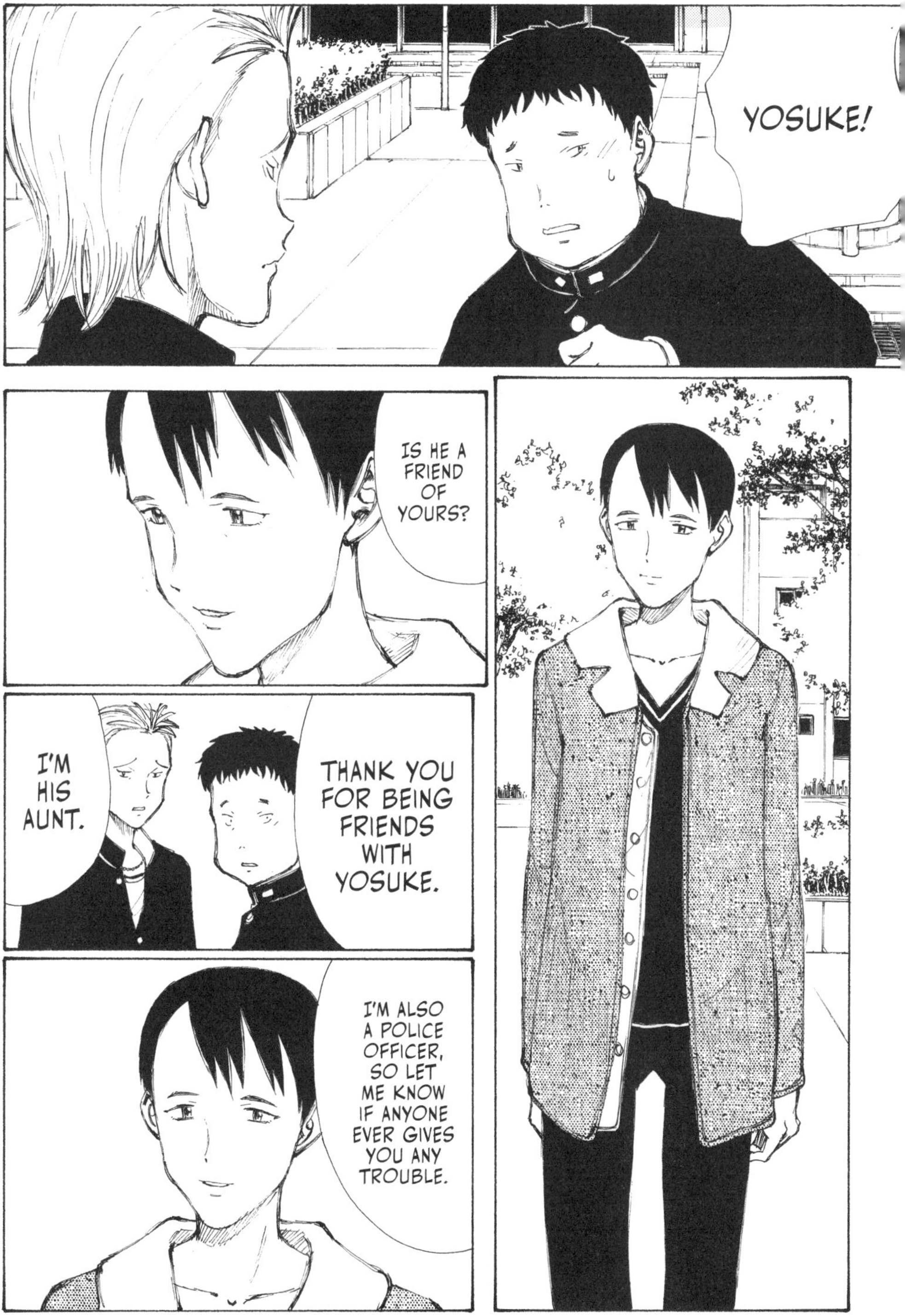
YOSUKE!
IS HE A FRIEND OF YOURS?
THANK YOU FOR BEING FRIENDS WITH YOSUKE.
I'M HIS AUNT.
I'M ALSO A POLICE OFFICER, SO LET ME KNOW IF ANYONE EVER GIVES YOU ANY TROUBLE.

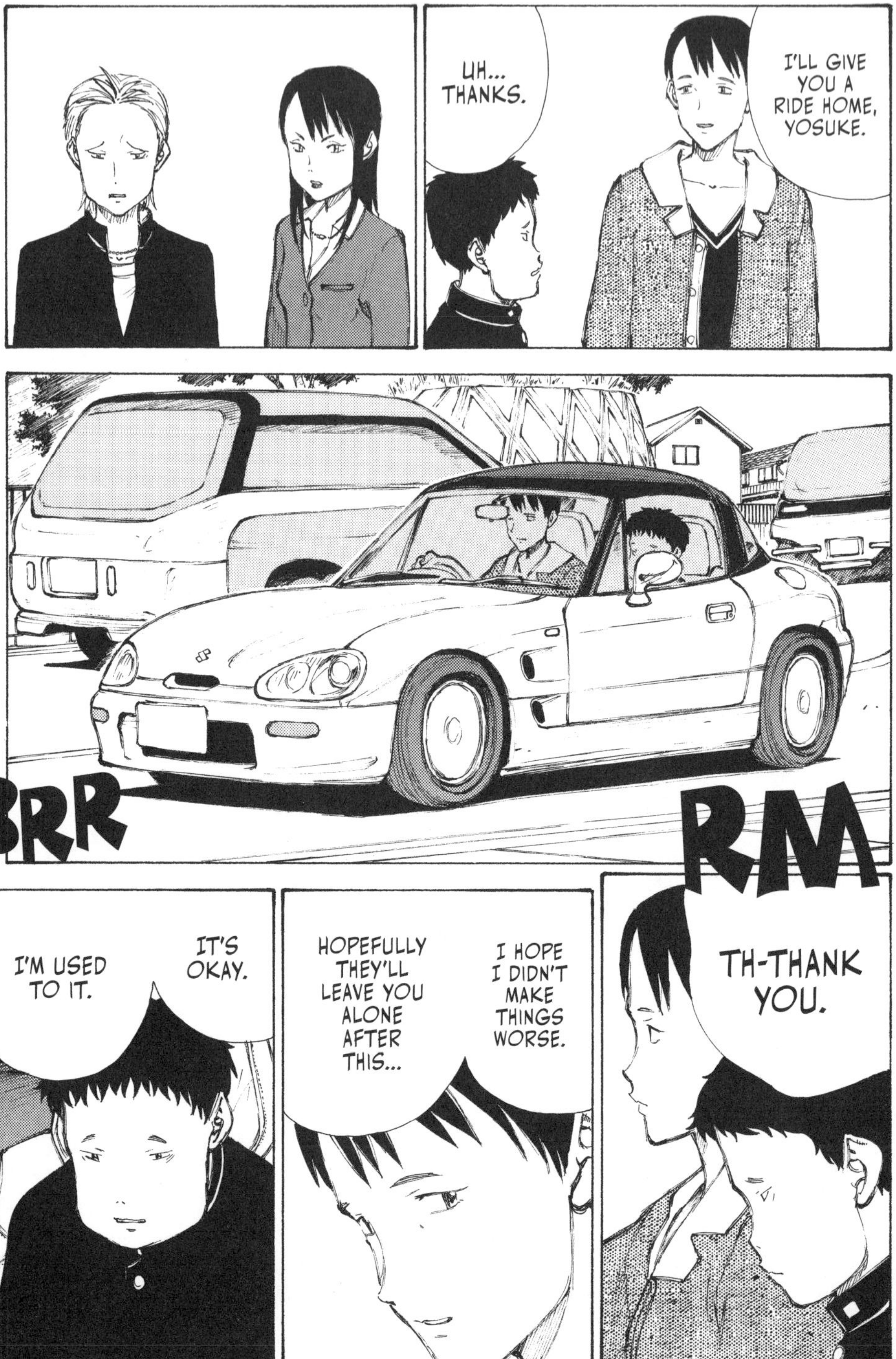
I'LL GIVE YOU A RIDE HOME, YOSUKE.
UH... THANKS.
BRR
RM
TH-THANK YOU.
I HOPE I DIDN'T MAKE THINGS WORSE.
HOPEFULLY THEY'LL LEAVE YOU ALONE AFTER THIS...
IT'S OKAY.
I'M USED TO IT.

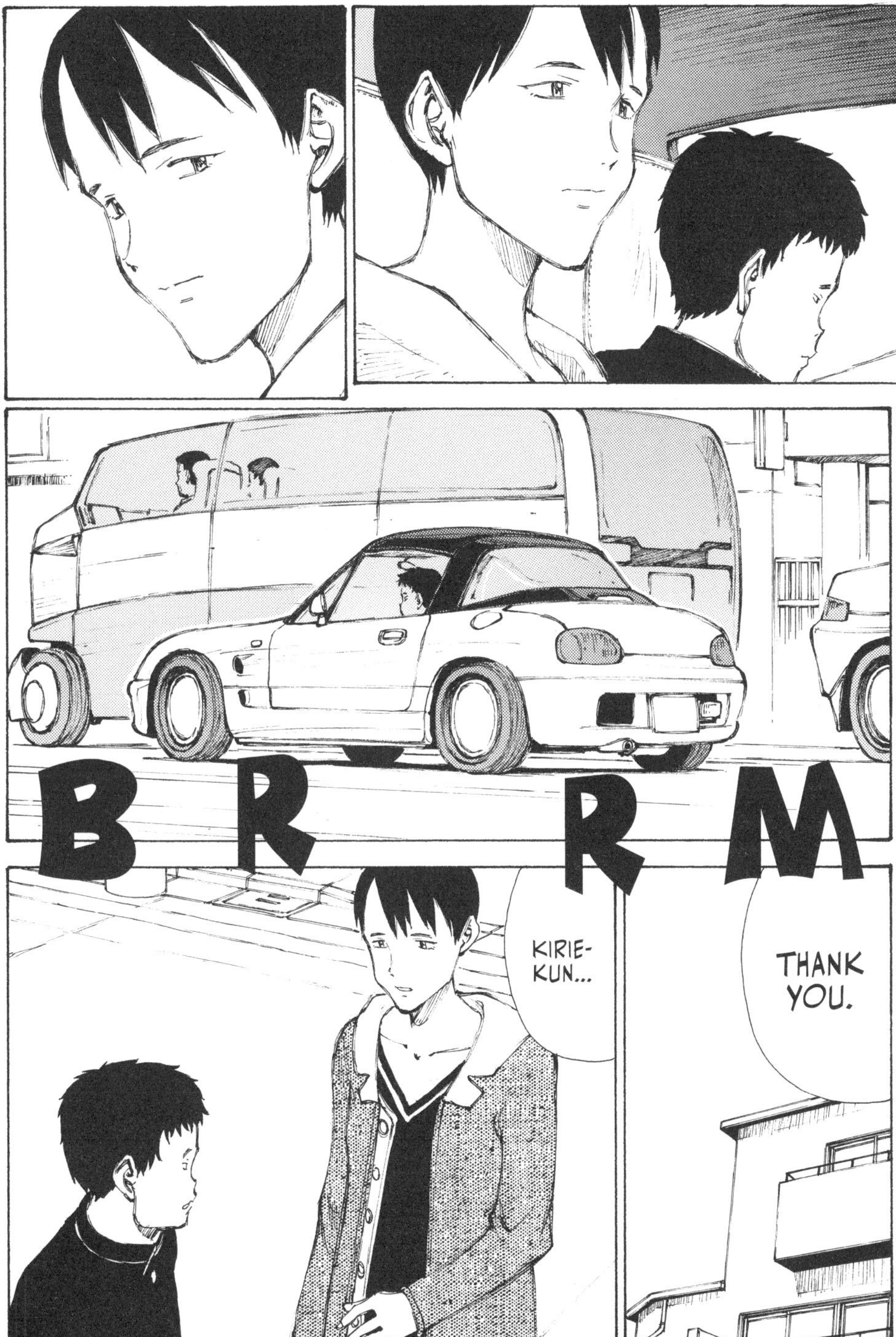
BRRM
THANK YOU.
KIRIE-KUN...

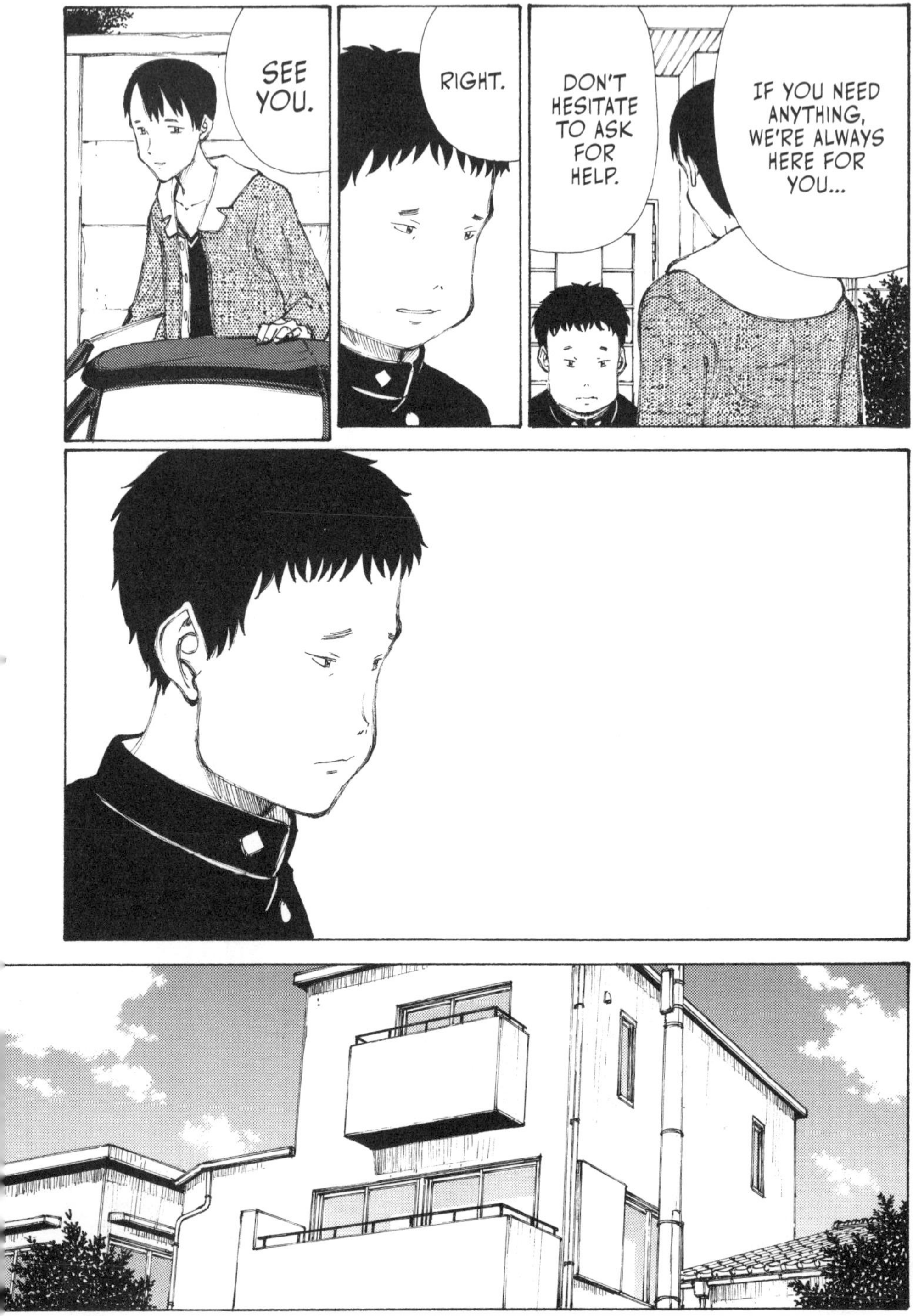
IF YOU NEED ANYTHING, WE'RE ALWAYS HERE FOR YOU...
DON'T HESITATE TO ASK FOR HELP.
RIGHT.
SEE YOU.

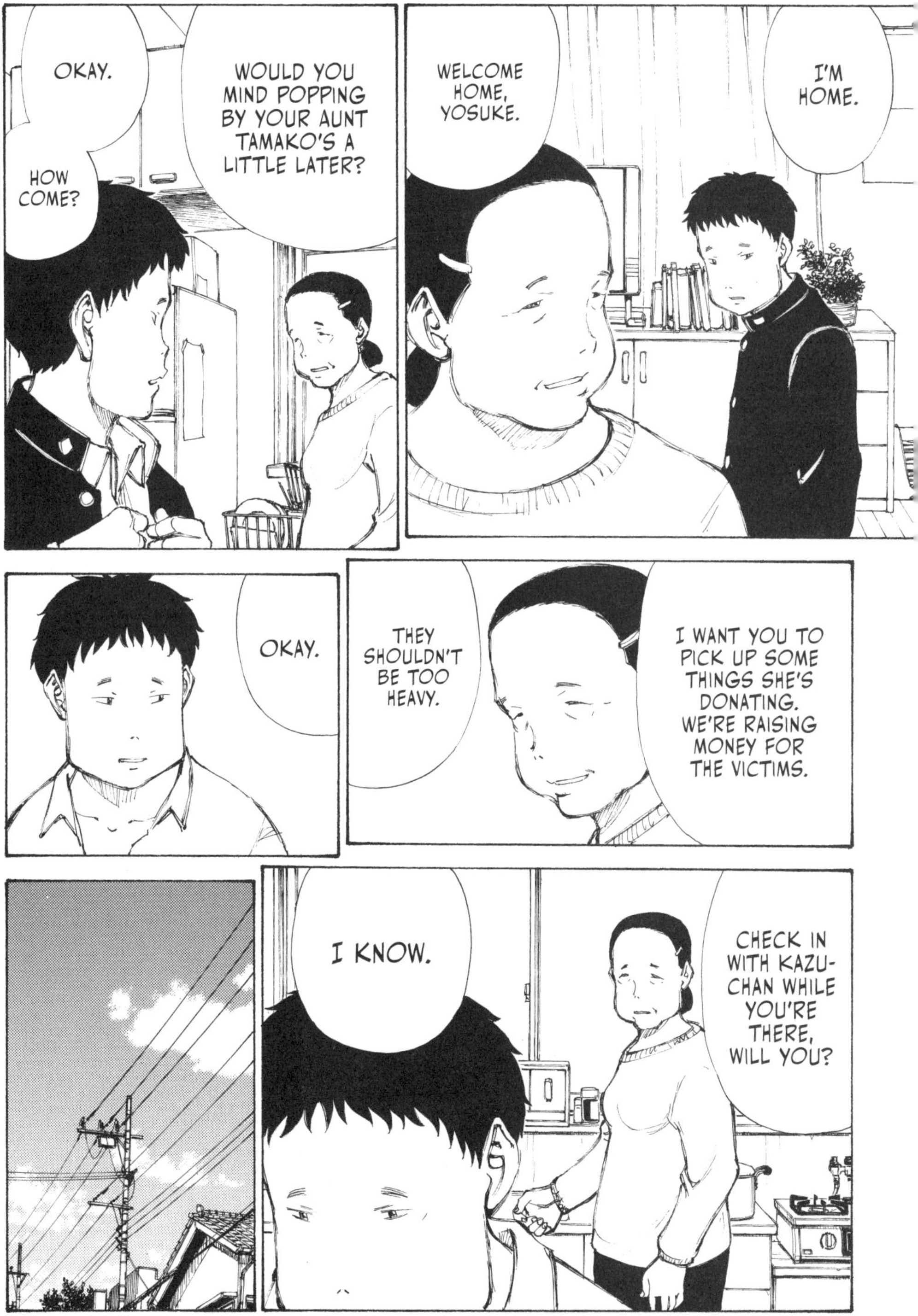
I'M HOME.
WELCOME HOME, YOSUKE.
WOULD YOU MIND POPPING BY YOUR AUNT TAMAKO'S A LITTLE LATER?
OKAY.
HOW COME?
I WANT YOU TO PICK UP SOME THINGS SHE'S DONATING. WE'RE RAISING MONEY FOR THE VICTIMS.
THEY SHOULDN'T BE TOO HEAVY.
OKAY.
CHECK IN WITH KAZU-CHAN WHILE YOU'RE THERE, WILL YOU?
I KNOW.

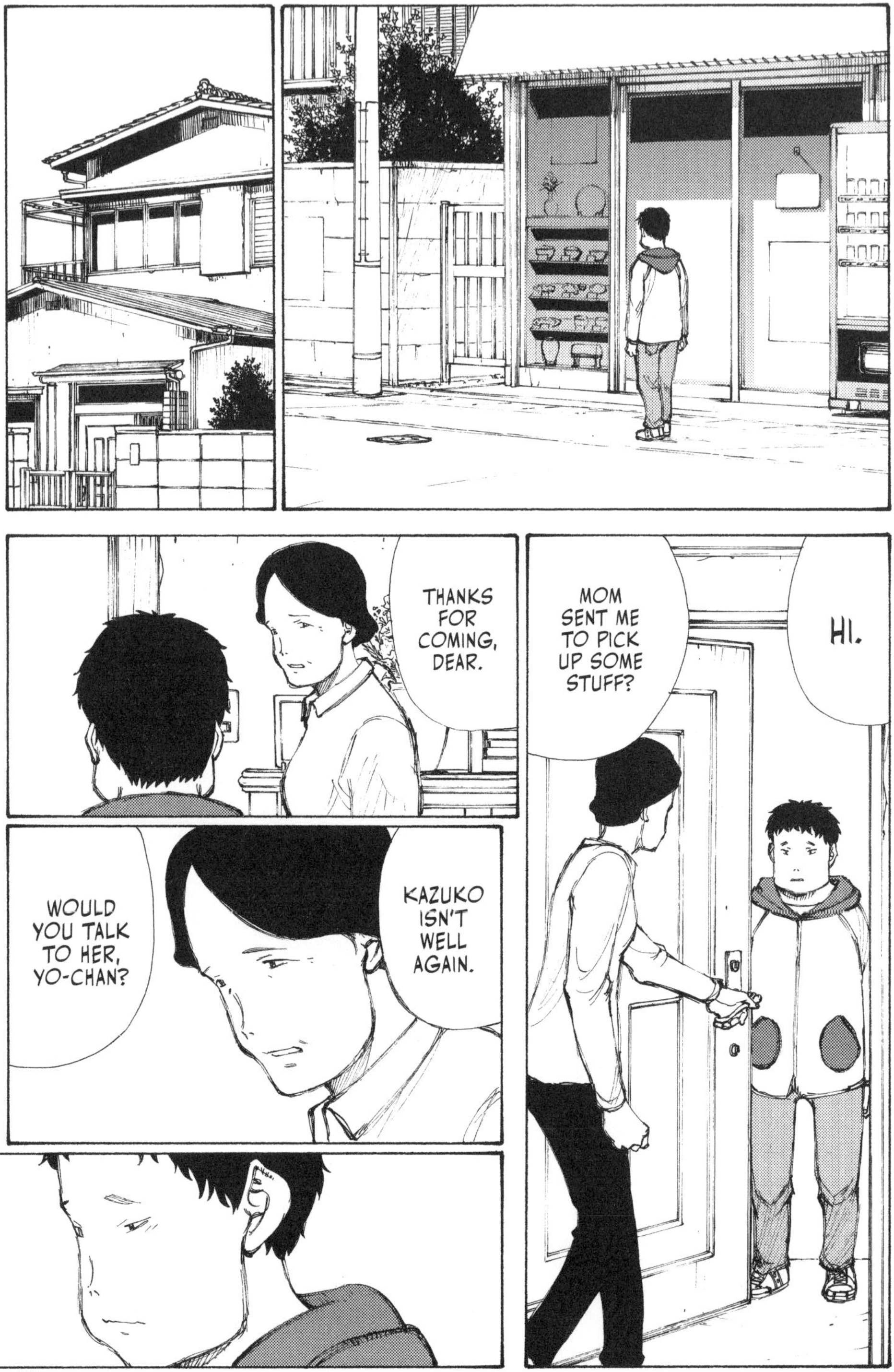
HI.
MOM SENT ME TO PICK UP SOME STUFF?
THANKS FOR COMING, DEAR.
KAZUKO ISN'T WELL AGAIN.
WOULD YOU TALK TO HER, YO-CHAN?

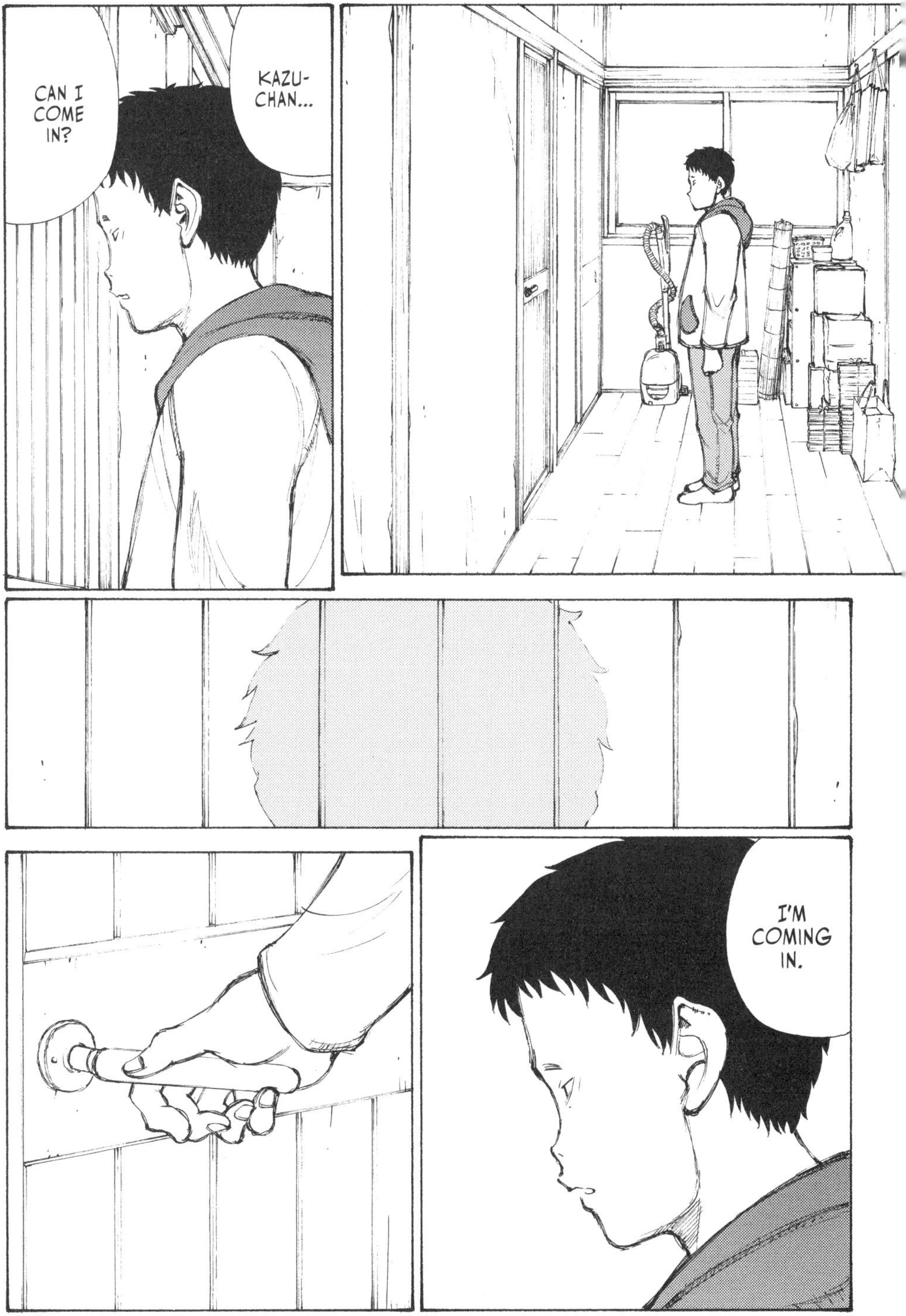
KAZU-CHAN...
CAN I COME IN?
I'M COMING IN.

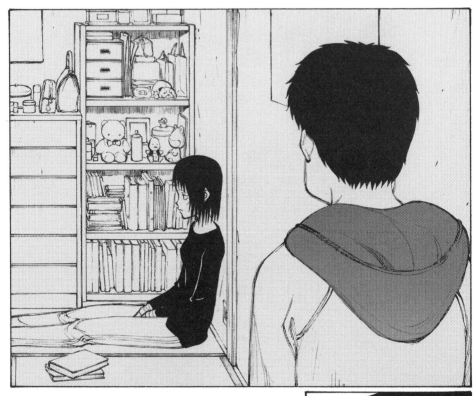

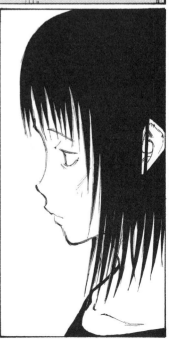

DID YOU DO IT AGAIN?

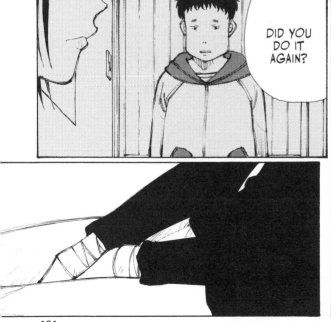

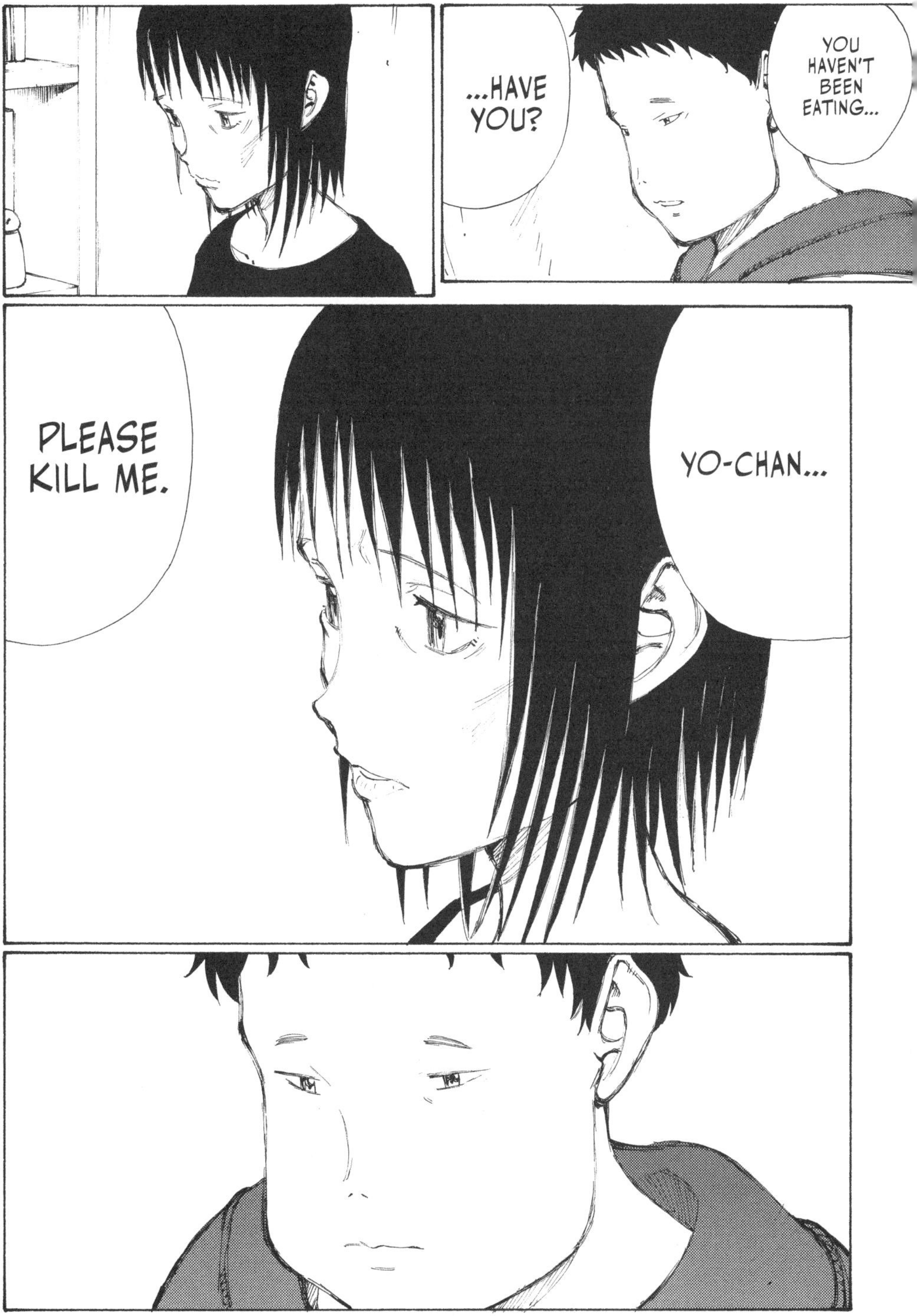
YOU HAVEN'T BEEN EATING...
...HAVE YOU?
YO-CHAN...
PLEASE KILL ME.

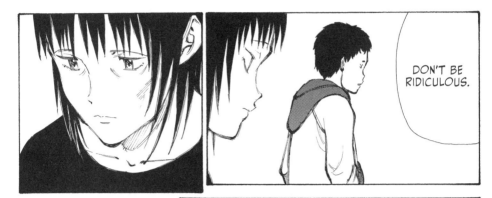

DON'T BE RIDICULOUS.

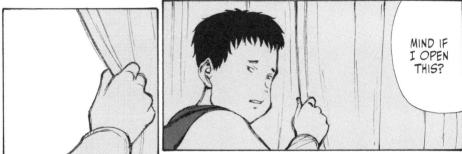

MIND IF I OPEN THIS?

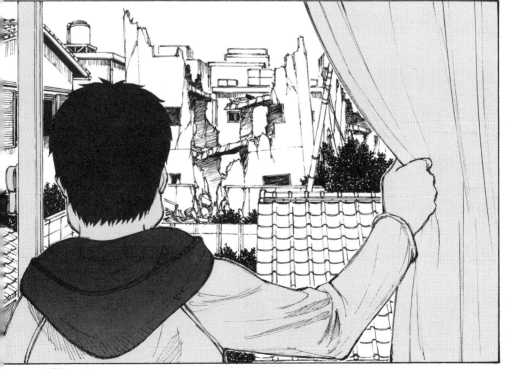

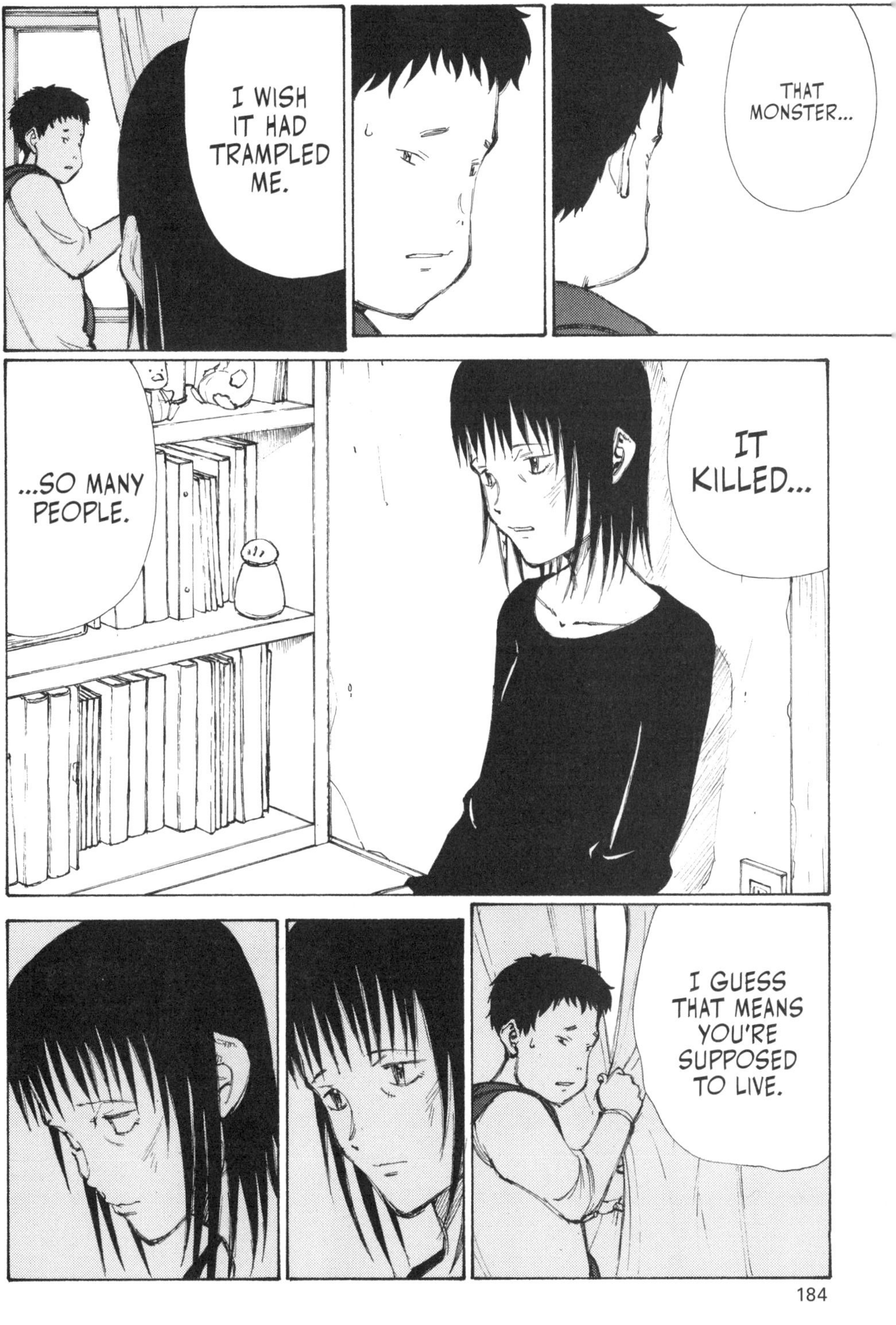
THAT MONSTER...
I WISH IT HAD TRAMPLED ME.
IT KILLED...
...SO MANY PEOPLE.
I GUESS THAT MEANS YOU'RE SUPPOSED TO LIVE.

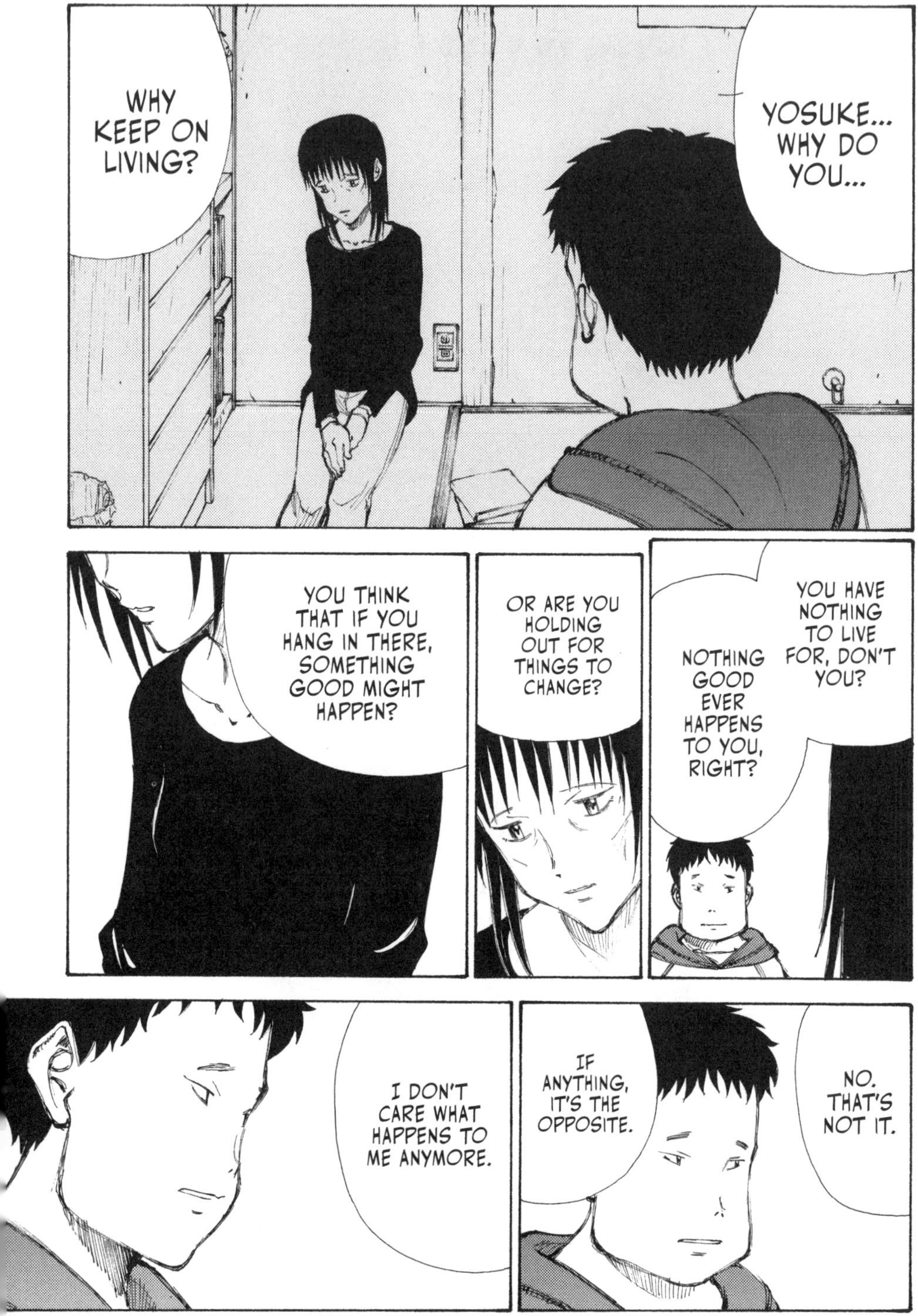
YOSUKE... WHY DO YOU...
WHY KEEP ON LIVING?
YOU HAVE NOTHING TO LIVE FOR, DON'T YOU?
NOTHING GOOD EVER HAPPENS TO YOU, RIGHT?
OR ARE YOU HOLDING OUT FOR THINGS TO CHANGE?
YOU THINK THAT IF YOU HANG IN THERE, SOMETHING GOOD MIGHT HAPPEN?
NO. THAT'S NOT IT.
IF ANYTHING, IT'S THE OPPOSITE.
I DON'T CARE WHAT HAPPENS TO ME ANYMORE.

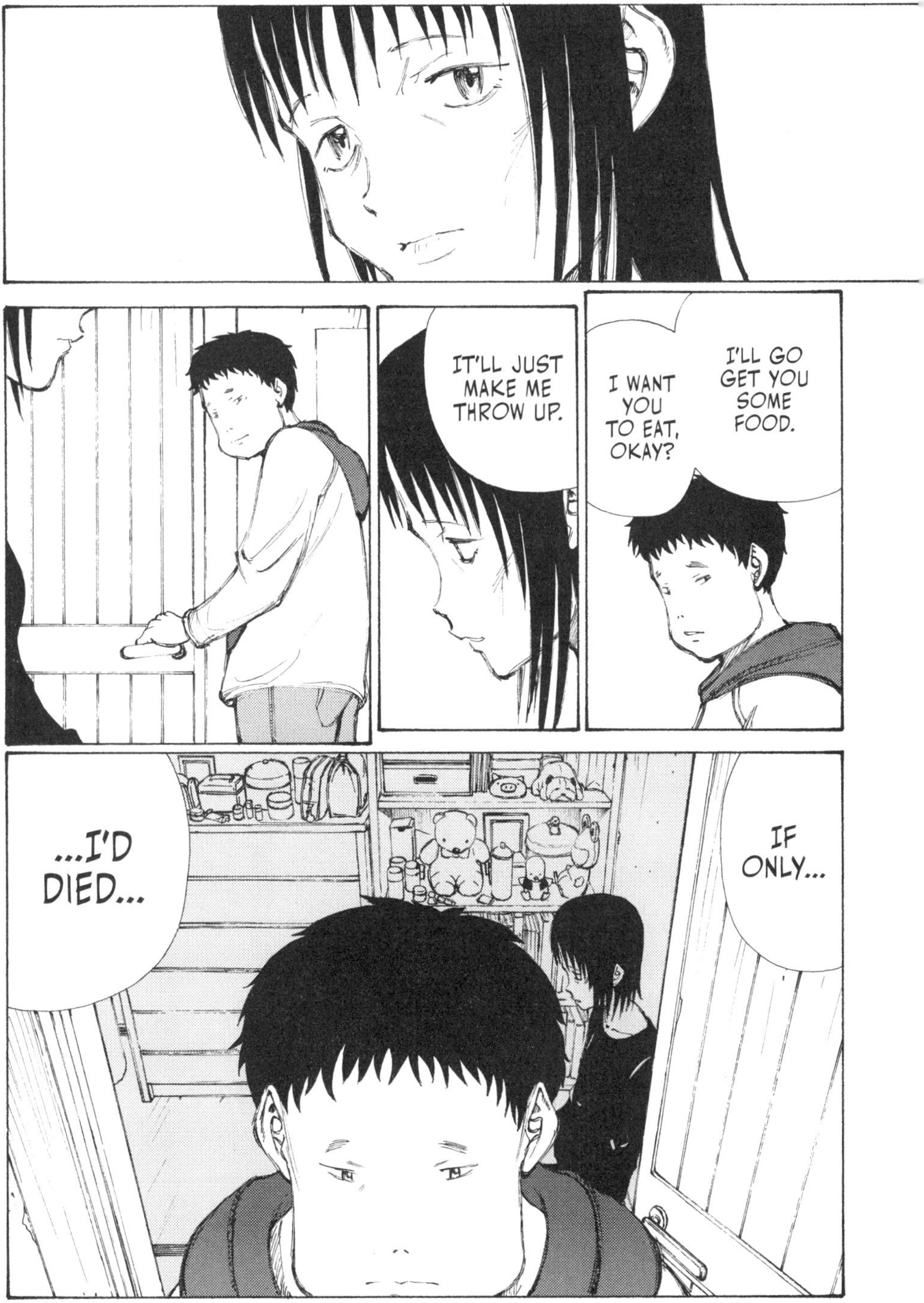
I'LL GO GET YOU SOME FOOD.
I WANT YOU TO EAT, OKAY?
IT'LL JUST MAKE ME THROW UP.
IF ONLY...
...I'D DIED...

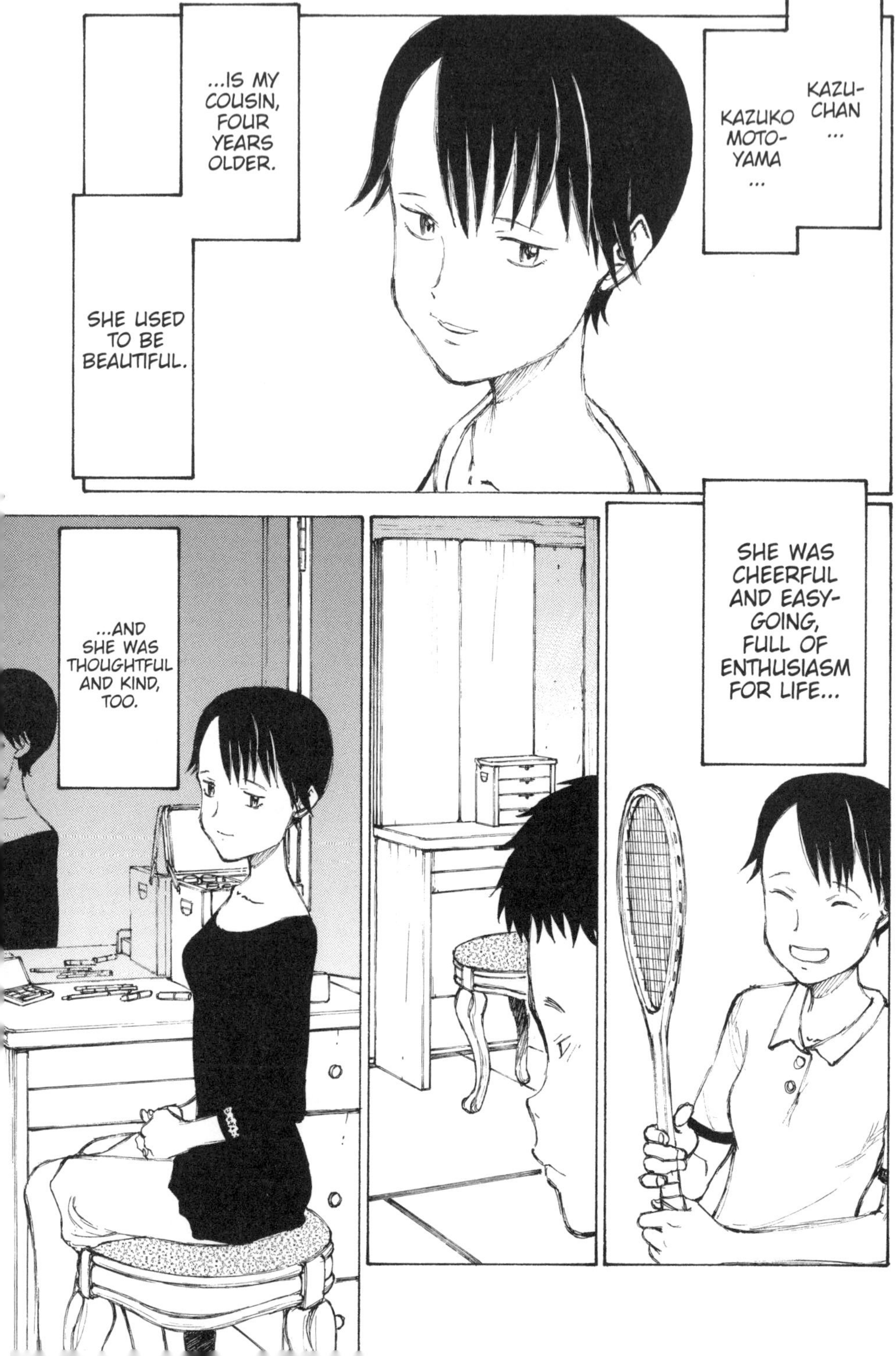
KAZU-CHAN...
KAZUKO MOTO-YAMA...
...IS MY COUSIN, FOUR YEARS OLDER.
SHE USED TO BE BEAUTIFUL.
SHE WAS CHEERFUL AND EASY-GOING, FULL OF ENTHUSIASM FOR LIFE...
...AND SHE WAS THOUGHTFUL AND KIND, TOO.

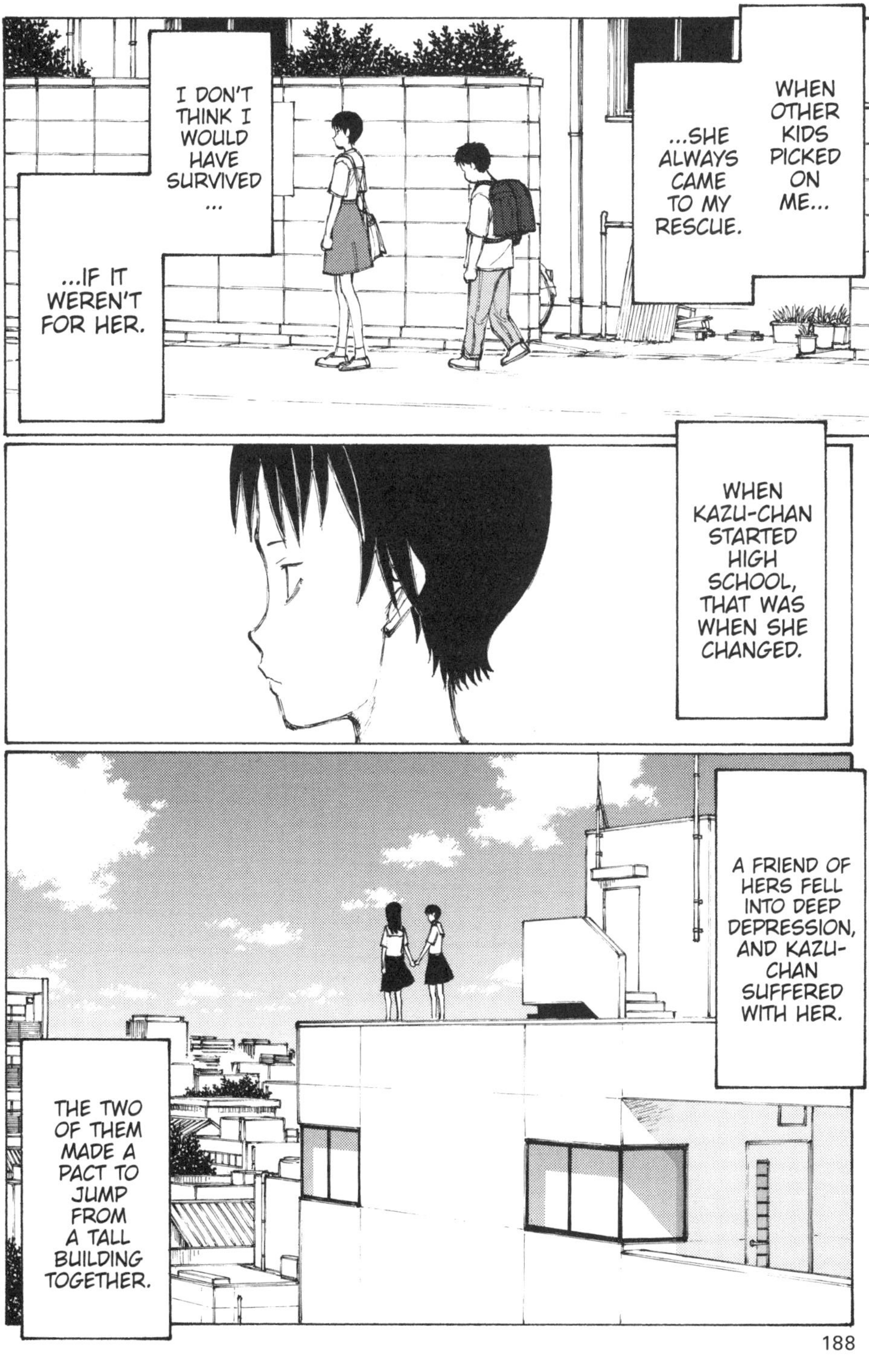
WHEN OTHER KIDS PICKED ON ME...
...SHE ALWAYS CAME TO MY RESCUE.
I DON'T THINK I WOULD HAVE SURVIVED...
...IF IT WEREN'T FOR HER.
WHEN KAZU-CHAN STARTED HIGH SCHOOL, THAT WAS WHEN SHE CHANGED.
A FRIEND OF HERS FELL INTO DEEP DEPRESSION, AND KAZU-CHAN SUFFERED WITH HER.
THE TWO OF THEM MADE A PACT TO JUMP FROM A TALL BUILDING TOGETHER.

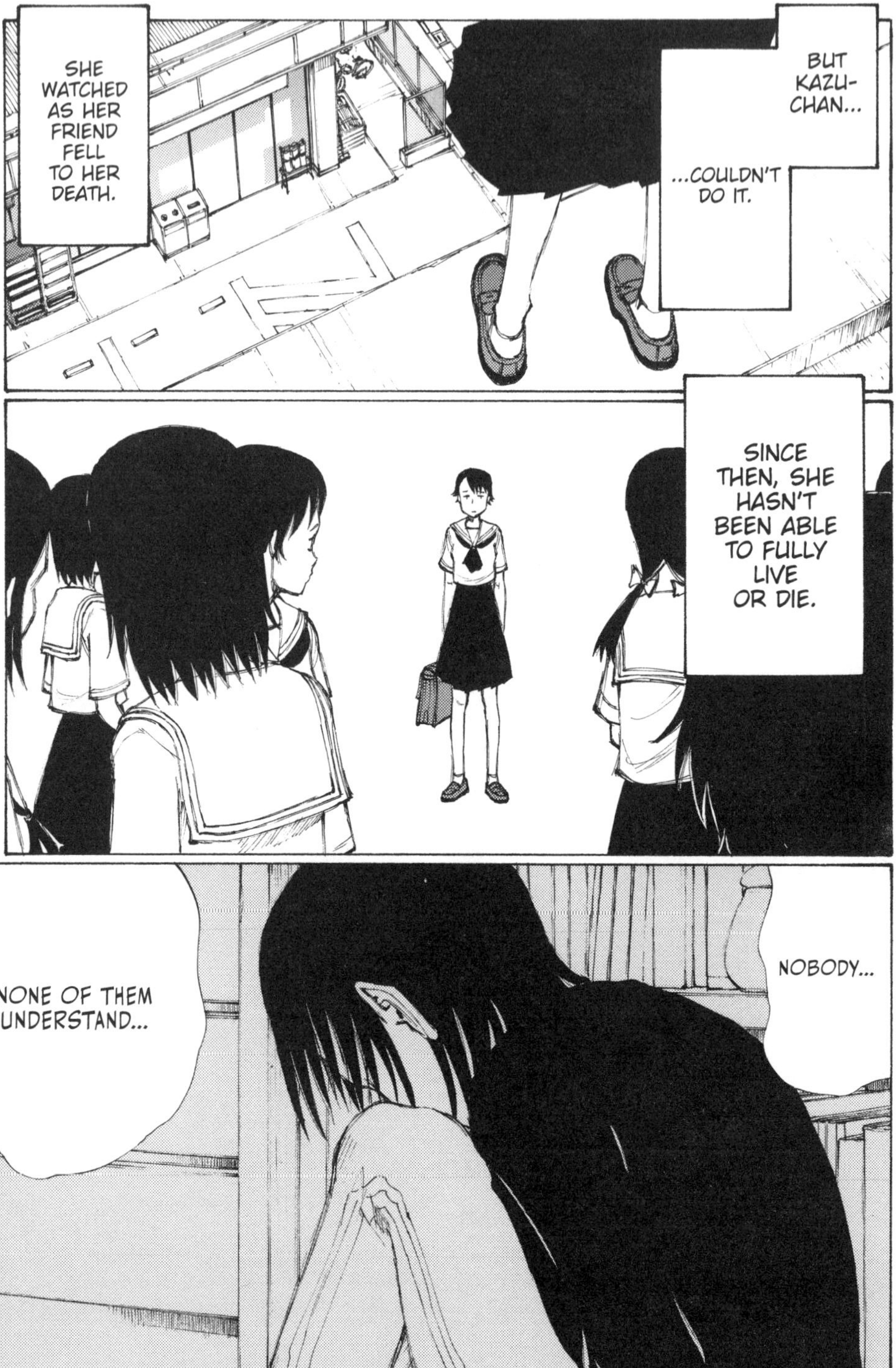
BUT KAZU-CHAN...
...COULDN'T DO IT.
SHE WATCHED AS HER FRIEND FELL TO HER DEATH.
SINCE THEN, SHE HASN'T BEEN ABLE TO FULLY LIVE OR DIE.
NOBODY...
NONE OF THEM UNDERSTAND...

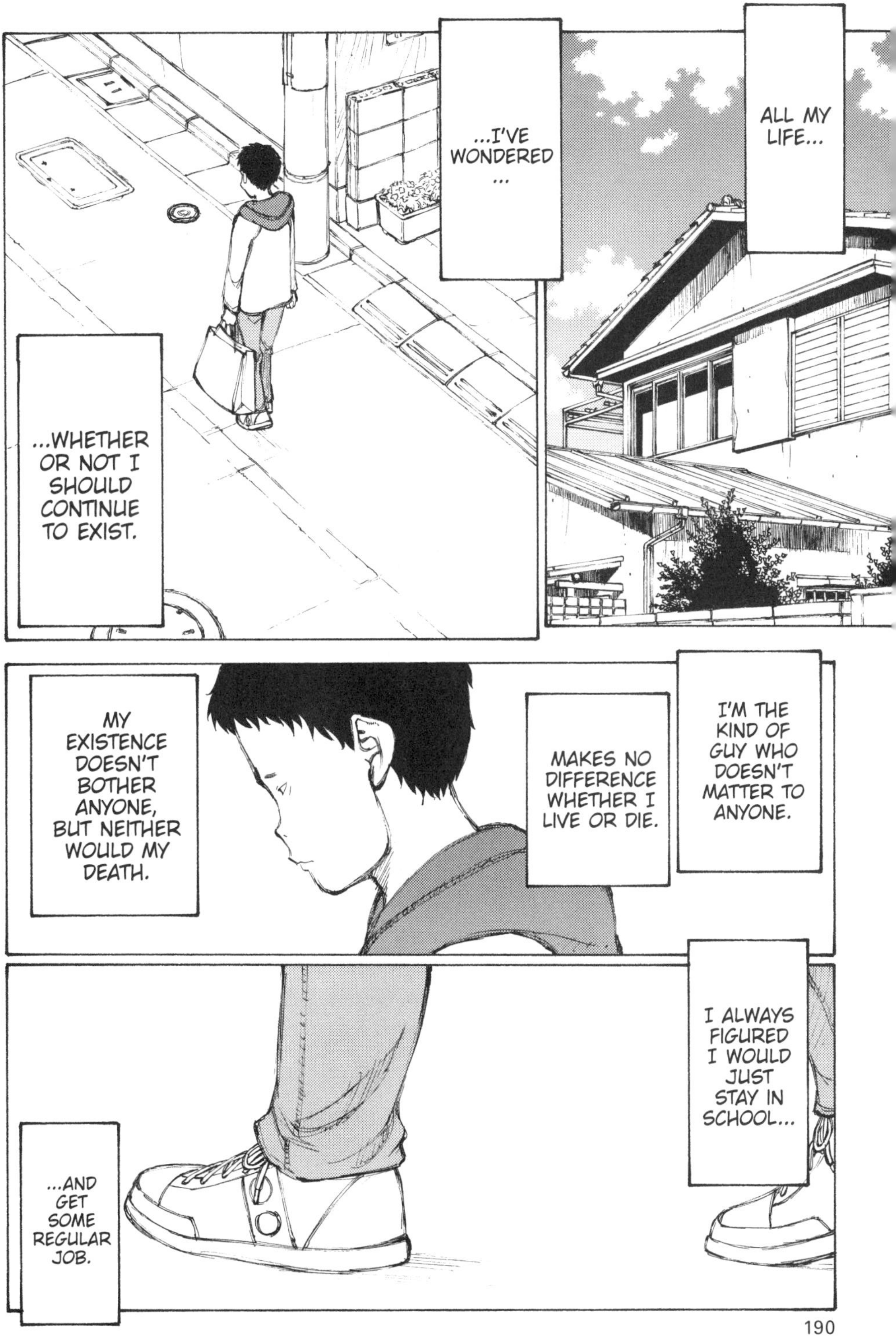
ALL MY LIFE...
...I'VE WONDERED ...
...WHETHER OR NOT I SHOULD CONTINUE TO EXIST.
I'M THE KIND OF GUY WHO DOESN'T MATTER TO ANYONE.
MAKES NO DIFFERENCE WHETHER I LIVE OR DIE.
MY EXISTENCE DOESN'T BOTHER ANYONE, BUT NEITHER WOULD MY DEATH.
I ALWAYS FIGURED I WOULD JUST STAY IN SCHOOL...
...AND GET SOME REGULAR JOB.

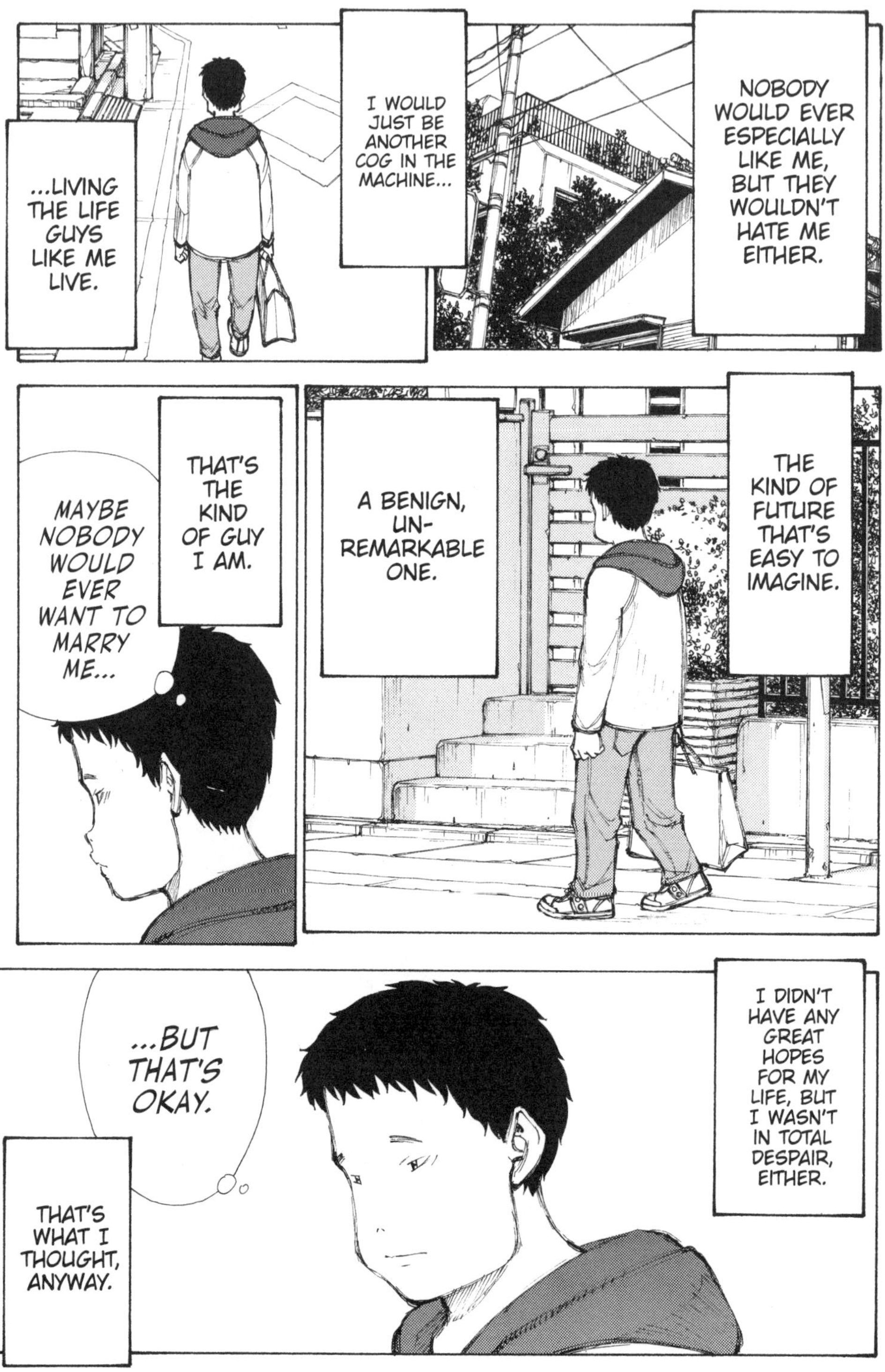
NOBODY WOULD EVER ESPECIALLY LIKE ME, BUT THEY WOULDN'T HATE ME EITHER.
I WOULD JUST BE ANOTHER COG IN THE MACHINE...
...LIVING THE LIFE GUYS LIKE ME LIVE.
THE KIND OF FUTURE THAT'S EASY TO IMAGINE.
A BENIGN, UN-REMARKABLE ONE.
THAT'S THE KIND OF GUY I AM.
MAYBE NOBODY WOULD EVER WANT TO MARRY ME...
I DIDN'T HAVE ANY GREAT HOPES FOR MY LIFE, BUT I WASN'T IN TOTAL DESPAIR, EITHER.
...BUT THAT'S OKAY.
THAT'S WHAT I THOUGHT, ANYWAY.

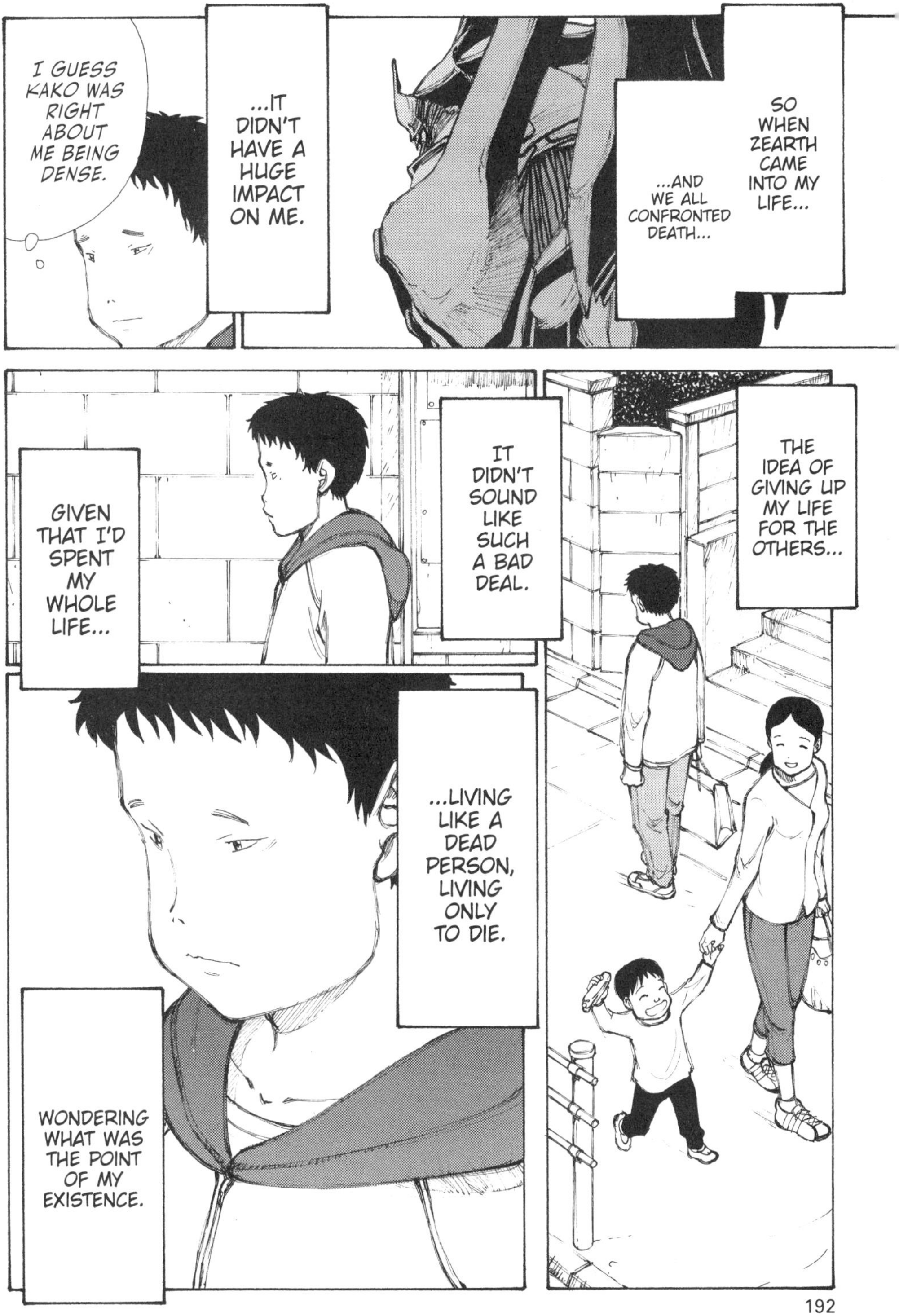
SO WHEN ZEARTH CAME INTO MY LIFE...
...AND WE ALL CONFRONTED DEATH...
...IT DIDN'T HAVE A HUGE IMPACT ON ME.
I GUESS KAKO WAS RIGHT ABOUT ME BEING DENSE.
THE IDEA OF GIVING UP MY LIFE FOR THE OTHERS...
IT DIDN'T SOUND LIKE SUCH A BAD DEAL.
GIVEN THAT I'D SPENT MY WHOLE LIFE...
...LIVING LIKE A DEAD PERSON, LIVING ONLY TO DIE.
WONDERING WHAT WAS THE POINT OF MY EXISTENCE.

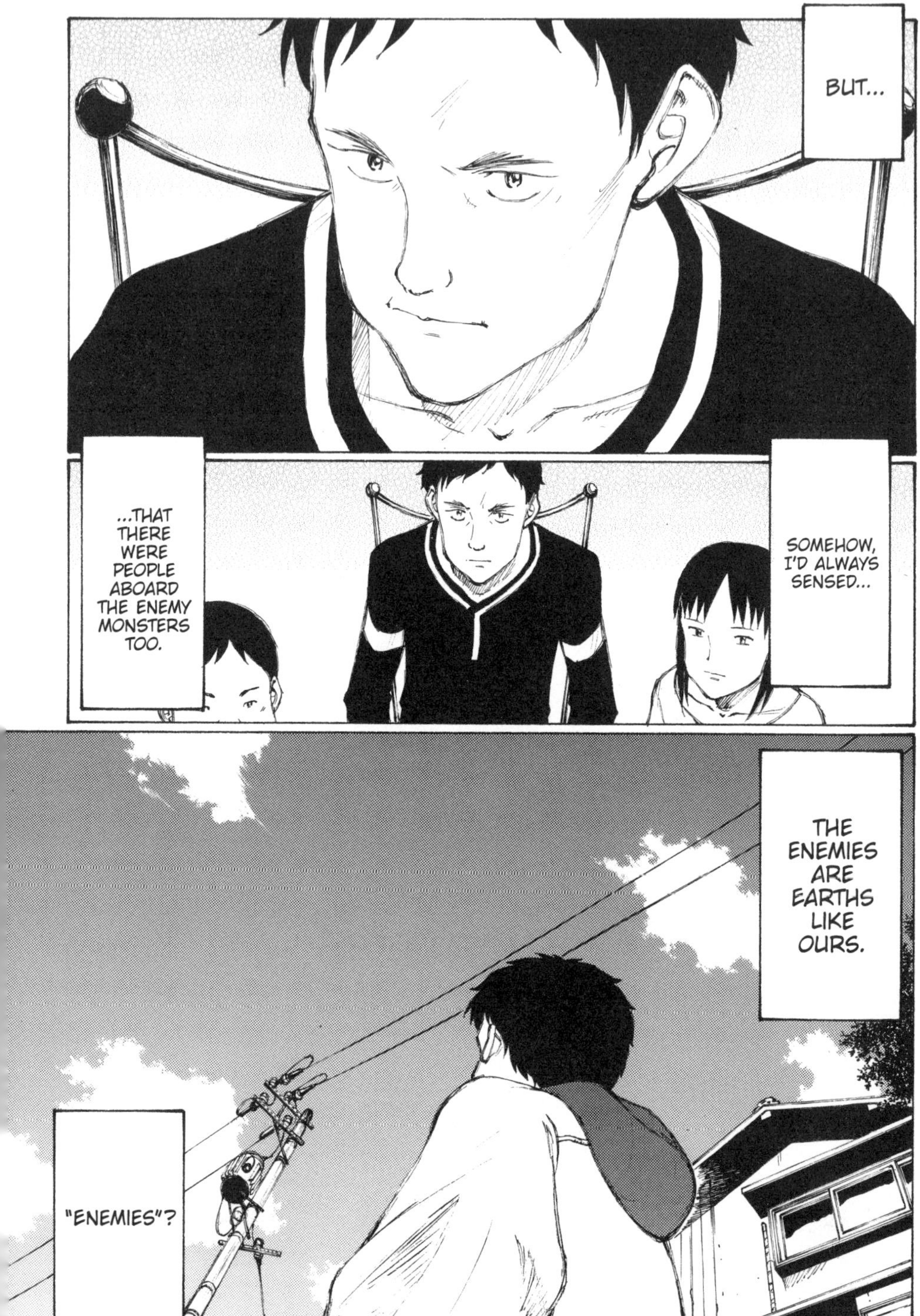
BUT...
SOMEHOW, I'D ALWAYS SENSED...
...THAT THERE WERE PEOPLE ABOARD THE ENEMY MONSTERS TOO.
THE ENEMIES ARE EARTHS LIKE OURS.
"ENEMIES"?

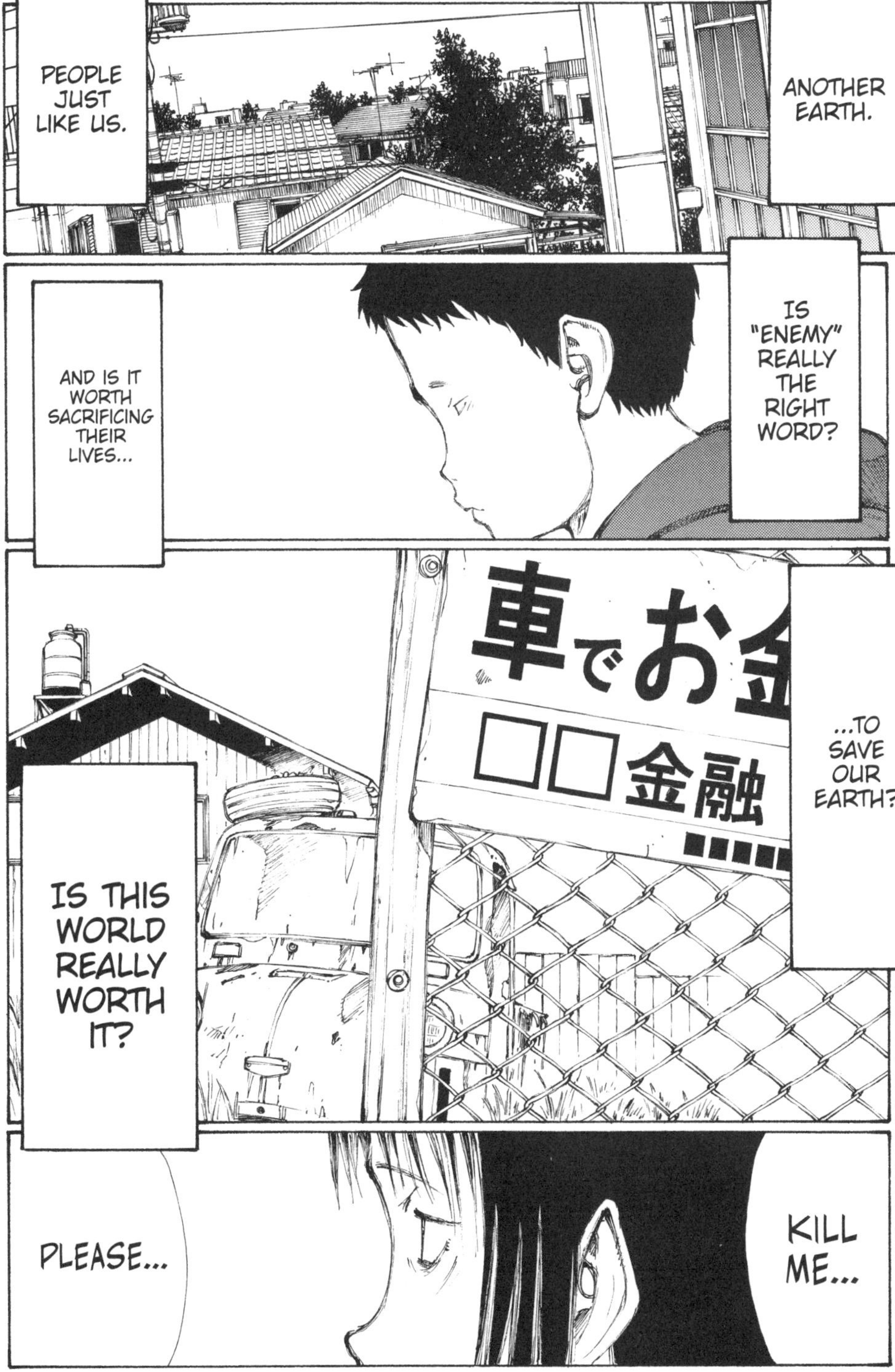
ANOTHER EARTH.
PEOPLE JUST LIKE US.
IS "ENEMY" REALLY THE RIGHT WORD?
AND IS IT WORTH SACRIFICING THEIR LIVES...
...TO SAVE OUR EARTH?
車でお金
□□金融
IS THIS WORLD REALLY WORTH IT?
KILL ME...
PLEASE...

Sign: Have a car? Get a loan! XX Financing

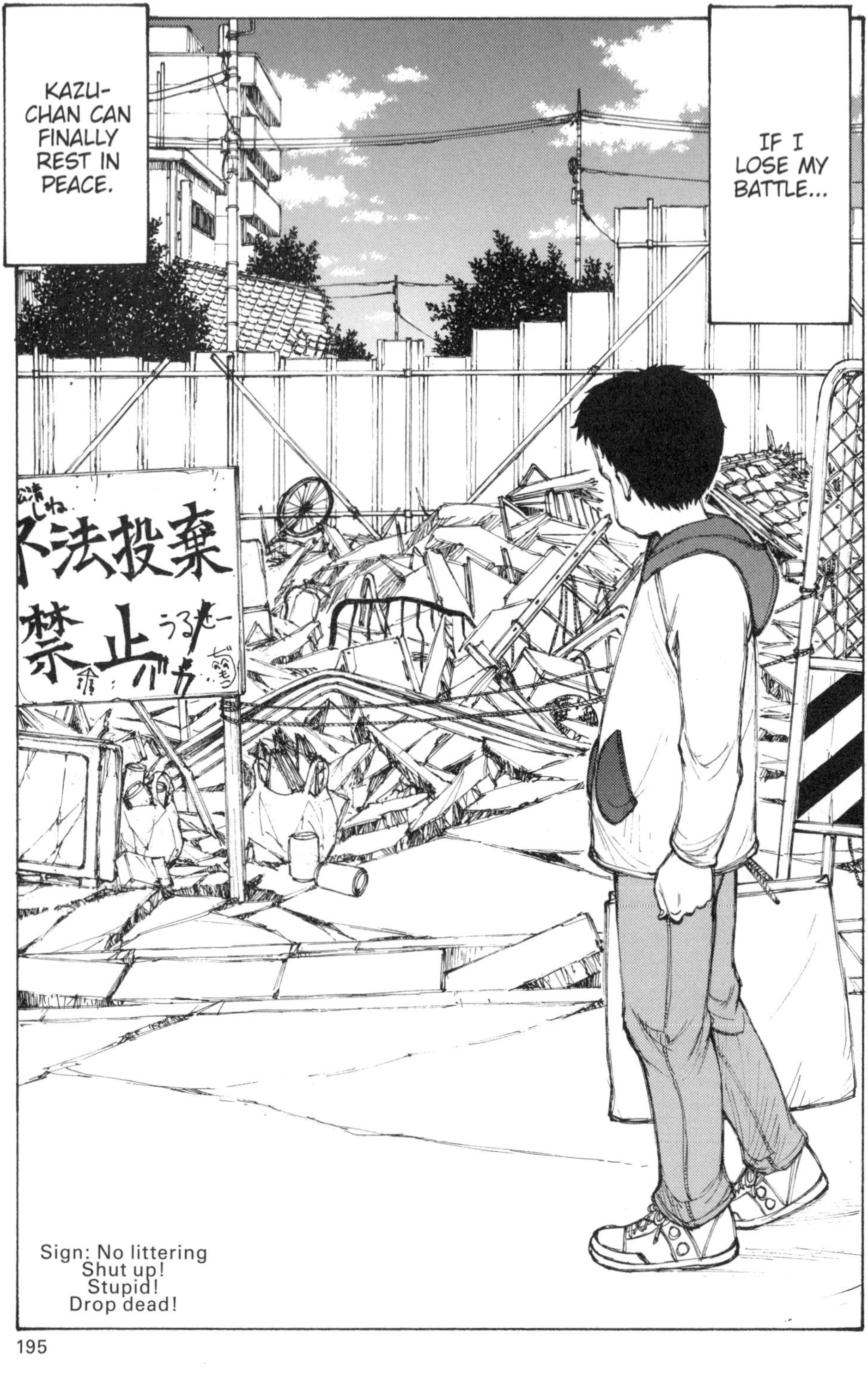
IF I LOSE MY BATTLE...
KAZU-CHAN CAN FINALLY REST IN PEACE.
法投棄
禁止
うるせー
バカ
Sign: No littering
Shut up!
Stupid!
Drop dead!

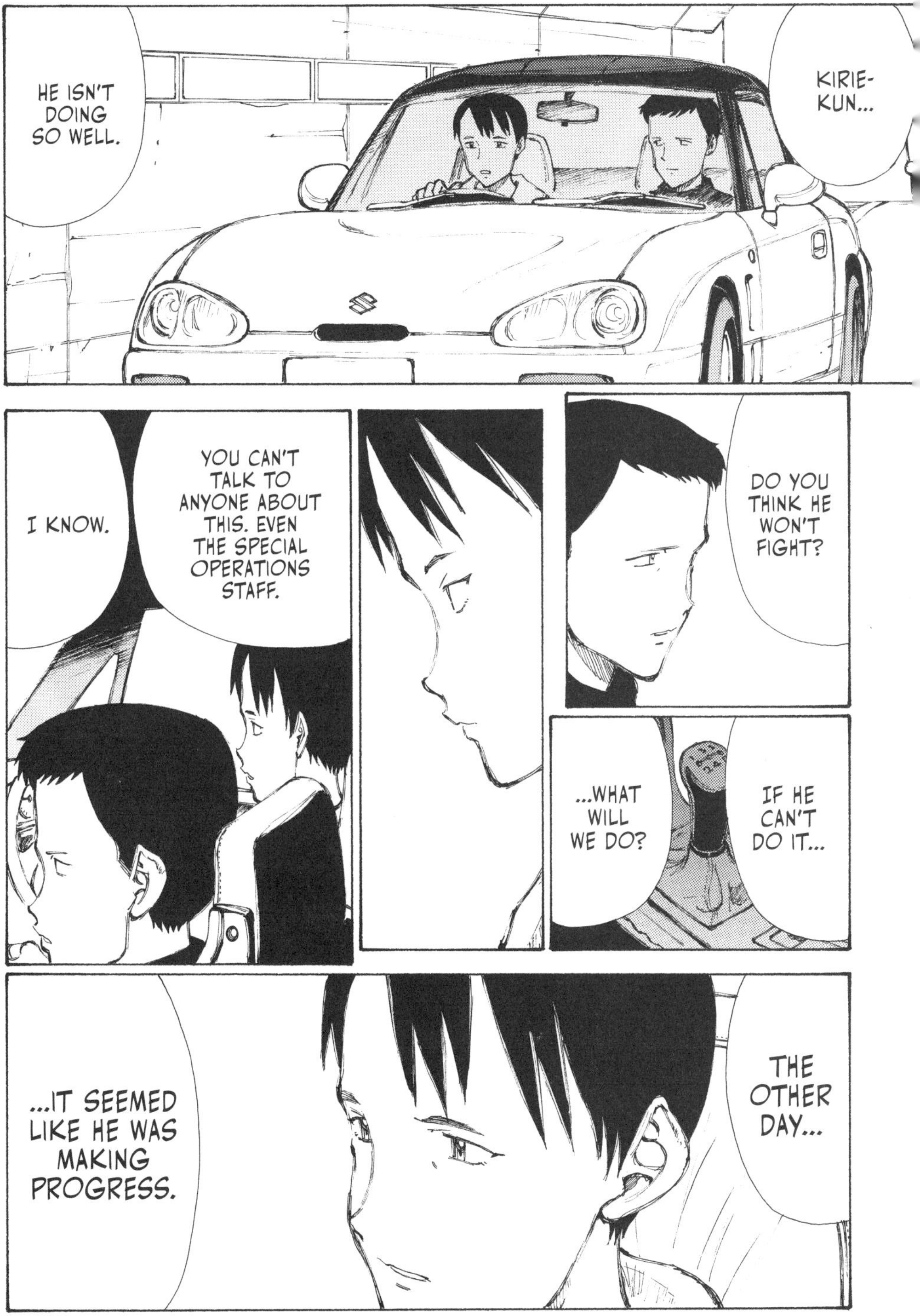
KIRIE-KUN...
HE ISN'T DOING SO WELL.
DO YOU THINK HE WON'T FIGHT?
IF HE CAN'T DO IT...
...WHAT WILL WE DO?
YOU CAN'T TALK TO ANYONE ABOUT THIS. EVEN THE SPECIAL OPERATIONS STAFF.
I KNOW.
THE OTHER DAY...
...IT SEEMED LIKE HE WAS MAKING PROGRESS.

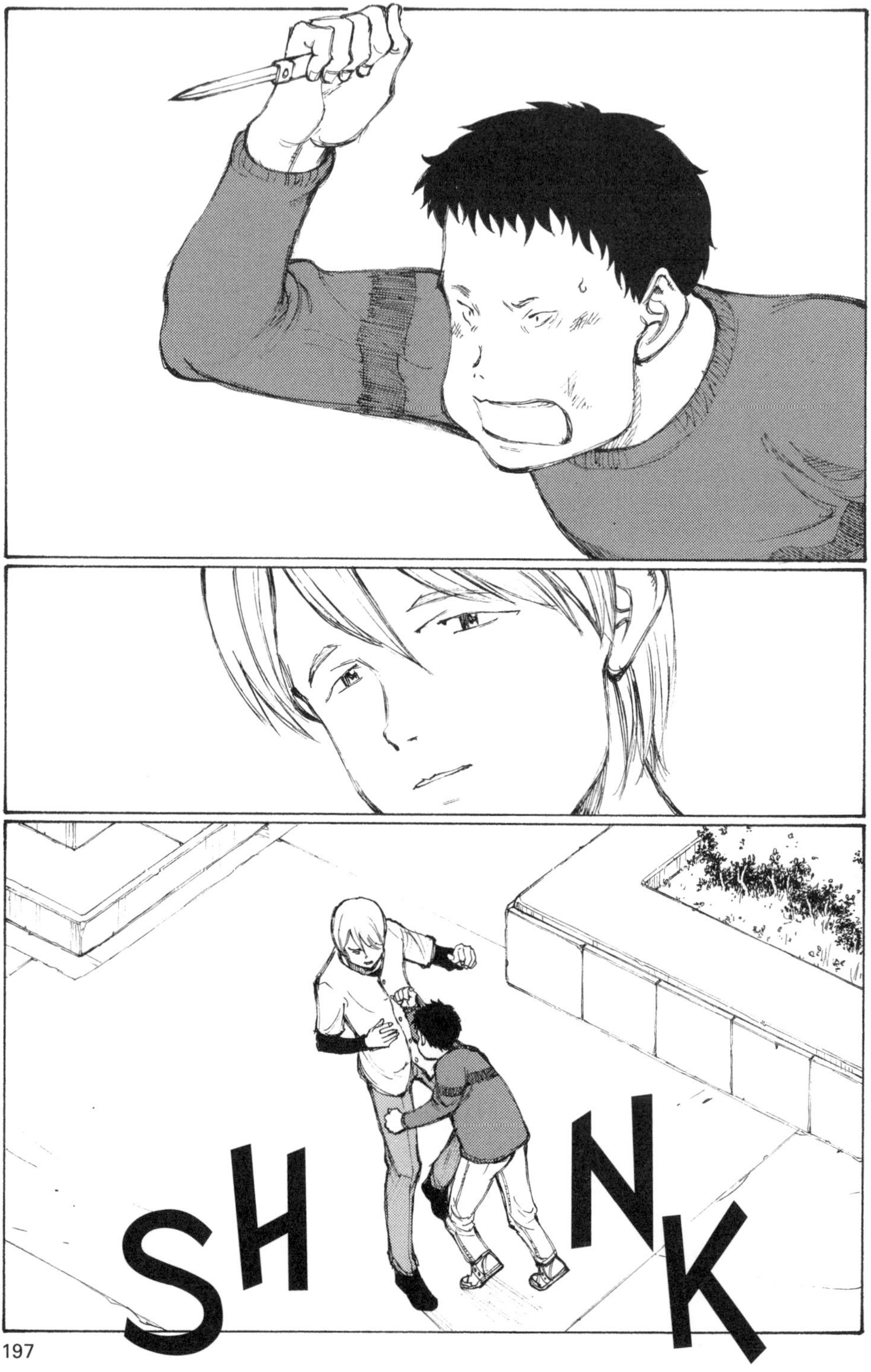
SHINK

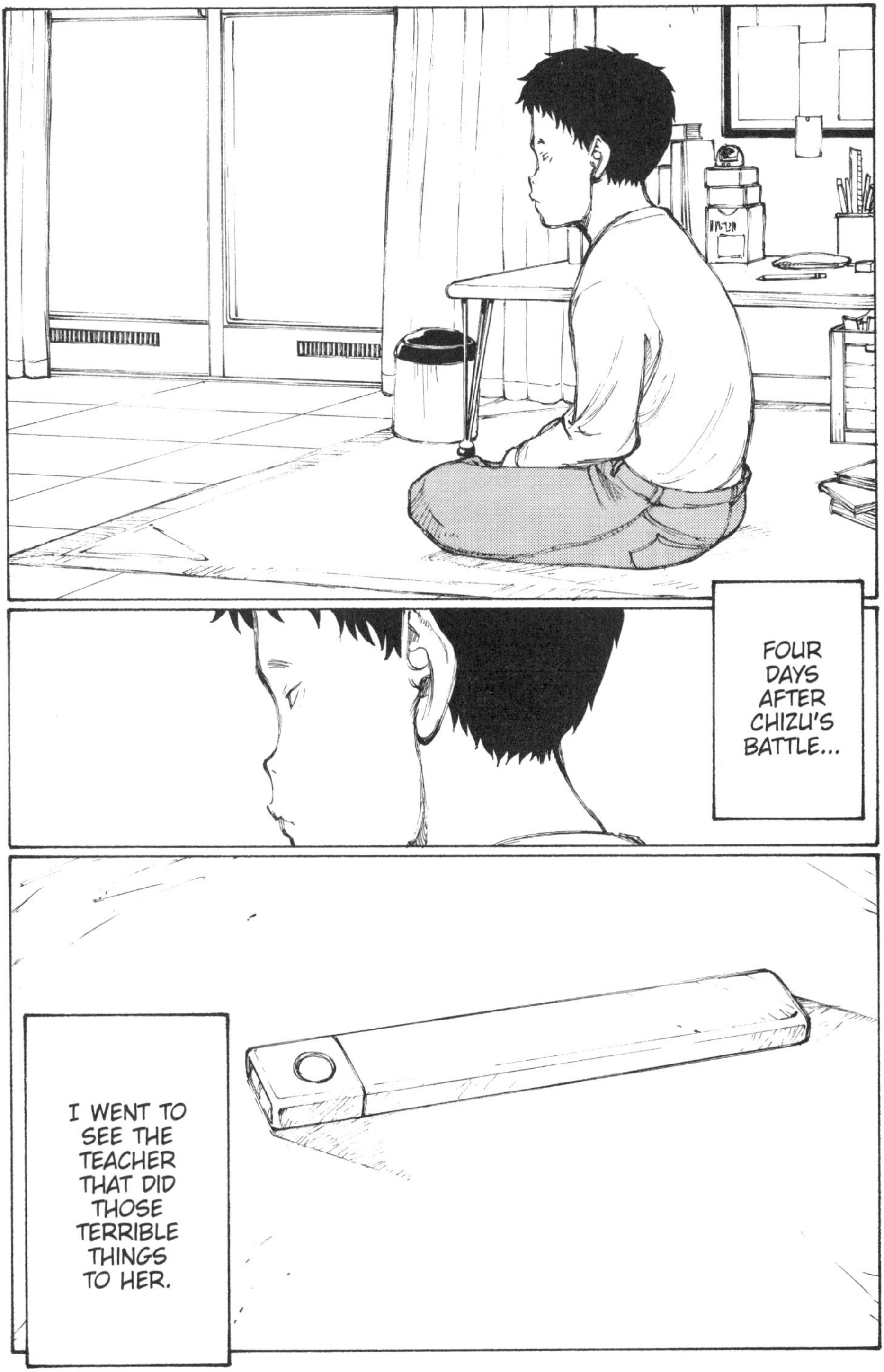
FOUR DAYS AFTER CHIZU'S BATTLE...
I WENT TO SEE THE TEACHER THAT DID THOSE TERRIBLE THINGS TO HER.

BOKURANO OURS

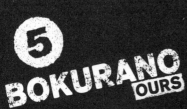

BOKURANO: OURS
VOL. 5

VIZ SIGNATURE EDITION

STORY & ART BY **MOHIRO KITOH**

Original Japanese edition "BOKURANO"
published by SHOGAKUKAN Inc.

Original Japanese cover designed by
CentralG7 Yutaka Kimura and Hiruki Masuda

TRANSLATION Camellia Nieh
TOUCH-UP ART & LETTERING Jose Macasocol
DESIGN Sam Elzway
EDITOR Chris Mackenzie

Printed in Canada

Published by VIZ Media, LLC
P.O. Box 77010
San Francisco, CA 94107

10 9 8 7 6 5 4 3 2 1
First printing, January 2012

VIZ SIGNATURE
WWW.SIGIKKI.COM

PARENTAL ADVISORY
BOKURANO: OURS is rated T+ for Older Teen and is recommended for ages 16 and up.

RATED T+ FOR OLDER TEEN
ratings.viz.com

www.viz.com

My parents are clueless.

My boyfriend's a mooch.

My boss is a perv.

But who cares? I sure don't.
At least they know who they are.

Being young and dissatisfied
really makes it hard to care
about anything in this world...

solanin

STORY & ART BY INIO ASANO

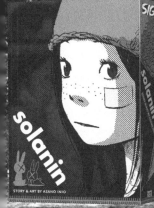